# GROWTH AND ETHNIC INEQUALITY

JUST FAALAND     J. R. PARKINSON

RAIS SANIMAN

# Growth and Ethnic Inequality

## Malaysia's New Economic Policy

HURST & COMPANY, LONDON
ST. MARTIN'S PRESS, NEW YORK

*in association with the*
*Chr. Michelsen Institute, Bergen, Norway*

First published in the United Kingdom by
C. Hurst & Co. (Publishers) Ltd.,
38 King Street, London WC2E 8JT,
and in the United States of America by
St. Martin's Press, Inc.,
175 Fifth Avenue, New York, NY 10010.
All rights reserved.
© the Chr. Michelsen Institute, Bergen, Norway, 1990
Printed in England

ISBNs
1–85065–095–0 (*Hurst*)
0–312–04933–1 (*St. Martin's*)

**Library of Congress Cataloging-in-Publication Data**

Faaland, Just.
    Growth and ethnic inequality : Malaysia's new economic policy
(NEP) / Just Faaland, Jack Parkinson, Rais B. Saniman.
        p.     cm.
    Includes bibliographical references and index.
    ISBN 0–312–04933–1
    1. Malaysia—Economic policy.   2. Malaysia—Economic conditions.
3. Malaysia—Race relations.   I. Parkinson, J. R. (John Richard)
II. Saniman, Rais B.   III. Title.   ·
HC445.5.F33     1990
338.9595′0089—dc20
                                                            90–41066
                                                               CIP

# PREFACE

Since Independence (Merdeka) in 1957 the economy of Malaysia has been growing as rapidly and persistently as practically any other country in the world. Along with this growth, in fact underpinning it, has gone a transformation of large proportions in the structure of the economy. Malaysia, which three decades ago was considered by observers as a somewhat sleepy, pristine society, blessed with natural resources of land and minerals, has now developed into a vigorous, dynamic economy where industry has replaced agriculture as the largest sector in both production and exports (but not employment), yielding a per capita annual income of approximately US $2000 equivalent, more than twice that of Thailand. In this process of massive growth - inevitably with its ups and downs mostly in response to changing fortunes in world markets - Malaysia has also shown its ability to adjust the course so as best to make up for both ill fortune and mistakes and to seek out and exploit new or changing opportunities. Malaysia is without doubt a real economic success story, holding its own well within the group of ASEAN countries, which itself is a most impressive growth area in the world economy.

Twenty years ago, after the vicious riots of 13th May 1969, Malaysia set for itself what was called the New Economic Policy (NEP), which is the subject of this book. The NEP was designed and adopted in a determined effort to ensure that the fruits from further development of the country would redound to all its citizens in an equitable manner, not disproportionately to the immigrant communities of Chinese and Indian origins, as against the Malays and other indigenous groups (collectively referred to in Malaysia as the Bumiputra). The political leadership at that time, also in some responsible non-Malay circles, recognised, that the Bumiputra feeling of losing out, of being left behind economically in their own country, had to be met and had to be seen to be met by clearly stated policy objectives and effective policy instruments. This was all the more imperative, it was felt, because the established political foundation for the Malays in the country would also be endangered if they continued to lag far behind economically.

We have attempted to give a full account of the emergence of the NEP and to explain the need for it in terms of the history of the country. The formulation of the NEP is treated in some detail, drawing on documents prepared in 1969 to lay the foundations for a shift in development strategies. Four of these documents are reproduced at the end of the book for reference and scrutiny. The account of the nature of the new strategies and the reasons for them is followed by a discussion of the shifts in policy that occurred as successive plans were unfolded. This is a preliminary to an appraisal of the effectiveness of the NEP during the past twenty years, followed by an up-to-date account of the stances taken by the major political parties in relation to the NEP and to the fact that the Outline Perspective Plan, which has guided the NEP through most of its history, ends in 1990. The final chapter is concerned with the continued need to reduce ethnic inequalities and with policies that might be followed to achieve this in the next one or two decades. In view of the wide-ranging character of the issues covered in the various chapters, we have endeavoured to make them self-contained, even though this has entailed a measure of overlapping between chapters and of unavoidable repetition.

The three of us have come to the task of preparing this account of the NEP with different and complementary experience and credentials. Faaland wrote some of the basic documents during his stay there in 1969 and 1970. Both he and Saniman were included at the time in a small group of analysts and administrators working to the National Operations Council, the Prime Minister's Department and later also the Department of National Unity. Saniman continued for many years in Malaysia helping to build one of the central institutions for NEP implementation, until in late 1983, he joined the OECD Development Centre in Paris where Faaland was President at the time and where we could pursue our interest in an analysis of Malaysia as one of our tasks. During that period also Parkinson joined our work in Paris as a consultant. His particular responsibility in this venture has been to provide perspective on the analysis, including an international perspective, and to take part in the selection of material, the elaboration of the analysis and the presentation of the study.

The support and facilities of the Chr. Michelsen Institute over many years have been crucial for the progression and completion of this book. Faaland had leave of absence from the directorship of the Institute from mid 1968 to the end of 1970 for his planning advisory work in Malaysia, Parkinson has been an associate fellow of the Institute for many years and Saniman was a full time visiting fellow in 1971-72. This has provided invaluable opportunities for us to draw on the resources of the Institute for this work, particularly the rich facilities of the library, including documentation from the early efforts to develop the NEP in Malaysia, and the Institute's exemplary secretarial services, all of which has been put at our disposal generously, efficiently and expeditiously.

Last, but not least, we express our sincere thanks to the many individuals and institutions in Malaysia who so liberally have provided us with help and advice in this venture.

*Bergen, January 1990*            JUST FAALAND  
                                       JACK PARKINSON  
                                       RAIS B. SANIMAN

# CONTENTS

## FOUR SELECTED DOCUMENTS FROM 1969-70

# TABLES

# BOXES

# DIAGRAMS

# ACRONYMS

| | |
|---|---|
| ABIM | *Angkatan Belia Islam Malaysia* (Islamic Youth Movement of Malaysia) |
| ADB | Asian Development Bank |
| ASEAN | Association of South-East Asian Nations |
| CIC | Capital Investment Committee |
| DAP | Democratic Action Party |
| DNU | Department of National Unity |
| EPU | Economic Planning Unit |
| FAMA | Federal Agricultural Marketing Authority |
| FELCRA | Federal Land Consolidation and Rehabilitation Authority |
| FELDA | Federal Land Development Authority |
| FIDA | Federal Industrial Development Authority |
| FLDA | (See FELDA) |
| GDP | Gross Domestic Product |
| GNP | Gross National Product |
| IADP | Integrated Area Development Programme |
| IAPG | Inter-Agency Planning Groups |
| IBRD | International Bank for Reconstruction and Development |
| ICA | Industrial Co-ordination Act |
| IDDP | Income Doubling and Distribution Plan |
| IMF | International Development Fund |
| IMP | Industrial Master Plan |
| INTAN | *Institute Tadbiran Awam Negara* (National Institute of Public Administration Malaysia) |
| MAPEN | *Majlis Perundigan Ekonomi Negara* (National Economic Consultative Council) |
| MARA | *Majlis Amanah Rakyat (*Council of Trust for the Indigenous People) |
| MARDI | Malaysian Agricultural Research Development Institute |
| MCA | Malaysian Chinese Association |
| MHFS | Malaysian Home and Foreign Service |
| MIC | Malaysian Indian Congress |
| MIDF | Malaysian Industrial Development Finance Bhd. |
| MIER | Malaysian Institute of Economic Research |
| MIPS | Malaysian Industrial Policy Studies |
| MP | Malaysian Plan (preceded by indication of Plan number) |

| | |
|---|---|
| MTR | Mid-Term Review (preceded or followed by indication of Plan reviewed) |
| NAP | National Agricultural Plan or Policy |
| NECC | National Economic Consultative Council |
| NEP | New Economic Policy |
| NFPE | Non-Financial Public Enterprise |
| NGP | National Growth Programme |
| OPP | Outline Perspective Plan 1970-1990 |
| PAP | People's Action Party |
| PAS | *Parti Islam Se-Malaysia* (Islamic Party of Malaysia) |
| PETRONAS | *Petroleum Nasional Berhad* (National Petroleum Company) |
| PNB | *Permodalan Nasional Berhad* (National Equity Corporation) |
| RIDA | Rural and Industrial Development Authority |
| RISDA | Rubber Industry Smallholders Development Authority |
| UMNO | United Malays National Organisation |

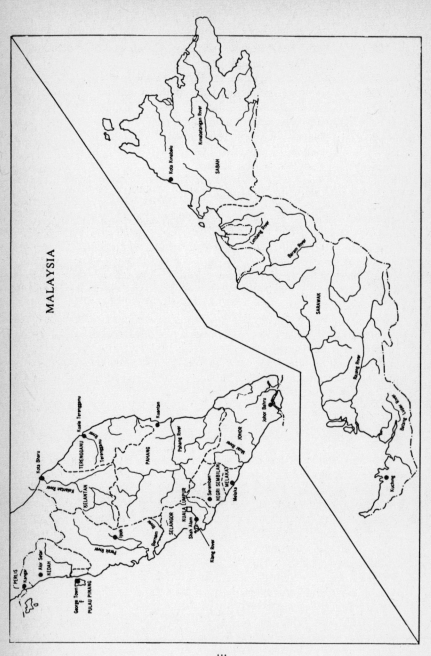

MALAYSIA

PERLIS
Kangar
Alor Setar
KEDAH
George Town
PULAU PINANG
Perak River
Ipoh
Berman River
Kota Bharu
Kelantan River
KELANTAN
Kuala Terengganu
TERENGGANU
Terengganu River
PAHANG
Pahang River
Kuantan
SELANGOR
KUALA LUMPUR
Shah Alam
Klang River
Seremban
NEGRI SEMBILAN
MELAKA
Melaka
JOHOR
Muar River
Johor Bahru

SABAH
Kota Kinabalu
Kinabatangan River
Labuan River
Baram River
SARAWAK
Rajang River
Batang Lupar River
Kuching

xviii

# CHAPTER 1

# THE SETTING

Malaysia is a country with a pronounced pluralistic society and a dualistic economic structure. Deep rooted demarcations permeate the society in population structures and locations, political organisations, economic activities and religious beliefs. The diverse structures have their own momentum and dynamics, with their strengths and weaknesses. While there are strong common elements of goodwill, institutions, and activities in everyday life, fostered by successive national policies, clear demarcations are all too evident in the fabric of the society. They express themselves in many forms — often divisive, confrontational, and politically destabilising and damaging to the country as a whole. It is the cardinal policy of every successive administration since Merdeka (Independence) to reverse and eventually to eradicate these various divisive structural forms, so that long term political stability and a cohesive united Malaysian nation may eventually emerge.

## Geography

The Federation of Malaysia is in South East Asia and covers a total area of 330 thousand square kilometres. It is bounded in the North by Thailand and the Philippines, in the South and East by Indonesia and in the West by the Indian Ocean. It was formed in 1963, then comprising the Federation of Malaya, including Singapore, together with the Borneo Territories of Sabah and Sarawak, but excluding the State of Brunei. Singapore left Malaysia in 1965, and is now an independent republic. The Federation of Malaya or Peninsular Malaysia as it is known to-day, covers an area of 132 thousand square kilometres, and is made up of eleven states: Perlis, Kedah, Penang, Perak, Selangor (with the Federal Capital Territory of Kuala Lumpur), Negri Sembilan, Melaka, Johor, Pahang, Terengganu, and Kelantan. Each state has a Sultan or a Governor; the Federal Territory of Kuala Lumpur has a Mayor. The Sultans elect one of their number as the Yang Di-Pertuan Agong or the King on a five year rotational basis. Kuala Lumpur is the capital of Malaysia while Kota Kinabalu and Kuching are the capitals of the states of Sabah and Sarawak respectively. At the closest point, Sabah and Sarawak are separated from Peninsular Malaysia by about 864 kilometres of the South China Sea. The topography of both Peninsular Malaysia, Sabah and Sarawak is characterised by rich coastal plains giving way to a rugged mountainous interior. In Peninsular Malaysia a mountainous spine known as the Main Range runs from the Thai border southwards to Negri Sembilan, effectively separating the Western part of the Peninsular from the Eastern part. Gunong Kinabalu, 4175 metres high and located in Sabah, is the highest mountain in Malaysia and in South East Asia. About four-fifths of Malaysia is covered by tropical rain forest. The climate of Malaysia is governed by the regime of the north-east and south-west monsoons which blow alternately during the course of the year. Being in the tropics, the average temperature throughout the year is constantly high, above 25 degrees celsius; the humidity likewise is high and the rainfall heavy. The main economic activities of Malaysia include the production and processing of oil and gas mainly from offshore areas and the production of rubber, palm oil, and tin from the rich plain. Industrial activities were initially connected with processing these basic raw materials. Malaysia has been pursuing an outward industrialisation strategy and is now engaged in producing, and exporting, such goods as electronic products, air conditioners and finished products arising from its heavy industrialisation programme. Of equal importance are the peasant activities in the traditional sector, in which a substantial proportion of its population is still engaged. These include rice farming, smallholder cultivation of rubber and coconut, and inshore fishing.

## Ethnic Plurality

The major ethnic groups are the Malays, Chinese and Indians. The Malays of Peninsular Malaysia, together with the Bumiputra of Sabah and Sarawak, are collectively called Bumiputra (the translation meaning: sons of the soil). In this study, where focus is mainly on Peninsular Malaysia, we use the term "Malay" and "Bumiputra" where convenient interchangeably.

The total population of the whole country estimated in 1988 stood at 16.9 million, out of which 13.9 million were in Peninsular Malaysia, 1.4 million in Sabah and 1.6 million in Sarawak. Within

Peninsular Malaysia, the Malays or the Bumiputra constituted 8 million of the total, the Chinese 4.4 million, the Indians 1.4 million and the balance of around 100,000 comprised significant minority groups — Thais, Pakistanis, Eurasians, Europeans etc. The non-Malays (primarily the Chinese and Indians) are found predominantly in the developed West Coast of Peninsular Malaysia. The majority of the Malays are in the relatively underdeveloped Malay Belt, comprising the States of Perlis, Kedah, Kelantan, Terengganu and Pahang. The non-Malays are located in the main towns and urban centres, and in the industrial parts of the country, including the main ports; the Malays are mostly located in the rural areas, as a hinterland to the urban and other growth centres, while a great many Indians are located in the rubber plantations. The total population of the country has been growing at an annual rate of 2.5 per cent, with the Malays registering the highest rate of growth of 3.0 per cent per annum, followed by the Indians at 2.2 per cent and the Chinese at 1.7 per cent. The Government has now introduced a new population policy with the objective of reaching a total population of 70 million by the year 2100.

While the terms Malays and Bumiputra, Chinese and Indians are generally used for practical purposes as if they each denoted a homogeneous group, they are, in fact, highly differentiated. For example, the term Malay as used for Peninsular Malaysia includes the Orang Asli (the aborigines). As a group, the Malays are similar, however, to the peoples found in Indonesia and the Philippines, generally known as peoples native to the Malay world or the Malay Archipelago. The Chinese community itself is subdivided into various clans depending on the places in Mainland China from where their forefathers originally set out to emigrate. Most Chinese Malaysians derive from South China, with the Cantonese and Hokkien forming the largest dialect groups. Although the "Babas" or the "Straits Chinese", residing mainly in Melaka and Penang, have been in Malaysia for hundreds of years, and speak the Malay language perhaps even better than the natives, they have successfully maintained their separate identity. The Indians hail primarily from Southern India and Sri Lanka, with significant Sikh and other minorities. All the communities have their separate languages, culture and religions. They are bound together by the national language, called "Bahasa Malaysia" which is similar to the Indonesian language. The Malay language, Bahasa Melayu, is now the main language used in government. English is taught and spoken widely in the country, and indeed it is the main language of commerce and industry. Nearly 100 per cent of the Malays are Muslim, while the

Chinese and Indians belong to various denominations, including Bhuddism and Christianity. Because of their educational, religious and cultural orientations, events outside of Malaysia, such as in the Middle East, China and India, have tended to influence the attitudes of the various communities within the society. Some still maintain close ties and remit funds to families and relatives in China and India, in a similar fashion to the Pakistanis and the Bangladeshis working in the Middle East remitting portions of their earnings to their home villages.

The history of ethnic pluralism began to be significant when the British took control and dominated the Malay states. They encouraged unrestricted and large scale immigrations of the Chinese and Indians in order to exploit the tin fields, reputed to be amongst the world's richest, and to open new lands for rubber estate cultivation. This process started in the second half of the nineteenth century and continued until the Great Depression, when it stabilised. According to Anand[1], estimates put the population of Peninsular Malaysia at 250,000 in 1800, 2,000,000 in 1900, and 6.3 million in 1957, the year Peninsular Malaysia achieved its Independence. According to Snodgrass[2], the composition of the Malays in the total population dropped significantly over the years. In the Straits Settlements (i.e. Penang, Melaka and Singapore) the Malays made up 52 per cent of the population in 1871. This percentage fell to 41 per cent in 1891 and to 25 per cent by 1931. In the Federated Malay States (i.e. Perak, Selangor, Negri Sembilan, and Pahang) the Malay share of the population fell from 56 per cent in 1891 to 37 per cent in 1931. Also in the Unfederated Malay States (i.e. Perlis, Kedah, Kelantan, Terengganu and Johor) the Malay population declined in the early decades of the 1900s but remained a majority of 69 per cent in 1931. These large scale and unrestricted immigrations swamped the Malays. Recent population projections, however, show that the ratio of the Malay population is now increasing, due to higher fertility rates compared to those of other communities and also it seems to immigration from Indonesia. The population of Malaysia is now projected to reach 22.5 million in the year 2000.

[1]   S. Anand, *Inequality and Poverty in Malaysia — Measurement and Decomposition*, Oxford University Press, 1983, p. 2.
[2]   Donald R. Snodgrass, *Inequality and Economic Development in Malaysia*, Oxford University Press, 1980, p. 26.

## Economic Dualism

From the early years of British rule the method of production in the country was organised into two distinct and parallel types. One was the large scale production and commercial activities of the joint stock companies of the English, like Guthrie, Harrisons and Crosfield etc. They extracted tin, using modern technology, and produced rubber and palm oil on a large-scale plantation or estate basis. These activities were concentrated in the rich Western parts of Peninsular Malaysia where most of the tin deposits were found, and where the soils were suitable for rubber and palm oil cultivation on a large scale. The produce was exported to the international markets via the main ports of Singapore and Penang, again located in the West Coast and in the calm waters of the Melaka Straits. The reverse flow consisted of the importation of capital and consumer goods needed by the country. These activities were also organised by the same trading companies or by subsidiaries established for the purpose. The commercial activities of the companies were based on modern technologies and research, using up to date organisational methods and international marketing procedures. They were, therefore, very much part of the mechanism of international trade and exchange. The companies had their shares floated and traded on the stock exchanges of London and elsewhere. Their operations in the Peninsular were backed by such powerful banks as the Chartered Bank and the Hong Kong and Shanghai Bank. The companies were, therefore, the avant-garde organisations of the modern sector of the Malaysian economy. The profits and wages derived from these activities were relatively high, compared with those obtainable elsewhere in the economy. The presence and activities of these organisations had a modernising influence with considerable impact on local culture and value systems.

The second mode of economic life, running side by side with that of the Western production and organisation systems, was based on traditional methods which had evolved locally over the centuries. It depended on peasant agriculture, consisting mainly of padi farming, coconut farming, coffee farming and inshore fishing. It was not an orderly or structured way of nationally planned development, but one that evolved more haphazardly, in a disorganised way from the exigencies of daily life at the household and village level. The produce was locally consumed and not intended for sale in the international markets. This system of production was very much part of the way of life in the Malay Belt, that is in the North and in the Eastern states of Peninsular Malaysia. In the West Coast, peasant agriculture extended into rubber smallholdings. The rubber sheets and latex they produced were sold to middle men who were mostly agents from the main trading centres. To that extent, this particular sector of peasant agriculture was drawn into the modern sector and was affected by fluctuations in the prices of rubber. This became important as time went on and the economy progressed. Tin mining with sophisticated machinery was not embarked upon by the village based small scale producers, partly because large scale capital investment and modern organisation were needed for operations of the "European" type. Mining was mostly carried out by hand, using local techniques of extraction. The tin produced in this way was sold to trading agents. The use of banks and organised credit facilities was not widespread. Modern organisational methods, production techniques, marketing tools, international trade and exchange instruments were practically unheard of outside foreign firms until Malaysia obtained Independence and the Government turned its attention seriously to this particular sector.

While the organised modern sector based on Western systems of production and organisation was well integrated into the modern world economy and trading system, and prospered accordingly over time, the peasant unorganised system was very much isolated as an enclave on its own, connected only indirectly to the outside world. As the modern sector expanded and developed into an urban, commercial and industrial sector, the traditional sector stagnated or even deteriorated, as the pressure of population on land worsened over time with the increase of the population. The Islamic inheritance law, practised by the Malays, also had its impact on the size of the land holdings of the farmers. The duality deepened over time as the differential rates of productivity of the two sectors widened with the introduction in the modern sector of increasingly sophisticated technology. Differentials in productivity, wealth, jobs and income of those engaged in the two sectors widened. As time went on the imbalances extended to cultural and sociological differences. The dualism permeated to the whole fabric of society, affecting the goods market, the capital market and the labour market, as well as the machinery of government. In this respect the structure of production of the Malaysian economy was similar in its effects to those of other developing economies which were former colonies of metropolitan powers.[3]

The Europeans, the Chinese and the Indians were mostly engaged in the high productivity modern sector of the economy, as

---

[3] J. Faaland and J.R. Parkinson, *The Political Economy of Development*, London: Frances Pinter, 1986, p. 74.

entrepreneurs, managers and employees in firms, estates, and trading companies, while the Malays were mostly engaged in the low productivity traditional sector of peasant agriculture and fishing. The non-Malays inhabited the rich West Coast plain of Peninsular Malaysia where most of the commercial activities were to be found, while the latter were mostly located in the Malay Belt where generally they were much poorer. Most of the roads, railways, modern communications, schools, hospitals, etc. were built on the West Coast. Technology from international sources flowed into the country via this seaboard. As the Chinese and Indians formed an economic layer below the Europeans in the modern sector, they benefited from these developments and were in a position to take over from the foreigners when they later divested themselves following Merdeka.

The only Malay involvement in the modern sector was in the civil service, both at the Federal and State levels, where it was reserved for them by the British, and in the police and the military to which the non-Malays were not attracted because of the relatively low wages paid there compared with earnings in the tightly organised communal private sector. Social and economic discrimination against the Malays by commercial and industrial circles controlled by the non-Malays took many forms. In business, the British and Chinese banks refused to have anything to do with them, for they were regarded as having no suitable experience. In wholesale, retail, and export and import business, they were kept out by associations and guilds. Even if the Malays sought jobs in the private sector, they were kept out by clan, language and cultural preferences and barriers. The many Chinese and Indian shops refused to employ Malays. Until recently, Indian shops imported labour from India when they were short-handed. As for urban jobs outside the government, only the lowest types of manual labour were open to the Malays: such jobs as trishaw pedalers, drivers and watchmen.

Competing hypotheses and theories abound with explanations as to why the Malays were trapped in the backward traditional rural sector of the economy, so losing control of their country and destiny. We have drawn attention to the intense discrimination in many forms and guises against the Malays, deliberate or justified on grounds of low education, inability to speak the Chinese or Indian languages etc. Other attempts at explanation include anything from assertions about "the lazy native" and "the backward sloping labour supply curve", to the enervating influence of the humid tropical climate, in contrast to the special drive inherent in the immigration culture. Other explanations extended to the neglect and exploitation of the rural areas, and to the effects of adverse terms of trade.

The argument which inspired the NEP was that the "trickle down" effect had shown itself not to work in Malaysia, as indeed it had failed to do in most other developing countries. In the case of Malaysia, if it worked at all, the main beneficiaries of the trickle down effect were the non-Malays who were next to the Europeans in the existing order, in terms of economic ranking, educational standards and organisation and, therefore, were relatively more advanced than the Malays. They were the ones who were in the position to seize the new opportunities created through development. For the Malays, the competition was too unequally stacked against them. The Malay community was the poorest and the least advantaged and would continue to be so, trickle down or not. The economic gap between the non-Malays and Malays was irreversibly set to widen over time as productivity differences between the modern and traditional sectors increased. The system had to be changed if Malays were to be given a chance to participate and benefit from the rapid economic development of the country that was taking place.

## History and Politics

The plurality of the population and the dualism of the economy fell neatly within ethnic demarcations, and constituted the fundamental underlying basis which shaped the political interactions of the country before and since Merdeka. These demarcations evolved from the days of pre-British rule, but certainly intensified after the British took control. In order to have a better perspective of the nature of the problems which prompted the government to introduce the NEP, it is necessary to touch briefly upon the relevant parts of the country's history.

Historically, despite the stresses and tensions in the economic and social fabric, the Malays adapted well to change and absorbed foreign influences into their society. Their ability to adapt to changing conditions stemmed from the fact that their country was at the cross roads of intra-island and international trade. Melaka and Penang have been trading centres from early times. People there were used to foreigners and knew how to interact with them. Islam came through these trading centres and other ports. By all accounts, the Malays, in the ports and trading centres along the waterways of Peninsular Malaysia, were traders, artisans, craftsmen, as well as agriculturalists and fishermen, much as they are found even to-day in parts of the states comprising the Malay Belt, where they have been shielded from the intense competition and superior technology of the immigrants. Successive waves of Chinese and Indian traders and immigrants came and settled in these ports. Subsequently they expanded to the mainland, for example, into Johor from Singapore at the encouragement of the Sultan. Some of the descendents of the immigrants inter-married locally and became rulers, influential courtiers and administrators in the Malay administrations. While adapting to changing conditions, the Malays retained their identification and intellectual and emotional ties with the Islamic world. They did not feel that they were seriously threatened by the immigrants. When the British took over Penang and Melaka there were already large settlements of non-Malays in these territories. Yet, by all accounts inter-ethnic relations were amicable and harmonious.

The generally good record of ethnic relations, in spite of the multi-racial, multi-religious and multi-lingual character of the population, rested on the premise that the British and the non-Malays did not openly challenge Malay political sovereignty in local matters and daily life. An effort was made not to provoke the acquiescent Malays. The different groups lived and worked quite separately. The Europeans had a monopoly of the lucrative international trade, and were the owners of major plantations and tin mines. When they first came, they recognised that the Chinese and Indians were useful. These communities provided a ready infrastructure for European economic activities, and serviced them efficiently as middlemen and intermediaries vis-à-vis the Malays. The wealth accumulated by the Chinese also provided a good market for British products. The British naturally encouraged Chinese immigration. The immigrants soon displaced the Malays who were pushed further and further from the towns and urban centres. In the process, the political and economic status of the Malays deteriorated in step with the ascendency of economic power of the Chinese and later their political power as they actively entered the political process.

Increasingly, the Malays registered their concern about the rising level of the immigrant population, but there was not much they could do to reverse the flow, as they were not masters of their own destiny. They had lost control of their country, except for ceremonial matters concerned with Islam and the Malay *adat* (culture). However, in the 1940s, the Malays, under the leadership of Dato Onn bin Jaafar of Johor, were galvanised into action, when the MacMichael Treaty was forced upon them. The plan was to create a Malayan Union, where among others changes, the status of the Malay Rulers, the autonomy of the states, and the rights of the Malays would be abolished. In its place a "Majlis Penasihat Pusat Malayan Union"

(Central Council of Malayan Union) would be formed. The Sultans would sit as members of the Council in an advisory capacity to the British Governor General, who would be the Chairman of the Council. Starting from a position of indirect rule of the Malay States, the British government would thus assume direct and complete political control of the country. The country would be governed directly from Whitehall, through the Governor General, as a colony. Thus, the role of the British as the "protector of the Malays" and the rationale for the advancement of political intervention into the affairs of the Malay States, and on which most of the Malay Sultans anchored their trust, came to its logical conclusion. Some felt that if Sir Harold MacMichael had been subtler and more tactful in his advocacy of the Malayan Union Scheme, it would probably have been accepted with acquiescence, as some of the rulers had already signed the Treaty, although registering some protests.

In the years before the proposed introduction of the Malayan Union Scheme, the response of the Malays to the encroachment of their political and economic power, was uncoordinated, weak and disunited. When the Malays saw the threat, they might have been expected to sink their differences and organise themselves into a common front. But for a long time they continued to quarrel among themselves. This theme of Malay quarrels and disunity is a predominant feature of Malay history. In the first place, it was the deadly and fratricidal quarrels among the Malays that gave the British the opportunity to intervene in the affairs of the Malay states and, later, these quarrels led to the eventual takeover of the country. All that the British colonial administrators and business companies had to do to enhance their political and economic interests, was to exploit and deepen this basic weakness in the Malay culture and values.

Faced with the Malayan Union scheme, however, the Malays, at last, after centuries of quarrels for power, disputes over territories, collection of river tolls and fees, managed to come together and unite to fight the common threat. This was the first time in their history that this had been done on any scale and it was to prove short-lived. After four decades and in recent years, the Malays resumed their historical pattern of fraternal quarrels. But while Malay unity prevailed, much was achieved to strengthen the position of the Malay community. UMNO (United Malays National Organisation) was formed in 1946, and most Malays rallied to its banner. Under UMNO's leadership, mass demonstrations and protests were organised. The Malays were able to persuade the British to replace the Malayan Union Scheme by a new political arrangement more favourable to them, called the Federation of Malaya. This was done in 1948. Under the Federation arrangement, the sovereignty of the Sultans, the individuality of the states, and special Malay rights were upheld. Citizenship was made more restrictive than was intended under the Malayan Union Scheme. A British High Commissioner was appointed, rather than a Governor, and he symbolically derived his authority from the Sultans rather than from the Crown. The Federation was a victory for the Malays, in fact the first major victory since the British landed in Penang in the 18th century.

The MCA (Malaysian Chinese Association) was founded in 1949 to protect and advance the cause of the Chinese vested interests. In a similar way, the MIC (Malaysian Indian Congress), formed in the same year as UMNO (1946), had as its primary objective the protection of Indian vested interests. The three major communal parties formed the Alliance Party and evolved a working relationship which has become the hallmark of Malaysian politics ever since. Together they obtained Independence from the British in 1957. The working relationship was based on the balance of a division of responsibilities: the economic prominence of the non-Malays and the political supremacy of the Malays.

The heart of the carefully structured balance, arrived at by the political leadership of the communal parties, was the "Bargain of 1957". Starting from opposite positions, the non-Malays demanded equal political rights with the Malays, including citizenship, a secular state, and continued official use of English in addition to the Malay language. The Malays on the other hand, concentrated on recognition of their special position as the indigenous people of the country and on acceptance of measures to accelerate their socio-economic progress in competition with the more aggressive immigrants. The Malays feared that they would be swamped by new non-Malay citizens, so losing their political hegemony, which they saw as a counter-balance to the economic strength of the Chinese. The essence of the compromise was that the Malays would make substantial concesssions with respect to citizenship, while the non-Malays would recognise the special position of the Malays, evidently without limit of time.[4] The agreements reached by the political parties were subsequently incorporated as an integral part of the Federal Constitution.

In 1963, Singapore, Sabah and Sarawak joined the Federation of Malaya converting it into the wider Federation of Malaysia. The Constitution incorporating the results of the "bargain" were extended

---

[4] Snodgrass, *op.cit.*, p. 46.

to these component states with important modifications in line with their demands and circumstances. In general, the new states enjoyed greater autonomy than the Malay states of Peninsular Malaysia. It soon became clear, however, that some provisions of the Constitution agreed to by the Alliance were not acceptable to Singapore, which pressed for the adoption and implementation of the concept of "Malaysian Malaysia", as opposed to the "Malay Malaysia" which was championed by UMNO. In 1965, Singapore opted out of Malaysia, and became a Republic. After Singapore left, the battle for "Malaysian Malaysia" continued to be fought within Malaysia by the DAP (Democratic Action Party, representing the Chinese opposition).

Malaysia's parliamentary system is built on the British model with a Prime Minister and a Cabinet responsible to Parliament. The basic constitutional document is the Federal Constitution. The prime minister has considerable power. He is, however, constrained by the political forces within his party and the coalition parties. Much of his ability to move the system, therefore, depends upon his own standing and his capacity to satisfy his party constituency and members of the Coalition Government, initially the Alliance and later the Barisan. The supreme policy objective of successive governments has been to achieve national unity and political stability by finding a *modus vivendi* with ethnic plurality and economic dualism. This was pursued through political pragmatism, protection of the "bargain", efforts to preserve communal harmony and to anticipate and manage potential conflict. At the same time the government embarked on successive five year development plans, based on a free enterprise system and with foreign investment, to develop the economy with the intention of creating prosperity for all Malaysians, while simultaneously accelerating Malay economic development. Sensitive communal issues were as far as possible depoliticised, racial extremism was curbed, and commonalities were emphasised so as to forge intercommunal links and integration. So long as the balance struck by the "bargain" was kept, the system worked. In 1969, this delicate equilibrium was violently upset by the communal riots which erupted in Kuala Lumpur and elsewhere in the country. Politically and ethnically the country retrogressed with racial feelings running high. Twelve years after achieving independence the country faltered.

## The Riots of May 1969

The 1969 riot was only the tip of the iceberg of a far more serious and deep seated problem of a structural nature confronting the society arising from Malaysia's past. Ethnic plurality, economic dualism and inequality were too ingrained in the fabric of the society. The "bargain" provided a balance and an equilibrium, but in the run up to the 1969 election it was broken. First, the opposition parties, particularly the DAP and the Gerakan (a political party with Chinese affiliations) questioned the rights of the Malays, including the use of the Malay language and other things, agreed to as part of the "bargain" and entrenched in the Constitution. Second, the DAP campaigned militantly on the theme of "Malaysian Malaysia", again settled by the "bargain" and written into the Constitution. Third, the immediate gains in the form of easier access to citizenship for the non-Malays were demonstrated by their increased political strength in the polls after 1957, and the majority of them voted for the opposition. The attempts by the government to implement the other provisions of the "bargain", such as the Malay language, met with vehement opposition by the Chinese community. Fourth, Malay aspirations to improve their economic status vis-à-vis the non-Malays did not materialise as expected. The Chinese appeared to win hands down. For every one step the Malays took, the non-Malays seemed to take two and were forging ahead. Huge contracts, which were part of the implementation of development plans, went to Chinese firms. Having been relegated to the status of economic inferiority, the Malays were now in danger of being reduced to political inferiority as well by the results of the recent election.

The worst fears of many Malays, particularly the educated ones, appeared to be confirmed. The "bargain", as it now turned out, was seen as hardly better than a "sell out". Many in UMNO at the time were vocal in pressing for a more radical solution to the Malay problem. To add insult to injury, the DAP and the Gerakan celebrated their victory by parading also through the predominantly Malay area of Kampong Bahru in Kuala Lumpur. It seemed to the Malays that racial harmony could be maintained only if the Malays kept on giving in. Their fight for equality in their own country was not only belittled, they were not even supposed to discuss it, since, it was argued, such discussions would only spoil the climate for private investment, local and foreign. Malay reactions to the humiliations were swift and predictable.

The one major lesson to be drawn by the non-Malays from the 1969 racial riot was that to challenge the position of the Malays as entrenched in the Constitution, overtly or obliquely, before the Malays could feel economically secure, would be counterproductive. It would be resisted by the Malays who felt that their backs were to the wall and the very life and survival of their community was at stake with no possible alternative to resistance. The "bargain", such it was, had given the country some balance and stability, for the common good of all. Any attempt to undo it before the Malays achieved a measure of economic parity could only lead to instability and break-down, economically, socially and politically.


## The Challenge

The NEP was launched as part of the overall strategy of Tun Razak (the then Prime Minister) to re-unite and rebuild the country after the traumatic experience of 1969. Besides its objective of creating prosperity for all Malaysians, so that no community would experience a sense of loss and deprivation, it equally stressed the important objective of uplifting the economic status of the Malays, in line with the spirit and intent of the "bargain" and the Constitution. In formulating the policy, the lessons of past policies were valuable, namely that the efforts of the previous years were not sufficient to redress the economic position of the Malays vis-à-vis the non-Malays, even if implementation could be improved. Indeed past policies had increased the gap between the Malays and other groups. It was the basic underlying assumption of the NEP strategists, as proved by the recent riot, that too much poverty and too much inequality, stacked against the Malays, could only bring further discontent and trouble. The need was to shift and integrate the Malays into the main stream of development of commerce and industry, and prevent them from becoming permanently marginalised in the backward sectors. It was a daunting task. Every one knew that the Malays had a long way to go, after being left behind for centuries in a peasant economy with all the economic, sociological, cultural and religious problems this entailed. The Second Malaysia Plan, the first phase of the NEP, summarised this basic philosophy when it stated (pp. 3-4):

National Unity is unattainable without greater equity and balance among Malaysia's social and ethnic groups in their participation in the development of the country and in the sharing of the benefits from modernisation and economic growth. National Unity cannot be fostered if vast sections of the population remain poor and if sufficient productive employment opportunities are not created for the expanding labour force.

In other words, economic growth alone, no matter how rapid it was, would not be enough. Distribution must be a parallel or twin objective of equal importance for any acceptable economic policy.

The conviction that extreme inequality in Malaysia can lead only to political chaos, was subsequently amply and disasterously corroborated by evidence and experience from other countries, in South East Asia most notably from the Philippines.

CHAPTER 2

# FOUNDATION AND FORMULATION

## The Constitution

Article 153 of the Constitution sets out a set of special rights of the Malays and also other articles deal with their rights and prerogatives under the Constitution (see Box 2.1). These parts of the Constitution represent a central element of the social contract, or as some call it a social bargain, entered into by the dominant political parties when the Constitution was drawn up.[1] While the Malays see these provisions as sacrosanct, some non-Malays question whether they are relevant and binding even to-day. On any reasonable interpretation

[1] Milne and Mauzy describe the bargain in these terms, see *Politics and Government in Malaysia*, revised edition 1980; Times Books International, Singapore: "The Alliance, in particular the UMNO and the MCA, had hammered out proposals which in effect represented a "bargain" over the relative constitutional position of the two major races" (p. 36).... "Article 153 is an extension of past practices of the colonial government, and has actually been used to continue policies which were already in force before independence, for instance, as regards admission into some branches of public service and for particular types of licenses, such as those for road haulage and hired passenger vehicles. At first sight the existence of Article 153 appears to be strange. Why was it necessary to make constitutional provision to protect the Malays when they were the largest racial group in Malaya and constituted a majority of the electors? The answer is not contained in the Constitution. Different kinds of answers can be given; that the Malays, being "indigenous", should have special consideration; that the rights were already there under the British and should not be terminated; that they are a trade-off for the concessions to the non-Malays on citizenships; that they are needed to enable the Malays to achieve a greater degree of economic equality" (p. 39)..... "Essentially the bargain provided for Malay political domination in return for a free enterprise system which would allow the continuation of Chinese economic power. Specifically, it offered liberal citizenship requirements as a major concession by the Malays in return for non-Malay concessions on special rights, religion and language. In the short term, this package deal satisfied the major claims of each community. Though there was a determined effort to maintain the myth of equality between the component parties of the Alliance, it was clear from the beginning that political power had primacy over economic power, that the UMNO was the senior partner of the Alliance, and indeed, that the cornerstone of any policy would be based on the precept of Malay (UMNO) political dominance. Within these boundaries there could be bargaining, compromises and accommodation on specific issues among the elite" (p. 130).

the meaning of these provisions in the Constitution would be that the economic and social well being of the economically weak Malays is to be protected and promoted as compared to that of the more advanced non-Malays. In return for this privilege, the Malays gave unequivocal concessions in terms of political power by granting Federal citizenship to the non-Malays. In addition, the non-Malays were assured that they were free to conduct their businesses unimpeded and also to retain and develop their own cultural and linguistic heritage and separateness. In other words, while the Constitution made special provisions for the Malays, the non-Malay citizen had his rights guaranteed under the Federal Constitution. By design, and as proved over time, as long as the parties did not renege on their commitments, the bargain at Merdeka was a balanced one, judging from the durability of the Alliance Government.

One tangible result of this exchange was that there was an avalanche of non-citizens applying to become Federal citizens. As the record shows (see for instance Milne and Mauzy: *op. cit.*, p. 40), in one year alone, in 1958, 800,000 became Federal citizens with all the rights and privileges that went with it. To this extent, Malay political power was eroded in terms of voting strength. This was an intended consequence, accepted by the Malays. However, as a matter of record, and not acceptable to the Malays, it has also meant that the descendants of the then new non-Malay citizens have come to question and challenge why they, as citizens of Malaysia and of no other state, should carry what they consider a burden, even though their forefathers had purportedly made a pledge at some point in the remote past, even before some of them were born. What matters, they feel, is now. They sense that Government efforts to help the Malays under the Constitution amount to discrimination against the non-Malays in their own country of citizenship and even of birth. They may feel that they are but second class citizens in their own country. Understandably, they campaign for what they see as equal rights in various forms and guises.

The Constitution did not specify in full the manner in which the Malays were to be helped to achieve economic parity with the non-Malays. While in Articles 153 and 89 it is stated that the Malays should be given extra transport and business licenses, extra educational privileges, prior right of employment in the civil service and the armed forces, and also that Malay Reserve land should be made nonalienable to non-Malays, no quantitative targets or timetables were set for the achievement of the objective of economic parity in the future, in exchange for the tangible and immediate right of citizenship for the non-Malays and their descendants. The

BOX 2.1:   Extract from FEDERAL CONSTITUTION (as of 25 January 1989)

**3.       Religion of the Federation**

(1) Islam is the religion of the Federation, but other religions may be practised in peace and harmony in any part of the Federation.
......

**32.      Supreme Head of the Federation, and his Consort**

(1) There shall be a Supreme Head of the Federation, to be called the Yang di-Pertuan Agong, who shall take precedence over all persons in the Federation and shall not be liable to any proceedings whatsoever in any court.
......

**89.      Malay reservations**

(1) Any land in a State which immediately before Merdeka Day was a Malay reservation in accordance with the existing law may continue as a Malay reservation in accordance with that law until otherwise provided by an Enactment of the Legislature of that State.

(2) Any land in a State which is not for the time being a Malay reservation in accordance with the existing law and has not been developed or cultivated may be declared as a Malay reservation in accordance with that law. ....

(3) Subject to Clause (4), the Government of any State may, in accordance with the existing law, declare as a Malay reservation —
(a)       any land acquired by that Government by agreement for that purpose;
(b)       on the application of the proprietor, and with the consent of every person having a right or interest therein, any other land;

and shall, in accordance with the existing law, immediately declare as a Malay reservation, in a case where any land ceases to be a Malay reservation, any other land of a similar character and of an area not exceeding the area of that land.

(4) Nothing in this Article shall authorise the declaration as a Malay reservation of any land which at the time of the declaration is owned or occupied by a person who is not a Malay or in or over which such a person has then any right or interest.

(5) Without prejudice to Clause (3), the Government of any State may, in accordance with law, acquire land for the settlement of Malays or other communities, and establish trusts for that purpose.

(6) In this Article "Malay reservation" means land reserved in alienation to Malays or to natives of the State in which it lies; and "Malay" includes any person who, under the law of the State in which he is resident, is treated as a Malay for the purposes of the reservation of land.
......

**90.      Special provisions relating to customary land in Negri Sembilan and Malacca, and Malay holdings in Trengganu**

(1) Nothing in this Constitution shall affect the validity of any restrictions imposed by law on the transfers or lease of customary land in the State of Negri Sembilan or the State of Malacca, or of any interest in such land.
.....

**152.     National language**

(1) The national language shall be the Malay language and shall be in such script as Parliament may by law provide:
Provided that:
(a)       no person shall be prohibited or prevented from using (otherwise than for official purposes) or from teaching or learning, any other language; and
(b)       nothing in this Clause shall prejudice the right of the Federal Government or of any State Government to preserve and sustain the use and study of the language of any other community in the Federation.
........

**153.     Reservation of quotas in respect of services, permits, etc., for Malays and natives of any of the States of Sabah and Sarawak**

(1)  It shall be the responsibility of the Yang di-Pertuan Agong to safeguard the special position of the Malays and natives of any of the States of Sabah and Sarawak and the legitimate interests of other communities in accordance with the provisions of this Article.

(2)  Notwithstanding anything in this Constitution, but subject to the provisions of Article 40 and of this Article, the Yang di-Pertuan Agong shall exercise his functions under the Constitution and federal law in such manner as may be necessary to safeguard the special position of the Malays and natives of any of the States of Sabah and Sarawak and to ensure the reservation for Malays and natives of any of the States of Sabah and Sarawak of such proportion as he may deem reasonable of positions in the public service (other than the public service of a State) and of scholarships, exhibitions and other similar educational or training privileges or special facilities given or accorded by the Federal Government and, when any permit or license for the operation of any trade or business is required by federal law, then, subject to the provision of that law and this Article, of such permits and licenses.

(3)  The Yang di-Pertuan Agong may, in order to ensure in accordance with Clause (2) the reservation to Malays and natives of any of the States of Sabah and Sarawak of positions in the public service and of scholarships, exhibitions and other educational or training privileges or special facilities, give such general directions as may be required for that purpose to any Commission to which Part X applies or to any authority charged with responsibility for the grant of such scholarships, exhibitions or other educational or training privileges or special facilities; and the Commission or authority shall duly comply with the directions.

(4)  In exercising his functions under this Constitution and federal law in accordance with Clauses (1) to (3) the Yang di-Pertuan Agong shall not deprive any person of any public office held by him or of the continuance of any scholarship, exhibition or other educational or training privileges or special facilities enjoyed by him.

(5)  This Article does not derogate from the provisions of Article 136.

(6)  Where by existing federal law a permit or licence is required for the operation of any trade or business the Yang di-Pertuan Agong may exercise his functions under that law in such manner, or give such general directions to any authority charged under that law with the grant of such permits of licences, as may be required to ensure the reservation of such proportion of such permits or licences for Malays and natives of any of the States of Sabah and Sarawak as the Yang di-Pertuan Agong may deem reasonable; and the authority shall duly comply with the directions.

(7)  Nothing in this Article shall operate to deprive or authorise the deprivation of any person of any right, privilege, permit or licence accrued to or enjoyed or held by him or to authorise a refusal to renew to any person any such permit or licence or a refusal to grant to the heirs, successors or assigns of a person any permit or licence when the renewal or grant might reasonably be expected in the ordinary course of events.

(8)  Notwithstanding anything in this Constitution, whereby any federal law and permit or licence is required for the operation of any trade of business, that law may provide for the reservation of a proportion of such permits or licences for Malays and natives of any of the States of Sabah and Sarawak; but no such law shall for the purpose of ensuring such a reservation-

(a)     deprive or authorise the deprivation of any person of any right, privilege, permit or licence accrued to or enjoyed or held by him; or

(b)     authorise a refusal to renew to any person any such permit or licence or a refusal to grant to the heirs, successors or assigns of any person any permit or licence when the renewal or grant might in accordance with the other provisions of the law reasonably be expected in the ordinary course of events, or prevent any person from transferring together with his business any transferable licence to operate that business; or

(c)     where no permit or licence was previously required for the operation of the trade or business, authorise a refusal to grant a permit or licence to any person for the operation of any trade or business which immediately before the coming into force of the law he had been *bone fide* carrying on, or authorise a refusal subsequently to renew to any such person any permit or licence, or a refusal to grant to the heirs, successors or assigns of any such person any such permit or licence when the renewal or grant might in accordance with the other provisions of that law reasonably be expected in the ordinary course of events.

(8A)  Notwithstanding anything in the Constitution, where in any University, College and other educational institution providing education after Malaysian Certificate of Education or its equivalent, the number of places offered by the authority responsible for the management of the University, College or such educational institution to candidates for any course of study is less than the number of candidates qualified for such places, it shall be lawful for the Yang di-Pertuan Agong by virtue of this Article to give such directions to the authority as may be required to ensure the reservation of such proportion of such places for Malays and natives of any of the States of Sabah and Sarawak as the Yang di-Pertuan Agong may deem reasonable; and the authority shall duly comply with the directions.

..........

objective of racial economic balance was left vague with all hoping and praying that somehow the problem of inequality would one day be resolved by itself and would go away, never to return. It was as if the major terms of the bargain were conveniently — and selectively — forgotten. Yet, the economic disparity problem was and remains a sensitive racial issue. It is usually mentioned, if at all, in a hushed tone for fear of being labelled a racist or one who raises "sensitive national issues".

The stark reality of the situation is that the Malay problem has not gone away by itself, nor is it conceivable that the problem could be solved just by granting an extra number of transport licenses and other rights as specified in the Constitution. The complex problems of mass Malay economic poverty and relative backwardness are embedded in the economic system of the country, reflecting more than a century of neglect, discrimination and exploitation by the colonial masters. As Tunku Abdul Rahman, the Father of Malaysian Independence and one of the founders of the Constitution, has said:[2]

> Our experience had shown that in the states run by the British, the Malays had no place: their rights were ignored and disregarded. Even their schools were relegated to the lowest rung of the educational ladder giving "vernacular" education over three or four years — at the end of which all they could do was to eke out a hand-to-mouth living. A few rich Malays could afford to send their children abroad for higher education, but the huge majority were looked down upon by everybody. The plan would have reduced all Malays to the level of human scum.

After Merdeka, attempts were therefore made by the government to help the Malays, bearing in mind the interests of the non-Malays. Again quoting Tunku Abdul Rahman:[3]

> The Malays required help in raising their standard of living, so in the first five year development plan we agreed on extensive development because the people of the kampungs (villages) had been completely neglected by the British. To be fair, however, an equal area of land was given to the other communities with the government providing funds and facilities. Next, it provided economic help and business facilities for the Malays, though the government had to subsidise them as the Malays need time to learn commerce and business.

[2] See *Far Eastern Economic Review*, 21 July 1988, p. 17.
[3] *Idem.*

Among that generation of politicians and national leaders, Malay, Chinese and Indian, it was also generally understood that it was part of the social contract that the non-Malays would help and teach the Malays how to get into business and commerce. In short, the non-Malays were to give a helping hand to the laggard Malays and pull them along with the progress of the country. This was part of the generally believed gentlemen's agreement that existed between them.

However, judging from historical and statistical records — and laudable individual effort and generosity notwithstanding — the non-Malays as a group did not come forward with a genuinely helping hand to the Malays in the private sector. The Democratic Action Party (DAP), the Malaysian Chinese Association (MCA), the Gerakan or other Chinese Associations and Guilds, or for that matter the Malaysian Indian Congress (MIC), did not come up with statesmanship initiatives or collaborative plans, programmes and projects to help the Malays, so as to create an identity of interests among the racial groups, even though such initiatives would have been in their own self-interest, providing security and insurance for the future. In fact, the contrary was generally the rule. The non-Malays discriminated against the Malays in business in terms of contracts, in employment etc. in favour of their own kind. The Malays were regarded as being inferior and lazy and capable of only doing the mentally and physically less demanding jobs. They were also deemed to be unresponsive to the profit motive and lacking in initiative and, when given a job, the Malays were considered incapable of carrying it out seriously over a long haul, as compared with the other races. At the most, Malays were given decorative posts for cosmetic and public relations purposes, particularly if the company concerned had dealings with government departments in which the majority were Malay officers. In practice, therefore, the Malays had given the non-Malays inalienable rights under the Constitution in exchange for what turned out to be little more than vague and empty promises by the non-Malays. As we discuss in a later chapter, even these promises are now being denied by some sections of the non-Malay community.

In the public sector some government expenditures were designed to promote the income earning capacity of the Malays, and various kinds of direct controls were applied, such as employment quotas and preferential licenses. Specialised institutions were set up, such as FAMA (Federal Agricultural Marketing Authority) and MARA (Council of Trust for Indigenous People, a lending institution) with specific objectives to help Malays establish themselves. Employment quotas did create jobs for thousands of Malays, but could not effectively touch the vast majority of the Malay population in the kampongs. The specialised institutions also provided some Malay employment, but they were operated too inefficiently to have any significant, favourable impact on rural marketing, credit and the like. The end result of these efforts was that population growth wiped out much of the few gains that were made and Malay kampong income failed to rise significantly. In turn, the political effect was to push many Malay politicians and intellectuals toward advocacy of increasingly radical solutions.

These political trends within the Malay community were quite apparent to the Chinese and Indian communities and were a source of increasing concern. Also important, the original socio-political contract struck by the dominant political parties, which provided a favourable climate particularly for the Chinese businessmen, had little appeal to the majority of the Chinese and Indians who were professionals, teachers and labourers. This majority  experienced rising incomes, but the number of new jobs created did not keep pace with the number of new entrants into the labour force and hence general unemployment in the country rose. Rightly or wrongly, this job squeeze was blamed increasingly on those policies of the government that were intended to improve the prospects of the Malays, in particular on the direct controls favouring the Malays. Furthermore, the Chinese and Indian communities were increasingly able to express their dissatisfaction through the ballot box as a result of the Merdeka Agreement. In the 1969 general election, a substantial majority of the Chinese and Indian communities voted against the Government. A feeling in the Malay community of losing out, of having been outplayed by the more dynamic and well organised Chinese in the commercial and industrial fields, had been growing for some years. The fear that the Malay population might be relegated to a permanent status even of political inferiority, in addition to economic and social inferiority, seemed to be confirmed by the outcome of the 1969 election. There was a ready illustration of this across the causeway. What had happened to the Singapore Malays, who were driven to near extinction numerically, politically and economically, increased the fear of the Malays in Malaysia and seemed to confirm the inevitable fate awaiting them in their own country unless something more effective was done to speed up their capacity to grow and prosper.

The Malaysian tragedy of May 13 which followed the election of 1969 threw the country into a state of national emergency. Among other things it showed that the past economic strategy had clearly failed to bring the economic and social status of the Malays to anywhere near that of the non-Malays. The measures which had been taken during the years since Merdeka to alleviate the economic status of the Malays were shown clearly to have been too weak and insufficiently comprehensive to make a real dent on the problem. In May 1969 it became clear that something new had to be done to help the Malays to get onto the bandwagon of economic progress in line with the rest of the population. Otherwise the trends were very clear for anyone to see — over a few generations the Malays would eventually lose out on both counts, politically as well as economically.

## Rukunegara, National Unity and the NEP

With the tragedy of the 1969 riot fresh in the minds of the people, with so many dead and with the disruptions and dislocations it caused, the government under YB[4] Tun Abdul Razak, as Chairman of the National Operations Council, realised that the achievement of national unity and racial economic integration was the most critical problem confronting the country. The political leadership had no illusion that the problem would be other than extremely complex and difficult to solve. A new course had to be charted to forge a cohesive and united Malaysian nation which would be based on equal justice and fairer share of the fruits of economic development for all Malaysians, irrespective or race or origins. Only then, it was thought, would it be possible to avoid another tragedy similar to that which had erupted in 1969, and to establish lasting political stability. Towards this end, the national ideology of Rukunegara[5] was proclaimed to the nation on Independence Day in 1970 and is reproduced here in Box 2.2. The political statesmanship and foresight of this approach to nation building by means of consensus instead of confrontation and through frank but closed door discussions of sensitive national issues, has been demonstrated by the uninterrupted political stability of the country from 1969 to recent years.

The relationship of the Rukunegara to the provisions of the Constitution was explained by the former Lord President Tun Salleh Abas in his book: *Constitution, Law and Judiciary*, (p. 231) as follows:

[4] The letters YB signify a title (Yang Berhormat) roughly equivalent to "Honourable".
[5] The reader will note that "Rukunegara" and "Rukun Negara" are alternative spellings of the same concept.

Rukun Negara does not impose more obligations, nor does it confer more rights than what is already contained in the Constitution. Obeying the Rukun Negara, therefore, is no more onerous than obeying the Constitution itself. What a citizen has to do is merely to respect each other's rights and duties, customs, habits and culture, and not to accentuate certain sensitivities which may provoke violent reaction from another group. In other words, Rukun Negara is a passport towards achievement of not merely co-existence of the various races but the intermingling of the various races in this country harmoniously without danger of having to repeat an incident like May the 13th .... For anyone

---

BOX 2.2

## RUKUNEGARA

### DECLARATION

OUR NATION, MALAYSIA, being dedicated

to achieving a greater unity of all her peoples;

to maintaining a democratic way of life;

to creating a just society in which the wealth of

the nation shall be equitably shared;

to ensuring a liberal approach to her rich and

diverse cultural traditions;

to building a progressive society which shall be oriented

to modern science and technology

WE, her peoples, pledge our united efforts

to attain these ends guided by these principles:

**Belief in God**

**Loyalty to King and Country**

**Upholding the Constitution**

**Rule of Law**

**Good Behaviour and Morality**

who disagrees with the Malaysian Constitution he will always disagree with Rukun Negara. The accusation that Rukun Negara represents the ideology of the Malay capitalists, or will benefit only the Malay race, is just as patent as it is a false one.

The New Economic Policy (NEP) was formulated by the government after the riot of 1969 as the economic foundation of the Rukun Negara. Tun Abdul Razak, in his wisdom, was fully aware that, important though the ideals of Rukun Negara and consensus building might be, the battle for unity would be won or lost in the economic and social restructuring of the nation. The NEP was therefore designed with the intention of giving content and substance to the new Malaysian ideology of nationbuilding as embodied by the Rukun Negara. It was based on the construction of new alliances of moderate political elements within the society and on a new formula. But Tun Abdul Razak emphatically stated (in Second Malaysia Plan, p. v) that the NEP would not take away the rights of the non-Malays, citizens or non-citizens:

> It (the government) will spare no efforts to promote national unity and develop a just and progressive Malaysian society in a rapidly expanding economy so that no one will experience any loss or feel any sense of deprivation of his rights, privileges, job or opportunity.

His strategy was based on the redistribution of the increments of the expanding Malaysian national cake gradually for at least a generation. Beginning with the Second Malaysia Plan as the first phase, the NEP was launched with the hope that a new Malaysian society would gradually emerge with a common value system transcending ethnic, cultural and socio economic differences. As seen in the aftermath of the May 13 riots, the nation had no other choice. The alternative would be a return, sooner or later, to antagonistic racial politics and polarisation, disunity, anarchy and disintegration.

## The Birth of a New Development Strategy

### The Documents

Comprehensive and pioneering analysis, methodological innovation and search for statistical underpinnings characterised the emergence and development of what became known as the New Economic Policy (NEP). At the end of this book we reproduce four of the documents prepared in 1969-70 as part of this endeavour:

Document A: *Policies for Growth with Racial Balance* was written within a few weeks following the riots of 13th May 1969. It was a personal first assessment by the head of the Harvard University Development Advisory Service in Malaysia, working within the Prime Minister's Department. The document, which initially was given a limited circulation, was instrumental in formulating issues for debate and became a reference document in subsequent elaboration of analysis.

Document B: *Racial Disparity and Economic Development* was issued by the Department of National Unity in November 1969 and circulated throughout Government departments.

Document C: *The New Economic Policy* was issued in March 1970 by the Department of National Unity as a *Directive* to all Government Departments and Agencies, providing basic guidelines for the Second Malaysia Plan 1971-75.

Document D: *Employment, Production and Racial Economic Balance Targets for the SMP,* dated June 19, 1970 sought to ensure that the approaches and objectives of NEP were reflected in the formulation of the Second Malaysia Plan. It provided an operational methodology for a planning exercise which would supplement the prevailing demand and financial approach with production, employment and supply considerations and objectives in a manner that gave expression to the NEP concerns for restructuring of the economy.

All these documents had the full and determined support of the Chief Secretary of the Federal Government at the time, Tan Sri Abdul Kadir Shamsuddin, before they were released for circulation to other Government departments. They came to be part of the foundation for the search by Tun Abdul Razak, as Director of Operations and then as Prime Minister, and by the Department of National Unity (DNU) for an alternative development strategy which could provide the basic thrust of the NEP and of the Second Malaysia Plan (SMP), the framework of which was then under discussion by the agencies and committees directly connected with drawing up the plan.

Two further documents (not reproduced in this book) may be mentioned as indicating the range of activity that went into the reconsideration of strategies for the country after the 1969 riots. One was an effort to develop a set of attitudes as well as specific policy measures for change that could gain widespread support within each and all ethnic groups. These are contained in *Problems of Racial Economic Imbalance and National Unity*, August 1970, agreed by the Economic Committee of the National Consultative Council. The

Council itself had been formed in January 1970 to formulate guidelines for inter-racial cooperation and social integration with a view to developing a Malaysian national identity. It comprised representatives from Ministers of the National Operations Council, state governments, political parties, religious groups, professional bodies, public services, trade unions, employers' associations, the Press, teachers and minority groups. The DAP (Democratic Action Policy, the main Chinese opposition party), however, was not represented, either as a body or by individuals. The deliberations of the Council were purposely kept away from the media, so that sensitive issues could be thoroughly discussed and a true consensus arrived at for the benefit of all Malaysians, present and future. The Economic Committee of this Council was headed by YB Tan Sri Mansor Othman and included YB Tun Hussein Onn, Professor U.A. Aziz, Professor Sayed Hussain Alatas, YB Tan Sri P.O. Narayanan, YB P.G. Lim and Reverend Denis C. Dutton among other Malaysian personalities.

An effort in a different direction concentrated on the wider aspects of the problems of national unity; those that went beyond the economic dimensions. In a report of May 1970: *Social Science Research for National Unity*, a group of internationally renowned social scientists examined the ways national unity might be furthered in Malaysia and how, concretely, social science analysis can be of significant help to the Government. The report spelled out a limited action programme to increase the capacity of Government to draw on such wider analysis, specifically for anticipating needs, defining strategies, evaluating policy impact, presentation and justification of policies, and assessing receptivity to alternative policies. The preparatory work for the NEP went well beyond the concerns and expertise of economists and administrators!

The discussion which follows will centre on the arguments, rationale and recommendations of these documents, which collectively are termed here as the DNU documents. After the riot, two major schools of economic thought emerged on how to respond in the most appropriate way to the grave situation in the country. The first school, led by the EPU (Economic Planning Unit) and strongly backed by the Treasury, Bank Negara (The Central Bank), the Statistics Department and FIDA (Federal Industrial Development Authority), is termed for convenience the EPU School. The second school, led by the Prime Minister's Department and the Department of National Unity is termed the DNU School.

## The EPU Approach

The EPU School emphasised economic growth over other priorities. The higher the rise in the GNP, the assumption was, the higher the increase in the standard of living and in the general welfare of the population. This was a logical policy, as long as, somehow, the system distributed the fruits of development in a fairly equitable manner among the populace and regions. Indeed, this was the assumption of the EPU school explicitly or implied. The EPU school therefore advocated a policy of "return to normalcy" and more effective implementation of the policies and strategies of the 1960s. May 13 was seen as a tragic but passing departure from a basically healthy course of economic development. Provided growth could be accelerated, distribution would take care of itself via the 'trickle down effect'. Over time, the system would eventually come to a balance through the price mechanism, where necessary supplemented by limited budgetary allocations for the poor, mainly the Malays. Malaysia in the past had achieved one of the finest records of economic development through this path of development strategy. Judged by its record of rising overall prosperity, the country's performance surpassed that of many other countries in the world, developed or underdeveloped.

This exceptional success was achieved by the government's maintaining a policy of political stability with minimum interference in the economic affairs of the country. The policy of maximum economic growth, maximum industrialisation effort, attractive incentives for private local and foreign capital etc. had proved its effectiveness. Conservative fiscal and monetary policy gave the country internal price stability and a stable external exchange rate. A balanced budget, at least on the current account, was the major objective, while development expenditure was financed out of genuine savings from the Employee's Provident Fund (EPF) and other sources. The word "deficit financing" was taboo, never to be mentioned in the corridors of the Treasury or Bank Negara. Neither was deficit financing necessary at that time. Moreover, balance of payments surpluses resulted in accumulated foreign exchange reserves far in excess of what the IMF articles required. For example, under the Currency Board System Malaysia backed its currency with sterling deposits in London by 100 per cent to 115 per cent for every dollar that was in circulation. These foreign deposits were later diversified to include other currencies and gold holdings. But under the new Bank Negara regime this currency backing was raised even further and kept at excessively high levels. This state of affairs continued for many years. At times, even the IMF questioned the need for such a vast hoarding of precious foreign exchange deposits when some portions of those deposits could be utilised for investment purposes in the country. Nonetheless, Malaysians not unjustifiably took pride in proclaiming to the world at international conferences and other forums that their country was a model of how a developing country should pursue successful economic and financial management with a set of cautious, conservative and proven policies.

The conservative approach had its merits. The state of economic knowledge of the country then was not so well developed. Malaysia had only recently emerged from colonialism. Qualified economic thinkers and planners were few in number, and the understanding of the economic processes was still in its infancy. In such a state it was safer to continue with the old proven policies and to err on the safe side rather than to venture into the risky unknown. The policy of "growth first and distribution later" had also intellectual respectability. Its ancestors included the Harrod-Domar model and Arthur Lewis' teachings, which were then the intellectual vogue in the profession.[6] Most of the technicians in the government institutions responsible for preparing the macro economic policy of the country were brought up in this intellectual tradition, reinforced by their further training with either the World Bank, the IMF, the Bank of England or other central banks. The practice of regular and intensive discussions with the World Bank and the IMF in particular won for the policy the full endorsement and approval of these prestigious international institutions. Any substantive change in policy contemplated was preceded by consultations with the staff of the World Bank or the IMF.

Furthermore, the economic policy pursued in the country had the full backing of the powerful local non-Malay business community through their chambers of commerce and through their political parties, which were constituent components of the ruling Alliance government. In particular, the Minister of Finance, a post reserved at the time for the MCA, was a lever in economic policy making. Tun Tan Siew Sin, President of the MCA, was for many years the Minister of Finance. He was the model of a monetary disciplinarian.

---

[6] It should be pointed out that Lewis' seminal work sometimes has been somewhat misrepresented. Note his statement in *The Theory of Economic Growth*, London: Unwin University Books, sixth impression, 1963, p. 1: "First it should be noted that our subject matter is growth, and not distribution. It is possible that output may be growing, and yet that the mass of people may be becoming poorer. We shall have to consider the relationship between the growth and the distribution of output, but our primary interest is analysing not distribution but growth."

Without his approval no policy could be adopted, at least not if it required a budgetary allocation. The Prime Minister was the only person who could override his objections and this was done sparingly and with great circumspection. The checks and balances were always there, since the Prime Minister was from UMNO while the Minister of Finance was from MCA and the Governor of Bank Negara was essentially appointed by the Minister of Finance. The equally if not more powerful foreign owners of the major banks, plantations, mines etc., not unexpectedly supported the policy through their chambers of commerce and embassies, as it worked to their interests. Even the large majority of foreign experts seconded from international agencies to the Malaysian government were supporting this policy and strongly advocating its extension. A coincidence of interest between the local and foreign owners of the modern sector favoured the perpetuation of the past policy. With the relatively overwhelming intellectual resources at its disposal this group, which included the more highly educated non-Malay elite, was able to present its case both lucidly and convincingly. Additional support for the policy was also given by some "liberal" Malays whose arguments were essentially that the Malays were unresponsive to the profit motive and that, since the Malays would not work as hard as the Chinese and the Indians, there was no reason why they should achieve the same measure of economic success. In sum, the advocates of the return to normalcy had an easier analytical and presentational task both to the country and to the world at large than had those who were attempting to advocate a new departure.

One of the merits of the EPU approach to planning in the country was that it highlighted the growth and the financial problems of the country. But it did not deal directly with the Malay problem, neither could it be expected to do so in a systematic and comprehensive manner. The Malays were simply assumed to derive benefits along with the general growth of the economy and indeed, to some extent, they did. But they were not at all able to catch up with the non-Malays. In fact, the distance between them and the non-Malays was getting wider. The late Dato Raslan, the first Chairman of Bank Bumiputra and one of the key advisers to Tun Abdul Razak in the NOC (National Operations Council), in one of those numerous meetings held after the riot to discuss the Malay problem, compared what was happening to a Jaguar overtaking a Morris Minor, never to be seen again.

At most, therefore, the EPU approach and strategy dealt with the Malay problems of poverty and inequity indirectly. The weakness of this approach, as pointed out in one of the early basic documents for the NEP (Doc. B, page 279), is that failure to analyse and consider the nature and magnitude of problems inevitably leads to ineffective, conflicting and superficial policies.

## The DNU Approach

Proponents of the DNU School, on the other hand, interpreted the 1969 riot differently. To them it was clear evidence of a growing fundamental structural defect in the country which had to be corrected urgently if a repetition of the 1969 type of racial riot or worse were to be avoided in the future. They pointed out that during the past decade the Malays had not shared equally with other ethnic groups in the expanding economic product of the nation. If anything, disparities in income between the communal groups had increased. Large segments of the Malay population remained ill-prepared to participate in the modern economy and key governmental policies and major institutional, social, cultural obstacles militated against effective Malay participation. So long as marked imbalances of this nature existed in the economy, meaningful integration and national unity would remain just a dream. Therefore, in a *Directive* sent from the Department of National Unity to Government Departments and Agencies the emphasis was placed on national unity, which for planning purposes was regarded as synonymous with the correction of the racial economic imbalances and the eradication of the identification or race with economic functions (Doc. C, p. 307):

> ... changes in racial economic imbalances are accepted by the Government as significant and central indicators of national unity. ... Are there marked differences as between racial groups in productivity, consumption, income, wealth, entrepreneurship, opportunities, etc.? If so, are these differences felt or assumed to be felt by one group or another as evidence of having lost out or of having been left out in the development process, as prejudicing the future of their group in social or political as well as in economic terms? How have these racial balances changed over time? Formulated in this way the economic objective of national unity may be expressed as *the improvement of economic balances between the races, or the reduction of racial economic disparities*. (Underlined in the original)

Thus, the DNU School emphasised the correction of the lopsided economic balances against the Malays as the most important objective of development for incorporation into the Second Malaysia Plan framework. They were careful to point out, however, (Doc. C, p. 307) that indicators of economic imbalance could not be expected to be other than imperfect recorders of elements of national unity.

Three areas of imbalances were emphasised by the DNU school namely imbalances in income, employment and ownership of capital and assets (Doc. B, p. 272). They were conscious, however, that these could only portray the disparity problem in terms of economics. Other factors, such as health (including such things as mortality rates and the incidence of malaria), educational opportunities in the form of easy physical access and availability of good teaching also accounted for a good deal. They were also aware of other limitations, including concentrating the analysis only on West Malaysia, and distinguishing only between Malays and non-Malays, and these limitations ruled out many important national and racial issues in the interest of focusing on a number of critical problems of racial disparity.

The primary objective of improvement in the income balance as between major ethnic groups was supplemented by the objective of maximising employment creation for all Malaysians, irrespective of race, through labour intensive methods of production, as well as through the pursuit of economic growth via export led and rapid industrialisation. The DNU strategy, therefore, had wider objectives than did the EPU strategy. Besides growth and distribution, socioeconomic and political developments had to be taken as equally important factors in the integrated approach to development. The new strategy, it was asserted, if implemented consistently over time, would spread the fruits of development widely to all sections of the community irrespective or race, class or region. Viewed from this perspective growth was only one of the elements. The overall objective was national unity and survival. If a trade-off was necessary, the objective of improvement in economic balance as between major ethnic groups would not be sacrificed in favour of growth, other things being equal.

The problem of economic imbalances arises primarily from income and productivity differentials between the Malays and the non-Malays. The sum total of the wide differentials expressed themselves in many ways, in the traditional/modern sector dimension, in the low/high productivity activities, in the rural/urban distinction and in the identification of race with economic functions. According to the DNU School, government policies since Merdeka had been ineffective in dealing with the problem, in part because the imbalances had not been sufficiently reflected in the analysis, formulation and implementation of the policies. Indeed, the governmental policy of relying nearly exclusively on the private sector for economic development had led to a lopsided development, which itself had become part of the problem — rather than the solution — of the racial economic imbalance situation. The DNU school therefore argued for an alternative development strategy that would lead to a correction of the imbalances. The main requirement was to develop policies that would be generally effective in raising income of Malays and providing for their entry into the modern sector on the basis of equal opportunity and non-discrimination. The new strategy of balanced participation placed primary emphasis on the objective of parity, secondary emphasis on overall growth and national income. Rather than aiming for such mitigation of disparity as was consistent with maximum growth, the strategy of balanced participation aimed for such growth as would be consistent with reducing racial disparities. This was of course the inverse order of the maximum growth strategy of the EPU School.

Economic imbalances in three specific areas considered to be the main issues of the problem, namely income, employment and ownership, were in focus for analysis and prescription. To quantify racial disparity in terms of productivity and income levels between the Malays and non-Malays, statistics of national accounts, population and employment for the eleven states of Peninsular Malaysia and for sectors were used. Similarly at industry level, statistics of employment by racial composition together with total output were used to show the differences in productivity between the Malays and non-Malays. Combining these data after making adjustment for known and assumed differences in earnings and productivity between the Malays and non-Malays, estimates of value added by race in the various sectors and industries were derived. Aggregating the output, the total employment and the value added by race in the various sectors, national figures in productivity and income differences were then derived. Estimates of ownership of assets, for which statistical data at the time were scarce, were carried out as a separate exercise. Again combining the three elements of productivity, income and wealth differences, it was possible to obtain a rough picture of the disparity ratio between the races in the economy: nationally, by region, by sector and by industry.

While the DNU School and the EPU School agreed that growth had to be an indispensable element in a policy of economic development and that the implementation machinery should be improved, the DNU school argued that the situation in the country required radically new treatment. Within the framework proposed, separate and specific targets were recommended for participation of Malays in each major modern sector and subsector activity, down to the unit level in manufacturing, finance, plantations, mining, construction, wholesale and retail trade, new estate developments etc., for incorporation into the Second Malaysia Plan which was then in the preparatory stage. Document D was an early effort by the DNU school to show how in practice this type of planning might be oriented. This would make the SMP an integral part of the NEP to speed up the participation of the Malays at all levels of modern sector activities. While thus recommending a new set of policy objectives, which subsequently became part of the New Economic Policy, the DNU school acknowledged that the economic balance objective and the growth objective were interconnected and in some ways could be conflicting. Yet, it was shown that the two objectives of restructuring and growth were simultaneously attainable in the context of the New Economic Policy.

Proponents of the DNU school argued for a decisive and strong policy for change and asserted (Doc. A, p. 269 ): "A timid and cautious financial and economic approach to Malaysia's present problems is doomed to fail", and then went on to state that:

> the danger is that the government and the administration will try to remedy the nation's political problems by singlemindedly pursuing goals such as "reduce unemployment" or "reduce Malay unemployment" and "raise the rate of growth of GNP". The current *ad hocism* of economic policy discussion and decision making badly needs to be replaced by analysis and consideration of the framework and means of a policy that is relevant to the basic issues of racial balance in economic development and growth. It is relatively easy to state the need for better balance and particularly the need to ensure that the Malay community enjoys a fair share of the opportunities and fruits of development. It is easy to point to imbalances and inequities. The real challenge is to propose a set of policies — not just minor isolated measures — that gives promise of success to correct the imbalances and the inequities. This requires imagination and hard work. It also requires direction and organisation.

## Differences in Approach

The differences between the two schools in both diagnosis and prescription went very deep. They were based not only on economic analysis but reflected also differences in respect of social philosophy as well as the parts of the society and the body politic with which the members of the two schools were associated. The EPU School which strongly advocated a return to normalcy and conventional planning methods, had an easier analytical and presentational task than did the DNU School. The continuation of the policies of 1960s were well defined and well understood, and had brought prosperity to Malaysia, albeit the Malays were largely left out in the development and modernisation process. The new strategy advocated by the DNU School on the other hand was still general and vague. It was a pioneering effort and was breaking new grounds. Not unexpectedly it met with resistance and even hostility.

In terms of economic approach, the EPU School used the methodology of demand analysis of the Keynesian type. Demand components of the GNP, namely public and private consumption and investments and foreign trade were projected over the proposed plan period. GNP forecasts were then derived. Allocations of resources, budgetary impact of the allocations, including projections of liquidity in the banking system, were then made consistent with the forecasts made for the other variables. This approach highlighted the issues of growth and finance such as the balance of payments of the country, level of foreign exchange, prices, etc. But it did not provide much insight into the serious issue of the rising general unemployment level in the country which affected all Malaysians, particularly the young among them. Neither did it address or attack the racial economic imbalance problem directly, serious as it was, as shown by the widespread racial rioting in 1969. Rather, the issues of employment and unemployment and of racial economic inequality were treated as residual problems, to be dealt with indirectly as a by-product of the growth policy. In so far as the economic imbalance problem was concerned, if the growth achievement was satisfactory and subsequently led to a partial solution of the imbalances so much the better. If not, then attempts to do so should be made in the next round. However, in no way or at any time should the concern for the residual problems be allowed to interfere with the growth performance of the economy. Such a system naturally works out to the advantage of the non-Malays, as they include the more economically advanced of the population and therefore are better placed to capture any opportunities that are being created in the economy. The Malays, being late starters with serious handicaps, could not possibly be expected to compete on equal terms and still come out at par with the non-Malays. The competition was just too hopelessly unequal against them.

The DNU School on the other hand approached development planning more from the production side of the economy. The new methodology was intended to supplement rather than replace the demand analysis of the EPU School. The purpose of the new approach was to highlight the general unemployment problems of the country, as well as the structure and the intractability of the Malay economic imbalance problem in terms of productivity and income differences between them and the non-Malays. The joint application of the two approaches would have brought out not only the issues of growth and finance but also equally important the issues of employment and of racial imbalances. Unless and until this was recognised in policy and planning analysis, the social and political bargaining and balancing process could not really take place, nor could an explicit choice of development strategy be made by the Government with clarity and finality and in the full knowledge of the implications of the choice. The DNU methodology allowed the problems of racial economic balance to be analysed directly and comprehensively. Consistent policies, programmes and projects which were needed to be formulated in order to achieve the targeted reduction in the disparity ratios within a time frame could also be developed and their progress of implementation monitored accordingly.

Three main sets of economic problems of the Malays were focused on and analysed by the DNU School for possible policy prescriptions. First, they analysed the nature and structure of the problem of economic imbalances between the Malays and the non-Malays in terms of income, employment and ownership of wealth. Second, they traced the developments of these imbalances over time since Merdeka and extrapolated them into the mid 1980s under certain assumptions. Third, they dealt with the problems of mass Malay poverty which was mainly rural poverty. All the three problems were of course interlinked. Moreover, it was realised that in a full analysis of the development and change of the society, other relevant factors had also to be taken into consideration. By explicitly limiting the analysis to the three sets of issue, other important national and racial issues were excluded from consideration. However, the advantage that was gained was the clear concentration on a number of what were felt to be the critical problems of racial economic imbalance and of Malay poverty.

The DNU school, in approaching the issues from the production side, developed what was essentially a pioneering method which provided a framework for comprehensive and yet specific analysis of the problem, both at the macro and micro levels. On this basis, prescriptions could be made which were consistent and which would stand together and be mutually reinforcing. This was in contrast to the uncoordinated and at best implicit manner in which such policies were developed and implemented in the pre-NEP days. Although article 153 of the Constitution specifically states that the Malays should be helped, this provision had never been translated into a comprehensive strategy with specific programmes and projects. There were many statements of noble intentions, promises, goodwill and friendship by Malay and non-Malay politicians alike. But these were again not reflected in concrete policies and plans; at least they did not add up to an integrated programme of action for attacking the Malay problem.

As the EPU itself and most of the team of foreign advisers to EPU were unconvinced of the new approach, refinement and further elaboration of the new approach had to be continued in the DNU. Conventional economic planning work continued in the EPU. In the DNU, the Minister Tan Sri Gazali Shafie was enthusiastic about the fresh approach. The Prime Minister, Tun Abdul Razak, and the Chief Secretary gave it their full support within the constraints that they had to face. To them and the moderate elements in the society as represented in the National Consultative Committee, the NEP concept as proposed offered hope to rebuild the country on a fairer basis for all Malaysians which would guarantee its long term stability.

However in terms of economic expertise the Department of National Unity did not have the capacity to carry out and sustain the work, particularly after the end of 1970, and the leadership drifted back to the EPU. In an environment where it was not welcomed in the first place, work on the imbalance problems were relegated to a role subordinate to the conventional planning priorities of the EPU. There were brave individual attempts, but as a guiding methodology of planning it largely fizzled out. The statement of noble ideals and intentions were still there in all the major documents. A part of the work initiated in the DNU was taken over by the Implementation Coordination Unit (ICU) in the Prime Minister's Department. This unit itself was a product and part of the overall strategy of the new approach to reorientate the government departments so as to enable them to undertake the wider role of expanded planning in the country. But again it was not a planning agency as such. Its main function was to modernise and streamline the government departments and agencies.

## The Problem Defined

### Ethnic Economic Imbalances

The main problem was that the Malaysian economy had a dualistic structure. Massive accumulated wealth in the modern sector existed side by side with mass rural poverty and underemployment in the traditional sector. Even if the population had been otherwise homogeneous, the gaps between the rich and the poor were too wide for the society to continue to exist without some form of social explosion sooner or later. To compound the strain, the gaps had been widening instead of narrowing since Merdeka. The Bumiputra who constitute more than half of the population, had received less than one-third of the *increase* of GNP which accrued from growth in the economy in the period from Merdeka up to the riots of 1969. The momentum had therefore been building up instead of being diffused by the post-Merdeka economic policies. The problem had taken on an ugly racial dimension.

As a summary statement of the nature and magnitude of the racial economic imbalance problem a number of generalisations regarding the "wealth and prosperity of Malaysians" were advanced in an early document of the DNU school (Doc. B, p. 273). These were that

the *average* Malay has a lower standard of living than the *average* non-Malay;

Malays form a much higher proportion of population in rural areas than in towns;

Malays populate the relatively poorer States and occupations to a higher degree than do non-Malays;

Malays form a higher proportion of the work force in low productivity traditional agriculture and a lower proportion of the work force in high productivity modern industry and commerce;

within given industries and enterprises Malays — as compared to non-Malays — typically hold lower-echelon positions;

placed in similar physical situations the motivation, inventiveness, energy and productivity of Malays in many activities fall short of those of non-Malays;

Malays own (or have property rights over) only about one third of land under agricultural cultivation;

Malays have a significantly lower share of ownership of industrial and commercial capital.

Population figures with GDP estimates by States were produced and analysed. They brought out in clear numerical terms how strongly the Malay population was concentrated in the poorest four Northern states of Terengganu, Kelantan, Perlis and Kedah where average GDP was the lowest. These states were dominated by agriculture and fishing activities of the unorganised traditional type. The four

Western states of Negri Sembilan, Selangor, Perak and Penang, where the non-Malays were the majority, had the highest GDP per capita. Modern commerce, industry, mining and plantation activities in the country were mainly centred in these states. The three Southern states of Pahang, Johor, and Melaka had median incomes per person, roughly equal to the national average, and the population in these states were about evenly distributed in terms of racial composition. In sum, the Malays lived largely in the parts of the country that were relatively untouched by economic development and modernisation, while the non-Malays largely lived in the prosperous states.

To examine the situation further, but from another angle, that is in terms of patterns of income, productivity and employment, the national economy was divided into rural and urban sectors which were further subdivided into modern and traditional sectors. To this fourfold division one additional sector, namely the government sector, was added. Definition of the sectors was as follows (Doc. B, p. 277):

*The Modern Rural Sector* which comprises the estates, commercial forestry, trawling, and about half of the mining operations.
*The Traditional Rural Sector* which comprises all agriculture, forestry, fishing and mining, not included in the modern rural sector. This sector also includes the mass of underemployed and fully unemployed rural workers.
*The Modern Urban Sector* which comprises modern type of industry, construction, trade and commerce, etc.
*The Government Sector* which includes Federal, State and local government administration, public educational and health services, etc., as well as the police and military forces.
*The Traditional Urban Sector* which comprises the urban petty traders, stalls, small artisans, personal servants and the multitude of activities requiring little or no initial skill or training for entry. This sector also includes the unemployed urban work force.

While the grouping was in some respects arbitrary, its main purpose was to give a picture of the dualistic structure of the economy as between rural and urban settings and, within each, the distribution as between the traditional, low productivity, relatively stagnant and economically backward activities where the Malays were predominantly located on the one hand, and on the other, the modern, organised, relatively capital requiring and more highly specialised and productive sectors where the non-Malays were mostly engaged. It therefore enabled a general analysis to be made in terms of income, employment and ownership and control of wealth by each group. Each category was given estimates of value added, and of total employment and its racial composition. Combining these data, estimates of value added were derived by industrial and racial groups, see Table 2.1, drawn from Doc. B, Table B.3.

Average income of workers in the five sectors outlined above ranged from highest in the Modern Urban Sector to medium in the Modern Rural Sector and the Government Sector and lowest in the Traditional Urban Sector and Traditional Rural Sector. The estimates confirmed that Malays were the poorest in the country, reflecting in some part the fact that the majority of them were engaged in the traditional rural economy. Even in the Traditional Sector, where they dominated, non-Malay incomes were higher. The figures also confirmed that in the modern sectors, both urban and rural, the levels of income were considerably higher. The Malays were the least represented in these sectors. In the Government Sector where the Malays were the majority, their income was higher than in the rural areas but lower than in the modern sectors. Most important, 43 per cent of the non-Malay workers were concentrated in the modern sectors, as against only 16 per cent of the Malays.

Although the differences were large, they still represented an underestimation of the actual situation for two main reasons. First, within a given industry or enterprise non-Malays on the average had a higher share of the higher echelon and higher income jobs than did the Malays. For example in modern industry and commerce there were relatively more non-Malays in positions of clerical staff and foremen, while the Malays were relatively more prominent in the general labour categories. Second, non-Malay workers were more productive. They saved and invested a larger share of their earnings than did the Malays. Even allowing for the weakness of the statistical data available, the fact emerged very clearly that the non-Malays were participating in the modern, urban and rural, higher productivity activities to a far greater extent than the Malays .

The racial composition of the labour force differed very significantly among the five sectors. Malays outnumbered the non-Malays in the traditional rural sector. In the traditional urban sector the reverse applied. In the modern rural and urban sectors the non-Malays outnumbered the Malays. In the government sector Malays outnumbered the non-Malays. While half of the non-Malay working force were employed in the modern sectors, including Government, less than one-third of the Malays were in those sectors. Further analysis of the structure of employment revealed that the traditional rural sector was by far the less efficient in terms of productivity of its labour, which largely was Malay. The productivity of labour in

TABLE 2.1

MALAY AND NON-MALAY VALUE ADDED AND EMPLOYMENT BY SECTOR

Data for 1967 as available or estimated in 1969-70

| | Value added per Worker | | | | Employment (thousands) | | | |
|---|---|---|---|---|---|---|---|---|
| | Malay | Non-Malay | Total | Malay as percentage of non-Malay | Malay | Non Malay | Total | Malay as percentage of total |
| Modern Rural | 3455 | 3920 | 3785 | 88 | 103 | 248 | 351 | 29 |
| Traditional Rural | 1135 | 1440 | 1215 | 79 | 928 | 327 | 1255 | 74 |
| Modern Urban | 4125 | 5160 | 4885 | 80 | 142 | 393 | 535 | 27 |
| Traditional Urban | 1280 | 1805 | 1675 | 71 | 142 | 420 | 562 | 25 |
| Government | 2400 | 2400 | 2400 | 100 | 185 | 112 | 297 | 62 |
| Total Economy | 1750 | 3000 | 2375 | 58 | 1500 | 1500 | 3000 | 50 |

the modern urban sector, which was largely non-Malay, was four times as high. As expressed in Doc. B, p. 279: "Overall there is a productivity and income differential in favour of the non-Malays which may be expressed by a ratio of nearly 7 to 4 or by the absolute difference of $1250... The enormity of the task to create balance is evident."

Equally lopsided, ownership and leadership of the modern sector were almost entirely in the hands of the non-Malays before the NEP, see Tables 2.2 and 2.3 for manufacturing industries.[7]

Industrial ownership, management and technical staffs were almost entirely Chinese except for a few Europeans and Americans. Commerce at all levels, foreign and domestic, was either in British or Chinese hands with the latter increasingly dominant. There were few Malay estates. Malay participation in construction was largely confined to unskilled and semiskilled jobs. The entrepreneurs themselves were overwhelmingly Chinese. University graduates in the sciences, medicine and engineering were almost entirely Chinese or Indians. Only in government service were there large numbers of Malays in managerial type positions. Even there the Malay role was heavily concentrated in the area of general leadership. Technical jobs remained largely in the non-Malay hands. Only in the armed forces and the police were the forces led and staffed by the Malays.

## Mass Malay Poverty

Mass Malay poverty both in absolute and in relative terms vis-a-vis the rest of the population is the outcome of large imbalances in terms of income, employment and the ownership of wealth. Since the vast majority of the Malays lived in the rural areas and were engaged in the least productive sector of the economy, mass Malay poverty was caused largely by conditions of rural poverty. Mass rural poverty was not homogenous, however, and it had to be recognised that there were several different groups whose social and economic situations and needs differed. It was necessary to distinguish various groups: rural Malays on the East Coast and in Kedah and Perlis; rural Malays on the West Coast except Kedah and Perlis; urban semi-skilled and unskilled Malays; and educated Malays, particularly those with University degrees and MARA education.

---

[7] The data in the tables are derived from *Problems of Racial Economic Imbalance and National Unity*, Report of the Economic Committee of the National Economic Council, August, 1970. Similar data were subsequently presented in the *Second Malaysia Plan 1971-75* and its *Mid-Term Review*.

## TABLE 2.2
## PAID FULL-TIME EMPLOYMENT BY OWNERSHIP
## IN MANUFACTURING INDUSTRIES
Data for 1967

| Ownership | Total employment | Malaysians | | Non-Malaysians |
|---|---|---|---|---|
| | | Malays | Non-Malays | |
| Malays | 1569 | 1223 | 301 | 45 |
| Non-Malays | 57455 | 13444 | 41467 | 2544 |
| Total Malaysians | 59024 | 14667 | 41768 | 2589 |
| Non-Malaysians | 34304 | 10453 | 20486 | 3365 |
| Total | 93328 | 25120 | 62254 | 5954 |

Twenty years ago, the numbers of Malays in towns and with education were quite small and they therefore constituted only a small minority of people in poverty in those categories. Rural Malay poverty groups were large, however, consisting primarily of those engaged in rubber smallholdings, in traditional paid cultivation and, in traditional inshore fishing.

Among all these rubber smallholders, padi planters, fishermen, etc., there was again a large majority who belonged to the sub-strata of the really poor, the hard-core poor, who could not be reached by traditional policy initiatives. These were the ones who lived below the poverty line, subsisting on meagre and inadequate incomes from whatever they could get from the environment. To make it worse, prices of their produce were controlled by the middlemen, where monopolistic and monopsonistic pricing conditions prevailed. Government taxation policy, such as the rubber cess levied on the rubber smallholders, discriminated against them in favour of the big rubber plantations. In fact, these Malays were subsidising the urban population as a result of the pro-urban policies of the British colonial government and their extension after Merdeka and also the unfavourable terms of trade which the agricultural sector received vis-a-vis the other sectors of the economy. These rural Malays, who formed the bulk of the Malays in the total population, were the ones who were the most vulnerable, the ones who were in need of most help and yet the last to receive any help. Many lived in remote areas inaccessible by modern roads, without electricity, water supply and

TABLE 2.3
PAID FULL-TIME EMPLOYMENT BY CATEGORY
OF WORKERS IN MANUFACTURING:
Data for 1967

| | Total | Malaysians | | Non-Malaysians |
| --- | --- | --- | --- | --- |
| | | Malays | Non-Malays | |
| 1. Factory workers | | | | |
| (a) skilled | 35177 | 7830 | 24950 | 2397 |
| (b) unskilled | 36865 | 13473 | 21837 | 1555 |
| 2. General workers | 7226 | 2357 | 4532 | 337 |
| 3. Clerical workers | 7078 | 732 | 5970 | 376 |
| 4. Technical and Supervisory | 4076 | 562 | 3124 | 390 |
| 5. Managerial and Professional | 2910 | 266 | 1941 | 703 |
| Total | 93332 | 25220 | 62354 | 5758 |
| Percentages | 100.0 | 27.0 | 66.8 | 6.2 |

modern health and sanitation facilities among others. They were the ones who were most prone to diseases because of inadequate calories and other malnutrition. Many of the urban people did not even know that such conditions existed since many of them had never visited these remote villages even once in their life.

Neither were these hard-core poor Malays able to present their case to the world at large, as were, for instance the National Union of Plantation Workers, whose president was an active member of the ILO in Geneva. Moreover, they were not organised like the urban workers. Most of the kampong people were either illiterate or their education was limited to that of the village Malay schools. In any case they were too polite to make any noise — or unaware of what would be effective noises to make — in order to make their plight known. Such behaviour and protestation would have been considered ill mannered by the "Pengulus" (headman) and the hierarchy in the

Malay value system. Those who were fortunate enough to have relatives working in the urban areas, in the government or in Singapore were able to supplement their meagre incomes by remittances from these relatives (in a similar fashion to Bangladeshi and Pakistani workers remitting money to their villages from abroad). But for the rest they plodded on silently. As part of their life they concentrated their efforts and energy, as they had done for centuries, on the salient features and the finer points of their religion and their other cultural intangibles. In this they were led on by the local "ulamas" (religious leaders) and later by politicians who capitalised on Islam to enhance their own political careers. The resulting intense religious and political controversies, which subsequently occurred in later years among the Malays, engaged a disproportionate amount of their attention and energy. This had three main effects. First, it split the Malays into various groups, second, it diverted their attention from their economic plight and their future, and third, it further segregated the various races from each other.

## Components of Income Disparity

It is difficult to quantify with any precision the extent of racial income differentials in Malaysia as between the major ethnic groups; it is even more difficult to be certain about the causes and dynamics of such income inequalities. It is helpful, however, analytically and as a basis for action, to distinguish between at least three components; first, the extent of outright poverty, that is life below what the statisticians term the poverty line; second, the racial income imbalance for those Malaysians who are living beyond or above the poverty line; and third, income inequalities within each ethnic group.

The fact that outright poverty in Malaysia is preponderantly (though not at all exclusively) a Malay phenomenon is clearly a factor in the perception that Malays generally are economically disadvantaged as against other racial groups. It was a very major factor twenty years ago when one in two of the Malay population was found to be living in poverty thus defined, as against one in four today, while the prevalence of outright poverty for non-Malays was and is much lower.

Also the more comfortably-off Malays felt that they had no real opportunity to move ahead with the other ethnic groups in trade and finance, in construction and industry, in entrepreneurship and the professions. The Malays were well acquainted with the opportunities of service in the army, police or public administration, but the modern and expanding sectors of business, industry and trade were regarded as the preserves of the other ethnic groups and, of course, the foreigners. Few Malays had the formal education required to enter the professions and the modern world of trade and business, they lacked both skills and opportunities to gain experience to prosper and succeed, they had no network of contacts for finance and markets, for supplies of inputs and for outlets for products. The apparently rewarding activities of Malaysian Chinese and Indian traders, money lenders, market operators and even workers in new industries and construction were highly visible, if often somewhat misleading, evidence of success, progress and fortune that somehow eluded the Malays. This they ascribed in large measure to discrimination by those groups that were already established and they strongly, even violently, voiced their demand for rectification of the injustice they felt through political action; hence the New Economic Policy.

In respect of distribution of assets and income within the racial groups the picture is not very clear. Growth, development and modernisation had progressed much further with the Chinese Malaysians than other ethnic groups. Considerable differences had shown themselves already in the 1960s and were in part reflected in the way this group of Malaysians organised themselves in political parties. For the Indian Malaysians, there were indeed great differences in standards of living between the many who worked on the estates and the few who had moved into the professions and comparative affluence, but their dissatisfaction found expression more in vigorous trade union action than in the establishment of different political parties which Malaysian Indians would join. For the Malays, there were conspicuous differences in the life styles that could be afforded, notably, of course, between the bounties and riches of the ruling Sultans and their extended families and the ordinary life of the Malay in the kampongs. Yet, this was a traditional and accepted difference in the Malay community which at the time was hardly even raised as a serious political issue. Such diversity of political affiliation among the Malays as did occur had more to do with the acceptance or otherwise of alleged moral and religious consequences of modernisation and development for the Malays.

## The Problem in Perspective

Again emphasising the recognised weakness of the data used and the fact that the computations of income and productivity differences deliberately underestimated rather than overestimated differences, the inescapable conclusion of the enormity of the problem of racial economic imbalances was clearly driven home. The Malays were the poorest in their own country measured by any criteria that one wished to use. The sum total of all the major imbalances expressed themselves ultimately in terms of income levels, in differences in the standard of living, in effective control of the economy and in the last analysis in political power itself. The computations confirmed that on average the level of income of the non-Malays stood perhaps twice as high as that of the Malays. What this meant was that a decade after Merdeka the Malays, in spite of the privileges accorded to them under the Constitution, primarily in Articles 89 and 153, were, in actuality, the ones against whom the system discriminated. Far from gaining ground, the Malays were actually losing relatively to the rest of the population. The actual tangible gains and the fruits of Merdeka, instead of going to them, went more to the non-Malays. Apparently, it made no difference whether the Malays were under the British colonial masters or managing their own economic destiny, they came out at the bottom anyway. What effectively happened at Merdeka was that a system of external British colonialism was substituted by a permanent system of internal discrimination.

These findings were not essentially new. The disparity was so glaringly visible that it had been a constant underlying concern of the Government since Merdeka. One had only to visit any Malay kampong or fishing village, or drive outside Kuala Lumpur or any of the large urban centres in the country to confirm the fact visually. But in accordance with the EPU approach the basic realisation of the problem had not been expressed in explicit and pervasive policies, nor had the government and the administration instituted or carried out any thorough and comprehensive analysis of the qualitative and quantitative elements of the disparity problem.

What was new and highlighted by the new approach however was that racial economic disparities were deeply entrenched in the structure and dynamics of the economy and that they had a momentum and logic of their own. They were too serious to be solved indirectly as a residual or as a by-product of a growth policy, however successful otherwise, or through exercises in exhortation and persuasion, or as a result of pious intentions or of short term measures to find employment opportunities for selected groups, or of specific but uncoordinated efforts to help the Malays. In fact, past policies might even have been counter productive at times in terms of racial balance. In any case their implementation came nowhere near adding up to a policy to deal with the disparity problem effectively. The overall findings of the new approach led to one major policy conclusion: the racial economic disparity problem had to be confronted and attacked firmly and explicitly and over a long period of time.

## Towards a Solution

There is no doubt that the state of inequality was explosive. It could not have been tolerated for long by any definition of a civilised society based on the principle of justice and compassion for the poor and the underprivileged. It was simply and clearly unacceptable. Sooner or later, such imbalances would have led to a social explosion, even if the population had been homogeneous without the added factor of the races. The solution to the problem was to raise the productivity and income levels of the laggard individuals, groups and races towards that of the rest of the population. It was not only a question of the Malays having to work harder like the non-Malays, as they were admonished by those who were elected by them. The Malays were even told that they were genetically defective because of incestuous marriages and inbreeding. These assertions ignored the facts of Malaysian history and the experience of other countries, developed or developing, struggling with similar problems to uplift their peoples from poverty and backwardness. In fact, the Malays did work hard; being poor they had to do so to survive. Most of the virgin jungles of the country, in places like West Johor, Sungei Manek, Tanjong Karang etc., with all the infestations of malaria and other diseases, were opened by Malays with the simple tools of the "parang" and the axe, not with bulldozers. They turned these jungles into prosperous farm lands. But there were limits to what they could do by themselves to keep up with the productivity increases in the modern sector. Beyond a point it would be of no avail to work hard on the diminishing plots of rubber and padi smallholdings, fragmented over time due to the Islamic inheritance law. They could hardly go deep sea fishing with the 'sampan' and simple nets and without capital equipment, new skills and other supporting facilities. How could they become innovative inventors or management experts with a standard four Malay school education?

According to the DNU School, the solution had to be found through the enhancement of productivity and incomes of the Malays to bring them up to those of the non-Malays by ensuring — over time — that Malays could enter the sectors of higher productivity in the economy in increasing numbers, so escaping from traditional, usually rural, unrewarding activities. In such a manner, effective equality and non-discrimination could eventually be established without depriving the non-Malays of their rights, or giving them a legitimate sense of loss and deprivation. Malays would, in other words, participate increasingly in the production of the Malaysian "cake" and gradually share more equally in the product with the other racial groups. This, then, would give more meaning and real economic content to the spirit and intent of Article 153 of the Constitution.

At the macro level, the new strategy of development advocated by the DNU School was based on four major elements (Doc. A, pp. 251 ff.): a thorough going land reform and support to smallholder farmers; a major effort to accelerate land development; a redirected and increased educational effort; and a policy of rapid industrialisation. In addition a number of measures of a shorter term nature were envisaged to provide Malay employment, increase their incomes and stem migration to the towns. The nature of these programmes would have to vary according to the various groups of Malays at which they were aimed. Reforms would be needed both *within* sectors (such as policies to raise the level of productivity and incomes of Malays in each sector where they earn their livelihood, especially in the Traditional Rural Sector) and shifts *between* sectors (e.g. relocation of Malay workers in such a manner as to gradually obtain a better occupational distribution, more comparable to that of the non-Malay working groups).

## Intra-Sectoral Reforms

Intra-sectoral reforms were those associated with raising Malay incomes within each of the main sectors, especially in the traditional rural sector, and included (Doc. A, p. 255) improved extension services to assist multicropping and intercropping, and assistance with processing and marketing. On a different note, attention was called to price policies which acted to the detriment of agriculture. These included protection given to local industry, located mainly in West Coast States, which raised prices to the agricultural sector, as well as arrangements affecting the agricultural sector itself. Subsidies to smallholders for replanting rubber were, in effect, considerably less than the cesses paid by the smallholders themselves, while the estates were subsidised. It is not surprising that such policies were dismissed as making no sense at all.

Also included in this category of measures to increase rural income were rapid land development schemes of the FELDA (Federal Land Development Authority) type. Estate agriculture development was therefore recommended to proceed at such a pace that a high proportion of the increase in the rural labour force, for example in East Coast states, could be given opportunities for gainful employment in land clearance, development and settlement. Secondly, the land development programmes needed to give the settlers large enough holdings to provide them with attractive incomes, allowing for the probable advances in technology as well as in general incomes. The allocations of land for new settlers were therefore recommended to be increased to at least 50 per cent above what at the time was the practice. Equally important, the recommendations went on, these new development schemes should be developed and led for the most part by the Malays themselves. They should of course be accompanied by large scale programmes for infrastructure development, including road building, feeder road construction and the like. The measures described should raise the willingness of the Malays to remain in the rural areas. This would stem the flow of rural to urban migration which was aggravating the social conditions in the urban areas.

Intra-sectoral reforms in the Modern Sector involved moving Malay workers proportionally up the echelons to the top executive levels. This would require a series of steps to be implemented, including education, training etc., both by the private sector and the Government. New institutions had to be established and the curricula of the existing ones re-directed to enhance Malay skills and to meet the demand of the Modern sector. The target groups in this category of policies were the urban semi-skilled and unskilled Malays, and the highly educated Malays, that is graduates of universities and other higher educational institutions. It was a well known fact that Malay workers were at that time discriminated against by the non-Malay employers in industries and business organisations. Therefore it was deemed necessary to make it mandatory for employers, particularly in the pioneer industries, to employ Malay labour increasingly over time at all levels as the Malays upgraded their skills. The really highly educated ones were thought to be capable of getting employment on their own or at least there was sufficient demand at the time to absorb them into employment in industries and in government. The trouble with this group was that they preferred to work in Kuala Lumpur rather than returning and serving the rural areas and thereby increase their productivity.

The importance of institutional changes for improving rural income was stressed by the DNU School. For many years the Government had given great emphasis to the introduction of technological change. While the results in terms of concrete physical progress were impressive, the impact on incomes and on incentives had not been satisfactory. Attempts by the government to mechanise agriculture and bring modern technology to the rural producers had been to a certain extent nullified because the very instruments of modernisation ended up in the hands of the rural capitalists whose monopolistic position was thus further reinforced. The basic objective of institutional change was to alter the relationship of the rural capitalists and the rural workers so as to create the opportunity for incentives to become effective. Such incentives would lead the traditional workers to increase their productivity by extensive adoption of technologically advanced methods of production. This would thus increase their incomes directly by the redistribution arising out of the institutional reforms and would further sustain increases in income from gains in productivity. Without institutional reform the incentive effects could be negated and the whole effort fail.

The rural capitalists and the rural producers were mutually associated in a system of institutional relationship. Rural capitalists include rural traders, both buyers and sellers, landlords, boat lords, fishing net lords and other owners of rural capital who rent to rural producers. Rural producers include landless workers, tenant farmers, owner farmers and peasants. The bulk of the rural capitalists were non-Malays, mainly Chinese, while the bulk of the rural producers were Malays. This aspect tended to create racial tension. Recognising that rural poverty was the main cause of Malay poverty stemming from low productivity, neglect and exploitation, it was only logical that these institutional relationships had to be rearranged to give the rural producers a better deal.

One set of measures proposed included legislative provisions that would give security of tenure to the landless. Existing legislation providing for producers' rights against landlords required firm enforcement through registration with the proper authorities. Other measures included giving due rights to those who were in employment in rural areas. For example, the relevant legislation providing for benefits to labour in the urban areas should be extended to the rural areas. Other measures included improving the system of division of the farm produce between the landlord and the tenant (the Bagi Dua system), the provision of rural credit and the introduction of marketing reforms.

If the measures recommended were in fact implemented, the DNU School concluded, the rural sector would rid itself of the problems of low productivity, neglect and exploitation. Rural income, predominantly being Malay, would rise and mass Malay poverty would decrease over time. Yet the warning was given (Doc. A, p. 253) that:

The major barriers to land reform in any country are political. Only a major and continuing effort will do the job. Many countries have land reform legislation, but few have land reform.

## Inter-Sectoral Reforms

Inter-sectoral reforms were mainly associated with the problem of changing the employment pattern to reflect the multiracial composition of the country. To a large extent, employment and type of employment determine income levels. The quantitative evidence presented showed that non-Malays were participating in the modern urban and rural sectors to a far greater extent than the Malays. Restructuring of Malay employment, to make it more comparable to that of the non-Malay working population, was therefore recommended. By so doing, the distribution of income would become more equitable in line with the distribution of employment.

To restructure employment, four main strategies were recommended. First, there was the unhindered movement of labour from rural to urban areas without any direct action on the part of the State beyond the provision of information of some welfare services to workers arriving from the rural areas. Second, there was the strategy of compulsion whereby firms would be required to employ certain proportions of workers of a specific ethnic group. Third, there was the strategy of a massive education and training programme directed towards future employment requirements in the educational institutions and in public and private sectors. Lastly, there was the strategy of active and direct participation by Government in the private sector in order to provide wider opportunities for training and employment for Malays.

To embark upon such a four-pronged strategy, the government was urged, with its power and resources, to re-order its priorities, formulate appropriate policies and programmes and create effective machinery for their implementation. It was necessary for example to set up an organisation to deal with all the problems arising out of guidance, placement, welfare, supervision, the training of workers for industrial jobs and teaching them how to live as industrial workers, and also helping them to adjust to the necessary changes from rural life to urban life. Also, existing government policies requiring pioneer companies to employ a racially balanced work force would need to be firmly implemented and extended also to non-pioneer companies in other industries. Other policies were to be put in place to encourage the employment of Malays in industries. There should also be an inspectorate within the Ministry of

Commerce and Industry to ensure that firms employed a certain proportion of workers of a specific ethnic group.

The strategy of inter-sectoral reforms also included the restructuring of financial capital and other capital assets. The survey of manufacturing industries carried out in 1970, for example, indicated that Malays owned less than 4 per cent of the total number of establishments in the manufacturing industries, compared with 79.6 per cent owned by non-Malays and 16.7 per cent by non-Malaysians. In the rubber estate sector, Malays owned less than 1 per cent of the total acreage compared with 48 per cent owned by the non-Malays. The disparity extended to palm oil production, coconut plantations etc. If the Malays were to be enabled to participate effectively in the capital ownership of industries and other modern sectors of the Malaysian economy and thereby reduce the racial economic imbalance position, restructuring had to be effected in all of them.

The distribution of wealth affects income levels. It also affects the rates and levels of savings. In order to increase Malay incomes and savings it was necessary that there should be redistribution of capital assets in modern industries and commerce. In part, this process could be effected through the redistribution of shares in modern companies. In order to enable the Malays to participate effectively in the capital ownership of industries in the modern sectors, a number of steps were recommended. First, the government was urged to review its policies so that more appropriate measures could be introduced for the Malays to establish themselves in the modern sectors. This included the provision of wider incentives. Second, government was urged to reserve a certain proportion of shares in pioneer companies to Malays and to implement these provisions firmly. Measures were needed not only to enable the Malays to retain their holdings but also to increase the number of Malays who would benefit from such a policy. It was also recommended that this policy should be extended to other important industrial and commercial companies. Third, it was recommended that the government should play a more active role in the establishment of industries in order to hold, on behalf of the Malays, the capital of such organisations until the time when the ownership of the organisations could be purchased by the Malays. Fourth, the government was asked to set up technical consultancy services to help emerging Malay entrepreneurs. Fifth, the almost wholly non-Malay private sector was asked to cooperate in these efforts by setting up joint ventures in the modern sectors to include Malay partners. A certain proportion of the agencies concerned with distribution were also reserved for the Malay partners.

## Elements of a Strategy

The overall objective of the DNU strategy was to raise the productivity of the Malays individually and collectively to that of the non-Malays over a long haul. At least, the system should be designed, so as to allow for an increase in their productivity in step with that of the non-Malays, so avoiding any further widening of the productivity differentials. This entailed raising the productivity of Malays, as well as moving those in the rural sectors, to the higher productivity sectors of commerce and industry. It was also necessary for the Malays to increase their ownership and control of capital assets in various sectors of the economy. Rural poverty, being mainly Malay poverty, could simultaneously be alleviated in the process.

### Growth vs. Distribution

In recommending a new set of policy objectives, approaches and targets, the DNU School fully recognised that the objectives were interconnected and in some ways might conflict with the maximum growth objective that had been pursued by the government. They pointed out that it was crucial for policy formation and for continuity and persistence in its implementation, as well as for analysis, to recognise the possibility that the strategy of maximum growth might compromise balance between the races, while the strategy of balanced participation might compromise growth. There was also the possibility of conflict in terms of the use of resources. The burden of taxation to raise resources in support of the Malays could become counter productive in terms of overall investment, growth and entrepreneurship. Devoting financial and real resources to increase the productivity and economic capacity of the Malays could to some extent mean forgoing development in otherwise more productive lines of activity. It might be possible to have some growth and some mitigation of disparities, but at some level and in particular situations the two objectives might become basically competing. The disparity which already existed was so deep seated that the economic distance between the races would be bound to widen unless determined policies to give the disadvantaged groups, mainly Malays, considerably greater participation in the modern sectors were followed, even though these policies might tend to contain the short term rate of growth and development of the overall national economy. However, for a longer term future, effective policies to contain or even lessen racial disparities would be consistent with an overall rate of growth in the economy, estimated at 6 per cent or more annually, which would be better than in the period since Merdeka.

In the past, the strategy had been to concentrate on growth of overall production and aggregate income creation. This strategy (as explained in Doc. B, p. 281) did not exclude consideration of disadvantaged groups; moreover, a rapid expansion in resources could provide the means to support and subsidise the lower income groups, particularly the rural population, the Malays, those in low productivity occupations and the unemployed.

Yet, in fact, this policy had worked to worsen the racial economic imbalance situation. In principle, transfers and subsidies to the disadvantaged groups were essentially of two types: those that raised their levels of private and collective consumption above what their own production efforts permitted, and those designed to raise the levels of productivity, production and income earning capacity of the disadvantaged groups. In practice, however, such transfers did not take place on balance. In fact a reverse flow occurred, largely from the poor rural Malays to the richer urban non-Malays.

## Redistribution vs. Participation

The net impact on the traditional sector was adversely effected by a number of measures and policies that had been designed and implemented in accordance with the maximum growth strategy. The traditional sector subsidised the modern sector by paying several production cesses on the rubber smallholders which were higher in total than what they were receiving in return. The health programmes for Malay villagers were inferior to those for urban populations and modern sector workers. Rural people on the whole had a lower quality of teachers and educational facilities for their children. The rural Malay population was paying a good part of the cost of subsidising and protecting industry which was owned and operated by the non-Malays without compensating benefits in terms of jobs and income. The list could go on. Even though there were some offsetting factors, the overall balance of advantages worked in favour of the modern sector, that is against the Malays. There certainly was no redistribution taking place in favour of the Malays. Even if the balance of advantage was improved in favour of the Malays, it would be unrealistic to expect, given the enormity of the distance between the Malays and non-Malays, that such an adjustment process would ever resolve the problem.

The second type of transfers (those to raise productivity) required the mobilisation of resources produced in the modern sector for investment in improved production facilities and capabilities for the disadvantaged groups. This type of transfer involved giving priority in public development and operating expenditures to rural over urban areas, to Malay entrepreneurs over non-Malays, to smallholders over estates and so on. In total or on balance, this type of priority had not been given since Merdeka, although there were some good special but partial efforts being made. The needs of the urban sector were so strong that the government had little left for the rural areas. Whatever transfers had been made, they were not sufficient or adequate to bring about a better production and income balance between the races.

Thus government policy, based on consumption subsidies and assistance to production, failed to attain a better balance between the races. The DNU School therefore insisted on the necessity of having a policy aimed at balanced participation of Malays in the modern sector of the economy. This would give them a fair and even chance to participate directly on terms of equality and non-discrimination. In consequence, deliberate policies were designed to increase Malay participation rates in all sectors of the economy as one of the means of reducing the disparities and enabling them to participate in the development of their own country as equal partners. Having to sit on the side lines watching the train of progress and modernisation go by, leaving them further and further behind, was unacceptable. Malay productivity was to be fostered by deliberate public action to increase it in line with that of the other races. Development in accordance with this new strategy of active Malay participation in the modern sector of the economy (as explained in Doc. B, p. 282) was intended to place primary emphasis on the objective of parity and secondary emphasis on overall growth. The alternative would have been to concentrate on growth and accept the limited contribution this could make to reducing racial disparities.

The DNU analysis projected an increase in Malay participation rates in all modern sectors. The Malays would therefore share in both the fruits and costs of development. But in so doing they would have to sweat it out like the others if they wanted progress and development.

## Role of the Government

Perhaps the single most important characteristic of the New Economic Policy was the determination with which the Government would be ready to set up new institutions, use new instruments of policy and adopt special measures to ensure that the national objectives could be achieved. Government was assigned a leading role together with the private sector in order to realise the overall new strategy of development. Unbridled private sector activity, it was felt, had not benefited the Malays either in terms of income or employment. The principle was put forward, therefore, in Document C, p. 310, of adopting a more positive and active role for the Government, of operating through public sector enterprise and through firm policies affecting development in the private sector.

It was clearly recognised, however, that there would have to be limits to Government interference with the modern private sector, particularly industry; otherwise it would not be able to play its role in the modernisation of Malaysian society, both Malay and non-Malay. Government was therefore assigned a multiple role of statesman, innovator and catalyst in the efforts to restructure the society. Government had to exercise its power, political and economic, to ensure the rapid emergence of a racially balanced participation in modern economic life of the country. While in the past, Government direct participation in the private sector had not been aimed at all decisively towards solving the problem of economic imbalance, this would now have to be changed. In other words, the government, including State Economic Development Corporations, statutory bodies and other government agencies, would pave the way for Malay entry into the modern sector in terms of employment and ownership. Moreover, government active participation at an early stage would also present opportunities for the eventual entry of Malays in fields which, otherwise, at a later stage, might prove difficult for new entrants. It would also provide physical evidence of the participation of the Malays in the development of the modern sector.

## Role of the Private Sector and Industrialisation

Although unbridled private sector activity in the past had worked to the detriment of the Malays in terms of balance, the DNU School, as noted above, warned that clear limits must be set on the amount of government interference in the private sector, particularly in industry. Industrial growth was considered crucial over the long run if the various schemes described were to be financed. Sources of government revenue were heavily dependent on the modern sector and growth of the modern sector was in turn greatly influenced by the pace of industrial growth. A further implication of the growth foreseen was that the Malaysian economy would be increasingly export oriented. The DNU School emphasised (see Doc. A, p. 268) that, if the goal of rapid industrial growth was to be met, liberal policies had to be adopted that would not seriously hamper the operations of Chinese entrepreneurs.

The critical role of industrial growth in creating employment was stressed as large numbers of new entrants were expected to come into the labour market, both Malay and non-Malay. A rapid increase in unemployment among young Chinese and Indians would be as politically explosive as would a comparable increase in Malay unemployment. So (as concluded in Doc. A, p. 265) to increase employment over the long run was to concentrate on raising the rates of industrial growth.

## Role of Education

Education was given a central role in the new development strategy (Doc. C, p. 317) because it was regarded as a vehicle to modernise society and attain social goals, and as a way to achieve equal opportunities for all and promote national unity. It was regarded as of particular importance for the rural population and for urban unskilled Malays. It was also regarded as an essential element in creating a leadership elite and, for the Malays, the means to take their rightful place in society.

There was a clear need to revise rural school curricula to make them more relevant to rural needs. Also, the establishment of three additional universities was urged. Acquirement of skills was indispensable for increasingly sophisticated tasks. The targets could be realised only if the Malay labour force could be given training to perform skilled tasks through basic education and other formal instruction as well as practical on the job training. The dangers to the system from irrelevant education were also pointed out (Doc. A, pp. 264-265). It was felt that there would be a wide range of skills amongst educated Malays, but also that many would not have the abilities needed to achieve economic and political leadership of the country. There could be a danger, therefore, that their education would be conducive to highly volatile political demagoguery, as had happened in so many developing countries, and to leadership for politicial disintegration, a much less demanding task than that of achieving integration and growth.

Specifically in education the role of the government was to embark upon a more vigorous dynamic training programme for the Malays, especially in the management, technical and scientific fields. This would involve the modification of the existing education system in order to provide more facilities for the rural areas with particular emphasis on modern sciences and technology. It was proposed to establish regional colleges to ensure a supply of qualified students for advanced training in all fields of modern sectors. Cooperation from the private sector was expected in the provision of training programmes to facilitate the absorption of Malays into gainful employment. Such training programmes could be undertaken with industrial firms or jointly by firms in a particular industry. The government was urged to offer partial financing for a workable scheme of in-service training which could be designed by the private sector in close consultation with the relevant authorities.

## Complementary Policies

In formulating the NEP the Government emphasised three basic objectives of economic policy: (i) the promotion of national unity and integration, (ii) the creation of employment opportunities and, (iii) the promotion of overall economic growth. As stated in the Government *Directive* (see Doc. C) the overriding objective was to be the promotion of national unity and integration. This, in turn, was interpreted mainly in terms of improvement of economic balances between the races. It was recognised, however, that indicators of racial economic balance reflect many important aspects of national unity only imperfectly, rather like economic growth rates as indicators of improvement in general well-being. It was envisaged, therefore, that planning for improvement in racial economic balances needed to be supplemented by analysis of changes in other social relations: in urban harmony or tension as otherwise evidenced, in racial settlement patterns for squatters and for residents in given areas, in racial elements of interrelationships between retailer-customer, employer-employee, producer-trader, lender-borrower etc.

Creating the conditions for national unity, like development itself, was seen as a multidimensional process, which in the situation of Malaysia had strong economic dimensions, but also elements that went beyond economics and required analysis and policy based on insights that would need to be derived from other disciplines of social studies. Towards this end a social science team of experts were invited in early 1970 to prepare a report on how social science could best contribute to the reconstruction of the Malaysian society. As these experts saw the situation, the pursuit of national unity would have a three-fold goal: first, the avoidance of communal violence and the reduction of communal tension; second, the achievement of a better racial economic balance; and third, the promotion of a deeper, common, national identity, as a basis for national unity. Five important functions were identified for social science research that would be effective in informing and assisting policy makers in their task: (i) to help anticipate tensions and demands that may require a policy response; (ii) to help develop options for policy response; (iii) to assess the impact and effectiveness of old and new policies, (iv) to help in the presentation of such policies to make them better understood and more acceptable to opinion makers and (v) to help determine receptivity in different groups of the population and thus to guide policy makers in their choice of options available. At the time of the formulation of the NEP itself, therefore, there was a search for complementary programmes that went beyond the central and explicit economic objectives and policy measures of the NEP. This reflected the realisation, first, that the objectives and specific measures of the NEP would have consequences on the social fabric that went beyond the straight economic dimensions and, second, that the NEP as a programme of economic action could not encompass the full range of social engineering that might advance the cause of national unity.

## Potential Impact of NEP

In order to assess how the strategy outlined above would work, the DNU School carried out a number of simulations designed to assess the character and extent of racial disparities in the 1970s and to see how they might change in the 1980s if there was a strong political will to deal with them, and if economic developments within Malaysia and in the rest of the world were favourable. Although a "conservative" estimate of the extent of the original disparity was made, other assumptions bordered on rather heroic optimism (Doc. B, p. 287). There was a deliberate overestimate of the extent to which and the speed with which the basic production structure could be modernised, an ambitious set of targets relating to the degree of participation of the Malay work force in the developments and a rate of growth of the economy which would be consistent with the assumed policies to ensure Malay participation. In their pioneering efforts, rudimentary data, such as they were, had to be used as best they could. The age of the computer still being in infancy, the calculations were made laboriously by hand. In spite of these limitations, it served its purpose. To date the main findings and their validity have yet to be refuted, notwithstanding all the high-tech machines that are now in use, the availability of data and the state of economic knowledge on the Malaysian economy. Regrettably, this analysis has not been developed and appreciably extended, in spite of the importance of the issues these problems have for national survival. (However, some scholars and outsiders, particularly from the World Bank, have produced valuable insights into one part of the problem, namely the general income distribution issues, and we refer to their findings elsewhere.) Two main sets of projections were made by the DNU School: one was a medium term outlook to 1985 (see in particular Doc. B); the other focused on the short term to 1975 and gave more detail (see in particular Doc. D). The former were intended to show the magnitude of the task of restructuring set for the NEP, the latter was intended for use as a basis for discussions by the various planning committees which were then drawing up the detailed plan of the Second Malaysia Plan. After refinements by the committees such quantitative targets, it was hoped, would be used and incorporated as an integral part of the Second Malaysia Plan.

## Racial Economic Disparities

For ease of reference a summary of findings from these computations for the medium term outlook to 1985, as detailed in Doc. B, is presented here as Table 2.4. In 1967 the average income in absolute terms was estimated to be at $3000 for non-Malays as against $1750 for Malays. This disparity could be expressed by a ratio of roughly 7 to 4 in favour of the non-Malays. To bring this ratio to 7 to 5 by 1985, (by which time the Malaysian overall economy would have grown very considerably, to $5120 per capita for the non-Malays and $3645 for the Malays) the effort required from the government to restructure the economy, if it could be done at all, was monumental. Non-Malay income would increase, but Malay income would increase at a faster relative rate. Even so the absolute ringgit difference between the non-Malays and the Malays would increase (from $1250 to $1475); thus, even these optimistic projections showed a worsening of the disparity in average incomes in ringgit terms by no less than 18 per cent over the period. When calculations were made for only those who were actually employed, i.e. not including the unemployed (of which there would be relatively fewer amongst the Malays), the reduction in the disparity ratio possible by 1985 became less pronounced.

The improvement in the racial economic disparity in terms of income assumed, first, that increased job opportunities in the modern rural sectors were reserved for Malays; second, that new land development schemes would be opened up at three times the rate

TABLE 2.4
EMPLOYMENT, VALUE ADDED AND DISPARITY BY MAJOR SECTOR
FOR MALAYS AND NON-MALAYS 1967 AND 1985

| | | Employment (in thousands) | | Value added per worker in 1967 | | | Disparity of non-Malay over Malay income in | |
|---|---|---|---|---|---|---|---|---|---|
| | | Malay | Non-Malay | All | Malay | Non-Malay | All | Value | Ratio |
| Modern rural sector | 1967 | 103 | 248 | 351 | 3455 | 3920 | 3785 | 465 | 1.15 |
| | 1985 | 185 | 265 | 450 | 7115 | 7300 | 7260 | 275 | 1.04 |
| Traditional rural sector | 1967 | 928 | 327 | 1255 | 1135 | 1440 | 1215 | 305 | 1.27 |
| | 1985 | 1150 | 400 | 1550 | 2080 | 2760 | 2250 | 680 | 1.33 |
| Modern urban sector | 1967 | 142 | 393 | 535 | 4125 | 5160 | 4885 | 1035 | 1.25 |
| | 1985 | 380 | 720 | 1100 | 7925 | 9520 | 8970 | 1595 | 1.20 |
| Traditional urban sector | 1967 | 142 | 420 | 562 | 1280 | 1805 | 1675 | 525 | 1.41 |
| | 1985 | 385 | 915 | 1300 | 1955 | 2255 | 2135 | 300 | 1.15 |
| Government sector | 1967 | 185 | 112 | 297 | 2400 | 2400 | 2400 | - | 1.00 |
| | 1985 | 400 | 200 | 600 | 4085 | 4085 | 4085 | - | 1.00 |
| Total Economy | 1967 | 1500 | 1500 | 3000 | 1750 | 3000 | 2375 | 1250 | 1.71 |
| | 1985 | 2500 | 2500 | 5000 | 3645 | 5120 | 4380 | 1475 | 1.40 |

implemented in 1967 with settlement and economic exploitation reserved for Malays; third, that industrial and commercial expansion in the rural areas and smaller towns would be subjected to preferential and discriminatory, restrictive and supportive policies which would ensure that this growth would take place largely with Malay entrepreneurship, ownership and workforce; and fourth, that Federal and State government organisation would act more vigorously and comprehensively to ensure Malay participation, if necessary through direct Government operations. Even with all these measures implemented vigorously, the *absolute* income and productivity differentials would increase markedly, they would not fall. This just confirmed that disparity was so ingrained that it would not possibly be removed within a decade or two. Indeed, it would not be eliminated even within this century without firm, consistent and quick implementation of the strategy recommended. If there were no shift in strategy and policy, the disparity would get even worse.

## Labour Force, Employment and Unemployment

The achievement of the improvement in the disparity ratio described in the foregoing section would be dependent upon an overall employment creation of 3 per cent annually, while the labour force itself was assumed to increase by 3.3 per cent annually. The Malay share of the active, employed labour force in all major categories of activities was projected to increase. By 1985 the labour force was estimated to be 5 million, compared with 3 million in the base year of 1967. Malay and non-Malay total labour force was shown to be of roughly equal size in 1985, as was the case also in 1967. To assess the growth of job opportunities, estimates of labour absorption by the various sectors were made, starting with *the rural sectors* which were computed to be able to create an additional 400,000 jobs by 1985. At the same time, productivity per rural worker was projected to increase significantly. As a result, less than 40 per cent of the increase in the labour force emanating from the rural (modern and traditional) sector could be absorbed productively within the rural economy itself.

It follows that there would have to be outward movement of workers in very large numbers from the rural areas, who seek jobs in the traditional or modern urban sectors, or in government, or just join the ranks of the urban unemployed. Assuming that all the increase in employment opportunities in rural sectors were allocated to the Malays, the non-Malays would still outnumber the Malays in the modern rural sector by a ratio of 3 to 2. Even with an aggressive policy in favour of the Malays, with its consequent harsh unemployment effect on the non-Malays, the Malays would still lag behind the non-Malays.

In 1967 *the non-Government urban sectors* accounted for 1,100,000 workers, with 100,000 of them being unemployed. By 1985 the labour force in these sectors were projected to more than double, but as many as 375,000 of them would be without jobs. In the urban areas in 1985, the non-Malays would outnumber the Malays by a ratio of over 2 to 1 as against nearly 3 to 1 in 1967.

In total the non-government modern and traditional urban sectors were projected to provide gainful employment in 1985 to about twice as many as in 1967. The structure of the urban economy as projected would change very considerably over the 18 year period. While in 1967 manufacturing contributed well under one-quarter of total value added in non-government urban sectors, in 1985 it would contribute 40 per cent. This type of structural change within the urban sectors was projected to be more pronounced for Malays than for non-Malays, reflecting in particular the more rapid relative growth of the Malay labour force in the urban economy.

Projections for *the Government sector* were made separately, but for classification purpose government employment was considered as urban in nature and orientation. This sector comprised administration, education, health etc., as well as the police and military forces. Together these activities gave employment to 300,000 people in 1967, over 65 per cent of whom were Malays. By 1985, the personnel in this sector were projected to double, as considerable expansion was expected due to the need to make increased provision for security, health services, education etc. It was also assumed that as the result of deliberate policy action the Malay share of total Government employment would increase moderately to a ratio of two Malays for each non-Malay.

The impact on the structure of employment of such changes, as described above, as between sectors and as between the races over the years, would be great. According to the projections, the level of unemployment would increase considerably over the period to 1985. While in 1967 there was a total of about 200,000 unemployed, equally distributed between the urban and rural traditional sectors, in 1985 unemployment was projected to reach 475,000 in total; 100,000 in the rural areas and as many as 375,000 in the urban areas. The overall unemployment percentage of the total labour force which stood at 6.7 per cent in 1967 would increase to 9.5 per cent in 1985. Total non-Malay unemployment would nearly triple, while Malay unemployment would double.

## Control of Capital Assets and of the Economy

In the initial stage of the elaboration of the NEP, no targets were set for restructuring the ownership of capital assets between Malays and non-Malays. But it was urged that such restructuring should in fact take effect as part of the overall strategy. This included a full review of the existing industrial policy to facilitate Malay entry into the modern sector. Restructuring of this sector was necessary because greater participation of Malays in ownership and control in the economy was as important in the long run for economic balance as was an equitable share in employment opportunities. It would be important, first, because Malay ownership and control would give a better guarantee of a high degree of Malay participation in employment at all levels, and second, because a considerable part of the value added in an enterprise would accrue to non-labour factors of production. For both these reasons the NEP indicated a number of measures to speed up the development of Malay entrepreneurship and to ensure a growing Malay share in ownership of means of production.

## Economic Growth

The combined effect of growth in the rural and urban sectors as described were such as to raise the gross national product for Peninsular Malaysia by an average rate of 6.4 per cent annually over the 18 year period to 1985. There would be marked differences between sectors, the projected rate of growth in the modern urban sector, including Government of well over 7.5 per cent as against a little over 5 per cent in the modern rural sector. Also the implied overall growth rate for Malays was 7.2 per cent as against 6 per cent for non-Malays. To achieve and sustain an overall growth rate of 6.4 per cent in GDP would represent a considerable improvement in the 5 per cent average rate of growth in the 1960s, particularly since, in accordance with the strategy of development adopted, the objective of rapid overall growth was assumed to be subsidiary to that of achieving better economic balance. All major sectors of the economy were projected to grow as part of this development, with the modern urban sector growing the most rapidly. The significance of this pattern of growth of output and productivity was great, both in terms of resource allocation and resource creation in general and in its effect on the economic balance between the rural and urban activities and in particular between the Malay and non-Malay labour force. One further implication of the pattern of growth foreseen was that the economy, also at the end of the period, would be clearly export oriented with manufacturing assuming the role of a leading sector. In fact, the growth of output in considerable measure was shown to be in the production of export crops. Also for manufacturing to grow as fast as was projected and for it to be consistent with racial balance objectives, policies had to be designed to step up production for exports considerably.

In the short term the overall economic growth projected for the SMP of 7.0 per cent in real terms would be a considerable improvement on the performance as well as the targets set for the First Malaysian Plan. The importance of economic growth was stressed because the realisation of the objectives to create employment opportunities and indeed the creation of sufficient resources for effective policies of economic balance would be impossible if the full growth potential within the context of the NEP were not fully realised. This was a most important point for economic policy. Indeed if the Government were to err on the side of financial and monetary conservatism, the basic political as well as economic potential for creating a foundation for national unity during the SMP would be lost without hope of resurrection.

## The Outlook for Medium Term and Short Term Achievements

Those were the major elements of the DNU School strategy. The benefits of the new development strategy, if implemented efficiently, would accrue to all Malaysians irrespective of race in terms of rising income, standard of living and employment. There would be a definite reduction in the disparity ratio although in terms of absolute income the disparity would be wider. Malay incomes and standards of living would rise, so would those of non-Malays. Employment would better reflect the racial composition of the population. However, since Malay incomes, standard of living and employment in the modern sector would start from a low base, they would fall far short of the levels of the non-Malays. But Malay income on the average could rise at a faster rate than non-Malay income so that parity might ultimately be achieved. Within the new economic structure the non-Malays would no longer enjoy a near total monopoly of the benefits of development to the exclusion of the Malays. Yet, by accepting the new strategy the non-Malays would also gain in terms of added security and stability. Defence of future economic concerns would be based on the identity of interests rather than on racial lines. An evening out of the racial economic imbalances would eventually lead to the eradication of the identification of economic functions with particular racial groups, while a new hierarchy would emerge, based on class and transcending racial lines. This would strengthen the forces of unity and, at the end of the day, could lead to the integration of the races into a cohesive Malaysian nation with its own Malaysian identity. Article 153 would then be superfluous.

The conclusions which emerged from the simulations were therefore very clear. On all counts, in terms of economic balance, employment creation and growth, the DNU alternative development strategy was superior to the one proposed by the EPU School. Yet, the results were also discouraging. In spite of the active policies in favour of the Malays, they would still lag behind the non-Malays at the end of the period in the mid-1980s. In absolute dollar terms the distance would widen in favour of the non-Malays although in terms of the disparity ratio there would be a drop from 7 to 4 in 1967 to 7 to 5 in 1985 (in favour of the non-Malays). In spite of the intensive employment creation policies proposed, general unemployment would still increase substantially, affecting adversely Malays and non-Malays alike with the latter getting the brunt. In terms of growth the result could be considered good. All this assumed that the new development strategy proposed was adequately understood and firmly implemented, including the realisation that the problem would persist, at least to the end of this century and perhaps longer, and that, in some ways, it would get worse before getting better. A half hearted or marginal implementation would make success, even to this extent, unobtainable.

## Coordination and Leadership

### Implementation and Coordination

The results predicted by the DNU simulations assumed full and firm implementation of the new development strategy proposed (Doc. C, pp. 317-318). There was insistence on the need to streamline administrative procedures and cut red tape. Decentralisation of administration with accompanying delegation was stressed and the need to consider the use of operationally independent agencies was suggested.

In view of the great importance which was attached to this aspect of the Malaysian development problem, the responsibility for implementation would have to be taken at the highest government level: the Prime Minister or the Deputy Prime Minister. Participation and coordination of various departments and agencies at both State and Federal levels would be needed. In addition, similar coordination and cooperation between the Government and the private sector was called upon. The machinery of implementation would need to ensure clear divisions of responsibility so that duplication of efforts and wastage of resources would be avoided.

## Role of the Political Leadership

The architects of the NEP were in no doubt about the magnitude of the task and the need for determined and consistent efforts sustained into the next century (Doc. B, p. 283). They were insistent on the political nature of the economic choices that had to be made. It was the Government that had to decide on major questions such as the choice between growth, economic balances and other objectives; only then could detailed programmes be worked out for the major areas of social and economic policy. Document B was designed to consider the *overall* strategy of development and to provide effective guidance for day to day work on economic planning and policy. Without firm political guidance no bureaucrats would dare to function, with the gallant exception of the brave few, in such a sensitive area.

Given the enormity and the sensitiveness of the racial economic problem, and the massive transformation of the society that would have to be undertaken in order to make a dent in the problem, firm political guidance was required. The choice of the NEP required the Prime Minister and his cabinet colleagues to exercise political statesmanship, skill and courage of the highest order. It required them to see their political objectives in a time perspective far beyond their own likely future in active politics, and to be prepared to allow the requirements of their long term perspective to override the exigencies of the day to day politics. It also called for cooperation and goodwill by all sections of the community. Although Article 153 of the Constitution states that the Malays should be given help in their efforts at development, by their very nature, the specific policy measures recommended in favour of the Malays would be felt by the others as "Unfair" and "Discriminatory". Cries of violations of human rights, communal rights, principles of democracy etc., could easily be raised. The DNU School summed up their view as follows (Doc. B, pp. 303 and 284):

> The choice of strategy is a political decision, but a choice must be made. Failure to change present policies represents as much a choice as does

adoption of a new strategy. ...In other words, a balancing act must constantly be performed so as to find a course which is economically, socially and politically viable .... It will have to be the job of the political authorities to strike the balance, it must be the job of the administration to analyse and present the constituent elements of the choice. In the past as well as to-day, the political choice is made without guidance and advice on its implications.

The overall conclusion of the DNU analysis in 1969/70 as it pertains to the role of political leadership was summed up as follows (Doc. A, p. 247 and Doc. B, pp. 284-285):

The main challenge that faces the government to-day is that of constructing a new alliance of moderate elements (Malay, Chinese, and Indian) within the nation. But the new alliance must be built on a rather different base from the old one. At the centre of this new arrangement must be a series of policies that will be genuinely effective in raising Malay incomes and providing for Malay entry into the modern sector on the basis of real equality. So far few such policies have arisen either from within or without the government ... Unless the Malays do in fact benefit from such opportunities for growth as exist or can be created in the rural areas where most of them work and live, the task of ever achieving parity will be well nigh impossible.

## The NEP in Summary

The main elements of objectives and policies of the NEP as envisaged by the DNU may be summarised in the following seven points:

*First,* a decisive reduction in both urban and rural poverty for all Malaysians irrespective of race. In 1969-70 it was clear to all serious observers, as well as to Government, that poverty remained high in many rural areas and occupations, largely but not at all exclusively populated by Malays, while the standards of living for populations in urban areas, often dominated by non-Malay inhabitants but increasingly by Malays were, in many cases, unacceptably low.

*Second,* a definitive reduction in the racial economic imbalances in terms of (i) income (ii) employment and (iii) wealth. This would be realised through programmes and projects:

a)     to effect changes in the economic system itself:  In contrast to the previous Plan, steps would henceforth be taken to ensure that the Malays would not be discriminated against from participating actively in all sectors of the economy at all levels with the other races. The system of 'apartheid' constructed against them, openly or indirectly, by the colonial masters would be torn down. The strategy was therefore one of active participation and equal partnership rather than of disruptive distribution and hand-outs to the Malays; like everybody else they would have to sweat it out and raise their productivity and thus ultimately gain a higher standard of living. However, the system would now be so designed that it would help rather than hinder them to achieve parity.

b)    to create new institutions and modify existing ones so as to facilitate the inter-sectoral and intra-sectoral transfers, particularly of the Malays, from low to high productivity activity.

c)    to develop the capability of the Malays: Vigorous programmes of education and training of the Malays would be undertaken so as to enable them to participate actively in the development process. For all Malaysians, education was assigned the important role of laying the foundation for the creation of a new common value system among the younger generations for the attainment of national unity and racial integration.

d)    to ensure that the Malays would find real opportunities to share more equally than in the past in the creation of new wealth as development of the country proceeded.

e)    to deal with the unequal levels of development in different regions: Regional development programmes would be stepped up in order to develop those underdeveloped states, such as Kelantan, Terengganu, Pahang etc., which were also predominantly inhabited by Malays. The number of integrated land schemes of the FLDA type would be increased. Peasant agriculture, such as padi farming and the like, would be affected by a series of reforms and reorganisation to enable farmers to increase their productivity and the marketability of their products, so as to raise the income and welfare of the rural poor and the Malays.

*Third,* a target rate for growth of GNP of 6.4 per cent in real terms was set for the period up to 1985. As demonstrated by the results of the DNU simulations, this target was considered achievable concurrently with a firm implementation of the poverty and restructuring objectives; it would give a rate of overall growth superior to the performance of the economy during the First Malaysia Plan. Moreover, such rapid growth was seen to be a necessary condition for the achievement of the overall targets. The necessity for high growth was self-evident. It would alleviate general poverty in the country by raising the general income level, provided growth was fairly evenly spread. It would enable the non-Malays to grow to their full potentials without hindrance while allowing for accelerating Malay entry into the modern sectors. The growth rate was also necessary to create those additional resources, required to undertake the economic and social reforms envisaged, without serious pain and dislocation to the system. To achieve such a high performance, the private sector was to be given the necessary incentives to spearhead the growth of the economy, especially in its rapid industrialisation efforts and export drive. The DNU found, however, that it would be possible to have both quite rapid growth and an improving racial economic balance, but warned that beyond a point the pursuit of these objectives could become competitive rather than complementary. The Government would therefore have to exercise its discretion in case of a severe conflict. The DNU, however, was clear in its view: since the pursuit of national unity was seen as synonymous with improvement in the state of economic balances between the races, the national unity objective should override the growth objective in case of such conflict.

*Fourth,* a full employment policy that would absorb the unemployed labour remaining at the end of the First Malaysia Plan while at the same time catering for new entrants to the labour market stemming from the rapid population growth and the making room for those wishing to move to new jobs in the modern sector of the economy. Economic growth had to be encouraged and guided along an employment intensive path. The rationale was simple. One of the causes of poverty, both urban and rural, was unemployment or underemployment of labour. Therefore, to eradicate poverty in a labour surplus economy a labour intensive policy of employment was required. The full employment policy, like the rapid economic growth policy, was therefore an indispensable and a strategic element of the NEP.

*Fifth,* an interventionist role for the Federal and State governments and their various agencies and institutions so as to ensure that the Malays obtained a fair opportunity to gain increasing entrance to, and equality within, the modern sectors. New institutions would therefore be set up and old ones sharpened to assist the Malays.

*Sixth,* the implementation of supplementary social policies for the avoidance of communal conflicts, and to find ways to achieve a common identity and the realisation of national unity. The elaboration of such policies would be based on a determined search for greater insight into the state of social relations, in particular their ethnic dimensions.

*Seventh,* the elaboration of a consistent policy package of the foregoing elements and the implementation of a comprehensive system for economic and social data gathering and analysis to ensure that the programmes and projects were properly monitored and in conformity with stated objectives and, where necessary, re-directed and adjusted.

The most important elements of the DNU strategy were the eradication of poverty and the correction of the racial economic imbalances. All the other elements were sub-elements or means to achieve the two overall objectives. The existing situation of mass poverty prevailing in the midst of the affluence of the few rich, of conspicuous difference in living standards along racial lines and of unequal involvement of different groups in the advance of the economy, was no longer acceptable. It was an explosive situation, as 1969 had proved; it was an affront to human dignity, especially in a country that was rich in resources. The improvement in racial economic balance and the eradication of the identification of race with economic functions was therefore deemed vital for the improvement in inter-communal relations.

At its core, therefore, the DNU strategy was much more than an ordinary five year plan. It set out to achieve no less than a complete social and economic transformation and to lay the foundation and framework for a new Malaysian order. It sought to achieve the emergence of a new Malaysian society which would transcend existing ethnic, cultural, religious and economic differences and provide for opportunities for advancement for all Malaysians. After 1969, it seemed there was no other option, otherwise the country would return to anarchy and chaos.

# CHAPTER 3

# NEP IN PLAN DOCUMENTS

## Introduction

It is the purpose of this chapter to trace how far the comprehensive integrated approach of the DNU School, elaborated in the previous chapter, was finally incorporated into the various Five Year Plans of the government, beginning with the Second Malaysia Plan 1971-1975. This is crucial to the analysis and assessment of the NEP. Was in fact the thrust of policy constantly on course, pursuing the original NEP objectives, as was repeatedly asserted throughout the 1970s and 1980s? Or did it deviate and revert back, whether by design or neglect, to the conventional development planning strategy of the type and practices of the plans adopted by the government between Merdeka before 1970?

## Second Malaysia Plan 1971-1975 (SMP)

The main aim of the government in launching the NEP, with the Second Malaysia Plan 1971-1975 as its first phase, was to translate into operational terms the ideology of Rukunegara. This was succinctly expressed by Tun Razak in the Foreword (p. v) to the Second Malaysia Plan:

> The Plan is a blueprint for the New Economic Policy. It incorporates the two pronged objective of eradicating poverty, irrespective of race, and restructuring Malaysian society to reduce and eventually eliminate the identification of race with economic functions... It will spare no efforts to promote national unity and develop a just and progressive Malaysian society in a rapidly expanding economy so that no one will experience any loss or feel any sense of deprivation of his rights, privileges, income, job or opportunity... To achieve our overall objective of national unity, Malaysia needs more than merely a high rate of economic growth. While devoting our efforts to the task of achieving rapid economic development, we need to ensure at the same time that there is social justice, equitable sharing of income growth and increasing opportunities for employment...

The Plan must succeed as it is vital to our suvival as a progressive, happy and united nation.

The quest for national unity and goodwill was particularly acute after the racial riot of 1969. The Second Malaysia Plan recognised that the search for national unity and identity was a multi faceted task. It would not be easy, particularly for a country plagued by divisions of race, religion, economic status and geographical divide. Most developing countries with more favourable circumstances have been groping to translate into reality the same dream but often without much success. In Malaysia it involved using a whole range of economic and social policies, from education and health policies to labour and employment policies and measures to restructure capital ownership, to set in train a social transformation that would provide some degree of fairness to the majority of the country's citizens. It could not be costless. During the transition, vested interests would oppose such a social transformation on the scale envisaged. Many a country has found that the opposition is too strong for such comprehensive reforms to go through. But the economic preconditions for a cohesive Malaysian society have never been in doubt. So long as large segments of the population, whether they were Malays or non-Malays, were by-passed in the development process, the dream to unite Malaysia would be unattainable. The Second Malaysia Plan was as close to attacking the problems of poverty and inequality directly as any policy in existence anywhere in the world.

The NEP found its practical planning expressions in the Second Malaysia Plan 1971-1975 and its Mid-Term Review. This is not surprising. The growth oriented strategy of the 1960s, no matter how well intentioned, had failed and was blamed by many as a major cause of the racial riot of 1969. The strategy of the past had failed simply because in fact, if not by intent, there was no place for the Malays in it, at least no place giving level-pegging with the non-Malays. It largely excluded them from participating in the development process of their own country. All sorts of reasons were put forward for this result. Given the circumstances after the riot, in particular the strong political momentum given by the Prime Minister to the DNU School, together with skilfull handling and dogged persistence by its members, the NEP approach could gain some advantage, albeit temporary; for a time, the EPU school fell into eclipse.

Among all the Five Year Plan documents of the Malaysian government, there is no doubt that the SMP and its Mid-Term

Review were the closest that came to adopting the central thrusts of the NEP. Other elements of policy, including those that primarily and directly are concerned with general growth, employment, education etc., were explicitly recognised within the NEP as important in themselves, but mainly as means to the end of rapid advance in terms of the two-pronged strategy of the NEP. The analysis in the Second Plan document utilised, at least in part, the DNU methodology of categorising the economy into high and low productivity sectors which, if it had been followed through in subsequent Plans, would have greatly helped to quantify the various problems and elements involved and to ensure that macro and micro elements of the policy were consistent with each other within the overall framework. More elaborate quantification in terms of targets and follow-up would have enabled the problems to be more amenable to solutions based on facts and thus would have helped avoid some of the subsequent bitter controversies over the NEP.

The SMP represented a break with major points of earlier economic planning. By incorporating elements of the DNU strategy, the framework of planning itself underwent some transformation, at least in rhetoric if not much in substance. In the analysis and policy recommendations to deal directly with the serious problem of inequality prevailing in the country, the SMP had no direct precedent in Malaysia or in other developing countries. Indeed, it was a forerunner of what was later known as the 'Strategy of Growth with Equity', or 'Redistribution with Growth' or the strategy of 'Basic Needs' to meet directly the necessities of the poor. In launching the NEP, the government was standing on high moral and social ground. It was a policy for all Malaysians with priority for the poor, the majority of whom happened to be Malays who therefore had to be given special attention. In the last analysis, the government was seeking to lay the foundation for long term political and social stability, drawing on the experience of 1969 and knowing full well that a price had to be paid in the short term.

In order to implement the Plan efficiently, measures were also proposed for the government to reorganise its implementation machinery, including setting up the Implementation and Coordination Unit in the Prime Minister's Department. It was also proposed that the programmes should be monitored closely for measurement and feedback so that the government could be fully informed whether implementation was proceeding in conformity with the Plan and whether corrective measures were needed should there be any deviation.

One major weakness in the Plan document, however, was that it did not set specific quantitative targets for the reduction of racial economic imbalances over the Plan period. This was left vague, not because it was technically very difficult to do so, the DNU papers had developed a methodology and provided some of the statistical evidence, see for instance Document D included at the end of this book. Rather, the planners had in fact yielded to various pressure groups within and outside the government who were opposed to the NEP and its effective implementation. In a typically Malaysian way, the issue was left in ambiguity, perhaps for later activation and implementation. In the event, the analysis and follow-up were left in limbo. With the significant exception of the quantitative targets set by the SMP (pp 41 and 42) that "within a period of 20 years, Malays and other indigenous people will manage and own at least 30 per cent of the total commercial and industrial activities in all categories and scales of operation", and that the "employment pattern at all levels and in all sectors, particularly the Modern Rural and Modern Urban Sectors, must reflect the racial composition of the population", other specific quantitative targets bearing directly on racial economic balances were not set. The absence of concrete and definite targets for the progressive reduction of ethnic inequality and imbalance in the structure of incomes, beyond vague words extending into an indefinite future, was later to prove a stumbling block to monitoring its implementation.

## Mid-Term Review of the Second Malaysia Plan 1971-1975

As the name implies, the MTR document was a thorough and comprehensive review of the progress of the SMP since its launching. After three years of implementation, Tun Razak was satisfied that the NEP, charting a new course of social and economic development, had proved itself to be workable and that it made good sense. A continuing climate of confidence had been maintained. The various sub-policies, programmes and projects of the NEP had been launched with determination. Output, incomes and employment had increased. The social and physical infrastructure had been expanded. New institutions had been established while existing ones were streamlined and strengthened to resolve old problems and to meet new needs. All this led to the acceleration of the process of eradicating poverty, the restructuring of the society, the speeding up of modernisation and the nurturing of confidence among the people. The success was all the more gratifying, since it was achieved in the face of the adverse impact on the country of the world-wide downswing of economic activity during 1971-1972. Based on the performance of the NEP in the first three years of the SMP, Tun Razak was confident that the goals of eradicating poverty and restructuring society in the context of an expanding economy were fully feasible and that the broad economic framework to achieve these targets was a viable one.

The MTR document was particularly important because it manifested a further step in the evolution of the NEP, in that it refined and further developed some of the major concepts and policies launched by the DNU and the SMP. It extended the framework of the DNU strategy into a 20 year plan to 1990, known officially as the Outline Perspective Plan or in short the OPP. It laid down the framework, as well as a set of production, employment and distribution targets for the NEP over a 20 year period as they bore on the overall objectives to eradicate poverty and correct the racial imbalances. It highlighted and illustrated the kind of policies and the degree of effort that would be necessary for the achievement of the objectives of the NEP within the time period set. It also recognised that for the remainder of the SMP as well as for the implementation of subsequent Plans, changing conditions would require policy modifications and flexibility to meet such changing circumstances. Working within the perspective of a consistent long term framework, the Government would have greater assurance that policies and strategies would be sensitive to such changes, thus ensuring that the overall long run objectives of the NEP would be attained. From the time of the publication of the OPP, it seemed, there was no turning back. No politician could dismantle the NEP openly and get away with it. At least in rhetoric, if not in real achievements, the NEP was securely in place in the economic and social life of the nation for at least a generation. Ever since then Malaysia has been living under this economic regime in one form or another. With hindsight it could be said the OPP is probably the high water mark of the NEP.

For the achievement of the broad objectives of the NEP, the OPP spelled out (p. 62) that policies, programmes and projects should be designed specifically to:

(i)   generate employment opportunities at a rate sufficient to reduce current levels of unemployment and eventually bring about full employment of the whole labour force;

(ii)  increase the productivity and income of all those engaged in low productivity rural and urban occupations by increasing their access to opportunities to acquire skills, land, capital and other necessary inputs and by eliminating underemployment;

(iii)  expand opportunities for those engaged in low productivity activities to move to more productive endeavours in agriculture, forestry, fisheries, mining, construction, transportation, manufacturing, commerce and service industries;

(iv)  reduce the existing inequitable distribution of income between classes and races:

(v)  modernise rural life and improve the living conditions of the poor in urban areas through the provision of a wide range of social services including public housing, electricity, water supplies, sanitation, transportation, health and medical services and recreational and community facilities;

(vi)  promote the creation of a commercial and industrial community among Malays and other indigenous people in order that, within one generation, they will own and manage at least 30 per cent of the total commercial and industrial activities of the country in all categories and scales of operation;

(vii)  ensure that employment in the various sectors of the economy and employment by occupational levels will reflect the racial composition of the country.

(viii)  expand education and training facilities, other social services and the physical infrastructure of the country to effectively support the attainment of the above objectives.

These objectives were all designed to meet the needs of the poor directly. It was not a question of waiting for the indirect benefits of a 'trickle down effect' to happen after growth and development had taken place. Priority was given to the urban and rural poor and to those who were excluded from the development process, which meant the bulk of the Malays. The programmes and projects proposed would strengthen the capacity of the poor to meet such basic needs as adequate nutrition, health, housing, education and transportation. Regional development would be stepped up in a manner that would reduce the marked economic disparity which then existed between the States. This would include the mobilisation of the untapped resources of the less developed States, the promotion of population migration to areas with greater economic potential and the expansion of infrastructure and social services in those States and areas which were largely underdeveloped. Also, the government sought to inculcate a spirit of self-reliance and a readiness on the part of people to participate actively in the whole range of socio-economic development programmes and improve their standard of living and that of generations to come.

According to the OPP two elements of the NEP were pre-eminent, the attainment of which was central to its success. The first was that the achievement of full employment by the creation of productive employment opportunities, as well as the expansion of the supply of skilled manpower, was important in the strategy to eradicate poverty and to correct the racial economic imbalance. At the time, there was overfull employment for Chinese labour, as it was concentrated in the fastest growing sectors, some unemployment for the Indians and a high rate of unemployment for the Malays. The full employment policy therefore formed the heart of the first prong of the OPP objectives. With the projected growth of the labour force of 2.9 per cent per year and sectoral employment targets rising at 3.2 per cent per year over the 20 year period, unemployment as a percentage of the labour force would be reduced from its 1970 level of 7.5 per cent for the country to about 4 per cent by 1990. The progressive reduction in the unemployment rate would be accompanied by reduction in the level of underemployment. But no targets were fixed for the distribution of employment by race except the statement that it had to reflect the racial composition of the population at all levels and categories of activities.

The second element was in respect of ownership of assets. The objectives of growth and redistribution of the ownership of economically productive assets in the country was re-affirmed, as was the target that by 1990 the Malays and other indigenous people would own and operate at least 30 per cent of the total. This ownership target was deemed important for several reasons, including the fact that salaries and wages only represented half the total of income of Malaysian households. Considering that Malays owned only about 2 per cent of the total equity assets in 1970, as opposed to the 22 per cent owned by the Chinese, assets also had to be redistributed as part of the effort to redress the income distribution situation. Assets comprised financial and physical assets, including land, in all sectors of the economy. To ensure that implementation would conform to this objective, the Government and its agencies would continue to provide the necessary infrastructural and financial assistance to the Malay community. It would also ensure that their savings were properly mobilised into productive channels. The key to the ownership objective was through the ownership of equity. As targeted in the OPP (p. 85 of the MTR of the SMP), the racial pattern of equity ownership by 1990 would be more balanced at the levels of 30, 40 and 30 per cent for Malays, non-Malay nationals and foreigners respectively.

The restructuring, which was required in the ownership of assets, should not be so implemented as to result in loss and deprivation on the part of the non-Malays. The process of restructuring was to be undertaken in the context of a rapidly expanding economy. The national product was projected to grow at an average of 7 per cent per year over the 20 year period. The OPP clearly stated (p. 63) that

> For operational purposes, therefore, rapid economic growth of the country is a necessary condition for the success of the NEP. It is only through such growth that the objectives of the NEP can be achieved without any particular group in Malaysian society experiencing any loss or feeling any sense of deprivation... Growth *per se*, however, as evidenced by past experience is not a sufficient condition to achieve these objectives... The NEP is thus designed to ensure that the Government is sufficiently equipped to influence the pattern of economic growth in directions which will bring about a more equitable sharing of the benefits of growth and development among all Malaysians.

Non-Malay ownership of share capital was projected to expand by nearly 12 per cent per year and to increase its share of the total to 40 per cent by 1990, nine times more than the 1970 level in absolute terms. Foreign ownership would increase by 8 per cent annually during the same period. In relation to total share capital, however, the expansion of the share of Malays and other indigenous people from under 2 per cent in 1970 to 30 per cent in 1990 would involve a sizable decline in the share of foreign interest from 61 per cent to about 30 per cent during the 20 year period.

To achieve such formidable undertakings simultaneously, the crucial need for a rapid rate of overall growth was stressed in the OPP. The private sector, in particular manufacturing and construction, was given attractive incentives for accelerated growth. A healthy investment climate was maintained by the government. Through intensive promotional efforts overseas the government sought to attract foreign capital and technology. But it recognised that international flows of capital were subject to factors over which Malaysia did not have full control. Therefore, its quest for sustained economic and social development was underpinned by healthy growth of domestically mobilisable funds and resources. The manufacturing and construction sectors were assigned the leading roles since they were regarded as the most promising in terms of productivity, value added and employment creation potentials. Targets assigned to the manufacturing sector included growth of value added and exports by 12.5 per cent and 15 per cent respectively per year during 1971-1975, the creation of employment opportunities in these sectors at the rate of 7 per cent per year, the promotion of small scale industries and the dispersal of industries to the less developed states. Malaysia's potentials for export-led industrial growth as envisaged in the Plan were bright. With development on the scale envisaged in the Mid-Term Review (p. 72) and according to the criteria established by the World Bank it was expected that Malaysia would be transformed from being an industrialising country in 1970 to an industrialised country by 1990, with manufacturing accounting for 35 per cent of total output and a little more than 20 per cent of employment.

The objectives of the OPP were ambitious but feasible. The Plan devised was a pragmatic one. It was thought through carefully, taking into cognisance the experience of the riot, the resource potentials of the economy and the unique and sensitive racial problems. The OPP objectives and targets were mutually consistent and, if implemented firmly, the results would be far superior to what could be achieved by the growth oriented policy of the First Malaysia Plan, notably in the reduction in political and social tension and ultimately contributing to national integration and a cohesive Malaysian nation.

## Third Malaysia Plan 1976-1980 (TMP)

The Third Malaysia Plan 1976-80 (TMP) was issued 6 months after the untimely death of Tun Abdul Razak, the main force for the New Economic Policy. The TMP presented itself as the second phase in the implementation of the NEP and confidently asserted (p. 34) that the NEP had proved its value and that its two pronged strategy had benefitted all communities and the poor, irrespective of race, while opening up new avenues of opportunity. In this favourable atmosphere, the TMP was seen as an extension of the Second Malaysia Plan. In rural areas, there would be a major effort to reduce the extent of the poverty affecting padi cultivators, rubber and coconut smallholders, shifting cultivators, fishermen, estate workers, residents of New Villages, agricultural workers and the Orang Asli. New employment opportunities would be created by means of land development, the establishment of growth centres and the provision of greater access to water supplies, credit, markets and advice from extension workers, accompanied by greater provision of electricity and other public services. The urban poor were to be helped by expanded employment in manufacturing and construction and with the promotion of small scale industries; they would also be benefited by the provision of low-cost housing and the provision of other public services. All Malaysians, but particularly the poor, were to be helped by increased provision of educational opportunities, health services and family planning services and housing. The TMP was all-embracing in the means it proposed to achieve its objectives and included support to private investment, both domestic and foreign, better utilisation of the human and natural resources of the country and expansion of the social and physical infrastructure of the economy.

The TMP also gave expression (p. 176) to the need to see rapid growth as a pre-condition for the achievement of the restructuring objectives of the NEP. The way to improve the lot of the poor was through rural modernisation: overall growth was itself a way to reduce imbalances in employment and to give the Malays greater representation in the modern sector of the economy; it could also be used to increase the share of the Malays in the productive capital of the economy and in corporate stock, which was almost negligible, and in the process the Malays would have the opportunity to establish themselves as a commercial and industrial community. Fundamentally, growth was necessary for the generation of resources. It followed that the process of restructuring employment and ownership should be accompanied by strengthening the investment climate and the prospects for overall economic growth. The plan stressed that the underlying objective was that of obtaining a fair distribution through rapid economic growth so that no one would be deprived of rights, privileges, income, jobs or opportunities.

Nevertheless, it was felt that there were limits to what growth alone could be expected to accomplish in the way of economic restructuring. There was also the danger that it could exacerbate racial imbalances. Government action was needed to ensure the expansion of education and training opportunities, so that the necessary range of skills could be acquired by the various racial groups. It was also necessary to bring about more ethnically balanced patterns of employment and ownership of capital; in public enterprises as well as in the private sector, and in relation to existing share capital as well as in new capital to be issued in connection with the planned growth in activity. It was envisaged that capital would be acquired in trust by government agencies for the Malays and other indigenous peoples. Specifically, the TMP (pp 49-50) declared that measures would be taken to:

- increase the share of the Malays and other indigenous people in employment in mining, manufacturing and construction and the share of other Malaysians in agriculture and services so that by 1990 employment in the various sectors of the economy will reflect the racial composition of the country;
- raise the share of the Malays and other indigenous people in the ownership of productive wealth including land, fixed assets and equity capital. The target is that by 1990, they will own at least 30 per cent of equity capital with 40 per cent being owned by other Malaysians;

The TMP confirmed the earlier analysis of poverty as being dominantly a Malay problem because this group of Malaysians were concentrated so heavily in the low productivity sectors. Among the poor Chinese, the majority were in New Villages, particularly those situated in remote rural areas. The bulk of the Indian poor were to be found in the agricultural estates. The two largest groups in poverty in the rural areas, mainly Malays, were the rubber smallholders and the padi farmers. The advantage of identifying these specific groups was that sharper focus could be trained on these problems and that specific measures could be tailored to meet the special needs of the groups.

The long term strategy for the alleviation of rural poverty comprised four basic elements: firstly, emphasis on the provision of assistance to the poor to enable them to expand their productive capital; secondly, to relieve population pressure in the most congested sectors of agriculture; thirdly, the provision of infrastructure like electricity, water etc.; and fourthly, the accelerated creation of productive employment opportunities in the secondary and tertiary sectors of the economy. With respect to urban poverty the government's redressal strategy was to implement policies which would enlarge the scope of employment of the poor and also the provision of basic needs such as housing etc. It was also specifically recognised that rapid growth would benefit the urban poor first before the benefits permeated down to the rural areas, since the former had more direct links with the modern sectors.

Furthermore, the TMP confirmed the analysis which had led to the NEP. The wide disparity in income was identified in the TMP (p. 6) as being caused by:

the unequal distribution in employment of the major racial groups among the various sectors of the economy and unequal distribution in the ownership and control of wealth in the country. In employment, the Malays were concentrated in agriculture where *per capita* product was the lowest among all the sectors and where the incidence of poverty was the highest, accounting for over 70 per cent of all household in poverty. On the other hand, the Chinese were concentrated in mining, manufacturing and construction where per capita product was 16.7 per cent higher than in agriculture and 60 per cent higher than the average for the entire economy. The number of poor households in these sectors accounted for only 9 per cent of all those in poverty. With respect to the ownership of wealth, available data indicated that only small amounts of share capital were owned by Malays and Indians compared to the holdings by Chinese, but overall foreign interests dominated. In 1970, Malays and Malay interests owned 2.4 per cent of equity capital, while Indians held 1.1 per cent. The Chinese, on the other hand, accounted for 27.2 per cent, Others 6.0 per cent whilst foreigners held 63.3 per cent. In the non-corporate sector of modern agriculture, Malays owned 47.2 per cent, Chinese 32.8 per cent, Indians 10.1 per cent, Others 1.8 per cent, Government 2.3 per cent and foreigners 5.9 per cent of the acreage under cultivation. In the non-corporate industrial sector which is composed of manufacturing, mining and construction, the ownership of fixed assets was as follows: Malays 2.3 per cent, Chinese 92.2 per cent, Indians 2.3 per cent, Others 0.8 per cent and foreigners 2.4 per cent. It should, however, be noted that 87.4 per cent of the fixed assets in the industrial sector were owned by corporate entities... While the resulting inequalities in the distribution of income between the major racial groups were in themselves matters of grave concern from the point of view of social justice, the socio-political implications of an economic system divided along racial lines were an even greater threat to national unity, social stability and economic progress. Whatever their proximate causes, the racial riots of May 1969 owed their origin to inadequate efforts to redress socio-economic imbalances which have characterised Malaysian society for so long. Coming on top of political independence, economic growth itself in the sixties had irretrievably affected the values, attitudes, ambitions and expectations of Malaysians of all walks of life and in particular those who were less advantaged. A society marked by significant economic imbalances was no longer acceptable. A concerted effort to accelerate the removal of these imbalances became imperative.

The TMP provided further data on the magnitudes of the imbalances to be corrected (p. 5):

In Peninsular Malaysia itself, data on the distribution of income indicate that inequalities exist among all racial groups with the pattern of distribution similar among the Malays and the Chinese but more unequal among the Indians and other racial groups in the country. The problem in Malaysia is compounded by the fact that average incomes between the major social groups vary widely. In terms of per capita income, the Malays received $ 34 per month or one half of the Chinese at $ 68, while the Indians obtained $ 57 or some 70 per cent more than the

Malays. Of all the poor households, about 74 per cent were Malay, 17 per cent Chinese and 8 per cent Indian. Of all Malay households, 65 per cent were in poverty compared with 26 per cent for Chinese households. In the case of Indian and other households, 39 per cent and 45 per cent had incomes below the poverty line.

In other words, the Malays were the poorest: the income gap as measured by the income disparity ratio between them and the others in 1970 was roughly two times, confirming that the findings of the earlier DNU studies had been properly characterised as underestimates of the magnitude of the problem.

While the TMP also presented some further, useful statistical anlalysis of the magnitude and complexion of the disparity problems, and retained the major elements of the NEP, at least by reference, it failed to carry forward and build the momentum of policy change as conceived in 1969/70, formulated initially in the SMP and further elaborated in the Mid-Term Review of that Plan, particularly in its Outline Perspective Plan (OPP), as described above.

For all its emphasis on racial balance, the TMP failed to move decisively into the elaboration of analysis of the imbalance issues and of the components of change to deal with them. No further targets indicating amelioration and gradual elimination of imbalances were set, no quantitative indicators of advancement which could be used to monitor and check the effectiveness of policy were elaborated. Granted, these were deficiencies in the SMP and the OPP as well; the point is that the TMP showed no evidence of imagination, determination and sheer effort of planners to come to grips with the problems, matching that which had characterised the first year or two following the 13 May tragedy. Thus the TMP marks a return to a more traditional plan strategy, albeit with the retention of some elements already introduced under the NEP. This is seen perhaps more clearly in retrospect than at the time.

With the death of Tun Razak and transfers to new assignments of other originators and protagonists, architects and administrators of the NEP, the EPU school regained the initiative. The DNU itself degenerated into what, perhaps a little unfairly, has been characterised at a dumping ground for has-been politicians and so-so civil servants. It organised national unity walks in the Lake Garden on some weekends, neighbourhood picnics and the likes. While these activities in themselves were constructive and useful, they were a far cry from what was the main challenge and opportunity, namely to ensure that the NEP was on course and that implementation conformed closely to its original objectives, since so much was at stake and so much depended on its success.

## Mid-Term Review of the Third Malaysia Plan 1976-1980

The TMP review document for the three year period 1976-78 devoted a substantial amount of its efforts to analysing the macro developments of the economy. While the GDP growth target was raised in the TMP to 8.4 per cent per annum from the 7.4 per cent achieved in the Second Malaysia Plan Period, the growth over the period 1976-1978 was as high as 8.7 per cent. Much of this success, however, was a result of the continued strong commodity prices of the country's major exports. The document expressed the concern that while the macro performance was satisfactory, poverty persisted and the distribution of income between the racial groups was still in need of improvement. It was estimated that the incidence of poverty in Peninsular Malaysia declined from about 43.9 per cent in 1975 to about 36.6 per cent in 1978, while the incidence of poverty in agriculture declined from about 63.0 per cent to about 54.6 per cent. The income levels of all races in the lower income groups improved between 1970 and 1976. But the document also showed clearly (p. 44) that while all had benefitted and while incomes of all racial groups had risen, and quite substantially at that, the gap between the mean income of the Malays and that of the others, especially against the Chinese, had widened in 1976 compared to the situation in 1970. In these terms, the Malays were worse off now than when they started out in 1969. With respect to the employment situation, some progress in the restructuring of the employment pattern was made, but quite obviously not enough to make any serious dent on the overall situation; the NEP notwithstanding, the income distribution had worsened since the year of the riots.

## Fourth Malaysia Plan 1981-1985 (FMP)

Several far reaching changes were introduced in the Fourth Plan period (and later in the Fifth Plan), so as to make the Plans different from what the country had seen so far. The changes introduced formed part of a long term strategy by which the government sought to push Malaysia into a higher growth path via the export led industrialisation route of the type so successfully adopted by the Asian NIEs. This ambition was given expression also by government exhortation to the people of the country to be more efficient, to be honest, sincere, trustworthy, hardworking, morally upright like the political leadership (leadership by example), to work harder and to export more to the world like did the Japanese and the Koreans, etc. However, the main concern of our analysis is to ascertain where the

Malays fit in into this wider and more ambitious scheme of things. Would it help move the Malays nearer to economic parity? Or would it increase the economic gaps between them and the rest of the population while the country was speeding away to ever higher levels of GDP? It has to be remembered that Korea and Taiwan, two of the most successful Asian NIEs whose experience is probably the most relevant to Malaysia, emphasised equity simultaneously with growth in their export led industrialisation drive. Would the same happen in Malaysia? Or would Malaysia follow the Singapore route, where the country successfully became industrialised without much participation by the Malays, or the Brazilian route, where rapid industrialisation led to marked increase in economic imbalances?

The Fourth Malaysia Plan claimed that it was a continuation of the previous two plans in implementing the NEP; yet, the paramount role of growth was again re-stressed as in the First Malaysia Plan. As in that Plan, the macro variables were analysed in detail from growth forecasts, balance of payments prospects, monetary analysis, price developments, international developments affecting the Malaysian economy etc. While these analyses and prescriptions were technically challenging and useful in themselves, they were also basically non-controversial, irrelevant or incomplete in terms of the objectives of the NEP. The problems that led to the racial riot of 1969 were largely neglected. In spite of further confirmation that Malay incomes were lagging and their relative position was little better, if at all, than in 1969 and therefore that new efforts and innovations would be needed to speed up the corrective processes, the supreme objective of national economic policy in the Fourth Plan was the pursuit of growth. The DNU strategy of a direct attack, as opposed to an indirect attack now said to be pursued, on poverty and the restructuring objective, as reflected in the SMP and OPP, was downgraded in the Fourth Plan into at most a set of derived objectives of growth. The order of importance and ranking of objectives was now clearly established, with growth first, only then with poverty and restructuring in that order.

The projections for the eighties showed that the Malaysian economy would have to face greater challenges. In order to attain the poverty and the restructuring objectives, the target rate of growth was set at 8 per cent per annum for the economy as a whole, with sub-targets of 8.3 per cent and 12.4 per cent respectively for Kedah and Kelantan. Sectoral growth targets were also set for the output of the agricultural sector, the manufacturing sector, the construction sector etc.

Progress in poverty reduction had led to a decline in the incidence of poverty from 49.3 per cent in 1970 to 29.2 per cent in 1980. Allocations for anti-poverty programmes which had dropped from 26.3 per cent of the total Federal allocations in the Second Malaysia Plan to 20.5 per cent in the Third Malaysia Plan were raised to 23.7 per cent in the Fourth Malaysia Plan. The incidence of poverty was projected to decline to 15 per cent of total households in Peninsular Malaysia in 1990, slightly below (i.e. better than) the OPP target of 16.7 per cent. The FMP projections also showed that the levels of poverty continued to be much higher in the rural than in the urban areas.

In terms of income distribution among the ethnic groups, the Malay mean income continued to be well below the national average. The mean income of the Malays was shown (p. 4) to have grown "at the highest rate compared with those of other ethnic groups during 1971-1979, reducing the gap between the Malay income and the national average from 34.8 per cent in 1970 to 32.7 per cent in 1979. Both the Chinese and Indian mean incomes were above the national average". No projections for the 1980s were made in the FMP showing how these vast gaps were to be corrected beyond the general statement (p. 4) that "much remains to be done to remove the large income disparities between them".

The share of total equity held by Bumiputra and Bumiputra interests relative to other groups had increased from 4.3 per cent in 1971 to 12.4 per cent in 1980. This was below the target of 16 per cent by 1980 as set out in the OPP. As also reported in the FMP (p. 64), the share of equity held "by other Malaysian residents grew from 34 per cent in 1971 to about 40 per cent in 1980 as against their target of 40 per cent by 1990".

The growth and structural changes envisaged for the 1980s were expected to generate employment opportunities such that by 1990 full employment of the labour force could be achieved. Employment was estimated to grow by 3.2 per cent per annum during 1981-1990, a rate higher than the labour force growth of 3 per cent per annum, leading to a progressive reduction in the unemployment situation. The new job creation was expected to be located in the manufacturing, construction, mining, services and agricultural sectors. The leading sector would continue to be manufacturing. It is interesting to note that at the beginning of the Fourth Malaysia Plan period a situation had emerged with labour shortages in specific skills, particularly in agriculture, padi cultivation, and in rubber and palm oil estates. The FMP claimed that up to 1980 there had been significant improvement in the distribution of employment in line with the restructuring objective. The trend was expected to continue to 1990. But it also noted that the Bumiputra continued to be the minority in important professions as well as higher paid occupations.

The process of the gradual downgrading of the NEP into a sub-policy of Malaysian development efforts became complete with the launching of the Fourth Malaysia Plan. The NEP, as initially conceived as an over-arching *national* policy, had been reduced to a policy of separateness directed to the Malays. The NEP as an overall pragmatic development strategy for the whole country for the achievement of the ideals of Rukunegara, national unity, social justice and political stability, had become a residual policy within the macro growth policy. A policy designed to correct racial imbalances and injustice prevailing in the country, containing key ingredients of general recommendations of the World Bank, ILO and other UN and other aid agencies for Third World countries, became bogged down in controversies. Not surprisingly, a prolonged and sustained campaign against the NEP was mounted by the local media and even by the foreign press. In part this may be explained by the prospect that, in one of its dimensions, Malay progress would be at the expense of British commercial interests and those of their plantations and other industries. Within Malaysia, the NEP was conveniently branded as a racist policy intended exclusively for the Malays and at the expense of the Chinese and Indian communities. Increasingly, the NEP became discredited. It is particularly noteworthy that the MCA, who has been UMNO's partner since Merdeka, one of the signatories of the Merdeka Agreement and a participant, albeit a reluctant one, in the formulation of the NEP, was the most vociferous in campaigning against the NEP. Far from helping, the MCA became obstructionist. We return to the attacks on the NEP and the criticisms of it, justified or otherwise, in Chapter 5.

## Mid-Term Review of the Fourth Malaysia Plan 1981-85

The Mid-Term review of the Fourth Malaysia Plan in 1982 and 1983 took place in an environment of severe global economic recession, increasing protectionism, high inflation and unemployment in the OECD countries triggered earlier by the oil shock. The prolonged recession and its severity had serious adverse repercussions on Malaysia's external trade and growth. Private sector investments dropped severely as a result. The government was facing budgetary and resource constraints which were financed increasingly out of internal and external borrowings. The country's debts were rising while the balance of payments situation was deteriorating. The level of unemployment was rising. So did social tension. Generally the

country was facing a difficult time as did most other developing
countries. While the government had to cut down on its development
expenditure, the Prime Minister nonetheless cautioned (p. v):

> Care has to be taken to ensure that the reduction and restraint in
> expenditures will not adversely affect the development programmes
> undertaken in pursuit of the objectives of the New Economic Policy
> (NEP). Malaysians must, however, accept the fact that we are facing
> difficult times and must, therefore, share the burden of the necessary
> adjustments if we are to consolidate our achievements and to prepare the
> foundation for a faster recovery and growth.

The government called for a re-thinking of the existing development
strategies and implementation. During the run up to the review it
also became apparent that the economy had structural weaknesses.
The main challenge for planning and management of the economy
for the future was to engineer an early recovery of the economy and
lay the basis for a sustained high rate of growth for the long term.
A series of new innovative policies and strategies were proposed,
including the *Look East Policy*, the *Malaysia Incorporated Policy*, the
*Industrial Master Plan*, the *Privatisation Policy*, the *Outward
Industrial Strategy*, the *New International Markets Drive*, the
*Restructuring of Agriculture* and the *National Agricultural Policy*.
The sum total of the impact of these policies and strategies was
expected to be a streamlining and strengthening of the economy, so
as to place it in a strong position to meet internal demands and to
compete abroad in the tougher international markets.

The NEP had also to be readjusted in the face of the economic
difficulties of the country and the Mid-Term Review of the Fourth
Plan (p. 13) indicated the need for more emphasis on growth.[1] This
implied less emphasis on the restructuring objective of the NEP,
placing it, at least in terms of proposed implementation, at the same
level as the Look East Policy, Malaysia Incorporated Policy and the

---

[1] "As the NEP targets under the OPP were formulated on the basis of a more
optimistic economic environment, readjustments to the NEP strategy will be necessary
to take into account an economic environment marked by growing difficulties. The
Government will continue to put emphasis on raising the rate of growth of the
economy as growth is a necessary condition for making further progress on the
objectives of the NEP. As labour absorption is an important element in the strategy
for poverty redressal, a much more concerted drive to raise output and employment
of the modern urban and rural sectors will be necessary. Employment growth in
manufacturing will assume an important role in further alleviating poverty and the
Government will, therefore, take appropriate measures to accelerate the rate of
growth, especially of exports from the manufacturing sector."

Privatisation Policy.

Progress in poverty eradication had a set back as a result of the global economic recession and falling commodity prices. The overall incidence of poverty was estimated to have increased from 29.0 per cent in 1980 to 30.3 per cent in 1983. This set back hit the Malays particularly hard: while rural poverty was estimated to have increased from 37.4 per cent in 1980 to 41.6 per cent in 1983, the incidence of urban poverty actually declined from 12.6 per cent in 1980 to 11.1 per cent in 1983. The Mid-Term Review of the Fourth Plan explained the various concepts of poverty with care and the difficulties involved in making international comparisons of poverty, emphasising that Malaysian poverty was not of an acute form as in some other countries (pp. 76 and 79). Famine, lack of shelter, starvation were rarities in Malaysia. Even so, there was no gainsaying the fact that the level of poverty had increased and the Malays were mostly the victims.

After more than 10 years of implementation of the NEP, income imbalances between the urban and rural areas, between the races, and between the regions remained wide. Chinese mean income was roughly twice that of the Malays, while Indian mean monthly income was roughly 1.5 times that of the Malays. While there had been some improvement in the 1970s, including a slight improvement in rural/urban income ratios, there had been a clear set-back in this respect in the early years of the 1980s. With respect to employment the progress in restructuring proceeded at a slower pace; this was explained by the dampening effect of the slower growth in employment creation. Unemployment among all races increased mainly as a result of the continued growth in labour force and the slower rate of job creation following the recessionary impact. While the overall employment pattern reflected the racial composition of the population, the Malays were still underrepresented in the secondary sector, particularly in manufacturing and commerce, the majority of them still being employed largely in agriculture. Bumiputra ownership of the corporate sector, including that held by the trust agencies, increased from 12.5 per cent in 1980 to 18.7 per cent in 1983. The share held by other Malaysians was reported to have increased to 47.7 per cent in 1983, as against a target for 1990 of "only" 40 per cent. The Mid-Term Review document fended off criticism of this development by observing that the specific targets of the NEP were to be regarded only as intermediate steps to the attainment of national unity and that the NEP needed to be complemented by greater self-reliance. It went on to suggest that the ability to manage the affairs of the country was also an important yardstick for assessing the extent of achievement of the objectives of the NEP.

## Fifth Malaysia Plan 1985-1990

The Prime Minister, introducing the Fifth Malaysia Plan (p. v), explained:

> The Fifth Malaysia Plan 1986-1990 represents the fourth and last segment of the 20 year Outline Perspective Plan (OPP), 1971-1990, for attaining the overriding goal of national unity... If we are to sustain our achievements and to continue our efforts towards achieving national unity, without at the same time creating a sense of loss or deprivation within the Malaysian society, it is imperative that the drive towards growth must continue unabated. Towards this end and taking into account our resources, a strategy of moderate growth with stability will be pursued. At the same time, we must not lose sight of the importance of continuing our efforts to redress glaring socio-economic imbalances and to alleviate poverty.

By the foregoing passage, it appears clear that by this stage in the evolution of the NEP, the search for national unity had been turned upside down from the original concept of the NEP as understood and developed after the riot of 1969. It is recalled that national unity was the uppermost objective of the NEP, and the proximate indicator of national unity was considered to be the extent and speed of correction of the racial economic imbalances through the implementation of successive Five Year Plans. The most important dimensions of these economic imbalances, as the DNU had shown, were the imbalances in income, employment and wealth. The magnitude and seriousness of these imbalances displayed in the original NEP work were subsequently confirmed by later Plan documents and by some major World Bank studies. However, by now the achievement of the restructuring objective clearly ranked well below the objective of growth. Once again the solution of the Malay problems of inequality and poverty was seen as a *residual* matter not at par with other objectives.

There is a hollowness to the statement of the development thrust of the Fifth Malaysia Plan (pp. 16-17), out of keeping with the words used:

> It cannot be overemphasised that the overriding goal of socio-economic development in the country is to ultimately bring about national unity. The rallying point for national unity is nationalism. Malaysians should

develop a deep love and pride for the country, and be guided by the Rukunegara. The plurality of this young nation continues to pose a great challenge to all Malaysians to participate in the moulding of this society into a resilient nation imbued with positive qualities of self-reliance, diligence, moral strength, and integrity. It is important to continue promoting national unity because of the emergence of some parochial interests and extreme views and values among certain groups that can work against nation building... The major task of economic development is to forge a nation which is united, and an important part of this task is to remove the glaring socio-economic differences among the major ethnic groups.

As evidenced by this statement, the definition of national unity had now been broadened and elevated to the philosophical level of nationalism and the love of one's country. While this is a widely shared ideal, it is, in this context, an abstract concept of no operational relevance. Certainly, no one can reasonably accuse the Malays of not being nationalistic or of having become less nationalistic after Merdeka. The Malays made great sacrifices to drive away the colonial masters who created the Malay problem in the first place; now they appear to be left living under a more permanent form of internal colonialism. When the tally is taken, after 20 years of the NEP, which ever way one measures, the Malays would still be at the bottom of the economic ladder. The challenge remains: how to design an effective strategy and how to formulate and implement concrete and practical measures to speed up the restructuring process so that the Malays are not permanently left behind.

The Fifth Plan emphasis on development for the second half of the 1980s was based on growth with stability. The reasons given for the need to stimulate growth were many. First, growth in the remaining years of the 1980s was expected to slow down compared with the achievements of 1970s. In order to sustain the achievement so far, in terms of reducing the incidence of poverty, expanding the employment creation capacity, and increasing Bumiputra corporate ownership, the economy had to continue to expand. Second, it was necessary to have rapid growth so that other groups in the Malaysian society would not experience any loss or feel a sense of deprivation in the restructuring process. Third, in view of unemployment having already reached the 10 per cent level, the demands on the economy to create jobs would have to be intensified. Last, public resources were already under strain due to budget deficits, balance of payments difficulties, and mounting local and foreign debts.

The star performer in the growth performance in the coming years was expected to be the manufacturing sector. To foster industrial development and to enable the private sector to perform its role as the generator of growth, future industrial efforts were to be based on the recommendations of the *Malaysian Industrial Policies Strategies* (MIPS) and the *Industrial Master Plan* (IMP). These master plans were designed to make the Malaysian industrial sector highly competitive and export oriented. Already by 1984 the manufacturing sector had surpassed the agricultural sector as the largest sector in the economy. In this renewed effort, the IMP identified the metal industry, engineering, chemical and processing industries as well as the electronics industry as the basic industries to serve to broaden the Malaysian industrial base. The strategy was also based on the establishment of selected heavy industries.

The impetus for growth, especially through the manufacturing sector, would be spearheaded by the private sector. This accounts partly for the *Privatisation Policy* and the efforts to trim the size of the public sector under the Fifth Plan. Private sector investment was expected to increase its share of total investment from 50.4 per cent in 1985 to about 62 per cent in 1990. The growth and expansion of the private sector activities would not only contribute to the overall growth of the economy but also, it was expected, facilitate the increase of Bumiputra participation in the economy. The rapid expansion in the equity of industrial firms envisaged would lead to increased participation by the Bumiputra commercial and industrial community (assuming of course there would be no slackening in the conditions in the allocations of these shares). The Fifth Plan stressed (p. 213) the need for private sector activities which, by providing employment and opportunities to develop skills, could contribute to the participation of Bumiputra in management, supervisory and technical occupations and involve them in the modern and high-productivity sectors of manufacturing.

With respect to the agricultural sector the *National Agricultural Policy* (NAP) was intended to provide the broad guidelines for the development of the sector up to the year 2000. Within these guidelines the ministries and agencies concerned were to draw up detailed plans for implementation. These include land development and the development of specific commodities, including food and industrial crops, forestry, fisheries and livestock products. The focus would be on land development, rehabilitation of idle land, and group farming, while institutional and human development would be re-oriented in terms of emphasis and content. The thrust of the NAP, as was explained (pp. 296-297), was intended to promote increased productivity, efficiency and competitiveness in the use and development of resources. Development efforts were to be directed to the modernisation and commercialisation of smallholders so as to revitalise agriculture within the private sector. The NAP aspired to obtain a rational use of basic productive resources through sectoral planning. But the full impact of the NAP measures, the government warned, would not be felt until well into the 1990s.

The government's overall view (summarised on p. 81) was that

> While a great deal had been achieved under the NEP much remains to be done for the remaining years of the Outline Perspective Plan (OPP), 1971-1990. Greater efforts will, therefore, be required to ensure continuing progress towards achieving the objectives of the NEP, especially in view of the difficult times that are anticipated. While the targets of the NEP may not largely be met, nevertheless, by the end of the decade, further progress will have been made in reducing the glaring and serious economic imbalances which plagued the country at the beginning of the NEP.

At the time of the run-up to the completion of the OPP, therefore, the Government appeared to be satisfied that the average income of Malaysians had improved, the incidence of poverty had declined, and the restructuring of the pattern of employment and ownership of wealth had moved some way ahead. Nevertheless, at this time unemployment stood at slightly more than 10 per cent of the total labour force, many of the unemployed were graduates, particularly Malay graduates, and income imbalances between ethnic groups and between urban and rural areas were still wide.

## Mid-Term Review of the Fifth Malaysia Plan 1986-1990

The Mid-Term Review of the Fifth Malaysia Plan 1986-1990 was the occasion for a final stocktaking before the country reached the end of the OPP period of 20 years to 1990. The pigeon had come home to roost. In terms of data and explanations on performance during the NEP, the Mid-Term Review is more forthcoming and explicit than other recent Plan documents, although the methodology utilised is the same as in the previous Plans. Not surprisingly, the achievements with respect to the Restructuring Objective of the NEP foreseen by 1990 fell short on all fronts and on all counts compared with the targets set in the OPP. This is the result of accumulated shortfalls over the last nearly 20 years, which could not be corrected within the space of another two years to 1990. At the time of the Mid-Term Review, therefore, it was already clear that the government would not be able to deliver in full measure on its promises to the Malays and to the nation in 1970 when the NEP was launched.

Understandably, the Government argued that it had to focus its attention on countering the impact of worldwide disruption and difficulties, seeking an effective response in terms of fiscal and monetary policies, and other measures to stimulate the economy on a path to recovery from a prolonged recession emanating from the international economy. As a matter of record, the Government's priorities have been very clear: growth and its attendant policies were given top priority, followed by anti-poverty measures, with the Restructuring Objective coming third where possible. The Government drew the conclusion (p. 7) as follows:

> The key lessons that were learnt from the recession of 1985-1986 and the successful adjustment and sustained growth that took place thereafter, are that prudent and stable macro-economic fiscal management is necessary for stable economic growth. Modest and sustainable deficits promote growth, shield the poor from the heavy burdens of fiscal austerity, and allows the private sector greater scope to play a leading role in economic activities. In addition the objectives of poverty eradication and restructuring of society would be better served in the context of stable growth which create continuous distributional opportunities. Substantial economic benefits can also be derived by a more efficient management of scarce resources.

In this respect the Mid-Term Review of the Fifth Plan runs in the tradition of pre-1969 plans. Clearly, the Mid-Term Review was not seen as an occasion to reinstate the Restructuring Objective at the top of the nation's agenda. It had to wait.

In respect of NEP objectives and targets for 1990 the Government concluded (p. 78):

> The difficult economic environment in the early years of the Plan interrupted the attainment of the NEP objectives. ..... Although poverty eradication aspects of the NEP will be nearly attained by 1990, efforts will continue to be taken to reduce the incidence and occurrence of poverty, especially by concentrating on the hard core poverty groups. The restructuring targets may fall short by 1990, requiring new approaches and re-thinking of strategies towards effective participation of Bumiputra in all economic activities. With continued regional disparities, growth in less-developed states will be promoted through better urban-rural linkages. The challenges ahead would entail policy shifts that will nurture self-reliance, resourcefulness, and positive commitment among all Malaysians, particularly the lagging communities.

New thinking and shifts in policy directions and thrusts would certainly be required if the restructuring problems were to be progressively solved at all. Yet, it appeared (p. 6) that the government had set its economic strategy in the final years of the OPP period dominantly in terms of sustained economic growth:

> The thrust of development policy for the remaining period of the Plan will be to achieve the full potential output growth that the economy can generate, focusing on increased productivity, efficiency and competitiveness. The private sector will play the leading role in the expansion of the economy while the public sector will act as facilitator to private sector expansion in an environment of stability. Based on the vitality of the current recovery in the private sector, the sustained external impetus and the supportive role of the Government, the economy is expected to grow by an average of 7 per cent during the 1989-1990 period. Industrial restructuring will continue to be the main thrust of future development.

This policy thrust, as announced, overrode other policy priorities, including the efforts in the direction of the Restructuring Objective. Yet, if the restructuring problems are ever to be successfully solved, they must be confronted directly, consistently and persistently. As the experience of the last 20 years has shown, the seriousness of the problem of restructuring yields to forceful attack. Pretence is the enemy of action.

## Summary

The closest to the original concept of the NEP, as proposed by the Department of National Unity after the riot, were the Second Malaysia Plan 1971-75 and the Outline Perspective Plan in its Mid-Term Review. Indeed the NEP reached its high point in the early years. Beginning with the Third Malaysia Plan, growth was gradually reinstated to its central role in the national economic policy. While in the original concept the restructuring objective was supreme, and growth was one of its sub-elements, though an important one, in subsequent Plans it was restructuring that became a sub-element of the growth policy. To that extent it was a complete reversal of priorities. In the following chapter we shall review the progress or otherwise over the past twenty years in the pursuit of the objectives of the NEP.

# CHAPTER 4

# IMPLEMENTATION

## Ambitions and Approaches

Any attempt to assess the success of the NEP comes up against an immediate difficulty: the NEP was never completely specified and the term "New Economic Policy", as currently used, is simply a shorthand description of the plans and policies that have been developed in the past two decades to deal with the restructuring of the economy. Such plans were drawn up with knowledge of the objectives and aspirations of the initiators of the New Economic Policy but they represent no more than an interpretation of the original aims. For a statement of these we have to turn to a seminal document, *Policies for Growth with Racial Balance*, which is reproduced in this book as Document A. This document has to be read in the knowledge that it was intended to set in train a continuing process of explicating new policies for the advancement of the Bumiputra and providing for the implementation of measures that would be needed to put these policies into effect. Document A is to be regarded, in many respects, as a declaration of intent, the first stage in getting acceptance of new policies and promoting their induction. It was intended to be followed by a second stage devoted to giving depth and substance to the policies, which was to involve all aspects of the work of the government departments concerned. This in turn was expected to lead to a third stage, that of giving form to the measures needed to implement the new policies and make them operationally effective. In order to make the proposals outlined in Document A operational, a *Directive*, providing basic guidelines for the formulation of the Second Malaysia Plan 1971-75, was sent from the Department of National Unity, on 18 March 1970, to all Government Departments and Agencies. This *Directive*, reproduced here as Document C, called for "explicit consideration of the implications of the national unity objective" (p. 308). It laid stress on racial economic balances and pointed to a number of differences that could exist between racial groups in such things as income, wealth and opportunities. The *Directive* went on to establish three basic objectives for the New Economic Policy, viz. "reduction of racial economic disparities; creation of economic opportunities; and the promotion of overall economic growth" (p. 308).

Of particular importance was the declaration that "The Government will use its licensing authority, budget and tax structure, financial incentives, specific regulations and other systems of incentives and controls to ensure that the private sector development reflects the objectives and needs of the country" (p. 310). The State governments were also to be drawn into "this new emphasis on a more dynamic role for the public sector" (p. 311).

In its details, the *Directive* emphasised the importance of advances in padi production in which the Malays were predominant, and which had shown small increases in productivity, and went on to make a series of recommendations relating to the agricultural sector of the economy, including fisheries. For manufacturing, mining and construction, the emphasis was on greater Malay participation fostered by giving preferences to Malay interests. There was also consideration of the "lopsided geographical distribution of manufacturing establishments" and the need to introduce corrective measures. Above all, support was to be given to Malay ventures. Development in the sectors of the community concerned with material welfare were to be flanked with progress in the promotion of medical and health facilities. Similarly with education.

There were many exhortations to efficiency with emphasis on coordination and implementation of policies. The *Directive* suffered from its length and diversity of recommendations but it reinforced the pressures on administrators to accept the NEP and pointed the way to its implementation.

Many of the recommendations of the *Directive*, although focused on the reduction of racial disparities and on the promotion of Bumiputra interests, were of such wide acceptability as to be included in any set of development proposals; it is, therefore, not inappropriate to ask what were the particular characteristics of the NEP and, for this, it is helpful to go back to Document A as being more indicative of the intended nature of the NEP than subsequent statements.

It was a cardinal principle of the New Economic Policy, as put forward in the document, that, if necessary, growth had to be sacrificed for equity. Such a sacrifice could not be absolute, but nowhere was it explained what reduction in growth was acceptable to ensure greater equality of income and provide a wider spread of opportunities for advancement. Perhaps this was not really necessary.

Many differences in the position of Malays and other ethnic groups manifested themselves; duality was many faceted, but the essential process of rectification consisted in helping the Malays (and incidentally others) in agriculture where they predominated, and working progressively to improve their presence in the modern sector of the economy, both rural and urban. One of the trade-offs could thus be a lower return to investment in traditional agriculture compared with other sectors, and a slower rate of progression in the modern sector in return for better conditions for the poor. Of course there would be other trade-offs, but the agriculture/modern sector exchange was the major one. It need not necessarily be disadvantageous; it was always possible that investment in agriculture would prove to be higher yielding than investment in the modern sector; if so, growth with equity would be attainable. This outturn was favoured, as we shall see, by turning agriculture itself into a modern sector. Nevertheless, the development of agriculture was not the ultimate solution to easing racial imbalances: major progress could be made only by developing other sectors of the economy. The issue here was not agriculture or industry but their relative progression over time.

It was intended to attain the objectives of the NEP by following certain main lines of action. These were directed, in the first place, to the rural areas, distinguishing the needs of the East and the West Coast areas of the country. The first major feature of the development programme proposed for the East Coast, Kedah and Perlis was concentrated on land ownership and tenancy with emphasis on the relationships between landlords and tenants. The second major feature was concerned with a much more rapid land development programme and the third feature with provisions for an ambitious programme for construction of infrastructure. A general characteristic of the proposals was the adoption of policies to assist rural farmers to increase their productivity and incomes.

Concern was expressed about several aspects of the programmes: possible effects on the price of rubber, the need to train and organise Malay workers for effective participation in the developments proposed so that it would be unnecessary always to use Chinese or Indian workers, and the need to provide large numbers of extension workers, administrators and technicians who were indispensable for the execution of programmes.

The proposals for the West Coast were broadly similar to those for the East Coast but the provision of infrastructure was regarded as of lesser urgency and particular emphasis was placed on smallholder rubber replanting.

For urban semi-skilled and unskilled Malays, employment quotas were recommended as a means to increase participation and promote training. The issues here were how high such quotas should be initially, probably below 25 per cent (Document A, p. 260) and how rapidly they could be raised, which was highly dependent on the rate at which training could proceed, for participation on a basis of glaring inequalities was not going to promote political stability. It was concluded that the "main hope for major increases in urban employment must come from rapid growth of industry and other sectors of the modern urban economy (transport, commerce, etc.)" (p. 260). Some measures were discussed for alleviation of the consequences of protracted unemployment, by giving preference, for example, to long-term urban unemployed, but it was accepted that not a great deal could be done to provide sufficient jobs to reduce the numbers of unemployed.

Education was regarded as perhaps the most basic means to ensure the Malays of their rightful place in society, and a variety of proposals were made for increased educational provision and suitable curricula. Preference for Malays to pursue suitable courses at University level was also proposed and considered in the context of increasing the availability of university education.

On one thing the author of *Policies for Growth with Racial Balance* was absolutely clear: industry was not to be impeded; "To make industry bear the brunt of a Malay income and employment policy will be to markedly slow its development and to seriously endanger the long-term economic future of the country" (p. 265). It was industry that could offer managerial opportunities for Malays; it was industry that could provide the means of growth in output and employment while financing investment and contributing to government revenues. It was industry that could reduce dependence on imports and, in the fullness of time, add to export earnings. In a readiness to sacrifice some growth for equity while at the same time insisting on industry as an instrument for growth, Document A had an element of ambivalence, perhaps because it was instinctively felt that the dilemma was more imaginary than real. Policies for the rapid advancement of industry were fully consistent with bringing Malays into that sector and exposing them to that experience. In fact, growth was seen as a necessary condition for achieving greater racial balance.

To this initial statement of the content of the NEP set out in Document A, may be added other elements, more evident in retrospect than in the sketch of them in the statement itself; so it is useful to put down in summary form what were the essentials of the policies advocated in the NEP as it developed and was interpreted. Some of these were general in compass, others more specific. Those of wide application comprised:

> The intention of the authors of the NEP to get politicians and administrators, and particularly administrators, to focus their attention on a different way of looking at the development strategy than had hitherto been adopted;

> Insistence on the necessity to develop effective policies to implement the new strategy;

> The need to look at statistics relating to the running of the economy in the light of new as well as old objectives and to provide new series of figures suitable for monitoring performance;

> Emphasis on acquiring greater racial balance at all income levels and not just at the poverty level;

> Recognition of the crucial contribution of growth to solving the racial problem.

More specifically, emphasis was placed on:

> Progress with agriculture, particularly that part of it in which the Bumiputra were engaged;

> The adoption of employment quotas in the modern sector of the economy;

> Measures to improve the distribution of assets in favour of the Bumiputra;

> The need for regional policies to redress some large economic imbalances;

> The importance of extending educational opportunities and health care;

> The need to eliminate basic poverty.

The overriding aim of all these policies was, of course, to rectify racial imbalances and particularly to improve the distribution of income in favour of the Bumiputra.

It is not possible to say in relation to any of these things, what the contribution of the NEP has been and what differences would have been evident if the NEP had never been devised. The success or failure of the NEP can not be evaluated in these terms. What can be done, is to see how far Malaysia has been able to proceed with the objectives detailed above since the NEP was first broached, and to judge whether progress appears to have been adequate in all the circumstances.

It was one of the strengths of the efforts to present the NEP that not only was it put forward persuasively in terms of policy but, in addition, it was backed up by quantitative illustration. This was the essential function of Document B, *Racial Disparity and Economic Development*, also included in this book. For our purposes, this has a double importance, for it not only reveals the magnitudes of the programme that was envisaged but makes it possible to relate it, in some measure, to the policies that were proposed and to the subsequent development of the economy.

The reasons why Malays had lower incomes than other ethnic groups are summarised in Document B. Malays were preponderant in the countryside rather than in the towns and they were concentrated in the poorer states; they were in low productivity sectors and within virtually all those sectors were disproportionately in lower-echelon positions; they owned only one-third of the land and had a significantly lower ownership of industrial and commercial capital. It appeared from the calculations in Document B that there was a productivity and income differential in favour of the non-Malays (as we have already seen) approximating to a ratio of 7:4. Even this was a considerable underestimate. It is evident that the differences were understated in the document with the deliberate intention of avoiding any accusation of bias. Subsequent work suggests that the differences were very much greater than these first estimates appeared to show.

Table B.3 in Document B (pp. 290-291) can be consulted for the basic calculations. Interesting though the details of these are, their value lies not so much in the statistical calculations as in the analytical framework that is developed and against which comparisons can be made.

Several types of structural shifts were envisaged in that table. It was not supposed that there would be much change in the proportion of Malays included in the traditional rural sectors. In 1985, as in 1967, Malays would account for about three-quarters of the total. In contrast, in the modern rural sector a marked change was assumed to take place; the proportion of Malay workers would change from 29 to 41 per cent. In the modern urban sector, the change was expected to be less marked in terms of proportions although it would be greater numerically because more people were employed in that sector. The process of reducing disparities was expected to take

place, to a substantial degree as a result of a shift in the employment
of Malays towards the modern sectors of the economy. It may be
estimated that this was expected to be of sufficient magnitude to
increase Malay incomes by about one per cent per year, on the basis
of the value added in the various sectors. The effects of occupational
shifts on other ethnic groups was small and the implication was that
an increase in the incomes of the Malays in the labour force (as
defined in the table) relative to those of the non-Malays, would
bring the ratio down from about 1.75 (as then calculated) to about
1.40. This took account of the need to accommodate nearly 0.5
million more Malays in the traditional sector in 1985 than in 1967,
presumably because there would not be sufficient new jobs to
employ them all.

What we are dealing with here is a type of dual economy
distinguished from others mainly because of its racial overtones, but
also because these had the effects of impeding entry to the modern
sector. This general model of development was explored by Sir
Arthur W. Lewis in a seminal article[1] and extended in subsequent
work by Fei and Ranis[2]. The essence of the process is a transfer of
labour from the traditional to the modern sector of an economy
under dynamic conditions that are changing in a number of important
respects. In the Malaysian context, the amount of labour needed to
produce a given output diminishes in both the traditional and modern
sectors of the economy as new technology is brought to bear.
Employment increases in total and may continue to increase in the
traditional sector of the economy for a time depending on the rate
of increase in population and the rate at which it can be absorbed
into the modern sector. As the development process gathers
momentum, employment in the traditional sector of the economy may
be expected to decline as a proportion of the working population and
probably in absolute amount, depending on the rate of labour
absorption into the modern sector and changes in activity rates.
Unemployment may increase or decline, the expectation being that
it will decline as a proportion of the labour force, as the absorption
of labour gathers force. Improvements in productivity in the modern
sector of the economy will, of course, condition the rate of labour
absorption by it, and may be helpful to employment or otherwise,

[1]  See, Lewis, W.A., "Economic Development with Unlimited Supplies of Labour",
*The Manchester School of Economic and Social Studies*, vol. 12 (1954), no. 2, pp.
139-191.
[2]  See, John C.H. Fei and Gustav Ranis, *Development of the Labour Surplus
Economy*, Homewood, Ill: Irwin, 1964.

depending on how costs and markets are affected. Such improvements in productivity will not be restricted to the modern sector of the economy; they will also affect the demand for labour by the traditional sector, again not in a wholly determinate fashion, but probably in the direction of reducing demand, as is abundantly evident in the evolution of developing countries.

This shift of labour from the traditional to the modern sectors of the economy may be expected to have considerable price effects which in practice may not be easy to predict. Nevertheless, as job opportunities open up in the modern sector and labour is attracted to it from rural areas, it is to be expected that remuneration in the traditional sector will gradually rise. Again, the models presumed that a surplus of labour available in the traditional sector would hold down remuneration for a time; it would be only after the surplus labour was absorbed that wages (or remuneration) would start to rise; then the increase might accelerate, depending on how productivity reacted to diminishing supplies of labour, whether there was induced technical change, and so on. In these models, it is probably not to be expected that remuneration in the traditional sector will speedily catch up with remuneration in the modern sector for the deployment of comparable skills, and it may never do so. The quality of life in rural areas and in the towns has to be taken into account: in Marshall's phrase the net advantages of working in particular occupations are what matters[3]. Differences in the cost of living in towns as opposed to the countryside have to be taken into consideration as well as the effects of inertia which may also play a part.

In the case of Malaysia, the period when the development of a modern sector has little effect on remuneration in the traditional sector might be expected to be shorter than in the land-hungry countries of Asia. Employment opportunities in rural areas could be augmented by measures to take additional areas of land into cultivation, as was proposed in the NEP. Increases in productivity may also serve to augment rural incomes, provided, of course, that they are not offset by corresponding reductions in prices, or imposed upon producers in order to meet competition from other countries.

Clearly these considerations are of considerable importance in relation to the agricultural export crops of Malaysia.

---

[3]   Alfred Marshall, *Principles of Economics*, 8th ed. London: Macmillan, 1938, p. 73.

## An Arithmetic Illustration

The development path of a dual economy of the Malaysian type may be portrayed with the aid of an arithmetic illustration. We assume a traditional and a modern sector with the characteristics shown in Table 4.1. The traditional sector is supposed to employ only Bumiputra and the modern sector, initially, only non-Bumiputra. In the process of development Bumiputra move from the traditional sector to the modern sector as employment expands there, along the lines of the Lewis model.

The division of the economy into a traditional and a modern sector in the form outlined above is, of course, a very considerable simplification of the real world, and is adopted only with the intention of illustrating the process of development and the factors that may affect the ethnic distribution of income in a dual economy of the Malaysian type, as the balance of employment moves towards the modern sector.

The figures of employment in the first column are no more than proportions, representing the division of labour between the traditional and the modern sectors. The figures for the capital stock are tied to the figures of output by an assumed capital-output ratio of 4:1 in both sectors. This, in turn, combined with a rate of growth of output per annum of 6 per cent in the economy as a whole, implies that net investment amounts to 24 per cent of GDP.[4] Another assumption is that the total labour force increases at nearly 3 per cent per annum and that this increase is absorbed into the modern sector whether it originates in the traditional or modern sector. Output per head in the modern sector is assumed to increase at 2 per cent per annum and at the greater rate of no less than 4 per cent per annum in the traditional sector (sufficient to increase output per head by 80 per cent over 15 years). The initial ratio of earnings in the modern sector to those in the traditional one is set at 2.2, corresponding to the ratio of the remuneration of Bumiputra to other ethnic groups round about 1970.

[4] This follows from the fact that an increase in output equivalent to 6 per cent of GDP requires supporting capital of 4 times this amount. Net investment of 24 per cent of GDP may be equivalent to gross investment of about 27 per cent of GDP (corresponding to the Malaysian economy over the period considered) assuming that GDP is increasing at about 6 per cent per annum and that capital needs to be replaced after 15 years. There is always a danger that national income accounting makes insufficient allowance for maintenance expenditure and, if so, this would require higher gross investment to keep capital intact. The above assumptions represent a first approximation to investment relations in the Malaysian economy from 1970 to 1985.

TABLE 4.1
TRADITIONAL AND MODERN SECTOR DEVELOPMENT IN A DUAL ECONOMY

| Sector | Employment | | Output per Person Employed | | Value of Total Output | | Capital Stock | |
|---|---|---|---|---|---|---|---|---|
| | 1970 | 1985 | 1970 | 1985 | 1970 | 1985 | 1970 | 1985 |
| Traditional | 50 | 50 | 1.0 | 1.8 | 50 | 90 | 200 | 360 |
| Modern | 50 | 100 | 2.2 | 2.9 | 110 | 290 | 440 | 1160 |
| Total | 100 | 150 | 1.6 | 2.5 | 160 | 380 | 640 | 1520 |

All the assumptions can, of course, be varied at will, but as they stand they can be used to capture some of the important changes that took place in the Malaysian economy over the period 1970 to 1985 and their likely effects on the ethnic distribution of income. The factors that appear of greatest relevance are changes in population, as they affect the labour force, relative price changes in the output of the two sectors (although these are not portrayed in the model), the rate of growth of output and productivity in the two sectors.

In spite of the limitations of the arithmetic illustration, it is sufficiently close to reality for some judgements to be formed as to how various parameters evolve as time goes on and to show some ways in which earnings per capita will change in the traditional and modern sectors of the economy as development proceeds. A striking feature of the assumptions made in the table is the considerable increase in average per capita income in the traditional sector of the economy. This is in keeping with the large increase in output actually realised in the agricultural sector of the Malaysian economy, over the period covered in the table, without, so far as can be judged from incomplete statistical series, much increase, if any, in employment. This has the effect of raising productivity considerably — by about 80 per cent in 15 years. In this respect, the arithmetic model could be deceptive in suggesting that Bumiputra engaged in agriculture had improved their incomes correspondingly if, for example, it turned out that much of the benefit had accrued to large estates operated preponderantly with foreign or Chinese capital and that the effect of higher productivity was to increase profits rather than the remuneration of labour. In practice, this does not seem to have been the case. A considerable part of the innovations effected in agriculture were designed to benefit small holders.[5]

---

[5] Consideration of figures of valued added in agriculture according to type of activity throws some light on these issues. Output of rubber at constant prices showed little change from 1978 to 1987. Much the same was true for coconut, fisheries and small-scale activities including output of padi, a primary activity of Bumiputra. There has been major growth in output of palm oil, cocoa and livestock, and to a lesser relative extent in forestry and logging, and to a numerically small extent in tea. The most striking increase has been in the yield and output of palm oil. This is produced by both estates and smallholders in roughly equal amounts and so may have been of considerable benefit to Bumiputra. It is also necessary to consider what effect the increase in agricultural output has had on wages. The evidence here is limited and confusing because wages and earnings fluctuate markedly, depending on market prices for the products. Nevertheless, it appears from the available statistics that there has been an increase in the remuneration of wage earners engaged in harvesting, probably more than matching the increase in the cost of living although this does not appear to be the case for factory workers.

Whatever the precise facts may be in relation to the traditional agricultural sector, there is a second, and ultimately, more powerful force at work in the transference of Bumiputra to the modern sector, where productivity and earnings are much greater than in the traditional sector. In the model, the expansion of the modern sector is sufficient to provide employment not only for the increase in the population born into that environment but also for an influx of workers from the traditional sector. This is assumed to be sufficient to take up the whole of the natural rate of increase of the labour force. If, in order to point the issue, we continue to assume that initially all the population in the traditional sector consisted of Bumiputra, and all of the population in the modern sector of non-Bumiputra, the transfer of Bumiputra to the modern sector by 1985 (where in the model they are assumed to earn the same as non-Malays) will improve the income distribution[6]. We can quantify this by observing that in order to equate the average per capita income of Bumiputra with that of non-Bumiputra in 1970, it would have been necessary to transfer 19 per cent of total income from one racial group to the other, whereas the same effect could be achieved in 1985 by the transfer of only 7 per cent of total income in that year (in effect using the Theil index to measure inequality between the two sectors)[7]. In another 15 years, the reduction in inequality would become much more apparent, assuming that the process of development continued along the same lines[8]; eventually, if the process were continued, inequality would become very small indeed.

---

[6] It is unrealistic to assume that the earnings of Bumiputra and non-Bumiputra are the same in the modern sector. The *Post Enumeration Survey,* carried out in 1970, (for details, see Sudhir Anand, *Inequality and Poverty in Malaysia,* Oxford University Press, 1983, pp. 230-236) shows, that with rare exceptions, earnings of Bumiputra in the same occupational classifications were markedly lower than those of the Chinese. This is an important qualification to the findings of the model and one to which we return below.

[7] The Theil index is generally described as an entropy index based on the notion of entropy in information theory. It is more easily understood as a measure of the proportion of income that would have to be transfered from those above the average income to those below it to achieve approximate equality.

[8] If the model were extended for a further period of 15 years on similar assumptions, the remuneration of non-Bumiputra would be about 7 per cent greater on the average than that of Bumiputra by the end of the period. This would imply, using the Theil index, that a transfer of about 4 per cent of total income would be all that would be needed to equate average Bumiputra and non-Bumiputra incomes. There are, however, several reasons for doubting whether the assumptions made above are robust enough to bear extension for 15 years into the future. It may well be that the growth of productivity in the agricultural sector will slow down and there may be a rise in capital-output ratios. A further complication is that our calculations assume that Bumiputra, industry for industry, and occupation for occupation, are as well rewarded as non-Bumiputra. In the past this has not been the case.

Clearly the process could be accelerated by increasing investment in either the modern sector or traditional sectors if this were practicable and resulted in increases in productivity and employment. It may be questioned, however, whether *net* investment could be increased much beyond 30 per cent of the GDP, and it may also be expected that the incremental capital/output ratio will tend to increase. We return to this discussion in Chapter 6 when we consider a somewhat similar model of development constructed by the Malaysian Institute of Economic Research.

The arithmetic model exposes the results that might be expected to emerge from the so-called trickle-down effect working in suitable circumstances. It is to be expected that there will be some considerable elapse of time before an acceptable distribution of income is attained, even with assumptions of a strong development effort, as made in the table. When, however, the model is faced with the reality of the Malaysian economy, it is evident that the gap between the Bumiputra and other ethnic groups has not closed so quickly as the model suggests would be the case. By 1985 in the model, the ratio between the incomes of Bumiputra and other groups closes to about 1: 1.3, whereas the gap relative to the Chinese ethnic group even as late as 1987 appears to have been much greater, about 1: 1.6. It is easy to dismiss this difference as being due to the imperfect specification of the arithmetic model and the considerable approximations that are incorporated into it. In a formal sense, this is, of course, correct, although the model was designed to follow the evolution of the economy with reasonable closeness. In order to throw some light on the factors involved, further investigation is needed into the details of the structural change that the Malaysian economy has undergone in the last 15 to 20 years.

## Structural Change and the Economy

It is evident from Document B, that the initiators of the NEP expected that there would be a considerable increase in rural employment (contrary to the assumptions of the model). It seems that this has not occurred, at least not on the scale envisaged, although the absence of comparable figures makes this difficult to establish with exactitude. Certainly, it does not appear from Table 4.2 that employment in agriculture has shown any great change since 1975; and the increase that has become evident recently is small and may be only temporary. Employment has expanded mainly through an expansion of the non-agricultural sector of the economy, so avoiding the necessity for many to seek employment in comparatively unrewarding rural occupations. In fact, the increase in non-agricultural sector employment has been of the order of 1.5 millions since 1975 and presumably much more since 1967.

It is evident from the table that over the ten years 1975 to 1985 there was a considerable increase in output per head in agriculture amounting to about 4 per cent per annum. In contrast, the increase in output per head in the rest of the economy was less than 1.5 per cent per annum. This has probably helped to improve the share of the Bumiputra in national income since the larger proportional increase in productivity in agriculture has occurred in a sector in which they are most active, although for the reasons indicated above, it is uncertain to what extent this improvement has been split between capital and labour and how much of it has been dissipated by a fall in prices of Malaysia's agricultural exports. The apparent fact that there was no increase in productivity in the residual sector of the economy, consisting mainly of services, must also have facilitated labour absorption there. Moreover, it is an outcome which reflects the function of this composite category as a first entry point of many rural migrants to the urban areas. Similarly the supply of labour to the industrial sector is highly elastic in conditions of a mobile labour force in the rural areas.

## Population and Employment

Another factor influencing employment opportunities is the number of people flowing on to the labour market. Over the period considered, the population has increased by about 2.5 per cent per annum and this will determine the increase in the labour force in future years. Table 4.3 summarises recent population movements on an ethnic basis.

What stands out in Table 4.3 is that the natural rate of increase of the Bumiputra population is substantially in excess of that of other racial groups. It is evident that the increase in the Bumiputra population is likely to make it more difficult to absorb the full increase in the Bumiputra labour force into the modern sector and that, in so far as this process is relied on to achieve greater equality in income, attainment of an acceptable degree of equality will take longer.

Between 1985 and 1988, the Bumiputra population was increasing by about 310,000 per annum and that of other ethnic groups by about 105,000. The figures for the period 1970 to 1988 are incomplete but we may estimate that the annual rates of increase over the whole of the period were of the order of 230,000 for the

TABLE 4.2

VALUE ADDED, EMPLOYMENT AND VALUE ADDED PER HEAD

Value added in million Ringgit in 1978 prices, employment in
thousands and value added per head in Ringgit in 1978 prices

| | 1975 | | | 1985 | | | 1975-85 |
| | Value added | Employ-ment | Value added per head | Value added | Employ-ment | Value added per head | Growth in value added per head |
|---|---|---|---|---|---|---|---|
| All sectors | 26446 | 4020 | 6579 | 47182 | 5468 | 8628 | 1.31 |
| Agriculture | 8146 | 1915 | 4254 | 11914 | 1953 | 6100 | 1.43 |
| Industry incl. mining | 9467 | 695 | 13622 | 20934 | 1267 | 16522 | 1.21 |
| Other | 8833 | 1410 | 6264 | 14334 | 2248 | 6376 | 1.02 |

Sources: Employment: *Mid-Term Review of the Third Malaysia Plan*, table 4.5 for 1975; *Fifth Malaysia Plan 1986-90*, table 3.5 for 1985. GDP: Department of Statistics, Malaysia.

Bumiputra and about 90.000 for the other ethnic groups.

The labour force increased by about 1.5 million persons between 1980 and 1988;[9] the increase being somewhat larger for the Bumiputra than for all other ethnic groups. This has to be seen against the rate of job creation. Between 1980 and 1988, roughly 1.25 million jobs were created, including, perhaps, 100,000 in agricultural employment, about 260,000 in manufacturing, 85,000 in construction, 350,000 in distribution and catering and 200,000 in government services. Since the number of jobs created fell short of the increase in the labour force by about a quarter of a million, unemployment nearly doubled. Part of this failure must undoubtedly be attributed to the reduced rate of growth of the economy evident in 1986 when the number of jobs created fell to about 80,000, compared with a more normal total of double, or more, this figure.

The effects of the marked slow down in job creation after 1985 fell unevenly on Bumiputra and others in the labour force.[10] Of the increase in jobs outside agriculture of little over 300,000 in the three year period to 1988, twice as many went to Chinese Malaysians as to Bumiputra, even though the numbers of Bumiputra already in place was nearly twice that of the Chinese. Clearly, when opportunities for entry to the modern sector get tight, there is discrimination against the Malays. It is not clear, however, how much of this was due to discrimination in the working of the market and how much should be explained by the relaxation that was introduced in the mid-1980s in the administrative pursuance of NEP objectives of restructuring employment.[11] Whatever the causation of the poor showing of the Bumiputra in getting jobs in the non-agricultural sector after 1985, the results are disturbing. Thus, for example, in the manufacturing sector alone, where the number of Bumiputra in 1985 exceeded that of the Chinese, the reverse applied by 1988: of the increase of 157,000 in jobs in manufacturing between 1985 and 1988, 29,000 went to the Bumiputra and 130,000 to the Chinese; the representation of the Indians and of other groups

[9]   See table 9.1, p. 195 in the 1988 *Yearbook of Statistics* for details.
[10]   Data used are derived from table 3.9, pp. 64-65 in the *Mid-Term Review of the Fifth Malaysia Plan* 1986-90.
[11]   It may be indicative of the importance of the administrative relaxation that in the projections in the MTR of the Fifth Plan for the final two years to 1990, when growth rates are again very high, the additional recruitment of Chinese labour to jobs outside agriculture is projected to be a higher share than it was shown to be in the earlier years of the decade.

TABLE 4.3
POPULATION MOVEMENTS BY ETHNIC GROUP

| | Population (in thousands) | | | | Growth (% per year) | | |
|---|---|---|---|---|---|---|---|
| | 1970 | 1980 | 1985 | 1988 | 1985/70 | 1985/80 | 1988/85 |
| Peninsular Malaysia | 9182 | 11442 | 12981 | 13959 | 2.34 | 2.56 | 2.45 |
| Bumiputra | 4841 | 6325 | 7349 | 8050 | 2.80 | 3.05 | 3.08 |
| Chinese | 3285 | 3869 | 4243 | 4435 | 1.72 | 1.86 | 1.47 |
| Indian | 981 | 1172 | 1306 | 1386 | 1.93 | 2.22 | 2.00 |
| Other | 73 | 75 | 83 | 88 | 0.86 | 2.05 | 1.97 |
| *Total Malaysia* | n.a. | 13764 | 15682 | 16921 | n.a. | 2.64 | 2.57 |
| Bumiputra | n.a. | 8098 | 9432 | 10354 | n.a. | 3.10 | 3.16 |
| Chinese | n.a. | 4419 | 4860 | 5092 | n.a. | 1.92 | 1.57 |
| Indian | n.a. | 1172 | 1306 | 1387 | n.a. | 2.19 | 2.03 |
| Other | n.a. | 74 | 83 | 88 | n.a. | 2.32 | 1.97 |

Source: *Social Statistics Bulletin 1987*, table 1.1, for 1970; *Yearbook of Statistics 1988*, table 3.6, for 1980-88.

declined. This can be most plausibly explained as the result of racial discrimination.

## Price changes

We have so far considered changes in productivity and employment as determinants of earnings in the different sectors of the Malaysian economy. We need also to consider price changes. The number of Bumiputra in the agricultural sector of the economy is large relative to other ethnic groups. Any change in the terms of trade between agriculture and non-agriculture which favoured the non-agricultural sector of the economy would be likely to act to the disadvantage of the Bumiputra and vice versa. We need, therefore, to check whether changes in the agricultural terms of trade provide some part of the explanation of why they have not been able to increase their incomes more rapidly, relative to other ethnic groups, than has been the case. Unfortunately, there is no reliable way of doing this. One possibility is to take published indices of producers prices for locally produced goods for agricultural and industrial products and to compare them. The result of doing so is to suggest a considerable improvement in agricultural terms of trade since 1972. However, apart from the crudity of the statistical calculations, to which there seems to be little alternative at the present time, it is possible that indices of producer prices reflect the position of small and subsistence producers inadequately, and, if so, the incomes of Bumiputra engaged in agriculture may not have benefited from relative price movements. But certainly, there is nothing in these rather crude calculations to explain why Bumiputra incomes have not increased more rapidly relative to the incomes of other ethnic groups than appears from other statistical data. Perhaps what should be made of this inconclusiveness is first, that price movements have the capacity to disturb ethnic balances and second, that it would be useful to have series of figures to monitor the effects of such changes.

## Growth in output

An assumption made in Document B was that total output would increase at the rate of 6.4 per cent per annum.[12] In fact, the rate of increase in output over the period 1970 to 1988 (the latest date for which an estimate is available) is 6 per cent or slightly above, so

[12] This assumed that the improvement in racial balance projected for 1985 would be effected.

TABLE 4.4
GROWTH OF GDP PER CAPITA 1950 TO 1984
FOR SELECTED COUNTRIES
(% per annum)

*Latin America:*

| | | |
|---|---|---|
| Argentina | 0.9 | (1950-84) |
| Brazil | 1.8 | (1950-84) |
| Chile | 0.4 | (1950-84) |
| Columbia | 1.2 | (1950-84) |
| Mexico | 1.3 | (1950-84) |
| Peru | 0.3 | (1950-84) |

*Africa*

| | | |
|---|---|---|
| Ivory Coast | 1.5 | (1960-84) |
| Egypt | 1.3 | (1950-84) |
| Ghana | -2.0 | (1957-84) |
| Kenya | 1.3 | (1963.84) |
| Tanzania | 1.3 | (1961-84) |

*Asia*

| | | |
|---|---|---|
| China | 2.2 | (1950-84) |
| India | 0.6 | (1950-84) |
| Pakistan | 1.4 | (1950-84) |
| Bangladesh | 2.1 | (1971-84) |
| Philippines | 1.3 | (1950-84) |
| Sri Lanka | 1.5 | (1950-84) |
| *Malaysia* | 2.8 | (1957-84) |

Source: OECD Development Centre data files, quoted in K. Griffin, *Alternative Strategies for Economic Development*, London: Macmillan, 1989, table 1.2, p. 5.

that the development of the economy has been very little different
from the expectations arrived at almost 20 years ago. Agricultural
output, as we have seen, has increased remarkably rapidly, by 4.4
per cent per annum over the same period, more than doubling, while
industrial output (including mining and other activities as well as
manufacturing) showed, as might be expected, a considerably greater
increase of about 7.8 per cent per annum.[13] In the rest of the
economy output increased by 4.8 per cent.

TABLE 4.5
ASEAN COUNTRIES' GROWTH PERFORMANCE
1965-80 AND 1980-87
(Average Annual Growth Rates of real GDP in percentages)

|                          | 1965-80 | 1980-87 |
|--------------------------|---------|---------|
| Indonesia                | 8.0     | 3.6     |
| Philippines              | 5.9     | -0.5    |
| Thailand                 | 7.2     | 5.6     |
| Singapore                | 10.1    | 5.4     |
| *Malaysia*               | 7.4     | 4.5     |
|                          |         |         |
| For comparison:          |         |         |
| All Middle-Income        |         |         |
| countries combined       | 6.2     | 2.8     |

Source: *World Development Report 1989*, Oxford University Press, 1989, pp.
166-167.

The growth of the Malaysian economy since 1950 comes out well
by comparison with developing countries of Latin America, Africa
and Asia at a similar stage of development, as is evident from Table
4.4. In comparison with other ASEAN countries, which probably
form a frame of reference more often consulted in the Malaysian
context, Malaysia's growth experience has been creditable, both
before 1980 and in the 1980s (see Table 4.5). While its performance
in terms of growth of GDP ranks below that of Singapore, it has
roughly equalled that of Thailand and Indonesia and exceeded that

---

[13] The increase in *manufacturing* output is, of course, much greater, about 10 per
cent per annum, starting from a low level.

of the Philippines. Performance in ASEAN countries, other than in the Philippines in the 1980s, has been consistently and markedly better than in the world's middle income countries generally, and even more so compared to the world's low-income countries (other than China).

The mid-1980s saw a set-back in economic development in most countries, including Malaysia and other ASEAN economies. The set-back in GDP, and in manufacturing, came in full force in 1985 in Malaysia and Singapore (as well as in Brunei which so heavily depends on the world petroleum market) and a year earlier in the Philippines. The significance of the setback for Malaysia is shown in Table 4.6.

TABLE 4.6
PERCENTAGE GROWTH RATE OF REAL GDP

| 1984-85 | 1985-86 | 1986-87 | 1987-88 |
| --- | --- | --- | --- |
| -1.0 | 1.2 | 5.2 | 8.7 |

Source: *Mid-Term Review of the Fifth Malaysia Plan 1986-1990*. Note that the figures relate to GDP at market prices; different rates of increase would be shown if comparisons were done on the basis of figures for GDP at factor cost (also at 1978 prices).

Output fell between 1984 and 1985. Recovery began in 1986 and growth accelerated to nearly 10 per cent in 1988. In 1989 it was nearly 8 per cent. In 1990, further growth is expected to take place although at a smaller rate than in 1989, reflecting lower growth rates in industrialised economies. It is evident, however, that the economy is showing great resilience. Manufacturing output was spearheading growth with increases in output estimated at 13 per cent in 1989 and 10.5 per cent in 1990. Construction was also expected to experience strong growth. In contrast the primary sector of the economy was expected to grow at 2-3 per cent per annum.[14]

The recession in 1985 caused unemployment to rise. This had an uneven impact ethnically. Unemployment already at 7.6 per cent

[14] For details, see the presentation of the budget proposals for 1990 by the Minister of Finance, YB Datuk Paduka Daim Zainuddin.

amongst Bumiputra increased to 9.2 per cent by 1988 and somewhat similarly for the Indian ethnic group where it rose from 7.0 to 8.9 per cent. For the Chinese the effect was less marked, with unemployment rising from an already comparatively low level of 5.6 to 6.0 per cent. It is evident that the Bumiputra and the Indians are much more vulnerable to recession than the Chinese.[15]

Subsequent increase in output has yet to make a significant contribution to a reduction in unemployment, as it did in Singapore and perhaps even in Thailand and the Philippines. Malaysia weathered the set-back of the mid-1980s without much change in domestic price levels, as did also Singapore and Brunei; however, price instability was more pronounced in Thailand, Indonesia and indeed in the Philippines.

Very significantly, in the mid-1980s, without exception, all developing countries which were supposed to have been able to escape world trends, including Korea, Hong Kong, Singapore, Thailand, Indonesia and the Philippines, fell victim to recession, with the Philippines experiencing negative growth. This is of considerable significance because countries like Hong Kong and the Philippines were very strongly growth oriented in their development strategies, countries with little or no concern for the kinds of objectives adopted in the NEP. They were, to say the least, monetarist and laissez-faire in their pursuit of economic growth. Yet they could not resist the downward trend. The slower rates of growth recorded by Malaysia can not reasonably be attributed to the NEP. Its economy slowed up like the rest, affected by deteriorating terms of trade as the prices of internationally tradable goods and services fell severely in response to recession in the OECD countries. The record of the 1980s in Malaysia by comparison with other developing countries, within the ASEAN or beyond, does not support the contention that the explanation lies in faulty allocation and inefficient use of resources and macro-dislocations due to the NEP in general, or to its restructuring objective in particular.

## Industrialisation

Overall economic growth alone is not a sufficient indicator of how well any country has done. Indeed, taken by itself it can be a misleading indicator of the performance and well-being of the

---

[15] For details see the *Mid-Term-Review of the Fifth Malaysia Plan 1986-1990*, table 3.9, pp. 64-65.

country and its people. It is of critical importance to examine both the elements of the process of growth itself and the uses made of the product. Is growth due to a cyclical boom of a particular single commodity, such as oil, or has it been achieved by increased investments and improved productivity in major sectors and subsectors of the economy as a whole? The level and structure of the Malaysian economy has been transformed from one that was predominantly agricultural to one that is industrialising. Indeed the industrial sector is now the largest sector of the Malaysian economy, with a substantial proportion of its manufacturing output, such as electronics, rubber products, textiles, air conditioners and other things, being exported to the world market.

This export-led industrialisation strategy, which was formulated early in the NEP phase, was greatly intensified and rationalised during the Mahathir Administration in the 1980s and is paying its dividends. Admittedly, the industrial base is still narrow, there are serious distortions in the market, and some subsectors of the manufacturing sector are still inefficient, high cost and often vulnerable to international competition and loss of protection. But with the series of reform and rationalisation measures instituted by the government, such as the introduction of the Industrial Master Plan, Look East Policy, Malaysia Incorporated Policy, Privatisation Policy, National Agricultural Policy etc. Malaysia is greatly ahead of most other developing countries in laying the basis for a modern, advanced economy. A network of institutions for a wider and efficient industrial base and for sustained long term industrial growth has been put in place and is functioning. With the national emphasis on increasing productivity, efficiency and hard work, Malaysia will continue to increase output substantially in the future.

## Structural Change in a Social Context

Social measures to improve the position of the Bumiputra population are an integral part of the NEP. In this section we look at a variety of aspects of social change including regional imbalances, the incidence of poverty and the provision of health and educational services which can improve the quality of life and provide opportunities for the future.

## Regional Imbalances

Differences between incomes of Bumiputra and other ethnic groups are at their greatest in rural areas; they are less in small towns and least of all in major centres of population[16].

In fact, regional differences are often quite marked as is evident from Table 4.7. In the Northern Region in 1988, Penang had an average income per capita 74 per cent greater than that of Kedah; in the Central Region, Wilayah Persekutuan (the Federal Territory) had an average income per capita 116 per cent greater than in Melaka; and in the Eastern Region Terengganu had an income nearly four times that of Kelantan; both have high poverty rates but Terengganu has oil. In other regions, the differences are less marked and the incomes of their States close to the average. Regional differences are a common feature of the economic world, developing or developed, and comparative figures may be very deceptive, as we have seen, but those revealed above are very considerable. It is to be expected that the incidence of poverty will be much greater in the poorer than in the richer states and this is broadly the case, but again caution has to be observed in generalising.

Households living below the poverty line, as measured for 1987, accounted for about one-third of the total number in Kedah, Kelantan, Perlis and Terengganu, the worst hit states. However, with the exception of Terengganu, the incidence was appreciably less than recorded in 1984. The reasons for extreme poverty are not totally apparent, although, when mining and quarrying activity (which includes petroleum production) is removed from consideration, a greater than average dependence on agriculture and a smaller than average representation of manufacturing appear to be important contributing factors.

It is evident that statistics of regional imbalances in GDP per capita and of the changes recorded over time, as given in table 4.7 require careful interpretation. Certain of the states have maintained a relatively well-off position in the table over the 25 years covered by it. A number of states which were relatively badly-off in 1963, have shown no improvement: Kelantan, Melaka, Kedah, Perlis and Johor. Some that were relatively well-off in 1963 have become less so by 1988: Negri Sembilan, Pahang, Perak and Selangor; for the latter two this reflects at least in part the very large drop in the price of tin. Some have moved against expectations and in a

---

[16] See Anand Sudhir, *Inequality and Poverty in Malaysia, Measurement and Decomposition*, Oxford University Press 1983, p. 98, and table 6.11, p. 230.

TABLE 4.7
PER CAPITA GDP OF STATES AS A
PROPORTION OF PENINSULAR MALAYSIA
MEAN GDP AT SELECTED DATES
(Ratios)

| States | 1963 | 1970 | 1988 |
|---|---|---|---|
| Johor | 0.97 | 0.98 | 0.88 |
| Kedah | 0.81 | 0.81 | 0.63 |
| Kelantan | 0.58 | 0.52 | 0.40 |
| Melaka | 0.82 | 0.69 | 0.80 |
| Negri Sembilan | 1.30 | 1.16 | 0.90 |
| Pahang | 1.10 | 1.04 | 0.76 |
| Penang | 0.67 | 0.78 | 1.09 |
| Perak | 1.03 | 1.07 | 0.77 |
| Perlis | 0.70 | 0.80 | 0.65 |
| Selangor | 1.53 | 1.49 | 1.47 |
| Terengganu | 0.69 | 0.60 | 1.54 |
| Federal Territory | - | - | 1.74 |
| Sabah | - | 1.25 | 1.06 |
| Sarawak | - | 0.99 | 0.92 |

Sources: *Mid-Term Review of the Second Malaysia Plan, 1971-75*, table 1-5, p. 18 and *Mid-Term Review of the Fifth Malaysia Plan, 1986-1990*, table 3.5, p. 48-51. (No adjustment appears to be needed for changes in geographical coverage. Note, however, that the figures for 1988 are compiled on the basis of 1978 prices.)

TABLE 4.8
## THE INCIDENCE OF POVERTY, 1987
(Percentages of households in poverty)

### Peninsular Malaysia

| *State* | | *Ethnic Group* | |
|---|---|---|---|
| Johor | 11.1 | Bumiputra | 23.8 |
| Kedah | 31.3 | Chinese | 7.1 |
| Kelantan | 31.6 | Indian | 9.7 |
| Melaka | 11.7 | Other | 24.3 |
| Negeri Sembilan | 21.5 | | |
| Pahang | 12.3 | | |
| Perak | 19.9 | *Stratum* | |
| Perlis | 29.1 | | |
| Pulau Pinang | 12.9 | Urban | 8.1 |
| Selangor | 8.9 | Rural | 22.4 |
| Terengganu | 36.1 | | |
| Federal Territory | 5.2 | | |
| Peninsular Malaysia | 17.3 | | |

### Sabah and Sarawak

| | |
|---|---|
| Sabah | 35.3 |
| Sarawak | 24.7 |

## OCCUPATIONAL POVERTY, 1987

| | Peninsular Malaysia | Sabah | Sarawak |
|---|---|---|---|
| Rubber smallholders | 40.0 | 68.3 | 62.5 |
| Padi farmers | 50.2 | 79.4 | 56.2 |
| Coconut smallholders | 39.2 | 73.3 | 44.4 |
| Fishermen | 24.4 | 44.2 | 27.5 |
| Estate workers | 15.0 | 53.4 | 7.7 |

deceptive manner: the improvement in the position of Terengganu has little to do with removal of poverty, only with the discovery of oil and gas, as is the case for Sarawak and Sabah. Such increments to production inflate recorded incomes but do little immediately to relieve poverty.

## The Incidence of Poverty

Another aspect of the incidence of poverty is shown in Table 4.8. This gives statistics of the proportion of families in poverty in States and according to ethnic divisions and selected occupation. Perhaps the main conclusion to be drawn from the table is that the NEP has done little to redress the poverty balance within States. Those States where poverty is most evident today, Kelantan, Terengganu, Perlis, and Kedah, Sabah and Sarawak were at the bottom of the poverty list when the NEP was introduced.

The extent of poverty has always been most acute in the primary sectors of the economy and, in consequence, in rural areas. The incidence of poverty in the agricultural sector of Peninsular Malaysia was estimated at 68 per cent in 1970. It has fallen since then but it was still 38 per cent in 1984 and, perhaps, about 34 per cent in 1987.[17] The groups most affected by poverty are also shown in the table. In spite of the very considerable increase in agricultural output and improvements in productivity of as much as 4 per cent per annum in the agricultural sector as a whole, a very high percentage of households operating as rubber smallholders, padi farmers and coconut smallholders are in poverty; fishermen and estate workers are less affected but the incidence of poverty there is still much greater than in urban areas. Absolutely, about 160,000 households in Peninsular Malaysia in the occupations mentioned above were in poverty in 1987 and a further 90,000 impoverished households were to be found in Sabah and Sarawak. In 1987, 650,000 families, in total, were in a condition of absolute poverty. The incidence of poverty is considerably affected by the prices that prevail for the major agricultural exports of Malaysia and unusually high prices can have the temporary effect of reducing poverty appreciably, with the concomitant effect that low prices increase it.

In Sabah and Sarawak, the incidence of rural poverty is much

[17] Figures shown for the incidence of poverty in the *Mid-Term Review of the Fifth Malaysia Plan*, table 3-6, pp. 52-53, are not so complete as those published for earlier years, in consequence any attempt to estimate the extent of the further fall is likely to be subject to error.

greater than in Peninsular Malaysia, with the exception of estate workers in Sarawak, if figures for 1987 are typical.

Poverty alleviation and its eventual eradication for all Malaysians, which is one of the main thrusts of the NEP, has met with considerable success, in spite of the reservations entered above. This conclusion is valid even after making allowances for the imperfections of the concepts and statistical measurements of poverty in Malaysia. Such deficiencies are recognised in planning documents and they in no way nullify the factual analyses as alleged by some critics. The prospect of achieving the target of redressing poverty is perhaps best summarised by the following lines from the Fifth Plan (p. 96):

> The OPP which was formulated in the early 1970s, has targeted that the incidence of poverty in Peninsular Malaysia is to be reduced to 16.7 per cent by the year 1990. By 1984, the available evidence has indicated that the incidence of poverty was about 18 per cent. Although it would be difficult to make precise estimates of the level of poverty by 1990, it would appear that the OPP target of about 17 per cent by 1990 is within reach.

The latest figures released by the Mid-Term Review of the Fifth Plan confirm the reduction of poverty over the last two decades. Unless there is an unexpected reversal of fortune, there is no doubt that it will count as one of the really remarkable success stories achieved by any developing country. However, it is true that the predominant poverty groups remain in the Malay dominated states, mainly because it is a largely rural phenomenon. This is not to minimise the poverty problems also of some non-Malay groups or residual poverty to be found in the urban areas, or that existing in the New Villages and in the estates, which predominantly affect the non-Malay population. But the problem of mass poverty is, and has been, mainly a Malay problem. [18]

[18] See for instance the summary statement in Sudir Anand's 1983 study for the World Bank, *op.cit.*, pp. 126-132, which includes the following:
The problem is overwhelmingly a Malay one, with 78.1 per cent of poor households being Malay. There are six Malay households in poverty for every one Chinese. ... More than half (51.4 per cent) of Malay households suffer from poverty, while the incidence among the Chinese is 14.7 per cent, and among Indians 24.8 per cent. Poverty is also overwhelmingly a rural phenomenon, with 87.7 per cent of poor households living in the rural areas. The four northern states of Kedah, Kelantan, Perlis, and Trengganu stand out as having above average incidences of poverty.

## Social Service Provision

The measures of poverty, as habitually designed, give uncertain weight to the provision of state services. While such provision may not be regarded by a household unable to feed, house and clothe itself as adequate recompense for the deprivation imposed by poverty, it provides benefits of value, including education as a form of investment in human capital.

Programmes for the alleviation of poverty generally require the use of government resources, and the ability to raise revenue is a first consideration. The proportion of revenue raised in taxes by Malaysia is at least average for countries in its income bracket and probably somewhat higher. The mid-1980s showed stagnant or declining revenues, reflecting the performance of the economy; this, in turn, acted as a restraining influence on expenditure, as total budget deficits had to be contained.

## Education

Education has received strong support, in keeping with Malaysia's real income per capita. Sufficient provision has been made available for pre-school centres to be established on a substantial scale  and it is gratifying, in the context of poverty, that government supported centres were established, in the period under review,  mainly in rural areas. Primary education enrolment is almost complete; the number of pupils per teacher, less than 22, is unusually low even though all the teachers may not be fully trained.  Enrolment in secondary schools has been increasing rapidly and amounted to 1.3 million pupils in 1988 — more than half the number in primary schools. The pupil-teacher ratio was little more than 20 to 1. The Bumiputra appear to be as well represented in secondary education as other ethnic groups and the same appears to apply to total enrolment in various forms of post-secondary education, including education to degree level undertaken within the country, although not to courses followed abroad where Chinese students, to some extent because of restricted entry to Malaysian institutions but also for other reasons, predominate. Teacher education appears to be well provided for.

In a strong effort to ensure participation of all ethnic groups in primary and secondary education, not only have classrooms been provided in rural and remote areas but hostels and teachers quarters as well. Other measures, such as scholarships, textbooks on loan and supplementary feeding have been made available to provide for poor students.

Of particular interest is the large numbers of skilled and semi-skilled workers that are now being trained.[19]

## Health

In matters of health, considerable progress has been made. In 1988, the Applied Food and Nutrition Programme was extended to about 47,000 households[20]. However, the expansion of health care has been slowed down because of budgetary constraints. It is believed to compare well in effectiveness, however, with other countries at similar levels of development, although, as always, there are considerable variations. The number of doctors in relation to population of 3.5 per 10,000 of population, or 2857 people per doctor, in 1987, compares unfavourably with other countries within the income bracket. The infant mortality rate compares well with similar countries, although there remains considerable scope for improvement. It is, however, very noticeable that for 1988, the rate for ethnic Chinese, 8.2 per thousand live births, is very much less than for those of Indian origin, 15.5, and Malay and other indigenous groups, 14.6. Not surprisingly, expectation of life at birth differs in the same way with, for example, Chinese women having an expectation of life of 74.0 years, calculated for 1980, against 69.4 for Malays and 67.0 for Indians. Rates for males were, as usual, lower for all ethnic groups. In all cases, however, life expectancy has been improving.

It should not be assumed that the differences in life expectation are due mainly to differences in access to health care, for many factors affect longevity; nor should it be assumed that poverty has restricted access of Malays and Indians to health care to any great extent. Jacob Meerman stated in 1980, on the basis of data for 1977, that "The basic conclusion to be drawn is that morbidity, not income, determines the demand for medical services. The need for medical care is met through the public system at little private cost"[21]. He went on, however, to qualify his remarks in relation to death rates for infants and recent mothers, which he suggested implied that there might be differences in the quality of health care received as

---

[19] See the *Mid-Term Review of the Fifth Malaysia Plan, 1986-1990*, table 4-7, p. 102.
[20] *Mid-Term Review of the Fifth Malaysia Plan 1986-1990*, p. 279.
[21] In *Malaysia, Growth and Equity in a Multiracial Society*, Baltimore: Johns Hopkins University Press, 1980, p. 143.

well as other factors. We might link these factors to regional differences in incomes with their ethnic contexts[22], for, it is understood, health clinics are in operation almost everywhere.

## Family planning

Growth of population is an important factor affecting the attainment of greater equality in the distribution of income in many respects. Rates of expansion of population vary considerably between ethnic groups, as is shown above; the Bumiputra population has been increasing at over 3 per cent per annum in recent years; the rate of increase of the Chinese population is much less, round about 1.5 per cent, and that of other groups is about 2 per cent per annum. It is, of course, true that the increase in the labour force for the next 15-20 years is already determined by the number of those growing up to adulthood, so that current efforts to restrain population growth can not affect the number of jobs immediately required, and it may be that in 20 or so years, sufficient modern sector jobs will be available to absorb present rates of expansion of the labour force. Nevertheless, irrespective of the direct effects on the absorption of the labour force, a reduction in the rate of population increase itself serves to accelerate development. With lower birth rates, less needs to be spent on building schools, on providing infrastructure and on investment in order to widen rather than deepen the capital structure. Thus, a continuing rise in population is indirectly, as well as directly, an impediment to modernisation and the improvement of productivity.

Present levels of mortality are low, so that a reduction in them is unlikely to be of much consequence in determining the balance between the availability of jobs and would-be entrants to the modern sector of the economy. A low level of mortality may be a factor tending to reduce planned family size, but it seems that amongst Malays, family size expectations have been revised markedly upwards[23]. Better health is itself a factor making for higher fertility, although the greater educational opportunities for women in

---

[22] For data on these relationships, see the *Fifth Malaysia Plan, 1986-1990*, table 20-2 p. 510.

[23] See the *Mid-Term Review of the Fifth Malaysia Plan, 1986-1990*, p. 82-83, Recent evidence (*Malaysian Population and Family Survey, 1984/85*) showed that over the past ten years there had been a marked upward revision in family size among the Malays and a concomitant decline in the proportion of couples practising family planning.

particular, will work in the opposite direction, as may the example created by the reduction in the family size of Chinese families where the total fertility rate is now approaching a level that will lead to stability in the Chinese population[24].

## An assessment of the NEP

We are now in a position to make an assessment of the performance of the NEP, as it has been interpreted over the years. In most major respects it has been a success and it has attained its objectives broadly to the extent expected of it in 1969. There is still a long way to go before its ultimate objectives will be fully realised, but this is not a reflection on the policies that have been followed so much as a recognition of the immensity of the task of bringing the Bumiputra population into parity with the Chinese. Another 20 years, possibly even longer, may be needed before racial balance can be adequately attained.

### Employment Creation and Restructuring

A key element in attaining greater ethnic economic equality is continued restructuring of employment. The facts that we have brought to bear show that it is not too difficult to build up the modern sector of the economy and reduce poverty there. The poverty that remains lies mainly in the countryside. This is in spite of a remarkable effort to adapt the pattern of agriculture to changing market conditions and technologies. The increase in agricultural output that has been achieved is exceptional but it has not extended sufficiently to the activities of many Bumiputra engaged in padi cultivation and other small-scale activities. This is in spite of the fact that the instigators of the NEP laid considerable emphasis on policies for agriculture, directed particularly to the poor. A principal aspect of this was the commissioning of more agricultural land.

Land development has proceeded at the rate of 1 million or more acres (400,000 hectares) per plan period under either Federal programmes (FELDA, FELCRA and RISDA) or State programmes, with some development proceeding as joint ventures with the private sector. Thus, in all, over 1.5 million hectares of additional land will have been brought into cultivation by the end of the currency of the

[24] *Mid-Term Review of the Fifth Malaysian Plan*, p. 82.

Outline Perspective Plan. This is a remarkable achievement, sufficient to extend the cultivable area by up to one-half. The extent of resettlement of families resulting from the schemes, however, has evidently been much less than the numbers that might be inferred from proposals for the allocation of 10 to 12 acres per smallholder. In the *Mid-Term Review of the Fifth Malaysia Plan*, it seems that the 105,000 hectares expected to be developed by FELDA in the period 1986-88, would result in the settlement of only some 18,500 families.[25] On this kind of ratio, a land development of hectares 1.5 million would be sufficient to cater for one-quarter of a million settlers. This is not a small figure compared with say 2 million seeking a living in agricultural employment, but it is not a panacea in the long run when larger holdings need to be operated by fewer people. The net monthly earnings of settlers for 1986-88 was estimated at $493 for oil palm, $545 for rubber schemes and $440 for sugar cane-growers. In 1988, earning were much higher at $871, $721 and $631, reflecting higher international prices[26], but even these levels will not be enough to meet aspirations in the long run. In 1987, mean monthly family income for the population as a whole was about $1,100 on the average.[27] Nevertheless, the significance of the land settlement schemes is to be found in the increase in the incomes of small holders that it has been possible to induce by a collective package of land development and delivery of expertise. Unfortunately, this seems not to have been extendable to the many Bumiputra engaged in padi cultivation and other small-scale activities. However, what has been accomplished provides a strengthened basis for further advance in future years.

The original plans for the NEP envisaged that there would be insufficient scope to absorb all of the natural increase in the labour force into the modern sector of the economy and that there would be, inevitably, an increase in the number of persons employed in agriculture. It is difficult to compare the original estimates of the growth of employment in agriculture with the outcome, as it now can be seen, because there have been considerable changes in the basis of the compilation of figures of employment. Nevertheless, it appears that the growth of employment in agriculture has been less

[25] P. 139.
[26] *Idem.*
[27] *Op. cit.,* p. 45.

than was expected and this is itself an indication of success.[28] It may be seen from Table 4.9 that about one-third of the working population is now employed in agriculture; although the figures are not comparable, the corresponding figure for 1970 was probably about one-half.[29]

This is a very significant change. It seems probable, although because of a lack of comparable figures we can not be sure, that the numbers of Chinese engaged in agriculture has declined, from, say, about one-fifth of the total at the end of the 1960s to about one-seventh. Thus, it may be surmised that they have succeeded in reducing their commitment to agriculture more rapidly than have the Bumiputra, who may even be employed in somewhat larger numbers than in 1970 and constitute 75 per cent of the agricultural labour force. The ethnic composition of the labour force, as it was estimated at the time that the Fifth Plan was drawn up, is also shown in table 4.9. A word of warning is necessary: figures for the ethnic composition of the work force and its dispositions do not seem to be available for 1988 on the same basis as in 1980, and the figures of total employment, that are available in the current employment series for 1985 and 1988, together with a projection for 1990, can not readily be matched to previous series. Any conclusions that are drawn have, therefore, to be regarded with an element of doubt as to how far they are valid in the light of statistical revisions.

The reduction in the proportion of the Malay labour force engaged in agriculture appears to have gone somewhat more slowly than was envisaged in 1969. At that time, it appeared, on the basis of the estimates of employment then available, that about two out of three were engaged in agriculture and it was hoped that it would be possible to bring this down to about 38 per cent of the employed labour force in 1990, as was intended in the Outline Perspective Plan.[30] By 1985 the proportion was reduced to just over 40 per cent and appears thus to have been following the desired trend, but since then, transfer of labour from the agricultural sector seems to have slowed, and may even have been reversed, perhaps mainly as a consequence of recession and reduced rates of employment in the

---

[28] A further factor is the influx of immigrants from Indonesia who find employment in the plantations (as well as in other sectors of the economy) and who may have entered Malaysia in considerable numbers.

[29] See *Mid-Term Review of the Second Malaysia Plan 1971-75*, table 4.4, p. 77.

[30] *Mid-Term Review of Second Malaysia Plan 1971-1975*, tables 4.4 and 4.5, pp. 77 and 79.

TABLE 4.9
EMPLOYMENT BY SECTOR AND ETHNIC GROUP,
1980, 1985, 1988 AND 1990 (est.) (000)

| Sector | Malays 1980 | 1985 | Chinese 1980 | 1985 | Indians 1980 | 1985 | Other 1980 | 1985 | Total 1980 | 1985 | Total 1980 | 1988 | 1990 |
|---|---|---|---|---|---|---|---|---|---|---|---|---|---|
| Agriculture | 1397 | 1429 | 313 | 318 | 185 | 188 | 15 | 18 | 1911 | 1953 | 1760 | 1908 | 1970 |
| Mining | 27 | 21 | 44 | 32 | 8 | 6 | 1 | 1 | 80 | 60 | 44 | 37 | 39 |
| Manufacturing | 309 | 353 | 381 | 394 | 61 | 75 | 5 | 5 | 755 | 828 | 855 | 1013 | 1157 |
| Construction | 106 | 148 | 144 | 206 | 17 | 21 | 3 | 4 | 270 | 379 | 429 | 356 | 407 |
| Electricity, gas and water | 21 | 27 | 3 | 3 | 7 | 9 | - | 1 | 31 | 40 | 44 | 45 | 47 |
| Transport | 110 | 147 | 73 | 88 | 25 | 28 | 1 | 1 | 209 | 265 | 244 | 261 | 273 |
| Commerce | 250 | 323 | 374 | 460 | 50 | 68 | 3 | 2 | 676 | 846 | 917 | 1070 | 1179 |
| Finance services | 29 | 39 | 43 | 55 | 6 | 7 | - | - | 78 | 102 | 199 | 212 | 221 |
| Government | 389 | 506 | 196 | 222 | 64 | 82 | 9 | 10 | 658 | 820 | 820 | 844 | 861 |
| Other services | 88 | 109 | 42 | 46 | 15 | 19 | 2 | 2 | 147 | 176 | 312 | 341 | 357 |
| Total employed | 2725 | 3102 | 1614 | 1827 | 439 | 496 | 39 | 44 | 4817 | 5468 | 5625 | 6088 | 6510 |
| Labour force | 2921 | 3397 | 1679 | 1932 | 468 | 542 | 40 | 46 | 5109 | 5917 | 6039 | 6622 | 7046 |
| Unemployment | 196 | 296 | 66 | 105 | 29 | 45 | 1 | 2 | 292 | 449 | 414 | 535 | 537 |
| Unemployment rate | 6.7 | 8.7 | 3.9 | 5.5 | 6.2 | 8.4 | 3.0 | 5.0 | 5.7 | 7.6 | 6.9 | 8.1 | 7.6 |

Sources: 1980 and 1985 (first ten columns), *Fifth Malaysia Plan 1986-90*, pp. 102-103. 1980 to 1990 (last three columns), *Mid-Term Review of the Fifth Malaysia Plan 1986-90*, table 3.9 pp. 64-65.

modern sector of the economy. The momentum of growth has since been regained and there has been an encouraging resurgence in industrial and associated production, but the presumption is that the transfer of the Malays out of agriculture will take longer than was hoped.

It is unfortunate that the movement of employment into the modern sector of the economy was slowed in the 1980s by world recession. One consequence has been a rise in unemployment. The Outline Perspective Plan set considerable store on the elimination of unemployment: "This development of full employment at a relatively high level of productivity is at the heart of the first prong of the NEP to reduce and eventually eradicate poverty."[31]

Unemployment, as we have argued above, is a common phenomenon in developing countries, reflecting the inability of development strategies to provide work opportunities; it presents dangers as well as being undesirable in itself:

A profile of the unemployed reveals some interesting characteristics, among others, unemployment was concentrated among the young, especially those with secondary education. The findings of the 1987 Labour Force Survey showed that about 70 per cent of the unemployed were below 25 years old, while 69 per cent had secondary education. An increasing number of the unemployed had also completed tertiary education, with the share rising from one per cent in 1980 to 3.6 per cent in 1987. Unemployment was also mainly short-term with 72 per cent of the actively unemployed being without a job for less than a year. Hard core unemployment, that is those waiting more than three years for a job, also declined from 6 per cent of the unemployed labour force in 1982 to 5.1 per cent in 1987.[32]

Hard core unemployment of this magnitude, that is about 25,000 people, particularly as it will include a number of young graduates, is a matter of considerable concern. It is also important to realise that high growth *per se* need not necessarily be accompanied by full employment. The nature of the growth and of the accompanying policy on manpower use ultimately determines the structure and level of employment. This is exactly the message that the DNU and the OPP were trying to convey from the start. Despite the success attained by the country in its efforts to eradicate poverty over the years, it continues to persist to an unacceptable degree. It is possible to point to a number of reasons for this, some of long-standing,

[31] *Op.cit*, table 39, pp. 64-65.
[32] *Mid-Term Review of the Fifth Malaysia Plan 1986-90*, p. 90.

others that may be of a more transient nature. The setback to the attainment of the full employment objective of the NEP is a phenomenon that may have elements due to world recession and which may now be declining as activity picks up. It is not to be expected, however, that in present conditions unemployment will fall to a very low level. Moreover, it is in the nature of economic development of a dual economy that unemployment will manifest itself, as rural workers will continue to move from the countryside to the towns in their search for more remunerative employment.

We have already shown that the number of jobs created in the modern sector of the economy in recent years has been inadequate in relation to the growth in the working population. When employment opportunities increase only slowly, access to those that do occur becomes a major matter. Insufficient and unequal access to adequate employment, both in the urban and rural areas, are among the major causes of poverty and inequality in most countries. In a developing economy like Malaysia, where there is a large backlog of surplus labour, carried over from successive five year plans, access to employment in the high growth and high productivity sectors becomes a major matter. Two major strategies were devised in the NEP to increase the chances of Malays getting jobs in the modern sector of the economy. They comprised policies to increase the allotment of employment to Malays in the modern sector of the economy and measures to increase the participation of Malays in the ownership of companies. It is to these aspects of the accomplishments of the NEP that we now turn.

## Employment of Malays in the Modern Sector

As we have seen, Document A advocated a cautious approach to bringing pressure to bear on employers to employ a minimum percentage of Malays in their activities. It seems that administrative pressure rather than formal legislation was used to ensure that Malays were employed in appropriate numbers. There was ample opportunity for this, since permissions of various kinds had to be given for the establishment and extension of activities in the modern sector of the economy. The ultimate objective was to ensure that Malays would be represented in the modern sector of the economy in proportion to their numbers in the community. Progress so far is indicated in Tables 4.10, 4.11 and 4.12.

Some comments may be made on the Table 4.10. Firstly, the proportion of Bumiputra in the more important sectors of the economy is such as to suggest that attempts to ensure that they are represented in minimal proportions in particular firms will be hard to administer. Secondly, within these composite categories it is only in commerce (largely wholesale and retail trade) that Bumiputra can be said to be greatly underrepresented. Thirdly, it is noticeable that, probably as a result of recession and of policies adopted to counter it, the Bumiputra share in manufacturing declined by 10 per cent between 1985 and 1988, while the Chinese share increased markedly. Finally, it might be tentatively concluded that the efforts to enforce employment of Bumiputra has had some success in circumstances that required considerable expansion of the labour force, but it also shows that such progress is tenuous in conditions of recession and of relaxation in administrative pressures.

Another aspect of ethnic employment is portrayed in the *Mid-Term Review of the Fifth Malaysia Plan*, in the form of an occupational distribution (as opposed to an industrial classification) of employment. The figures recorded for 1988 in table 4.11 are reproduced from that *Review*.[33]

It appears that the Bumiputra are represented in the professional and technical occupations, as a whole, in rough proportion to their labour force. In administrative and managerial positions they are seriously underrepresented, and this is also the case for sales. The same might also be said about Indian representation in administration and sales. In agriculture, as we have seen, the Bumiputra are overrepresented and the absolute magnitude of this is large.

In assessing the significance of these figure, it is necessary to be realistic. Increasingly, management positions call for a considerable range of skills, including technical and marketing skills, which take time to develop through education and experience, and the necessity to acquire this background will tend to slow the assumption of such positions by the Bumiputra. From a closer look at highly qualified professional workers, as is seen in Table 4.12 for 1988, it is evident that there is likely to be a dearth of certain skills amongst Bumiputra.

The relative deficiency of Bumiputra membership of professional groups is evident. The limited representation of architects, lawyers and engineers is likely to be one impediment to achieving control of enterprises in the modern sector and a factor affecting managerial appointments.

---

[33] See p. 66.

TABLE 4.10
DISTRIBUTION OF ETHNIC EMPLOYMENT IN
SELECTED SECTORS OF THE ECONOMY
(percentages)

| Sector | Ethnic Group | Year | | |
| --- | --- | --- | --- | --- |
| | | 1985 | 1988 | 1990 |
| Agriculture | Bumiputra | 75.0 | 75.2 | 75.2 |
| | Chinese | 15.5 | 15.1 | 15.1 |
| | Indians | 8.8 | 9.1 | 9.1 |
| Manufacturing | Bumiputra | 45.8 | 41.6 | 44.0 |
| | Chinese | 42.8 | 49.0 | 45.3 |
| | Indians | 10.9 | 9.1 | 10.3 |
| Construction | Bumiputra | 42.2 | 42.7 | 42.9 |
| | Chinese | 51.0 | 49.9 | 49.1 |
| | Indians | 5.8 | 6.3 | 6.8 |
| Transport | Bumiputra | 52.4 | 52.1 | 52.0 |
| | Chinese | 33.9 | 34.3 | 34.6 |
| | Indians | 13.0 | 13.0 | 12.8 |
| Commerce | Bumiputra | 36.4 | 35.0 | 34.7 |
| | Chinese | 55.2 | 57.7 | 57.7 |
| | Indians | 7.8 | 6.7 | 7.1 |
| Government | Bumiputra | 66.7 | 68.2 | 68.2 |
| | Chinese | 24.3 | 22.5 | 22.5 |
| | Indians | 8.5 | 8.7 | 8.7 |
| Other services | Bumiputra | 66.8 | 67.7 | 66.9 |
| | Chinese | 24.2 | 23.1 | 23.8 |
| | Indians | 8.5 | 8.7 | 8.7 |
| Total employed | Bumiputra | 57.7 | 56.9 | 56.6 |
| | Chinese | 32.6 | 33.7 | 33.6 |
| | Indians | 9.0 | 8.7 | 9.1 |

Note: The table is composed from table 3.9 in the *Mid-Term Review of the Fifth Malaysia Plan, 1986-90.* "Other" ethnic employees have been omitted.

## TABLE 4.11
### EMPLOYMENT BY OCCUPATION AND ETHNIC GROUP, 1988
(thousands)

| Occupation | Bumiputra | % | Chinese | % | Indian | % |
|---|---|---|---|---|---|---|
| Professional and technical | 247 | 56 | 137 | 31 | 51 | 12 |
| Administrative and managerial | 38 | 28 | 89 | 66 | 6 | 5 |
| Clerical | 320 | 55 | 207 | 36 | 51 | 9 |
| Sales | 245 | 36 | 385 | 58 | 40 | 6 |
| Service | 415 | 59 | 213 | 30 | 70 | 10 |
| Agricultural production | 1439 | 76 | 315 | 17 | 137 | 7 |
| Other production | 756 | 46 | 706 | 43 | 178 | 11 |
| Total | 3462 | 57 | 2052 | 34 | 533 | 9 |

Note: "Other" ethnic groups are excluded from the table but not from the totals on which the percentages are calculated.

TABLE 4.12

MEMBERSHIP OF REGISTERED PROFESSIONALS BY ETHNIC GROUP 1988

| Profession | Bumiputra | % | Chinese | % | Indian | % | Total |
|---|---|---|---|---|---|---|---|
| Architects | 192 | 22 | 676 | 76 | 14 | 2 | 888 |
| Accountants | 514 | 10 | 4079 | 82 | 315 | 6 | 4980 |
| Engineers | 4895 | 29 | 10512 | 63 | 885 | 5 | 16626 |
| Dentists | 307 | 24 | 569 | 45 | 361 | 28 | 1273 |
| Doctors | 1653 | 26 | 2258 | 35 | 2283 | 36 | 6393 |
| Veterinarians | 206 | 34 | 145 | 24 | 219 | 36 | 610 |
| Surveyors | 300 | 35 | 497 | 56 | 45 | 5 | 864 |
| Lawyers | 504 | 20 | 1249 | 49 | 754 | 29 | 2562 |
| Total | 8571 | 25 | 19985 | 58 | 4878 | 14 | 34196 |

Source:  *Mid-Term Review of the Fifth Malaysia Plan*, table 3-11, p. 67.

## Entrepreneurship and Ownership

An essential part of the NEP was to encourage entrepreneurship and capital ownership within the Bumiputra community. In this section we review a number of ways in which Bumiputra interests may have been promoted and assess their effectiveness. Not all of these were foreseen in the original formulation of the NEP.

Very considerable opportunities for developing Bumiputra managerial capabilites exist in the establishment of a large number of public corporations (or non-financial public enterprises (NFPEs) as they are called). Amongst them, PETRONAS, the national petroleum company, is highly profitable but over one hundred of the NFPEs have been experiencing losses and are currently the subject of study with the object of assessing their viability and the possibilities of privatisation. It may be concluded that the establishment of public corporations, while offering opportunities for Bumiputra involvement, is not without cost.

Allocation of government contracts also can be a means to favour Bumiputra interests. Some preferences are given in the letting of government contracts. For contracts amounting to not more than $50,000, Bumiputra may be given preference if their tender is not more than ten per cent above that of a non-Bumiputra bidder. Beyond this there is no formal provision for contracts to be allocated to Bumiputra interests although it is possible to envisage circumstances in which the nature or location of projects would make it more likely that they would be awarded to Bumiputra contractors; the declared target of involving Bumiputra in 30 per cent of higher cost contracts may be a further factor making for the administration of preferential allocations. There is no means of knowing, in the absence of published statistics, how far the letting of government contracts has been successful in bringing on Bumiputra entrepreneurship, particularly as, in some cases, contracts may have given rise to various degrees of sub-contracting to entrepreneurs from other ethnic groups. Various institutions have been set up to support Bumiputra entrepreneurs and provide them with training and facilities. These include, for example, MARA (Council of Trust for Indigenous Peoples) which provides about $ 11 million of loans per year and Bank Pembangunan (a development bank) which was established to support the NEP and which provides support for small entrepreneurs in a variety of ways, including administration of loans from the World Bank destined for small businessmen. The provision of finance may also be flanked with training programmes. Financially, the operations of Bank Pembangunan have given rise to considerable capital losses. A number of other development finance institutions are also in a position to support Bumiputra commercial and industrial activities.

There are arrangements for civil servants to retire early and to receive training and financial support to set up business enterprises. It is again hard to say how effective this has been in establishing viable Bumiputra controlled businesses.

The need to establish an Enterprise Rehabilitation Fund to salvage Bumiputra enterprises[34] affected by the recession provides an indication of the problems that are likely to be encountered in any effort to foster small enterprise. Such remedial action may be an unavoidable cost of attaining the social restructuring that is required. Without detailed study is is difficult to judge the efficacity of the total operation but it is to be presumed that Bumiputra involvement was increased by the supporting activities that were provided and that results would have been more evident had the recession not intervened.

The restructuring targets of the NEP were first defined in the Outline Perspective Plan.[35] It was realised that with the development and modernisation of the economy, the role of the corporate sector would increase as the structure and financial sophistication of the economy developed. It was concluded that the key to the ownership and control of wealth would be through the ownership of the equity capital of various enterprises. "A more balanced pattern in the ownership of assets in all sectors of the economy is necessary. The target of the government is that within a period of 20 years, Malays and other indigenous people will own and manage at least 30 per cent of the total commercial and industrial activities of the economy in all categories and scales of operation."[36] The overall target for the ownership of equity capital was set so that non-Bumiputra Malaysians would own 40 per cent of the total by the end of 1990 with foreigners owning the remaining 30 per cent. Intermediate steps for Malay ownership were fixed: 9 per cent of all share capital by 1975, 16 per cent by 1980, 23 per cent by 1985 and 30 per cent by 1990.[37] Restructuring of asset ownership extended to physical assets, including land, houses and commercial buildings as well as financial assets. However, there were no explicit quantitative targets for ownership of non-corporate assets. The analysis of the Economic Planning Unit in the early 1970s suggested that there had been a

[34] *Economic Report*, Ministry of Finance, Malaysia, 1989-90, p. 159.
[35] *Mid-Term Review of the Second Malaysia Plan*, p. 80.
[36] *Op. cit.*, p. 81.
[37] *Op. cit.*, p. 84.

worsening trend in the ownership of urban land against the Malays, whose holdings were already very low.

The target of 30 per cent for Bumiputra ownership of corporate capital by 1990 represented a considerable increase in the 1.9 per cent held in 1970. This change, it was argued, would lead to correspondingly more Malay participation in the modern high productivity sectors of the economy, increase their ownership and control of the sector, and improve the ethnic structures of employment and income. The 30 per cent corporate ownership target was not set just for its own sake, but as a means to an end, that of improving the distribution of income and of control of the economy. The target for non-Malay Malaysians was to be increased from 37 per cent to 40 per cent while the share of foreign holdings were to be halved from 61 per cent in 1970 to about 30 per cent in 1990.

The test of whether the NEP policies have succeeded or not in relation to capital ownership lies in the extent to which Bumiputra ownership has approached 30 per cent of capital ownership and, perhaps, also in the extent to which other ownership has changed in the direction of greater equality of holdings. What has actually taken place is shown in Table 4.13 and may be compared with the targets set in the OPP.

Compared with the target set for Bumiputra ownership of 30 per cent of the share capital of limited companies with reference to data in Table 4.13, it is generally assumed that only 19.4 per cent (in 1988) of the total capital is in Bumiputra hands and that further advances are necessary for the target to be achieved. This conclusion needs careful consideration and there are three reasons for thinking that the 19.4 per cent figure may be an underestimate of the position. The first of these is that the figure for Other Malaysian residents includes holdings of nominee companies amounting to 8.1 per cent of the total and part of these holdings may in fact be controlled by Bumiputra agencies.[38] A second reason for thinking that Bumiputra ownership may be more extensive than generally supposed is that "locally controlled" companies, which are also included under the heading Other Malaysian residents and amount to 13.1 per cent of the total in the table, can not be disaggregated further and assigned to specific ethnic groups. Still a third statistical doubt has to be expressed. The figures given for ownership are calculated in terms of par values and it is possible that this leads to an

[38] E.T. Gomez goes so far as to assert: "...it is well known that a significant proportion of such companies are owned by Bumiputras." See his *Politics in Business, UMNO's Corporate Investments*, Kuala Lumpur: Forum, 1990, p. 174.

TABLE 4.13

OWNERSHIP AND CONTROL OF THE CORPORATE SECTOR
1971 TO 1990 AS RECORDED AND (FOR 1990) PROJECTED

(Percentages held by ethnic group; figures relate to par values)

|  | 1971 | 1975 | 1980 | 1985 | 1988 | 1990 |
|---|---|---|---|---|---|---|
| Malaysian residents | 38.3 | 46.7 | 52.5 | 74.0 | 75.4 | 76.3 |
| *Bumiputra individuals* | 2.6 | 3.6 | 4.3 | 11.7 | 13.0 | 13.6 |
| *Bumiputra trust agencies* | 1.7 | 5.6 | 8.1 | 7.4 | 6.4 | 6.0 |
| *Other Malaysian residents* | 34.0 | 37.5 | 40.1 | 54.9 | 56.0 | 56.7 |
| Foreign residents | 61.7 | 53.3 | 47.5 | 26.0 | 24.6 | 23.7 |
| *Total* | 100 | 100 | 100 | 100 | 100 | 100 |

Source for 1971, 1975 and 1980: *Fourh Malaysia Plan*, table 3.13, p. 62. Source for
1985, 1988 and 1990: *Mid-Term Review of the Fifth Malaysia Plan*, table 3-12, p. 70.

understatement of Bumiputra ownership. It is well known that market values frequently deviate from par values and generally, in inflationary times in particular, market values are in excess and frequently considerably in excess of par values. This would not greatly matter in determining the ethnic composition of ownership if deviations from par values were random and not likely to affect one class of ownership more than another. This, however, may not be the case.[39] It is difficult to know what do with such doubtful and conflicting evidence. Two conclusions may stand out: first it would be unwise to accept that the NEP target for ownership of 30 per cent of quoted equity had or had not been attained until the matter has been investigated further and the criticisms put forward in this matter have been answered. Second, any change in policy related to ownership should perhaps also await the results of detailed and thorough statistical examination.

For the moment, taking the figures as they appear in the table as giving some indication of the trend, if not the proportion of Bumiputra ownership, some observations may be made. The first of these is the very small holdings of Bumiputra *individuals* revealed in the table. They are still far from constituting an equity-owning democracy.

It may also be observed that in the early 1980s, i.e. in the Fourth Plan period, there was a most remarkable increase in the percentage shares held by both Bumiputra (from 12.4 to 19.1 per cent) and other Malaysians (from 40.1 to 54.9 per cent) with a correspondingly dramatic reduction in the share held by foreigners (from 47.5 to no more than 26 per cent). The increase in the holdings by Malaysians must have required the mobilisation of large savings and borrowed funds. However, since 1985, there has been relatively little movement in the proportions of the shares held by the various groupings.

It is clear that Malaysian Chinese residents, individuals and groups,

[39] Professor K.S.Jomo, for example, asserts: "...if market values are considered instead of nominal or par values, the proportion of publicly listed foreign and Bumiputra shares would rise rather significantly, at the expense of the Chinese share." He goes on to add "that according to data from the Kuala Lumpur Stock Exchange Annual Handbook, incorporating information up to September 1988, 29.4 per cent of equity by *nominal value* was owned by Bumiputras... However, when market values based on closing prices at the KLSE on 1 March 1989 are considered, the Bumiputra shares... rose to 34.5 per cent..." See *Beyond 1990: Considerations for a New National Development Strategy*, Kuala Lumpur: Institute of Advanced Studies, Kuala Lumpur, 1989, p. 88. His source of information on the latter estimate is apparently Fong Chan Ong, *Malaysian Corporate Economy Restructuring: Progress Since 1970*, in Seminar "Dasar Ekonomi Baru dan Masa Depannya", Persatuan Sains Sosial Malaysia, Kuala Lumpur, 24-26 July, table 5.

have replaced foreigners as the dominant economic force in the country. The rise in Chinese shareholdings may not be fully matched, of course, by any corresponding increase in real investment in Malaysia, as is sometimes claimed; in part, it may simply represent a change in ownership through financial transactions.

There is no evidence that the modest increase in the capital holdings of Malays has been at the expense of Malaysian Chinese or Indians, as claimed and popularly promoted by the mass media in Malaysia. A thirty per cent capital holding which may be diffusely held is not a controlling interest and if capital issues are made on terms which properly reflect their market standing and expected profitability, they may even have been welcomed as a source of additional capital that would otherwise not have been readily forthcoming. The requirement to include Malay participation in the capital of companies may be open to abuse but, in principle, it is no different from any other mixture of holdings amongst shareholders determined by the functioning of a stock exchange.

It is not possible to assess the significance of capital ownership for the ethnic distribution of income because so much depends on the terms on which shares are acquired and partly because of the inadequacies of national income accounting which, evidently, can not be extended to the distribution of income between profits and other sources of income.[40] If shares are acquired on the open market when yields are low, the effect on income distribution may be relatively small. If, however, the gains from share ownership extend to greater involvement in managerial positions and other forms of employment, considerable gains may be made.

There has recently been a relaxation of requirements for Bumiputra involvement in the capital structure of companies. The reasons advanced for this are that they may constitute a discouragement to foreign investment and local enterprise. Concessions have been made to both local and would-be foreign investors who are now able to invest much more freely as regards the compulsory participation of Malays in the capital of foreign companies.[41] It is also government policy to disinvest itself of holdings in the trusts along "Thatcherite"

[40] In default, some speculative calculations can be made. Assume that half of the output of Malaysia is now in the hands of major companies; assume further that, after taxation, profits account for 30 per cent of total output in the "company" sector; then profits of companies come to about 15 per cent of the national income. 30 per cent of this is equivalent to 5 per cent of the GNP and would serve to boost the incomes of Bumiputra substantially.

[41] For details, see, for example, *Malaysia, Investment in the Manufacturing Sector*, Kuala Lumpur: Malaysian Industrial Development Authority, August 1989.

lines. This may not be a mistake in principle but it needs to be carried through in such a way as to respect Malay interests.

## Income Imbalance

With the perpetuation of the imbalances in the structure of employment and ownership of wealth in favour of non-Malays, it is a foregone conclusion that the income distribution has undergone insufficient rectification. The question is not whether there exists a marked difference in income between the Malays and the non-Malays, which even the most vociferous do not contest, but how great is the difference that remains. Has the disparity ratio or the gap been narrowed since the introduction of the NEP? It may be recalled that with respect to income distribution the objective of the OPP was, "to reduce the existing inequitable distribution of income between income classes and races". On this subject, a report of the Economic Committee of the National Consultative Council, submitted to the Council in August 1970, had this to say:

> The Committee is aware of the futility to achieve a utopian equality in the distribution of incomes. However, such evidence as has been produced before the Committee indicates a degree of inequality in the distribution of incomes that would be unacceptable in any modern state even if there were no problems of racial coincidence within this inequality.

The findings of the DNU estimates and simulations were summarised in chapter 2 above and are also to be found *in extenso* in Document B. The average income of the non-Malay in 1967 was estimated at $3000 per person compared to an average income for Malays of $1750 per person, giving an absolute difference of $1250, or a disparity ratio of 1.7. In the Second Malaysia Plan no specific targets were set for its reduction for a variety of reasons, including political pressure in the Alliance government by the MCA, and the reluctance of the EPU leadership and the Treasury to highlight the problem of racial economic imbalances on the grounds that it was a sensitive national issue best left in silence and — in any case — reliable statistics were not available. But the problem was there, and will continue to be there well into the 21st century whether one admits it or not. In spite of the seriousness of the problem, subsequent Five Year Plans did not set any quantitative targets for the progressive reduction of this disparity between the Malays and the non-Malays. It was left vaguely in suspension, with everybody hoping and praying that somehow it would fade away one day. Far from going away the essentials of the problem still remain. Not only is poverty still primarily a rural phenomenon, and thus largely a Malay problem, but its hardcore aspects are not susceptible to easy solutions. This is one reason why by any measure of average income, Malays fare badly against other ethnic groups, notably the Chinese, and why large and persistent disparities continue.

There are difficulties in comparing statistics for different years based on different sources and methodologies. It appears, however, from Table 4.14 that the disparity ratio of income as between Chinese Malaysians and Malays has been high ever since Merdeka and for Peninsular Malaysia has varied around two: from 1.9 in the late 1950s, according to the 1957-58 data, to as high as 2.3 or more in the late 1960s and to about 1.7 in the mid-1980s. When the NEP was initially conceived in 1969-70 it was estimated that at that time the ratio for non-Malay Malaysians to Malays was about 1.75 and that it might be possible to reduce this ratio to 1.40 by 1985. With more data and in retrospect, it has become evident that the racial income disparity issue was of a greater magnitude at the opening of NEP than was estimated at its initiation, and the situation in the mid-80s has also turned out to be more serious than foreseen after 15 years of NEP. The statistics of change during the 30 year period since Merdeka in household income by ethnic group given in Table 4.14 are consistent with the view that the racial economic disparities grew worse in the years up to the 1969 debacle and then have improved during the NEP period. While these statistics are not very robust, the changes are of sufficient magnitude to offer a partial explanation both of the riots of 1969 and of the impact of NEP as formulated and implemented. The trouble is that the improvement under NEP has at best has been limited. Clearly, the need for the NEP to-day is as obvious as ever; the task is even harder than foreseen and hoped when the NEP was initiated. Yet the conclusion that an NEP type strategy needs to be extended into the 21st century is also consistent with the simulations carried out by the DNU in 1969/1970.

Malaysia's income distribution, whether calculated for all households combined or for major ethnic groups separately, is worse than equivalent distributions not only in other ASEAN countries but also further afield. Thus, according to the World Development Report 1989, the poorest 20 per cent households in Indonesia, the Philippines, Thailand all had about 6 per cent share of all household income, while in Malaysia the figure was only 3.5 per cent. By contrast, the richest 20 per cent in Malaysia received no less than 56 per cent, while in the three other ASEAN members the equivalent

TABLE 4.14

HOUSEHOLDS MEAN INCOMES BY ETHNIC GROUP 1957 TO 1987

(PENINSULAR MALAYSIA)

(M$ per month and as percentage of Malay Mean Income)

| | 1957/58 | | 1967/68 | | 1970 | | 1984 | | 1987 | |
|---|---|---|---|---|---|---|---|---|---|---|
| | M$ | % | $ | % | $ | % | $ | % | $ | % |
| All Ethnic Groups | 199 | 138 | 217 | 167 | 264 | 153 | 1095 | 129 | 1074 | 124 |
| Bumiputra | 144 | 100 | 130 | 100 | 172 | 100 | 852 | 100 | 868 | 100 |
| Chinese | 272 | 189 | 321 | 247 | 394 | 229 | 1502 | 176 | 1430 | 165 |
| Indian | 217 | 151 | 253 | 195 | 304 | 177 | 1094 | 128 | 1089 | 125 |
| Others | n.a. | n.a. | 839 | 645 | 813 | 473 | 2454 | 288 | 2886 | 332 |

Source: For years to 1970: Sudhir Anand, *Inequality and Poverty in Malaysia — Measurement and Decomposition*, Oxford University Press, 1983, p. 30. For years 1984 and 1987: *Mid-Term Review of the Fifth Malaysia Plan 1986-1990*, pp. 42-43.

shares were about 50 per cent. The particularly skewed distribution in Malaysia reflects large differentials between ethnic groups but also a considerable — and generally growing — disparity within each group. This remains a serious shortcoming of policy design and implementation under the NEP.

A great deal has been written about inequality of income, its extent, the ways in which it can be decomposed into its constituent numerical causes, the factors that engender it and the way in which it can be expected to evolve through time and the strategies that can affect it. Amongst development economists, a Gini coefficient of 0.3, the measure of inequality that might apply in industrialised countries or, more certainly, in socialist orientated ones, might be regarded as good, while a coefficient of 0.5 might be considered to constitute a clearly undesirable pattern of in income distribution. One has to be careful about reaching such conclusions. Summary statistics of income distribution, even avoiding questions of their exact meaning, can at the best serve to draw attention to a potential cause of concern, if indeed such exists. It is a warning that policies should be orientated, if this is possible, in the direction of achieving greater equality in the distribution of income and within the effectiveness of policies that can be pursued to achieve this. It may be suggested that the reduction of inequality is not an aim to be considered without due consideration of the costs that might be incurred in pursuing it. The provision of basic needs and the removal of poverty may seem to many to be of greater moment than the elimination of inequality at least amongst those living out of reach of abject poverty. How far the sacrifice of future benefits in the interests of reducing or eliminating current poverty should go, is not an easy question to answer for reasons that have already been adduced. It may not always be a question that needs to be put. In rather special circumstances rapid growth with equity may be a practical possibility; Sri Lanka, up to a point, and Korea and Taiwan may illustrate what can be accomplished when circumstances are highly favourable and the political will is there.

## Conclusions

How then does the performance of the NEP rate in all the circumstances? The reduction of income inequalities is somewhat less than the arithmetic model introduced at the beginning of this chapter seems to suggest might have been possible. But probably the most important lesson to be learned is that the reduction of inequalities from a very high level to an acceptable one takes time

— short of revolution. Korea had the advantage of starting from a position of much greater equality and population homogeneity than was the case for Malaysia; consequently it was much easier to hold that position. If comparisons are to be made they need to take into account all relevant conditions.

In Malaysia, in spite of considerable efforts, poverty continues to rule to an unacceptable extent in rural areas: there are considerable differences in the prosperity of the states comprising Malaysia and the policies devised to reduce the incidence of poverty in such areas through the development of social services, education and the improvement of agricultural conditions need to be pursued with vigour. It is fortunate that poverty in Malaysia is not of the most severe type for, unless progress can be accelerated, there will continue to be many households with incomes below the poverty level for a number of years to come.

The efforts to improve education and training promise well. In the long run it is these that are most likely to ensure the establishment of an acceptable degree of inequality, whether racial or otherwise. There has been some disappointment in recent years with the contribution that the expansion of the modern sector of the economy has been able to make to the reduction of poverty and income inequality. In part, this has been the result of the impact of world levels of activity to which the Malaysian economy is widely open; but there is likely to be a continued renewal of growth and this should increase the absorption of Malays into the modern sector of the economy as, in the longer run, will shifting rates of population growth by curtailing the number of Chinese entrants to the labour market and, to a lesser extent, Malays. As the growth of the modern sector of the economy regains momentum, the movement of labour out of the agricultural sector will begin to make itself felt and this will be a further factor increasing the remuneration of Malays. It will also have consequences for the restructuring of agriculture itself which will have to put itself in a position to meet higher levels of remuneration through improvements in labour productivity.

In short, the NEP has achieved a very considerable level of success. This is not, however, a totally complete review of the government's performance in implementing its policies. Could it be thought realistically, that more could have been done? If the economy could have expanded more rapidly the extent of poverty and perhaps even racial imbalance might have been further reduced; but the rate of expansion was rapid and to have attempted more, even if the government had the instruments at hand to accelerate development, might well have caused the economy to overheat. Any attempt by government to increase the rate of development would almost certainly have required more government expenditure and more taxation and levels of expenditure can not be considered to have been low. More government expenditure would in all probability have had the effect of impinging on other activities; to substitute expenditure on, say, infrastructure required for production, for expenditure on, say, education or training, might well have been counterproductive in the long-run. It is always difficult to guess what the best distribution of expenditure should be in order to balance incremental present and future benefits. More is needed to be done to improve the position of Malays in rural areas and impoverished states, but as we have seen agricultural development was impressive and the temporal balance may again have pointed in the direction of delaying the reduction of immediate poverty with the intention of reducing it to a greater extent in a few years time, as a well supported modern sector began increasingly to take up the slack.

It might also be asked whether development was sufficiently pointed in the direction of supporting labour intensive techniques of production as has been advocated by so many developing economists.[42] However, while this may be an appropriate policy for countries with a very large labour surplus and limited opportunities to industrialise, it may not be a wholly appropriate policy for a country such as Malaysia, able to develop rapidly with the use of modern technology and to sell in world markets.

Criticism of greater validity can be directed to the administration of the measures to increase the involvement of the Malay population in company ownership which was not particularly successful and liable to abuse, a subject to which we return in chapter 6. Similar considerations apply to participation of labour in the modern sector and promotion there.

In short it was not possible for the NEP to eliminate poverty and attain racial balance in the time that it has been in operation, but a very substantial start was made which will continue to carry the economy forward into a new phase. What has to be realised in the Malaysian situation, is that structural change takes time, a considerable time, and that another 20 years of restructuring are necessary to approach racial balance in all its aspects, including

[42] Including Professor Gustav Papanek, for example, who is no stranger to Malaysia; see his papers "Industrialization strategies in labour abundant countries" in *Asian Development Review*, vol. 3 (1985), no. 1, and "Aid, Growth and Equity in Southern Asia" in J.R. Parkinson (editor), *Poverty and Aid*, Oxford: Basil Blackwell, 1983.

greater equality in income and opportunity in all echelons of the society and not just for those in poverty.

CHAPTER 5

# THE DEBATE

## Introduction

The general debate about development strategies in Malaysia, as elsewhere, is wide-ranging and inconclusive. There is no such thing as *the* best path to development; each strategy has its strengths and weaknesses. Each country must choose its own strategy, one that suits its own requirements, evolves from its own history, responds to its own particular socio-economic needs and effectively addresses the problems which require solution. The parties to the strategy debate in Malaysia are conditioned in their views and argumentation by their perceived economic and social interests, including in particular their ethnic backgrounds.

A near universal theme of debate about development strategies is the role of income and asset distribution between individuals and groups as against overall growth and modernisation as the major and direct thrust of policy. In Malaysia, this theme has a special dimension as an issue of ethnic inequality, and this is the main subject area of this book.

The NEP was the economic thrust of the overall political strategy to rebuild the country after the riot of 1969 and must be seen in its relation to political developments of the country. Indeed, the NEP was born out of a strongly felt need to create a new and viable basis for accommodating the various races into a cohesive nation and thus to avoid recurrence of such disasters in the future.

The debate over the NEP centres on two major aspects. It concerns, first, the purposes and design of the policy itself and, second, the implementation and outcome of the policy over the years and its relevance for the future. With respect to the first concern, the purposes of the NEP, the problems of inequality arising in the process of development are compounded in Malaysia and made more delicate by the inescapable fact that poverty and economic inequality in the society coincides with racial and religious demarcations. If that is not enough, the extent of inequality in the country is one of the worst in the world. The Malaysian problem is therefore both dangerous and explosive. What in other countries, such as Korea with a homogeneous population structure, is a straight forward problem of economic inequality, in Malaysia assumes a more serious and sinister character of racial hostility and antagonism.

With respect to the second concern, that is the implementation and possible continuation of the NEP after 1990, the positions taken are seemingly irreconcilable, with the non-Malays generally against the NEP and the Malays in favour. As will be amply demonstrated in the following, the debate, therefore, is between parties where one community is bent upon seeing the NEP abolished as soon as possible, while the other desires to extend it well beyond 1990.

Some of the many questions asked in the current debate are: whether the NEP has in fact achieved a measure of success, in terms of what it was intended to do; what have been the costs involved to the society arising from its implementation, not only in monetary terms, but also in terms of the perceived or alleged discrimination suffered by non-Malays; what in fact have been the opportunities to national advance that have been forgone; which have been the abuses and undesirable deviations; ultimately, have the policies pursued been necessary and justified in relation to accepted norms of social justice? In this chapter we report what we consider the basic positions taken by the various groups towards the NEP. But first we provide a summary of worldwide experience from different approaches to the task of development, as this bears on the choices for Malaysia.

## General Strategy

A number of alternative development strategies adopted in various developing countries may usefully be distinguished: monetarism and laissez-faire *versus* socialism; the open economy *versus* import substitution and protectionism; industrialisation *versus* agricultural development; distribution and basic needs *versus* growth.[1] While the thrusts of policy are different, depending on the strategy chosen, in practice the approaches taken have tended to overlap and combine, having a mixture of elements from two or often more of the strategies listed. Indeed, some developing countries in practice do not

[1] A similar set of categories is reviewed in Keith Griffin's study for the OECD Development Centre: *Alternative Strategies for Economic Development*, London: Macmillan, 1989. In the following pages we draw on parts of the analysis and argument of this authoritative and up-to-date study.

have what could be said to be a consistent and comprehensive development strategy; ad hocism and inconsistencies in strategies, policies and programmes are typical features of development as it unfolds in practice.

The outcome of a review and assessment of the effectiveness or otherwise of alternative strategies depends, of course, on the specific circumstances of individual countries at particular points of time in their development, but clearly also on the criteria applied for judgements, such as impacts on efficiency of resource utilisation; on savings, investment and growth; on human capital formation; on poverty and inequality, on the role of the State; and even on such basic aspects as participation, democracy and freedom. We shall quote some of the findings from a review of worldwide experience along these lines from the study by Keith Griffin (*op.cit.*), as they have a close bearing on the situation in Malaysia in general and for NEP in particular.

A central issue of debate in Malaysia has been concerned with the possibility of the constraint of overall growth by policies designed to contain and reduce inequality, specifically the NEP restructuring measures. Thus, it has been argued that the full potential for growth has not been realised in the 1970s and 1980s because of the NEP which contains elements of a redistributive strategy.[2] The assertion is that it is anti-growth with adverse effects on the development of the country and its standard of living and on the welfare of the general populace. Therefore, it is argued, the elimination of poverty and the improvement in ethnic distribution will be delayed via this path of development. Indeed it will stifle private sector initiative, create distortions and inefficiencies in the economy, and misallocate scarce resources among competing demands.

However, the weight of evidence accumulated over decades from development experience of Third World countries which have adopted a redistributive strategy suggests otherwise. In Asia, two of the most successful economies which adopted this strategy, South Korea and Taiwan, have been able to combine exceptionally rapid

---

[2] In the case of Malaysia see, for example, the criticism of the NEP by:
(a) Malaysian Chinese Association (MCA), "*The Future of Malaysian Chinese*", published by the MCA, Kuala Lumpur, 1988.
(b) Dato Malek Merican, "*Review of the NEP from Private Sector Perspective*". Paper delivered at Gemaputra Seminar Kebangsaan, Dasar Ekonomi Baru Selapas 1990, 24-26 March 1987, Kuala Lumpur.
(c) Lim Kit Siang, "*Crisis of Identity*", published by DAP, Kuala Lumpur, 1986.
We deal with these and other criticisms later in this chapter.

economic growth, sharply reduced inequality and widespread alleviation of poverty. Thus, for instance, in the case of Taiwan (Griffin, *op. cit.*, p. 181):

> Growth has been consistently rapid. Over the entire period for which data are available, 1952-1985, real GNP increased 8.6 per cent per annum and real GNP per head 6.0 per cent per annum. This of course is very much faster than the rise in per capita income experienced in most other Third World countries and demonstrates conclusively that there is no inherent conflict between rapid growth and an equitable distribution of income. Taiwan (like South Korea) has combined an exceptionally equal distribution of income and wealth with exceptionally fast growth. As a result, poverty as it is known in the rest of the Third World has virtually disappeared.

More generally, the experience from application of alternative strategies is summarised by Griffin (*op. cit.*) as follows:

> Aggregate growth rates have been highest in countries following an export-led industrialisation strategy (as in South Korea), or in countries following a redistributive strategy of development with a strong emphasis on exports (as in Taiwan), or in countries with an open economy which have enjoyed rapid expansion of exports (as in Botswana) or in countries following a socialist strategy of development. There are, in other words, a number of development strategies which are capable of producing above average rates of growth of total product and per capita income. The sectoral pattern of growth is more dependent on the specific strategy pursued. (p. 232)

> Above average income inequality is likely to be present under (i) monetarist strategies, (ii) open economy strategies based on the export of petroleum and mineral products, (iii) open economy strategies based on the export of agricultural products in countries where landownership is highly concentrated, and (iv) industrialisation strategies, particularly those based on producing consumer goods for the domestic market. ....Indeed, the distribution of productive assets, especially land, is fundamental. Those countries which have had a land reform (China, North Korea, South Korea, Taiwan) have succeeded in reducing poverty and inequality quite considerably, while most of those countries which have not (such as Brazil and the Philippines) have continued to have large numbers of people living in poverty even when they have managed to achieve rapid rates of economic growth. (p. 236)

As early as the late 1960s, disappointment began to set in with respect to the growth oriented strategy. Malaysia took its lessons from the traumatic experience of racial riots in 1969; hence was born the Malaysian NEP. Later, empirical evidence for other countries, which contradicted the assertions of the growth oriented strategy, was presented and analysed in a number of other studies, such as those for the World Bank conducted by Hollis Chenery and Montek S. Ahluwaliah etc.; for the OECD by David Turnham; by the various ILO Missions on behalf of the World Employment Programme; as well as others.[3] In 1972 and in 1973 during the annual meetings of the World Bank, McNamara as President of the World Bank made his now famous speeches in Washington D.C. and in Nairobi, which to all intents and purposes buried the growth oriented strategy, except as one dimension in combination with others, in particular strategies focusing on equity and distribution.

The redistributive strategy has many variants. The main concern of this type of strategy is to improve the distribution of wealth and income; it is designed to tackle head-on the problems of inequality by giving priority to the poor, the underprivileged and the weak. This strategy places emphasis on basic needs of the poor, raising the productivity of the economic system and providing more employment. Equally important, the strategy also involves the distribution of assets, including land reforms. In consequence, it runs

[3] See for example:
(a) Hollis Chenery, Ahluwalia Montek S. et al., *Redistribution with Growth*. A joint study by the World Bank's Development Research Center and the Institute of Development Studies at the University of Sussex. Published by Oxford University Press, 1974.
(b) D. Turnham, assisted by I. Jaeger, *The Employment Problem in Less Developed Countries: A review of Evidence*, Paris: OECD Development Centre, 1971.
(c) ILO, *Bibliography of published research of the World Employment Programme*, Geneva: ILO, 1978.
(d) John C.H. Fei, Gustav Ranis, and Shirley W.Y.Kuo, *Growth with Equity — the Taiwan Case*. Published for the World Bank by Oxford University Press, 1979.
(e) Irma Adelman and Sherman Robinson, *Income Distribution Policy in Developing Countries — A Case Study of Korea*. Published for the World Bank by Oxford University Press, 1978.
(f) World Bank Staff Working Papers no. 240, *Economic Growth and Income Inequality in Korea*, February 1976.
(g) World Bank Staff Working Papers no. 351, *Growth and Equity in Semi-Industrialised Countries*, August 1979.
(h) World Bank Staff Working Papers no. 309, (Revised), *Growth and Poverty in Developing Countries*, 1985.
(i) Gary S. Fields, *Poverty, Inequality and Development*, Cambridge University Press, 1980.
(j) Surjit S. Bhalla and Paul Glewwe, "Growth and Equity in Developing Countries: A reinterpretation of the Sri Lankan Experience", *World Bank Economic Review*, vol. 1 (September 1986), no. 1.

counter to established privileges and entrenched interests in the country; and understandably, it is likely to be met by their wrath.

As explained by Griffin, the central elements of a successful redistributive strategy are five in number (*op.cit.* pp 188-189):

i)    An initial redistribution of productive assets, particularly land;
ii)   The creation of local institutions which permit participation by the people in the selection, design and management of social and economic projects and programmes;
iii)  Investment in human capital — particularly in education, nutrition and health programmes — and the provision of essential social services and economic infrastructure;
iv)   The choice of an employment intensive pattern of development, led either by the export of labour-intensive manufactured goods or by rapid growth of agricultural output; and
v)    Sustained rapid growth of aggregate income per head.

Between them, these elements ensure a more equal distribution of income and wealth, rapid accumulation of human and physical capital, and fast growth of output and income.

The composite strategy does not necessarily require an exceptionally high rate of domestic savings. Nor does it necessarily require an unusually large state sector. It certainly is compatible with a capitalist system of production and exchange, although obviously not with *laissez faire*. The strategy's point of departure is an even distribution of the ownership of the means of production.

Redistributive strategies of development represent a genuine alternative to growth-oriented strategies in countries which attach priority to reducing quickly the most acute forms of poverty and to creating an egalitarian society. Problems of consistency in policy design must not be overlooked, however. Nor must the political preconditions for redistributive measures be ignored.

The account above of worldwide experience from the application of different development strategies has direct parallels in the course of debate in Malaysia. In a previous chapter (chapter 2) we have referred to the controversy between what we termed the EPU and DNU schools in the formulation of policies following the events of 1969; this also affected subsequent developments of the NEP.[4] The

---

[4] Ten years later, in 1980, D.R. Snodgrass characterised the EPU approach as the "Pro-Growth or Trickle-Down School", as contrasted to the "Pro-Redistribution or Interventionist School" of the DNU, see *Inequality and Economic Development in Malaysia*, Kuala Lumpur: Oxford University Press, 1980, p. 9.

deep division between these schools of economic thought affected the character of the various Five Year Plans and their implementation, as was reported earlier in this study (chapters 3 and 4). When the DNU was strong, as after the riot, the documents and planning strategy bore their stamp. Redistribution took precedence over growth although the latter was an indispensable part of its strategy.[5] The Second Malaysia Plan and its Mid-Term Review marked the high point of their influence. When the EPU regained the initiative with the eclipse of the DNU, the Plans and their implementation bore their hallmark. The NEP, as conceived by the DNU strategists, at times regained some lost ground but in neither form nor substance did the NEP become quite what had originally been intended. Moreover, the NEP strategy itself lost its way by substituting means for ends. For example, the 30 per cent share target for Bumiputra ownership was intended to achieve better distribution of assets and income, primarily as a means to create a Bumiputra commercial and industrial class on par with that of the non-Malays, while instead it was pursued increasingly as a statistical target on its own. Thus, too little attention was paid to the emerging inequality among the Malays.

The NEP increasingly became equated with UMNO and therefore the economic and political fate of the Malays. As a result, no politician of whatever personal power or race could hope to continue to stay in power, or for that matter no technocrat could hold on to his job, if he was seen openly attempting to dismantle the NEP. What opponents could do, however, was to give generous lip service to the objectives of the NEP in principle, but in practice seek to render it ineffective and discredited. This could be done in a variety of ways, such as holding back on necessary budgetary allocations, neglecting the auditing of the NEP by statistical monitoring which could have allowed timely corrective measures, over-emphasising its actual or asserted flaws and defects, and of course highlighting and stressing the supposed damage that it had done to the Malaysian economy with the passage of time. Outside the government, intellectuals, depending on their political and economic associations, and the mass media, controlled by the non-Malay power elite, mounted their sustained attacks to discredit the NEP in the eyes of the public and the world.

If we relate Malaysian experience to the classification used by Griffin, then the EPU-led strategy would represent a mix of three of his general approaches: *monetarism*, *open economy* and

---

[5]  See for instance Document A included in this book.

*industrialisation*. The first strategy of monetarism is basically laissez-faire, where economic change depends primarily on market efficiency and signals. Here the best, the toughest and the ones with a head start win the race. It is a strategy of the type: "Every man for himself and God for us all" as practised most clearly in Hong Kong. The second strategy of the open economy shares some features of monetarism, but with emphasis on the foreign trade sector: foreign trade supplemented by local and foreign private direct investment is seen as the leading engine of growth. The emphasis of the third strategy, that of industrialisation, is on rapid growth through rapid expansion of the manufacturing sector. While allowing for government intervention, this would be directed specifically to increasing production. In its pure form, this approach has no activist concern for re-distribution of wealth and income in favour of the low-income groups, quite the contrary, market forces would work so as to shift wealth and income toward groups with high marginal propensities to save. However, so the theory asserts, the poor would eventually benefit from this process when the fruits of growth would spread to them via the "trickle down" effect.

The NEP strategy, on the other hand, would fall squarely into the classification of a *redistributive strategy* with heavy doses also of the *open economy* and the *industrialisation* strategies. The NEP strategy is openly interventionist. Among others, it relies on the proper placing of various strategic institutions in the system to achieve an equilibrating effect. Indeed the NEP is one of the pioneers of the redistributive strategy itself, as currently being expounded by international development agencies, such as the World Bank, and as being practised in many countries of the Third World. As Snodgrass says (*op. cit.*, p. 286):

> Whatever happens, Malaysia and its New Economic Policy can certainly be seen as an example of the 'new meaning of development' — stressing greater national self-reliance and cultural awareness as well as redistribution of income, wealth and power — which is now beginning to gain international recognition...

Inevitably, the political parties in Malaysia have their own views about the appropriate development path to follow and we turn now to considering the stances of the protagonists in the major party affiliations.

## The Chinese Position

The general thrust of the Chinese attitude towards the NEP, as represented by their political parties, the DAP, MCA and Gerakan is quite clear cut. Despite variations in details, they support the poverty eradication objective of the NEP, as this also benefits the Chinese poor both in the urban and rural areas, particularly those living in the New Villages where the hard-core Chinese poverty is to be found. But the majority of them would like to dismantle the NEP restructuring objective. It is perceived to be discriminatory and unfair. Its implementation according to them is at their expense and therefore it is a burden on the Malaysian Chinese. It erodes their economic strength and threatens their livelihood and the very future of the Chinese community. It stifles their initiative and drive and therefore acts as a disincentive to Chinese private investment and therefore for growth of the economy as a whole in the long run. For all these reasons, the Chinese community strives for what they see as justice, equality and meritocracy; they urge an end to discrimination and Malay preferences, and demand that the government opens up all sectors of the economy, including the manning of the civil service, the armed forces, the police, etc. to reflect the multiracial composition of the population. Dato Kok Wee Kiat, the Vice President of the MCA and Deputy Minister of Trade and Industry, UMNO's partner in the ruling Alliance Government, perhaps summarised the mildest of their views when he said,

> The NEP came into being in 1970 with the tacit consent of all races. The consent was expressedly for 20 years. That 20 year period expires in 1990. When it expires in 1990, let it forever lie in peace. When it lies in peace, with it goes a terrible spectre of racial polarization. With it will be buried the "they" and "we" approach in our Malaysian way of life. Let Malaysians start all over again on the basis of unity, harmony and comradeship that gave us Merdeka in 1957.[6]

There are many strands of arguments put forward by the Chinese community against the NEP, ranging from those advanced by their political parties to the writings of their intellectuals and journalists, and to the complaints of the hawkers and taxi drivers, residents of New Villages etc.

The pattern of attack appears to be that the DAP acts as the shock troops and is the first to lead in the assault. Its supporters criticise

---

[6]   Dato Kok Wee Kiat, "Facing the Future", in *The Future of Malaysian Chinese*, Kuala Lumpur: Malaysian Chinese Association, 1988, p. 19.

government policies bitterly, ranging from abuses of human rights, corruption and the NEP, to discrimination against Chinese schools, language and culture. The DAP then makes alternative proposals, which would be quite impossible for the government to meet given the circumstances. The DAP then drops the issues or puts them on the back burner, and moves on to new and emerging issues. A number of years later, after the same issues have been softened up, the MCA returns to them and makes similar demands. By this time the issues can be raised with greater respectability and without the fear of being labelled a "Chinese Chauvinist". They will now be more acceptable to UMNO which may go to some lengths to meet them as the demands are now made by its main partner in the government. The same tactics, it seems, have been used with variations by the Gerakan, using a soft pedal and an approach aimed more at persuasion. In the following we consider only the main stance of the DAP, MCA and the Gerakan and their supporters.

## DAP (Democratic Action Party)

The DAP is the main Chinese opposition party in Parliament and State Assemblies. Milne and Mauzy describe the Party's aim contained in its manifesto (set out in its Setapak Declaration of 29th July 1967) as that of establishing a non-racial democratic society. As such it supported racial equality and the concept of "Malaysian Malaysia" while being prepared to make some concessions in accepting Malay as the National Language and giving some special rights to help rural Malays, rather than a Malay capitalist class, as might befit a party with its main support from urban working class Chinese.[7]

The Secretary General of the DAP, Lim Kit Siang has thrown further light on the objectives of the Party:[8]

> As democratic socialists, we are dedicated to the abolition of poverty and economic backwardness regardless of race. We want to create a classless community of Malaysians based on fellowship, co-operation and service, where there is no exploitation of man by man, class by class or race by race.

---

[7] Milne and Mauzy, *op.cit.*, p. 152.
[8] Lim Kit Siang, *Time Bombs in Malaysia*, second edition, Kuala Lumpur: Democratic Action Party, 1978, pp. 216-217.

We support any measure which will help better the lot of the Malay poor. But we are strongly opposed to the use of Malay special rights to enrich the new Malay rich to make them richer, while the mass of peasantry and poor are as exploited as ever.

There is gross social injustice and grave unequal distribution of wealth and income in Malaysia. Over the years, the feudal-compradore and tycoon class have become richer and richer, while the mass of peasantry and workers become more and more downtrodden.

The problem in Malaysia is complicated by an ostensible double coincidence. Firstly, the class divisions in our country appear very often to coincide with communal divisions, secondly, the disparity in incomes and productivity between urban and rural areas appear also to coincide along racial lines as towns are predominantly non-Malay while the mass of Malays live in rural areas.

The only effective way to uplift the living standards of the have-nots of all races is to execute meaningful socialist policies, untinged by racialism, as in carrying out radical land reforms, beginning with the abolition of absentee landlordism in the padi sector and distribution of land to the tenant farmers, the creation of a comprehensive and efficient rural credit, co-operative and marketing infrastructure to free the peasants from the triple curses of fragmentation, landlordism and credit indebtedness; greater diversification of agriculture and the economy; a modern and science-oriented education system to bring the peasants abreast with the techniques and know-how of twentieth-century era; and a greater rate of industrialisation.

Every Malaysian will support special rights to help the poor Malays, just as every citizen will support any special assistance to non-Malay poor, on the basis of need and not on the basis of colour or race.

Mr. Lim Kit Siang repeatedly maintains that the DAP accepts the objectives of the NEP, but with qualifications. In a speech in Parliament he said:

The DAP, and the large number of Malaysians who support the DAP, agree with the New Economic Policy objectives of achieving national unity through the two pronged process of eliminating poverty regardless of race, and the restructuring of the Malaysian society to eliminate the identification of race with occupation, vocation and location. We also accept the NEP pledge that in its implementation, 'no particular group experiences any loss or feels any sense of deprivation of its rights, privileges, income, job, or opportunity'. When the Second Malaysia Plan was debated in Parliament over 10 years ago, I said on behalf of the DAP in this House on July 14, 1971 that the DAP supported both prongs of the NEP .... What we do not support, however, is any attempt at selective restructuring, or the repudiation of the NEP pledge that there would be no discrimination against any racial group. A review of the NEP however shows that there had been selective restructuring....[9]

Since the launching of the NEP, the DAP has mounted a sustained attack on most, if not all, facets of the policy. A sample of these criticisms can be gauged from the following quotations taken from some of Mr. Lim's numerous speeches over the years. On the overall effect of the NEP. On national unity and the restructuring objectives he writes:

If national unity is to remain the overriding objective of the NEP, then I call on the Government to demonstrate by action to establish beyond doubt in any quarter, whether among Malays or non-Malays, that restructuring is a process of Malaysianisation of all sectors of Malaysian life, and not Malayisation![10]

It is also essential, if the Government is to regain the people's confidence, that the restructuring prong of the NEP is not meant for one race only, that it should progressively restructure all areas of national life, where there is pronounced identification of race with economic function, in particular the government services, armed forces and police.[11]

He also maintains that it is not true that the Chinese wealthy are the ones exploiting the poor Malays, since (at least in 1969) the economy was dominated by the foreigners.

It is thus clear that there is in fact a great economic imbalance between Malaysians and foreigners in the ownership and control of wealth in the modern sector of Malaysian economy. When the Government talks about Malay economic imbalance, it is always compared to the non-Malays. I would want to know why the Government had never compared this to the foreign ownership and control of wealth which is more significant.

A continuous harping on the theme of Malay/non-Malay economic imbalance, when in fact the majority of the Malays and non-Malays are poor, and the concentration of ownership and control of wealth in the

---

[9] Op.cit., pp. 162-163.
[10] Lim Kit Siang, Malaysia in the Dangerous 80s, Kuala Lumpur: Democratic Action Party, 1982, p. 68.
[11] Lim Kit Siang (1978), op.cit., p. 153.

modern economic sectors are in the hands of the foreigners cannot do the country and the goal of national unity any good.[12]

The recent Third Bumiputra Economic Congress, with its demand that the 30 per cent Bumiputra participation in commerce and industry should be raised to 51 per cent displaying an utter disregard to the sensitivities and legitimate aspirations of other races, must have by itself undone ten years of nationbuilding efforts by the schools — even among the school children themselves.[13]

The DAP is not opposed to Malay corporate ownership. What we in the DAP oppose is the Malay corporate ownership to exploit and to rob the Malay masses, the poor peasantry and the fishermen of their rights.[14]

On unemployment, Mr. Lim expresses the view of DAP in these general terms:

Finally, on the question of unemployment, the continued high rate of unemployment at 10 per cent is indefensible from the point of view of income distribution. For this would mean that this 10 per cent of the labour force have a zero share in the national income. As the Government planners themselves are incapable of creating full employment and give jobs to every Malaysian, then the Malaysian Government must take responsibility to assist and subsidise their livelihood from an unemployment fund. In a modern society, every man and woman must have a constitutional right to work. If he is denied that right through no fault of his own but because of the inadequacies of the national economic planners, then every such person must have the constitutional right to be looked after by the State. This is why an adequate rate of job creation must be one of the main objectives of our economic policy as unemployment is not only the principal immediate cause of poverty but also of social alienation.[15]

The list can go on to other sectors such as education, Chinese culture, language, etc.

According to the DAP, the major counter productive results of the NEP, in particular its restructuring objectives, have been, first, that Malaysia's economic growth has suffered and therefore the country has lagged far behind the other Asian NIEs, although Malaysia started off second only to Japan. This, DAP maintains,

[12] Lim Kit Siang (1978), *op.cit.*, p. 55-56. Note that in 1969 the Chinese owned 22.8 per cent, the Malays 1.5 per cent and foreigners 62.1 per cent.
[13] Lim Kit Siang (1982), *op.cit.*, p. 382.
[14] Lim Kit Siang (1978), *op.cit.*, p. 139.
[15] Lim Kit Siang (1978), *op.cit.*, p. 112.

shows the very high cost of NEP and reflects the many drags on the economy, such as the flight of capital, misallocation of resources, inefficiencies, etc. Second, the DAP contends that the NEP has created a Malay elite which is growing fat without having to work hard, preferring to earn through patronage. To use the DAP label, they are the UMNO-PUTRAS:

> The NEP has created multiple divisions in the Malaysian society. It has created disunity among the Malays because of the unequal distribution of wealth and income among the Malays. The NEP has created a small class of Malays with wealth, power and status. The majority of Malays in both the rural and urban areas are deprived and remain disadvantaged.[16]

To avoid these ills in the future, Mr. Lim demands *inter alia* that the ICA (Industrial Coordination Act) be abandoned:

> Firstly, (the Government) must repeal the Industrial Co-ordination Act, which typically represents what is wrong with the New Economic Policy implementation in eroding and removing legal protection for local investors, especially non-Malay investors, and the introduction and substitution of the concept of bureaucratic discretion in approving plans, licenses and applications. Vague terms of "national interest" can, from past experience, cover a multitude of sins.

> The repeal of the Industrial Co-ordination Act is therefore a prerequisite to regain confidence of Malaysians in the security of their investments in their own country![17]

Mr Lim is concerned that restructuring should not be seen as a programme benefitting one race only. In particular areas he argues that the resettlement programmes of FELDA should not be confined to Malays and that in order to avoid the identification of race with function, the armed forces should be restructured. He is strongly opposed to restructuring and criticises the award of scholarships and study awards to well-to-do Bumiputra families and the issue of taxi licences to Malays with connections and to defeated alliance candidates, who rent out their licences to genuine taxi operators in a form of parasitic exploitation. In the same vein, he is opposed to the allocation of land, timber and mining concesions to the rich and well connected with no benefit to genuinely poor Malays.[18]

---

[16] *The Rocket*, vol. 22 (1989), issue 5.
[17] Lim Kit Siang (1978), *op.cit.*, p. 168.
[18] Lim Kit Siang (1978), *op.cit.*, pp. 95-97.

As the above survey shows, over the years the DAP mobilised its efforts to attack and oppose every facet of the NEP and other policies of the government, ranging from alleged human rights abuses, through language policy, education policy, employment policy, housing and hawker problems, to under-representation of the Chinese as FELDA settlers etc. For good measure, DAP labelled the MCA as the "running dog" of UMNO. On numerous occasions DAP stormed out of Parliament and state legislatures in protests against the government. Parliamentary and Assembly speakers on many occasions had to order them out forcibly for behaviour and language unbecoming of legislators. DAP tactics in fact were disruptive and appeared to be designed to raise political temperature rather than to find common ground of goodwill and cooperation among the groups. The dangers of extreme actions by the Chinese if they come to feel that "they have their backs to the sea" are referred to by Mauzy.[19]

Cooperation between DAP and other interests is dificult. While the DAP joined the NECC, when it was established in early 1989, it subsequently withdrew, leaving it free to pursue its own National Development Policy (NDP) described below:

The New Economic Policy, with its accent on ethnic quotas and percentages, had worsened ethnic polarisation rather than contributed to national unity, retarded economic growth and aggravated social and economic inequities. A new approach is needed in the 1990s which can ensure that the national economic policy will further the most important objective of national unity. Such a policy should comprise the following ingredients:

-    Recognising that the majority of the Malays, Kadazans, Ibans, Muruts, Bidahyuhs and others are poor and from the lower income levels, they must be assured of getting even greater economic justice than under the NEP in the past two decades. Emphasis must be given to the underlying causes of poverty, like uneconomic holdings, inadequate credit facilities, a distorted marketing network, underemployment for the rural poor, and low incomes and poor housing for the urban poor. At the same time, the non-Malay poor would be given full assistance in the programme to eradicate poverty, raise incomes and living standards of the poor.
-    Reduction in the gross disparity in the distribution of wealth and income between Malaysians, rich or poor.
-    Reduction of ethnic differences among Malaysians, by emphasising and highlighting their common Malaysian nationality in all fields of national endeavour, whether political, economic, educational, social

[19] Mauzy, Daiane K., *Barisan Nasional — Coalition Government in Malaysia*, Kuala Lumpur: Maricans Academic Series, 1983, p. 148.

or cultural, so that Malaysians can fully inherit the wealth and strength to be found in our unique diversity.

- Recruitment into colleges and universities based on a mixed consideration of merit and equity, where socio-economic factors are given important account.
- The mobilisation and utilisation to the fullest of the human, natural and capital resources of the country for the development of the country.
- Elimination of Money Politics, Corruption, State Parasitism and all practices which retard economic efficiency, productivity and growth.
- Fostering and maintaining a democratic political system with full respect to the human rights of life, liberty and dignity.
- A common vision of all Malaysians in the year 2000 and the 21st Century so that they could work in unison towards this common destiny although they do not have a common past.

What the country needs, therefore, is a new policy to replace the New Economic Policy in 1990, which could be called the National Development Policy (NDP), which promotes national unity, economic growth and social equity. Instead of ethnic quotas and percentages and ethnic perspectives, they should be replaced by the Malaysian perspective and the principles of social equity and meritocracy.[20]

## MCA (Malaysian Chinese Association)

Since Merdeka the MCA has been UMNO's ally and partner in the Federal and State governments down to the districts and mukims (villages). Indeed the MCA was the political party which gained major concessions for the Malaysian Chinese, notably in terms of Federal citizenship, from UMNO during the Merdeka Round Table Conference. In exchange, the Malay position in the country was guaranteed by several special provisions in the Constitution. The "bargain" or the "social contract" of 1957 is now being disputed by the post Merdeka generations of Chinese. As far as they are concerned, they are Malaysians, born in Malaysia and as such entitled to the full rights and privileges of a national citizen. Some of them have never heard of article 153 of the Constitution, and even if they have, feel that it has nothing to do with them. This, they feel, is history of doubtful certainty. They cannot be held responsible for what their forefathers did or were presumed to have done. They should not be treated as step-sons in their country of

---

[20] *The Rocket*, vol. 22 (1989), issue 5.

birth. The Malays on the other hand say the social contract is sacrosanct and was given in exchange for the tangible concessions they made at Merdeka. According to them, the Chinese and the other non-Malays have not delivered on their promises, or at least in concrete tangible results the *quid pro quo* has not yet manifested itself. Indeed the opposite is true: instead of getting help they have been getting resentment of various degrees from the Chinese and other non-Malay communities at the government's efforts to strengthen them. However, as far as the Malays are concerned, the give and take attitude of the founding fathers at Merdeka seems to have been fair all round. The Chinese and the other non-Malays got what they wanted, and the Malays thought they got what they wanted. In any case the exchange was better than the provisions which were forced upon them by the hated MacMichael Treaty to set up the Malayan Union.

To sustain its legitimacy the MCA is placed in the difficult situation of having to play a delicate and balancing dual role. It has to please both its allies in the government, particularly UMNO, and at the same time its Chinese political base, whose basic positions seem to be at opposite ends of the spectrum. So it has to take on the role of a government and an opposition party combined into one. On the one hand, it is a member of the government and the cabinet, and an influential one at that, judging by the number of important portfolios and cabinet positions held by the MCA since Merdeka. They were therefore responsible with UMNO and MIC for the formulation and implementation of all the Five Year Plans of the government including the NEP. On the other hand they had to be seen to protect and advance the interests of the Chinese community to ensure that the future of the party would be guaranteed. Given the constant assaults, snipings and political pressures mounted at every opportunity by the DAP and the other more explicit Chinese interests standing in the wing against them, accusing them of giving away Chinese rights and interests and making them subservient to the interests of the Malays, the MCA has had to engage in serious competitive bidding for Chinese votes to stay in business. This was done by appearing to be the party that best champions Chinese rights and interests, in most cases beyond the bounds of the NEP. Sometimes the MCA has overplayed this role by taking on a stance more extreme than that of the DAP or that of the Gerakan. In its capacity as an opposition, the MCA has on occasion turned around and attacked some of the major decisions of the Alliance government and the cabinet, even though it has remained an important member of that government.

By openly mobilising efforts to criticise coalition policies, the MCA is acting, to say the least, in a manner that is shortsighted, inconsistent and even irresponsible. Disagreements should be ironed out in Cabinet before being presented to Parliament for approval and implementation. After that, the main task is to implement the agreed policy, to monitor it, and to make adjustments jointly if necessary. In the case of the NEP, even though the MCA had given its approval in the cabinet and Parliament jointly with its allies UMNO and the MIC, it sometimes reverted to attacking it. Over the years it mobilised efforts, including intellectual resources, to point out the flaws of the NEP, and campaigned for the early abolition of it. The combined government and opposition role played by the MCA has caused a number of crises in its relations with UMNO and raised the political temperature of the country on numerous occasions.

The demands which the MCA make on behalf of the Chinese community cover every aspect of society: politics, language, education, culture, civil service, the armed forces, land settlements, economics, etc. Politically they have aspired to reserve the right of MCA to fill the post of Finance Minister and they complain that in fact only the President of UMNO can be Prime Minister. In education they feel that Chinese schools have been neglected and that the Chinese are underrepresented in various institutions of learning. They complain of suppression of Chinese culture, and are disinclined to compromise on the use of the Chinese language. They protest about discrimination in employment in the civil service, the armed forces and in new land settlements and generally oppose the NEP, apart from its poverty provisions.

On the economic front, which particularly concerns us here, the demands of the MCA amount to scrapping the NEP with the exception of its poverty eradication objective, and replacing it by what is termed a Malaysian National Unity Perspective Plan. In the words of Dato Sri Dr. Ling, this plan would represent the MCA vision of the future.[21] The MCA think-tank would undertake to prepare such a plan for consideration and adoption as the country's post 1990 economic strategy and policy.[22]

Many reasons for replacing the NEP after 1990 have been put forward by the MCA and its intellectuals:

[21] See *Bernama News*, 31 July 1989.
[22] The intention seems to be to prepare a plan which basically would be a derivative of the associated Chinese Chamber of Commerce and Industry of Malaysia's plan, put forward in 1980, entitled "Towards faster growth and greater national unity".

*First*, the NEP is criticised as being anti-growth; it imposes too many constraints and burdens, including onerous rules and regulations which discourage Chinese private investments. The emphasis is on growth:

> Our first priority in these recessionary times should be a national growth programme to at least give us something to redistribute, and that we can no longer afford politically-motivated decisions that are economically unsound.[23] The *sine qua non* of restructuring is economic growth.[24]

*Second*, as formulated by Dato Kok Wee Kiat, the restructuring objective is objectionable, requiring sacrifices by non-Malays, including erosion of their cultural identity with the inevitable result being racial violence and loss of racial unity[25] In a paper appropriately called the "Erosion of the Chinese Economic Position" Dr. Lim Lin Lean develops this theme:

> It is, however the restructuring prong of the NEP that represents the primary cause of Chinese economic problems and insecurities....The interpretation of these targets and the implementation of the policy have, however, been subject to various abuses, deviations and acts of discrimination, such as to fuel the fears of the Chinese that the NEP is intended to bring about Malay dominance of the economy....Without corresponding attention to moving non-Malays into the sectors where they are currently under-represented, the identification of race with economic function will never be eliminated .... The costs of the NEP to the Chinese community have been high, if not punitive.[26]

*Third*, the structure of employment does not reflect the character of the Malaysian population, according to Dato Kok Wee Kiat:

> the non-Malays would expect and are entitled to employment opportunities equivalent to their share of the country's racial composition in the public sector, state administrations, non-financial public enterprises (NFPEs), armed forces, the utilities sector and other major areas of Malaysian economic and social life where they are severely under-represented.

---

[23] Dr. Lim Lin Lean, "The Erosion of the Chinese Economic Position", in *The Future of Malaysian Chinese*, Kuala Lumpur: Malaysian Chinese Association, 1988, p. 55.
[24] Chua Jui Meng, "The Malaysian Chinese - The Way Ahead", in *The Future of Malaysian Chinese*, Kuala Lumpur: Malaysian Chinese Association, 1988, p. 90.
[25] Dato Kok Wee Kiat, "Facing the Future", in *The Future of Malaysian Chinese*, *op.cit.*, p. 14.
[26] Dr. Lim Lin Lean, *op.cit.*, pp. 43-45, 53.

Similarly they would expect opportunities for management and control in all fields of the public sector in the same way that the Malays expect management and control opportunities in the corporate private sector. The non-Malays would also expect greater opportunities for them to participate in agricultural land ownership and in federal and state rurally oriented development schemes (including FELDA, FELCRA, RISDA, IADP projects, Regional development projects and so on)...[27]

*Fourth*, according to Mr. David Chua, the NEP threatens national unity because of serious defects in its implementation and the effects of restructuring in the field of education and culture.[28] This view is further reinforced by Dr. Ting Chew Peh. According to him there are three main causes of frictions in the society which militates against national unity:

First, the dissatisfaction of the non-Malay communities toward some government policies — the NEP, Education Policy and Cultural Policy....Second, there has been too much emphasis (in practice especially) on racial and ethnic differences in the allocation of opportunities — economic, educational and political....It is a negative factor in fostering "we-feeling" and national unity. Third, the attitudes of some groups who are still reluctant to accept the multi-ethnic nature of our society.[29]

*Fifth*, the statistics produced by the EPU on the implementation of the NEP, as shown in the Five Year Plan documents, are alleged to have been doctored to show that the Malays have underachieved their targets contrary to the actual situation on the ground.[30]

*Finally*, while growth first and distribution later is a main theme of all the proposals for the post-1990 economic strategy, as viewed from the Chinese point of view, Professor Fong stresses that policies must also be designed for the disadvantaged:

In our desire for rapid economic growth, there must be social justice and equitable distribution of the benefits of economic development to achieve national unity. To achieve this objective, it is proposed that affirmative strategies be implemented to help the disadvantaged groups — in

[27] Dato Kok Wee Kiat, *op.cit.*, pp. 16-17.
[28] David Chua, "The Chinese Education and Cultural Vision", in *The Future of Malaysian Chinese*, *op.cit.*, p. 65.
[29] Dr. Ting Chew Peh, "The Problem of National Unity", in *The Future of Malaysian Chinese*, *op.cit.*, p. 131.
[30] As reported by Rose Ismail, "Much Ado Over Statistics", *New Straits Times*, 6 August 1989.

particular the poor — so that in the process of economic growth, every group, whether by race or by social class, will achieve an equitable share of the benefits. The reward mechanism should be used in place of the forced restructuring strategy that has been adopted in the past.[31]

Dr. Lim takes up the same theme by stressing economic need and poverty rather than ethnicity as the overriding need.[32] Chua Jui Meng is less uncompromising, advocating the adoption of targets for non-Malay participation in specific sectors of the economy ranging from agriculture to services.[33]

## GERAKAN

The Gerakan's position with respect to the NEP is similar to that of the MCA. Its ideological orientation announced on the 15th April 1968, was described by Milne and Mauzy as comprising socialism and democracy with some recognition of the special rights of the Malays. Gerakan's first president was Professor Sayed Hussain Alatas, the current Vice-Chancellor of the University of Malaya, who apparently now is a strong UMNO supporter. On his departure, Dr. Lim Chong Eu took over and currently its leadership is in the hands of Dr. Lim Keng Yaik, who is also a Federal cabinet member. The Far Eastern Economic Review of 18th April 1985, reviewed Gerakan's view of the NEP as published in 1984 in the book *Strategies for Tomorrow — The National Economic Policy — 1990 and Beyond*. The Review states in part:

> This book echoes the concerns of many non-Malays regarding current policies and future plans. The articles, especially those which refer to the government's economic restructuring policies, leave the reader in no doubt that the party has serious reservations about the thrust of current government efforts. One of the most interesting features of the book is Gerakan's contention that the official figures on the racial distribution of corporate share ownership are inaccurate.

> The government is berated for its allegedly one-sided efforts to eliminate racial differences in income levels. Current programmes aimed at helping Bumiputras participate more fully in the manufacturing, construction,

---

[31] Professor Fong Chan Onn, "Economic Strategy for the Nation Towards and Beyond 1990", in *The Future of Malaysian Chinese*, *op.cit.*, p. 127.
[32] Dr. Lim Lin Lean, *op.cit.*, p. 55.
[33] Chua Jui Meng, "The Malaysian Chinese — The Way Ahead", in *The Future of Malaysian Chinese*, *op.cit.*, pp. 96-97.

banking, wholesale and retail trade, the book argues, have not been matched by corresponding efforts to assist Chinese and Indians in moving to other areas of the economy where they are under-represented, such as in agriculture and the civil service.

The book also includes a policy statement by Gerakan president Datuk Lim Keng Yaik in which he asserts that the NEP has not brought the country any closer to national unity. If anything, he said, ethnic polarisation has intensified with Malaysians becoming even more mindful of their respective ethnic backgrounds because of the official distinction made between Bumiputras and non-Bumiputras. As for policy to be pursued after 1990, when the economic restructuring targets of the NEP are scheduled to be achieved, Gerakan proposes that the NEP should be replaced by a National Economic Policy which emphasises redistribution of wealth to the poor, regardless of race.[34]

Like the MCA, Dr. Lim on behalf of Gerakan, asked the government to set up a body in the form of a National Consultative Council to evaluate the NEP. On the basis of this evaluation, "a new development strategy should be formulated for the next few decades".[35] He reiterated the Gerakan call for a National Economic Policy:

> under which there should be a shift in emphasis from restructuring of society to poverty eradication irrespective of race — after the NEP deadline expires in 1990. The Gerakan is of the firm view that the restructuring carried out since 1970 has been highly successful in that a class of Malay rich and a huge Malay middle class have been successfully bred via the NEP .... And in poverty eradication, need should take precedence over race for poverty knows no racial barrier. When poverty, irrespective of race, is eradicated then the foundation of national unity — which is the long term aspiration of the NEP — will be firmly laid.[36]

At the opening of the Gerakan's National Economic Seminar 1989 Dr. Lim gave his view in greater detail of what the elements of the post-1990 policy should be, stressing balanced growth, social justice and equitable distribution unrelated to race or religion with emphasis on poverty. Describing the Gerakan's three objectives as a policy

---

[34] Gerakan Rakyat Malaysia, *The National Economic Policy — 1990 and Beyond*, as reviewed by Bruce Gale in the *Far Eastern Economic Review*, 18 April 1985.
[35] *New Straits Times*, 7 June 1987.
[36] *The Star*, 7 June 1987.

of nation building for all Malaysians, Dr. Lim said the emphasis of the post 1990 policy should be on economic growth:[37]

> As we live in an increasingly competitive world, we must emphasis meritocracy, productivity and creativity. And this is only possible in a more liberal, deregulated and competitive environment where genuine entrepreneurship can flourish.

> Many among the poor Malays have not enjoyed much of the fruits of almost two decades of social engineering. On the other hand, the non-Bumiputras as a whole perceive they have lost out as a result of the NEP which is seen to have benefited a great many of the Bumiputras, especially the middle and upper strata of their community. Worse still, the non-Bumiputras see the gains by the Bumiputras as being obtained at their expense.

There is no doubt that despite variations in details, the trend of the proposals of the Gerakan is not dissimilar to that of the MCA.


## The Indian Position

### MIC (Malayan Indian Congress)

Historically the MIC was one of the constituent parties which fought for MERDEKA with the MCA and UMNO. It sought for the Indian community the same concessions and privileges as did the Chinese community, joining the "Social Contract of 1957". As a party it has taken what appears to be a more accomodating stance both on those provisions of the Constitution which together form the "Special rights of the Malays" and on the NEP. The official line taken by the MIC was reflected in its strength in the Alliance. For example, on the national language, the president of the MIC, Datuk Samy Vellu said at a MIC Youth Assembly:

> Bahasa Malaysia is our language. The Malays cannot claim it is theirs alone. Bahasa Malaysia does not belong to the Malays alone but to all of us and we are as jealous of protecting and encouraging its growth as anybody else. The MIC had frequently urged the Government to extend the teaching time of Bahasa Malaysia in Tamil Schools. After all these years it would be stupid for any one to question our commitment to

---

[37] *New Straits Times*, 3 April 1989.

Bahasa Malaysia or our loyalty to this country and expect us to undergo tests of fire to prove it.[38]

Increasingly, however, MIC has exerted strong pressure on the government for a greater share of the national cake for the Indian community. In response to a statement by Dato Musa Hitam, the then Deputy Prime Minister, that the government was considering fresh strategies to eradicate poverty and restructure society after the NEP period expires in 1990, Datuk Samy Vellu welcomed the new thinking. On behalf of the MIC he suggested six requirements for incorporation into the new strategy:

that it ensures larger goals of income growth, equity and employment;

ensures the economic development results in a massive spin-off and diffusion of benefits to all sections of the population;

that the benefits of advances in technology would be diffused to a larger section and proportion of the society;

ensures that industrialisation and economic development do not widen existing disparities in Malaysian society;

improves the learning capacity of all sections of society so that none are left behind; and

upgrades the human productivity of all communities so that every one can play a role in helping to improve the production base of the country.[39]

The MIC general assembly of 1986 focused on the NEP and passed no less than 13 resolutions regarding housing, citizenship etc. The Youth Section asked that the Barisan National set up a body to monitor the progress and implementation of the NEP. Malaysian Indians, according to the Deputy Vice President Datuk S. Subramaniam, have a rightful share of 10 per cent in the corporate and employment sector. He admitted, moreover, that much progress had been made already in certain other sectors, especially education:

The quota of Indian students in universities which at one time was between three and four per cent has been increased to nine per cent

---

[38] *The Star*, 24 August 1987.
[39] *New Straits Times*, 21 August 1985.

through representations made by the MIC. Although we have not reached the 10 per cent target, we are still working on it.[40]

In 1988 the Youth Section asked that the Indian community be defined as a deprived group so that it could benefit from all the programmes designed to eradicate poverty and restructure society.[41] Datuk Samy also has complained that the Indians in Kelantan have not been fairly treated on matters that concern their welfare, and the allegation has been made that the civil service has been practising discrimination against Indians in its recruiting and promotion procedure. On the whole, however, the attitude of the MIC towards the NEP has not been as hostile as that for example of the DAP or even the MCA. On the contrary, it has been positive. Dato Pathmanaban, who was involved in the NEP formulation and is now an Assistant Minister, summed it up on behalf of the party when he said: "It's still one of the finest strategies."[42] In this he was supported by Datuk Samy Vellu when he said simply: "Keep the NEP."[43]

## Views of Individuals

It is, however, something else with the intellectuals, professionals, academics and journalists within the Indian community, who carry influence locally and internationally far beyond their numbers. For example one of the vice presidents of the Gerakan is a former leading member of the PAP (People's Action Party) of Singapore. Some leading members of the trade union movement in Malaysia, like V. David, P. Patto and Karpal Singh etc. are key committee members of the DAP. The views of DAP towards the NEP have been reviewed above. From the university, the views of Mavis Puthucheary, K.S. Jomo and others, while not formally Indian views, reflect the concerns in the Indian community. Professor Jomo in his several publications expressed several doubts on the concept and the implementation of the NEP. In Penang, Dr. Chandra Muzafar through his publications in the *Aliran Monthly* champions the ideals of "Justice, Freedom and Solidarity". He has also proposed an

[40] *New Straits Times*, 7 January 1987.
[41] *New Straits Times*, 27 June 1988.
[42] *The Star*, 4 October 1986.
[43] *New Straits Times*, 17 March 1989.

alternative to the NEP.[44] With the Rukunegara as the basic foundation, the guiding principles of the Aliran post-1990 policy proposal are:

> In the nineties and beyond, we should go back to the Rukunegara's concept of a just society. This concept would express itself through various principles. More specifically we should try to:
> 1. Ensure that the basic needs of each and every Malaysian is met. This would include needs, such as food, clothing, shelter, employment, income, education, health etc.
> 2. Ensure that each and every Malaysian has access to basic amenities of life such as piped water, electricity, modern sanitation, etc.
> 3. Reduce vast disparities in wealth within sectors and communities and between sectors and communities
> 4. Eliminate the exploitation of the labour and skills of the weak by the strong in every sector of the economy.
> 5. Ensure that there is multi-ethnic participation at all levels and within each major sector and sub-sector of the economy. The eventual aim should be to achieve a pattern of participation which reflects the ethnic composition of the country. However, this has to be done gradually and without causing any disruption to ethnic relations.
> 6. Evolve any economic system which balances agrarian development, emphasising food production, with industrial development. The economic system should harness scientific knowledge, and at the same time absorb technology that is appropriate to our needs and aspirations.
> 7. Create a self-reliant economy which has its own autonomous strength, and is not overly dependent upon international economic forces.

From this survey of demands made by the MIC it is clear that the general trend of MIC policies have been generally supportive of the NEP so long as the Indian community also gets its proportionate share of the cake. This is but a just and fair demand. However, on balance it is probably not unfair to conclude that influential members of the Indian elites are *not* favourably disposed towards the NEP. Indeed, the thrust of their various stances are in line with a mixture of the philosophies of the DAP, MCA and the Gerakan.

The Indian community is therefore ambivalent in their views towards the NEP. On the one hand, as a political body, they are generally in favour of the continuation of the NEP but with modifications. On the other hand, influential individuals in the professions and in the universities continue to campaign against and

---

[44] "An Alternative to the NEP", *Aliran Monthly*, vol. 9, 1989, no. 5.

deride the NEP as at best an ill-thought out policy. Although numerically fewer than the Chinese, in terms of influence they have been very successful in their campaigns against the NEP.

## The Malay Position

With the exception of some minority views, such as those of PAS/ABIM and the Malay liberals, the Malays in general openly or implicitly are in favour of the NEP. On the whole the NEP is seen to benefit them, even at the expense of the non-Malays. NEP is, however, subjected to varying interpretations, definitions and intentions. The response by the Malays to the major issues raised by the DAP, MCA, Gerakan and MIC, has also been uneven, and certainly not as articulate as the views of the non-Malays.

The generally favourable attitude of the Malays towards the NEP, however interpreted, stems from two premises. First, the NEP has brought some actual improvements in their lot compared with the situation in 1969 when the NEP was launched. The standard of living in the country has improved, beyond any doubt even to the remotest village, and Malays have been able to penetrate into some key sectors and positions in the previously exclusive domain of the non-Malay and foreign modern sectors. So while they may bicker and quarrel among themselves over the details and spoils of the NEP, the Malays are generally in favour of the extension of the NEP beyond 1990. However, there is a widespread feeling of complacency prevailing among the Malay community, even though they are in fact doing little more than managing to run fast enough to stay in the same economic place vis-à-vis the non-Malays. This could eventually turn out to be an exercise in self-deception on a grand national scale and thus become the cause of their ultimate undoing.

Second, they are Bumiputra. The views of Tunku Abdul Rahman, the Father of Malaysian independence, are reported in *Bernama* after an interview to the following effect: The former Prime Minister stressed that the Malays were not just the prebumi or indigenous community but undisputedly the people to whom the country belonged. During the struggle for independence, other races had acknowledged the right of the Malays to call the country their country and the Federal Constitution, in its provisions under Articles 3 (Islam), 32 (Rulers), 152 (Malay language) and 153 (Special rights of Malays), had recognised the Malays as the indigenous people of the country. Those who wished to remain in the country had to accept the rights of the Malays or get out, as had happened in the case of Singapore when Lee Kuan Yew had wanted the same rights for all with his slogan Malaysian Malaysia. It was unfortunate that those who had migrated to Malaysia still wanted to regard themselves as citizens of their original country.[45]

The Tunku created Malaysia, such as it is, against all odds, dissensions within the rank and file within the Malay community, and severe opposition from the non-Malays, particularly from the Straits Chinese, who regarded themselves as British subjects. No-one is more concerned than the Tunku about fairness, equality, justice, and the future and prosperity of the country and the welfare of all the Malaysian communities. As leader of the UMNO delegation to the Merdeka talks, he was the one who agreed to the generous granting of citizenship to the immigrants. Indeed, he was accused many a time by the Malays for engaging in discrimination in reverse against his own kind, which contributed to his decision to withdraw after the racial riot of 1969.

## UMNO (United Malays National Organisation)

As far as UMNO is concerned, the NEP is equated with the party. Therefore, abolishing the NEP is equivalent to abolishing UMNO for it is the child of UMNO. Known to many who were involved in the early formulation of the NEP, shortly after May 13, 1969, Tun Razak held a series of meetings with his immediate advisers in Cameron Highlands (and also in Fraser's Hill where the Tun, a keen golfer but with a high handicap, played golf between working sessions with some of the participants) to map out the political and economic strategy for the reconstruction of the country after the riot. The basic strategy of the group rested on establishing a long term political and socio-economic policy for the nation. It was felt to be important to reduce politicking in order to promote racial harmony and to adapt the Westminister model of democracy to fit Malaysia's needs better. There could be no question of allowing the dominance of UMNO to be undermined.[46]

With respect to the political strategy, Tun Razak set about building political alliances with the other political parties out of which were born the expanded Alliance coalition and government. With respect to the socio-economic strategy, the NCC, comprising members from all communities and walks of life, was formed to hammer out a consensus policy for the post-riot era. The NCC reached an

---

[45] *Bernama News*, 6 November 1986.
[46] For details, see Milne and Mauzy, *op. cit.*, p. 177.

agreement which found expression in the NEP, the Rukunegara, and amendments to the Constitution. The overall motive for achieving a national consensus seems to have been the need to concentrate on implementing the Second Malaysia Plan and the NEP:

> when one looks at the coalition the overwhelming motive for it seems to be Tun Razak's goal of achieving a broad national political consensus in order to get fully down to the business of implementing the Second Malaysia Plan and the NEP.[47]

From the time of Tun Razak, successive governments under UMNO leadership have tried to implement the NEP. While in practice there have been deviations from its original objectives, at least in spirit it is there. With different administrations, also different priorities came to the fore. Under Dato Hussain Onn, security preoccupied the government and this concern is reflected in the Five Year Plan documents of his administration. Under Dr. Mahathir, the drive for industrialisation and for the NIE type of industrial structure often overrides other objectives. However, in his speech entitled "Let's be proud of our many successes under the NEP" when launching the NECC, Dr. Mahathir summed up the impact of NEP:

> Many of the economic successes were realised during the NEP period. Some quarters believe that the success would be more significant if there was no NEP. But the fact is that Malaysia has achieved good economic successes compared with other nations which had no elements such as the interfering NEP, as some people describe.[48]

The dominant theme of the Tunku was also very explicitly carried forward by Dato Abdullah Ahmad in a now well-known speech delivered in Singapore. To him the position is very clear:

> The political system of Malay dominance was born out of a sacrosanct social contract which preceded national independence. There have been moves to question, to set aside and violate this contract that have threatened the stability of the system... In the Malaysian political system the Malay position must be preserved and Malay expectation must be met. There is thus no two ways about it: the NEP must continue to sustain Malay dominance in the political system in line with the contract of 1957. Even after 1990, there must be mechanisms of preservation, protection and expansion in an evolving system... UMNO have met their side of the

[47] Mauzy, *op. cit.*, p. 71.
[48] *New Straits Times*, 20 January 1989.

bargain... Did the non-Malay, particularly the Chinese parties (referring to elections shortly held before the speech) in the Barisan National deliver? Not only did they not deliver, they compounded it by making the NEP the scapegoat for their feeble performance... The Malay obsession with political dominance is conditioned in no small measure by what has happened to the Malay minority in Singapore.[49]

The reaction to the speech of Datuk Abdullah drew shrill reactions from the non-Malays, including K. Das who complained angrily of racial threats.[50] In the eyes of K. Das, Datuk Abdullah's speech was a Malay conspiracy directed at the non-Malays. Tan Sri Dr. Tan Chee Khoon referred to shock waves[51] while Dr. Chandra Muzafar found the speech to be wanting in both logic and justice.[52] Dr. Mavis Puthucheary questioned whether there was in fact any such pact as the Social Contract.[53] Mr. Ong Hock Chuan went into detail on the history of the contract from the archives of the MCA[54] and Dr. Goh Cheng Teik, one of the key figures of the Gerakan and a cabinet member, denied the historical existence of such a contract saying that his earlier researches into the Tan Cheng Lock files in the National Archives had revealed no reference to consent by the MCA and the MIC to domination of the political system by the Malays. He claimed that the two parties had agreed to support a special constitutional position for the Malays and the use of Bahasa Melayu as the official language in return for UMNO's agreement on common citizenship. He went on to claim that Tun Razak designed the NEP as a policy instrument to restructure society and not as a weapon to dominate and suppress the non-Malay races. Rather, he claimed, the object had been to give the Malays some preference such as a handicap might provide in a golfing match.[55] The MCA Youth lodged a police report against Datuk Abdullah for the speech. The

---

[49] Datuk Abdullah Ahmad, *Issues in Malaysian Politics*, Speech delivered at the Institute of International Affairs, Singapore, 30 August 1986. The speech is reprinted, along with a number of commentaries and responses, in K. Das, *The Malay Dominance? The Abdullah Rubric*, Kuala Lumpur, 1987.

[50] K. Das, *op.cit.*, pp. 43 and 49.

[51] Tan Sri Dr. Tan Chee Khoon, "The Speech that sent Shock Waves", in K. Das, *op.cit.*, p.79.

[52] Dr. Chandra Muzafar, "Dominant Theory Defies Logic and Denies Justice", in K. Das, *op.cit.*, p.87.

[53] Dr. Mavis Puthucheary, "Was there such a Pact before Independence?" in K. Das, *op.cit.*

[54] Ong Hock Chuan, "The Birth of a Contract", in K. Das, *op.cit.*, p. 103.

[55] Dr. Goh Cheng Teik, "Race Relations and National Unity in Malaysia — A Reply to Datuk Abdullah Ahmad", in K. Das, *op.cit.*, p. 133.

MCA President Datuk Ling Liong Sik described the speech as "seditious, disloyal and treasonable."[56]

UMNO Youth's position towards the NEP is very firm. In February 1989 they held an economic congress (one of the many yearly such affairs held by the movement) to look into various aspects of national development, with emphasis on four main areas: national economic policy after 1990, privatisation, poverty and the development of human resources. Under the banner "Our share must equal our numbers", the resolutions passed include:

the implementation of policies to restructure society and for the distribution of wealth to be based on the population ratio;

the eradication of poverty to be carried out irrespective of race. But it must be reminded that poverty is still a Bumiputra phenomenon both in the rural and urban areas;

the level of economic achievement by Bumiputras to be enhanced;

the formulation of a long term overall systematic strategy for the development of human resources; and,

the Government to continue its active role in fulfilling the objectives of the New Economic Policy. It must therefore review the direction of the economic management of the country.[57]

Datuk Sri Najib Tun Razak declared that, since the Bumiputra make up 57 per cent of the population, "in a just and equitable society, the figure must reflect the division of the population between the Bumiputras and non-Bumiputras".[58] He stressed that from the historical point of view, the Malays had been accommodating and fair to the non-Malays and had made numerous concessions. According to him the redistribution of wealth had not really taken place. He therefore wanted a total approach to the issue, and assured that "UNMO Youth will not allow the Malays to lose their dominance because of their weak economic position".

Dr. Jamaluddin Jarjis, the chairman of the influential Economic Bureau of the wing, rejected the 20 year time constraint of the NEP and its 30 per cent target of corporate restructuring. The rationale

[56] Goh Say Eng and Chan Siew Wah, "MCA Youth Lodges Report on Speech", the *Star*, News Report, reprinted in K. Das, *op.cit.*
[57] *New Straits Times*, 20 February 1989.
[58] *Idem.*

was that the Malays, having been colonised for centuries with devastating effect on them and their economy, would find it impossible to reverse the trend in 20 years. Earlier, in October 1987, when the Chinese questioned certain aspects of Malay rights under the Constitution, UMNO Youth organised a mass demonstration under the slogan "HIDUP MELAYU" (Long Live the Malays), the same slogan used by UMNO in its fight for independence. During the mass demonstrations in Kampong Bahru, where the racial riot of 1969 was reported to have been at its worst, Datuk Najib said:

> We are fed up. He (referring to Dato Lim Kim Sai, the deputy leader of the MCA) has questioned the rights of the Malays ...We are giving the MCA a warning that if it is not happy with national policies collectively agreed to by the leaders of Barisan, it should leave the coalition.[59]

## PAS (Parti Islam Se-Malaysia)

PAS grew into a political party from having been a purely Islamic religious and welfare movement, out of its members' disillusionment and anger at UMNO's concessions to the non-Malays, especially over the citizenship issue prior to Malaysia achieving Merdeka. The party's ideology is explicitly based on two basic elements: Malay nationalism and Islam. As described by Safie Bin Ibrahim[60]:

> It should be acknowledged that the Malay nation is the rightful owner of Malaya. Secondly, the Malays should be granted special rights. The Constitution should stipulate that not a single interest will be tolerated if it contradicts with the interests of the Malays. Thirdly, Malayan citizenship cannot be conferred on individuals unless conditions have been laid down in advance which guarantee their sincere loyalty to Malaya. The party suggested ways and means to ensure that this citizenship can be withdrawn if there are indications of disloyalty. Fourthly, Islam should be the official religion of the country. According to the party this meant that the Islamic religion (Qur'an and Hadith) should be the guidance for the citizens and government, to be equally applied to all matters. Finally, Malay should immediately be made the national, official language of the country. According to the party this meant that the English language, as an official and second language, must be abolished as soon as possible, unless it is beneficial and necessary. These five basic principles were seemingly the collective product of the PAS leaders led by Dr. Burhan

---

[59] Asiaweek, 30 October 1987.
[60] Safie Bin Ibrahim, The Islamic Party of Malaysia, Its Formative Stages and Ideology, Kelantan: Selising, 1981, pp. 86-87.

ud-Din. The question of the Malay rights in terms of Islam was the main concern of the party and Dr. Burhan ud-Din. When Dr. Haji Abbas stated that 'Malays are absolutely the rightful owners of Malaya', then this was simply in line with what had been written by Dr. Burhan ud-Din in 1950 that 'anywhere in the world political rights belong only to the sons of the soil and Malaya belongs to the Malays'.

Milne and Mauzy describe PAS as originating as an Islamic — religious and Malay communal party. Its principal position was that Malaya belongs to the Malays, and this found its expression in its slogan: Bangsa (race), Ugama (religion), and Tanah Melayu (land of the Malays). In specific terms the party was staunchly Malay nationalist while combining Islamic modernist traditions with elements of socialism. Islam served as the unifying force of the party.[61] According to Mauzy, the party

> wanted Malay rights extended and entrenched in the Constitution, tighter and retroactive citizenship regulations, more restrictive immigration laws, Malay immediately as the national and only official language, the posts of Mentri Besar, Ministers, Governors, and Heads of the Armed Forces reserved for the Malays, and the establishment of a theocratic state. PAS accused UMNO of selling away the birthrights of the Malays, and said that the Alliance was dominated by the MCA. While the application of the party's theocratic and mildly socialistic ideas was never really explained, in its nationalism PAS had a clear unambiguous appeal as far as the Malay electorate was concerned.[62]

PAS to all intents and purposes therefore was effectively the counterpart of the Chinese DAP; the one wanted a Malay Islamic State, that is Malay supremacy, while the other wanted Malaysian Malaysia, i.e. effectively Chinese supremacy. In pursuit of its ideology, PAS has continued to criticise government policies, arguing that they have only succeeded in creating a wealthy Malay middle class and a handful of millionaires who are the symbols of the true character of the NEP. At the same time, the party has chastised the Government in strong language for its total failure to eradicate poverty. It also seeks to change the way of life of the Malays, including how they dress, etc., to conform to the Middle Eastern mode of living and thinking. It is worth noting that Tunku Abdul Rahman rejected the PAS concept of a Malay Islamic state

---

[61] See Milne and Mauzy, op.cit., pp. 143 and 145.
[62] Mauzy, op.cit., page 68.

completely and flatly as violating the Constitution, besides being impractical.

While the PAS was expressly formed with one of its main aims being the betterment of the Malay economic situation, it has not developed any comprehensive economic programme. As Dr. Chandra Muzafar says:

> For a party which for more than thirty years has argued for an Islamic alternative, it has done very little analysis for the character and content of the new society it wants to create based upon the Quran and Sunnah.[63]

> PAS talks of the importance of establishing industries, of creating jobs, of overcoming the problems posed by retrenchment, and yet it has not made any attempt to provide concrete suggestions on how policy makers and planners can go about meeting these challenges. It is a sad reflection of the party's approach to economic issues that even important leaders argue naively that the growing threat of unemployment can be resolved if only the people are prepared to work hard. Neither has PAS pondered upon some of the other equally crucial dimensions of an alternative economic system. What will be the relationship between labour and capital in an Islamic economy? ... This requires profound reflection on prevailing economic realities — the sort of reflection PAS has yet to undertake.[64]

Islam guarantees justice for every one, irrespective of ethnic origin or religious affiliation. In the eyes of the religion all human beings are equal and should be treated with love and dignity. PAS assured the Chinese that in its Islamic State they would have every right to pursue their economic activities without undue interference from the authorities. There would be no discrimination in employment, in State assistance or in the award of scholarships for educational purposes. Educational opportunities at tertiary level would be expanded to such an extent that all deserving students, whatever their ethnic origin, would be given places in the universities and colleges. Chinese education too would be preserved and even enhanced as part and parcel of PAS's commitment to the protection of Chinese culture. Chinese primary and secondary schools would be allowed to exist as independent entities. The party was even prepared to consider the establishment of a Chinese language university if this was what the Chinese community wanted. At the same time Chinese would have the freedom to develop their cultural dances, drama, music and art — as long as it did not threaten or tarnish Islam .... As Haji Abdul Hadi Awang, PAS Vice President and one of its more prominent personalities put it,

---

[63] Dr. Chandra Muzafar, *Islamic Resurgence in Malaysia*, Kuala Lumpur, 1987, p. 57.
[64] *Idem*, pp. 60-61.

"Even a Chinese Muslim or an Indian Muslim or any other Muslim can become Prime Minister provided he is pious and righteous".[65]

The fact of the matter is that the main problems for the Malays are poverty and inequality vis-à-vis the others in the country. PAS's political strength comes from the most poverty stricken states of Kelantan, Kedah and until recently Terengganu where the Malays predominate. Yet, when PAS was in control of Kelantan, it had the opportunity to devise comprehensive plans, programmes and projects to help the poor Malays of the state in accordance with its own teachings and ideology. However, the record is miserable. Haji Nakhaie Ahmad said when he left the party over policy differences with his peers:

> We have not succeeded in our struggle (to set up an Islamic State). We can talk and hold ceramah (lectures). But after that what? We are short of planners and implementors. We have preachers — plenty of them. But we have no politicians and technocrats to implement what we propagate .... People are more concerned with economic issues and economic problems than with political ideology. Political power is based on economic power. China has turned its back on Mao and the Soviet Union on Stalin. Progress has taken a new dimension. It's based on economic thrust.[66]

In its quest for political power PAS has now formed an alliance with *Angkatan '46* and with the DAP. A concrete plan has yet to be seen and discussed as to how, within such an alliance, PAS shall deal with economic growth and development, with the serious problem of Malay poverty and inequality, with the serious unemployment problems or with other social policies to lead Malaysia into the 21st century. The aim of the alliance as proclaimed by Tuan Haji Yusof Rawa, the PAS President, at the Party's Muktamar (General Assembly) in April, 1989, is to forge national unity based on Islamic values. Besides vague general statements of high principles, no concrete solutions on the lines articulated by the DAP for example, are offered. In an extensive interview with Utusan Malaysia, the new president, Haji Fadhil Nor, gave his views on a full range of topics concerning the problems facing the country, except those concerning the economic plight of the Malays or the NEP.[67]

---

[65] *Idem*, pp. 91-92.
[66] As reported in an article by Maria Samad in *New Straits Times*, entitled "PAS Crisis: Question of Style, Approach", 3 October 1988.
[67] *Utusan Malaysia*, 14 August 1989.

ABIM (Angkatan Belia Islam Malaysia) is the feeder organisation which supplies some of the leadership of PAS; indeed it could be viewed as the counterpart of the influential UMNO Youth. At least in matters concerning major issues facing the country, its general attitude may be described by the following passages from an outside observer:[68]

It is this feeling that Western thought and Western culture threaten the very existence of Islam that has helped to galvanize Islamic resurgence around certain antipathies. The animosity towards secularism is one of them; the antagonism towards decadent Western culture is another. Is there also some aversion towards Western or foreign economic dominance, which may have helped Islamic resurgence to grow? There is, undoubtedly. In January 1982, for instance, the Muslim leader, Anwar Ibrahim, who was then President of ABIM, warned against foreign economic dominance. He criticized the 'Look East' policy of the Government which calls upon the people to emulate the work ethics of the Japanese and South Koreans, especially their diligence and discipline. 'We should realize', he said, 'Japan has exploited developing countries. Efficiency in exploitation is Japan's greatest success. This is not a policy which we should emulate'.

Apart from philosophical denunciations of secularism, modernization and Western-oriented development, which are often described by ABIM officials as the major causes of the chaos that plagues Muslim countries like Malaysia, there have also been some specific criticisms of the more tangible dimensions of economics, culture and politics. ABIM, for instance, has sometimes lamented the overdependence of the Malaysian economy upon the international capitalist system. It has attacked the Government for allowing income disparities to grow, for allowing the perpetuation of poverty. It has criticized the leaders for undertaking all sorts of prestige projects: 'towns, arches, monuments, golf courses, skyscrapers... Also, we are always having festivals, ceremonies, meaningless visits. All these are paid for by the people, the majority of whom live below the poverty line'.

In summary, it would appear that PAS and ABIM have not addressed comprehensively the economic problems facing the Malay community in a manner as the DAP or the MCA have done for their community. PAS and ABIM will therefore have to think through what would be their policies and actions, and the expected impact they will have on the other communities and the country at large. Until and unless this is done, it is not likely that they could be taken

---

[68] Dr. Chandra Muzafar, *op.cit.*, pp. 22 and 49.

seriously as an alternative force that could be trusted to govern the country and bring with it prosperity and full employment. To compete internationally, which Malaysia must do to sustain its prosperity, research, productivity, organisations and labour skills are essential. PAS and ABIM must produce their plans to show how they propose to tackle this. Until then the one sure success of theirs is that they have split the Malay community into hostile camps. As Dato Abdullah Badawi has said: "PAS is more successful than the Communists in dividing the Malays."[69]  In the long run this trend will further diminish the relative strength of the Malays, both economically and politically.

## Angkatan '46

Angkatan '46 is a new party which came into existence in the wake of a series of crises faced by UMNO in 1987/88. Its president, Tunku Razaleigh Hamzah, was a former stalwart of UMNO. He served as an influential cabinet member under all Prime Ministers since the time of Tun Razak until his political disagreement with Dr. Mahathir which eventually led to his departure from UMNO to form Angkatan '46. He is therefore well-versed in the intricacies of the philosophy and the rationale of the NEP. Indeed he was one of the seasoned influential members of the cabinet who implemented the NEP under successive administrations. At this stage of the party's development, Angkatan '46 is preoccupied with building its organisation and capability. It is therefore too early to expect the party to be able to spell out in detail its programmes for improving the economic status of the Malays vis-à-vis the non-Malays. Politically Angkatan '46 has formed an alliance with PAS and DAP. PAS draws its support from the most conservative of rural Malays and the most fanatical Muslims, while DAP draws its support mostly from urban Chinese who abhor Islamic fundamentalism. Although both parties have moderated their stance, it is difficult to see how Angkatan '46 could draw up a comprehensive programme for the Malays that would also meet the opposing extreme and conflicting demands of both PAS and DAP. However, up to now two firm conclusions can be drawn from this new alliance and the realignment of the political forces in the country. First, with the emergence of Angkatan '46, the Malays are further subdivided and therefore their political base and power is fragmented: within the Malay community

[69] Utusan Malaysia, 9 March 1986.

itself there will now be a three-cornered fight for every Malay vote. To that extent it will weaken the strength of the community as a whole, with choice no longer confined to either UMNO or PAS. Whether the Malays are represented in the government by UMNO or by Angkatan '46 and PAS combined, the ability of either to push any policy for betterment of the Malay community would be that much weakened. Second, whether UMNO or Angkatan '46 and PAS combined win, the Malaysian Chinese, through MCA or the DAP, will be strengthened in their efforts to oppose the advancement of the Malay population. Which ever horse wins, the dinner is the same.

## The Malay Intellectuals and "Liberals"

The Malay intellectuals, not unexpectedly, have been concerned with the economic problems of the Malays. Indeed it is the fuel of their nationalist movement. However, the emphasis of their published writings has been on the poverty aspect of the problem. Surprisingly, the restructuring aspect has not been much written about, although privately it is the subject of much debate. One reason for this is perhaps that it is considered a sensitive subject. Who is to bell the cat without being mauled back?

The worry and unhappiness of the Malay intellectuals from the time of Za'aba to the present is reflected in many forms — in their writings, in their literature and poetry and of course in their politics. Indeed this concern has been one of the main driving forces of the earlier Malay nationalists and the recent Malay unity movements. The emphasis, however, has been different from generation to generation. The energy and effort directed towards the Malay problem is not surprising. First, the Malays formed their political power base. To continue to stay in office, something must be seen to be done, and the right words and the right promises and dreams must be conveyed to the Malays. Second, most of the Malay leaders, with the exception of those originating from the aristocracy and their relatives, came from the kampongs (villages); many were children of Malay school teachers or the children of petty administrators of functionaries in the government or its related agencies. They therefore know from first hand how it is to be poor and how difficult it is to get out from the pit. Indeed, while some were able to escape from the vicious circle of poverty, most of them still have relatives and friends left in the rural areas and on the fringes of the jungles and the riverine. One just has to observe the massive return to the rural home base on the eve of Hari Raya (Muslim festival at the end of the Ramadan fasting month) to see these linkages. Just in case some of them have forgotten their roots, or want to forget their roots because of their new found affluent styles of Guccis and Pierre Cardin and the social company they keep in the country clubs, during their short stay in the kampongs they are reminded again of their origins by the many unemployed rural youths queuing for jobs and by parents petitioning about their inability to provide a decent livelihood for their families and the difficulties they encounter. These are common experiences when one returns to the kampong. So the Malay better-off are reminded constantly about rural poverty and inequality vis-a-vis the modern sectors. Indeed it is two worlds existing side by side, or existing in the form of "dual organisation" to put it in the terms of Hla Mynt.[70] Malay poverty and economic inequality therefore form the basis of a permanent Malay revolution, as much as political inequality forms the basis of the non-Malay struggles for equality.

Nowhere was the concern for Malay poverty, especially rural poverty, and inequality more reflected than in the writings of Royal Professor U.A. Aziz. He profoundly influenced generations of young Malay economists and politicians from their early undergraduate days in the universities in Singapore and Malaysia and even those studying abroad. These graduates, imbibed with the mission to do better for their own kind and for the country, were able to translate some of his ideas into practical policies and programmes when they assumed important posts in the Malaysian administration and planning agencies. His main theory was that Malay poverty was caused by "low productivity, exploitation and victimization, neglect and urban-bias policies of the government".[71] These issues were further developed in other studies. Various categories of poverty were identified, such as the hard core poverty among the smallholders, padi farmers etc., and by regions. Detailed policy prescriptions for overcoming them were proposed. Far reaching specific institutions were established to deal directly with segments of these problems. Contributions were made in the works of S. Hussin Ali, Kassim Ahmad, Kamil Salleh, Zainal Aznam, Shukor Kassim, Chamhuri Siwar and Mohd. Haflah Piei, to mention but a

---

[70] Myint, H., "Organizational Dualism and Economic Development" *Asian Development Review*, vol. 3 (1985), no. 1.

[71] U.A. Aziz, "Footprints in the Sands of Time: The Malay Poverty Concept over 50 years from Za'aba to Aziz and the Second Malaysia Five Year Plan", in Chee S. and S.M. Khoo (eds.), *Malaysian Economic Development and Policies*, Kuala Lumpur: Malaysian Economic Association, 1975.

few. One would also include the works published by INTAN (Institute Tadbiran Awam Negara). Not unexpectedly, the proposed remedies ranged from socialist or Marxist solutions to those prescribed and recommended by international organisations like the World Bank and the Asian Development Bank. Without exception, all emphasised that in order to improve the economic status of the Malays it would be necessary to increase their productivity, remove the system that exploits them, introduce policies that would redress the inequities, and redirect government policies in favour of the rural areas. But then what would happen to the non-Malays and the country as a whole in the process of concentrating on the Malays? Therefore, the policies advocated by the Malay intellectuals were necessary but not sufficient in themselves. What was needed in addition was a comprehensive policy that would cater for the needs of the country as a whole, the needs of the Malays and of the non-Malays alike. Only then could the policy prescriptions be accepted by all and have the intended stabilising effect, socially and politically.

There were nevertheless some brave souls who dared to speak out their minds in public on the restructuring objective of the NEP. Dr. Mohd. Nor Abdul Ghani, the Director General of the Socio-Economic Research Unit of the Prime Minister's office expressed his views forcefully. The NEP, he declared, would be the last chance for the Malays to close the economic gaps existing between them and the non-Malays, because in the future the latter would know how to defend their entrenched rights, what they had already accumulated, and what they would feel rightfully belonging to them. The failure of the NEP would place the Malays so low on the economic ladder, that in order to correct it, nothing less than sweeping aside the principles of democracy in the country would be needed. Similarly, concern for the restructuring objective could be seen in the works of younger generations of writers and academics like Ahmad Idriss, Zulkifly Haji Mustaffa, Ishak Shaari, Mohamed Yussof Kassim, among others. Yet, in comparison with the poverty issue, the focus and analysis on the second prong of the NEP, it seems, was not given the importance that it deserved, considering that the very survival of the Malays, as Dr. Mohd. Nor had pointed out, could be at stake. A recent study by 15 Malays of the younger generation, based in the Kebangsaan University, is to be welcomed as an analysis extending discussion of ethnic poverty to considerations of inequality in income distribution in the middle and upper reaches of income distribution.[72]

An interesting and serious variant of the analysis of the Malay problem of poverty and inequality is provided by some members of the upper crust Malays who have done well under the NEP and think they can take the heat even if the NEP were now to be significantly softened. The privatisation policy of the government, the preferential share allocations, the large government awards for contracts etc., have made some of them into instant millionaires and multimillionaires. These are the ones who argue that the NEP should create more Malay millionaires, as if by creating a few more one could solve the problems of the Malays in the outlying rural areas or in urban low productivity activities. To make it worse, some members of the Malay *nouveaux riches* indulge in highly conspicuous consumption. One cannot miss their display of new found wealth and power, in the forms of their titles and medals, the number of expensive cars each one of them owns, the jewellery of their wives, etc. when one visits Kuala Lumpur or attends some of the glittering and opulent functions in the many five star hotels in the city. It is a major weakness of the outcome of the implementation of the NEP, not so much the strategy itself. Yet, these rich Malays are no less nationalistic than are their poorer cousins. Indeed some of them were at the forefront of the fight for Malay rights. Now that they have arrived, as it were, their prescriptions towards the Malay problem are markedly different, "objective" and less "racial", often condescending and patronising, not unlike the attitudes and admonitions of the non-Malays to-day and the colonials before them. They often take positions quite opposite to those advocated by UMNO, by its Youth wing and by the NEP itself.

The line of argument of the more thoughtful members of this group could be said to be typified by the consistent set of arguments presented by a well known Malay economist in the person of Dato Malek Merican. His extensive experience, ranging from the Treasury to the IMF and to the private sector, makes his arguments compelling. This is a voice of reason, logic and moderation, tempered by many years of practical experience on the ground. In many ways he reflects the rising worry and concern of many responsible Malaysians, Malays and non-Malays alike, who have the

---

[72] See *Setelah 1990: Ekonomi dan Pemebentukan Bangsa,* Universiti Kebangsaan, 1990.

welfare of the country at heart. To ignore his arguments would be to court risks.

In 1984 he questioned some of the weaknesses of the NEP implementation reflecting, amongst other things how long the PNB, rapidly becoming the biggest unit trust in the world, should continue to grow.[73] He also called for a more imaginative plan to foster Bumiputra entrepreneurship, stressing the need for Bumiputra entrepreneurs and managers and business organisations that could compete internationally as well as at home.[74]

In a later argument[75], he expressed his disillusionment with the NEP and proposed an alternative plan for the Bumiputras and the country for the post 1990 era, which for short he called the National Growth Plan or NGP. However, he was realistic and sensitive to the mood of the Malays when he qualified his recommendations:

> Looking at the performance to date and the likely performance to 1990, it would be difficult to convince the Bumis, especially the UMNO which form the core group in the National Front, that we can just terminate the NEP. Even non-Bumi Malaysians are willing to recognise that some form of affirmative action programme must be pursued to help Bumis to get into the main stream of business activities and a fair share of economic opportunity and material assets.[76]

According to Dato Malek Merican, one group of Malays "conceives the restructuring problems basically in terms of the NEP framework. They concentrate their arguments on the ultimate proportions of corporate equities the Bumis should own, whether the NEP restructuring effort should be pushed more vigorously or implemented more slowly."[77] Some of these feel particularly aggrieved that even the 30% target cannot be reached, and hence they argue that the government should be more aggressive in implementing this corporate policy, in particular that the Malays eventually should own 50% or more, This is the stance of the UMNO Youth. Others wish to see a 30-50 per cent target, but implemented without time constraint and as long as such a level of participation and ownership is not reached; in other words, the NEP restructuring programmes

[73] *New Straits Times*, 4 June 1984.
[74] *Idem*.
[75] Dato Malek Merican, *Review of the NEP from the Private Sector Perspective*, paper delivered at Gemaputra Sammar Kabangsaau, Dasar Economic Baru Selapas 1990, 24-26 March 1987, Kuala Lumpur.
[76] *Op.cit.*, p. 4.
[77] *Op.cit.*, p. 5.

should be continued. Many pragmatic Bumiputra are of this view, but they are realistic enough to recognise that other variables involved in the whole process of restructuring must also be taken into account. Finally, amongst the Malays who basically accept the NEP framework, there are some "who now argue that the NEP restructuring should be implemented in an anti-cyclical manner, i.e. slower during recessions and more vigorously during boom conditions".[78] Included in this latter category are leaders of the present government who made such statements during the recession in the mid 1980s.

There, however, also some Malays who, as Dato Malek explains:

worry about the adverse *impact on growth* if the NEP as presently conceived is continued to be implemented through the 1990s or even from now to 1990. They worry about the way the NEP as presently implemented seems to require restrictive regulations that breed *corruption* that erodes not only Bumi society but begins to impact on Malaysian national integrity as it pervades over wider areas. Some of them worry about the increasing emphasis on *Islamisation* as presently clarified which to date implicitly questions the need to refashion the Bumi individuals to make a success of the NEP programme.... (They) believe that the NEP restructuring concepts can only be applied during a period of strong growth like the 1970s, and even then for only a limited period of time before the negative impact inherent in a forced restructuring exercise slows down national growth ... (They) maintain that no growth or minimal growth *on a GNP per capita basis* means we cannot or should not implement NEP restructuring on a broad basis because we will be redistributing not through growth but taking or reducing what others own in the first place.... (They consider that) the NEP implementation is one of the basic causes of the slowdown in the rate of economic growth we now must envisage for the 1990s.... Through our eagerness to assist the Bumis and through Malaysian nationalism we have driven away more investments than we should.... The Malaysian government has now pronounced that the equity conditions relating to foreign investments made from October 1986 to the end of 1990 will not be changed in the sense that the foreign investors will not ever be required to sell their shareholdings to Malaysians. A company that has been approved under the new equity guidelines will not be required to restructure its equity at any time, even after the year 1990. This strong undertaking to promote economic growth came as a major shock to (those Malays) who continue to hanker to require all firms to sell at least 30% if not more, to Bumis.... Under pressure from the non-Malays, especially the MCA and.. (others), the Industrial Coordination Act was also relaxed, with its provisions

[78] *Op.cit.*, p. 6.

applying to companies having shareholder funds in excess of $2.5 million and engaging 75 or more full time employees.[79]

Dato Malek, himself an exponent of this latter group, is particularly concerned that corruption is now more rampant than before the NEP was introduced. This group of Malays point out:

> that many tenders, awards, licenses and approvals of share allocations were made on the basis of connections rather than to the lowest, most efficient or on some other merit related basis. They worry that Bumis and non-Bumis are beginning to believe that they should aim to become power brokers and influence peddlers rather than dedicate themselves to become the most efficient managers, producers and manufacturers.... (These Malays) are also concerned but uncertain about the implications on the NEP from the Islamisation programme that the Government is emphasising more recently. They feel that there must be certain contradictions between aspects of the two programmes as they affect the Bumis. Further clarification should be made about the Islamisation programme as it may impact on the flow of Bumi individuals who we hope will be the managers and entrepreneurs of the new Malaysia. To date the Islamisation programme seems to emphasise the need for the Bumis to be more religious, and to abstain from gambling, consuming liquor and being caught khalwating, on pain of being fined, imprisoned, caned or whipped in some states. In terms of the potential conflicts, there is also the emphasis that Muslims should not earn interest or be employed in firms that depend on interest. To make the NEP a success, we must envisage an increasing number of Bumi bankers and Bumi employees in the large and expanding banking industry... Reading some of the pronouncements of those preaching more intensive Islamisation, one wonders what sort of Bumi individuals, male or female, that we will be trying to fashion. Will they be able to be a participating partner with non-Bumis in joint ventures operating in Malaysia, and will they be able to relate closely with the foreign kafirs, be they Chinese, Japanese or Americans, who drink not only sake and gins but also eat foods which are definitely not halal to the pure?[80]

These reflections are based on keen and concerned observation of developments in the society. Clearly, there is a need for a serious soul searching exercise. As a result of the unsatisfactory developments that were deemed to have arisen from the implementation of the NEP, Dato Malek proposes as an alternative for the post 1990 era:

[79] *Op.cit.,* pp. 6, 7 and 10.
[80] *Op.cit.,* pp. 11 and 12.

to envisage a National Growth Programme (NGP) which will emphasise the need for national growth and an affirmative action programme to assist the Bumis to attain more equal opportunity and advancement in ways that are more consistent with the need to increase private sector investments and employment. The NEP emphasises restructuring of society and eradication of poverty. The NGP should emphasise the need to promote national growth and include a realistic programme to assist Bumiputra advancement.[81]

Areas recommended for Bumiputra to concentrate on for their advancement include education, small and medium scale business, financial and technical assistance to accelerate their advancement in the rural areas as well as in the urban areas, and measures destined to encourage efficiency and competitiveness:

The main difference however is that the National Growth Programme will do away with the forced restructuring aspect of NEP. The final salvation of the Bumis is not to be found in a system where Bumis get cheap shares in ways which will force non-Bumi Malaysians and foreigners to share their economic rewards and become less willing to invest in Malaysia ..... To put the emphasis permanently on restructuring, the provision of cheap minority shares from non-Bumi companies will only mislead the Bumis to a path of national economic stagnation, with all the implicit consequential tensions and risks.[82]

Dato Merican's proposal that a National Growth Policy should replace the NEP after 1990 falls into the category of "growth first and distribute later". The Malay dilemma would be solved only after the other problems are solved, not vice versa. Some basic questions are left unanswered: How would the Malays catch up with the non-Malays in terms of economic parity and within what time frame? Or is it implicit in this proposal that the Malays must accept that they are to be relegated to a permanent position of economic inferiority? With respect to the allegation that growth would be adversely affected by the NEP, the evidence from the past 20 years of NEP and from other countries contradicts this position. With respect to the effect of the implementation of NEP on corruption, and the implication for the resurgence of Islamisation in the country, the Malays must take up the challenge to contain such developments. A lot has been done concerning corruption, but there are glaring deficiencies in terms of "catching the big fish, not only the small

---

[81] *Op.cit.*, pp. 19 and 20.
[82] *Op.cit.*, p. 20.

fry". There are indeed reasons to fear that a process is in train which will further segregate an already divided society. National unity and racial integration, as envisaged by the NEP when it was launched, is not much nearer than in 1969, when racial mingling in daily life was more common and when the number of mullahs and semi-mullahs of an ultra religious bent was lower than it is to-day. Moreover, and important to the NEP, would Dato Malik's proposed National Growth Policy foster political stability on which private sector investments depend? NEP has fostered strong growth of the private sector and of GNP, perhaps not as fast as some may have wanted, but fast enough to enable Malaysia, if it so wishes, to join the ranks of the NIE in the near future. What use is it to have accelerated economic growth if it leads to intermittent chaos and instability?

In this review we must also report some of the views of Dr. Noordin Sopiee, the director of the Institute of Strategic and International Studies (ISIS), on the general political and economic development of the country since the riot of 1969.[83] According to him Malaysia has to face up to what may be called 10 commandments, which include, among others, the realisation that all Malaysians are in the same boat; the need for pragmatism, non-emotional and non-ideological approaches to problem solving; the spirit of give and take among the communities known in Malay as "lebih kurang" (give and take); the practice of democracy; the rule of law; the containment of extremism, be they social or political. Because the practice of these commandments has largely prevailed in Malaysia, the country has confounded the sceptics; Malaysia has not travelled the way of Lebanon, Sri Lanka, Northern Ireland or Cyprus. However, it is worth noting that these 'Lebih Kurang' approaches and practices have worked in the last nearly 20 years because the NEP had succeeded in "containing the rot" of poverty and inequality. Without it, Malaysia might again have gone the way it did in 1969 or, worse still, the way of the ill-fated countries just mentioned. To sustain the pleasant 'Malaysian Lebih Kurang' approach, its underlying foundation will depend on dealing effectively with the problems of poverty and inequality. A one-way traffic is not a Lebih Kurang approach.

With the approach of 1990 it seems that every one is sensing that an important historical epoch is coming to an end and that a new uncertain future is emerging towards the 21st century. In order to clarify the options available, many conferences and congresses have

---

[83] *New Straits Times*, 3 September 1989.

been organised to discuss the future of the Malays. One such congress, following the first held in 1988, was The Second Congress of Malay Intellectuals held at Universiti Kebangsaan in July, 1989. Its theme was "Memasuki Dasawarsa 90-an", that is "Entering the Era of the 1990s". It was organised jointly by 12 organisations on Malay language, literature, culture, economics, and education under the patronage of Education Minister Enche Anwar Ibrahim. Since this was the gathering of the elite Malay thinkers, and the issues raised by them reflected the issues foremost in their minds, it was an indicator of the temper and pulse of the Malays generally, spanning as it were a cross section of Malay concerns about their future. Papers on various topics, ranging from politics and Malay unity to the implementation of the NEP, were presented by leading speakers on their subjects of speciality. The upshot of it all was that more than 50 resolutions were passed on a wide spectrum of main issues facing the Malay community. Enche Anwar Ibrahim said in winding it up that the UMNO Supreme Council had set up a special committee to study the proposals and resolutions submitted by the Congress, presumably for eventual implementation or at least to be used as sensors and benchmarks when drawing up the party's national policies.

The Prime Minister in his inaugural speech to the plenary session recalled that the Malays were colonised for more than 400 years. Their masters divided them and their country, exploited them and changed their country's population composition. Now that independence had been achieved, the Malays had an opportunity to rebuild their society and chart their own progress. Although much had been achieved after 30 years of independence, the Malays still lagged behind, especially in the fields of economics and education. Therefore they had to strive harder for a better future, not only in these fields but also in other social spheres. The Malay intellectuals could and should not only contribute their ideas, but also lead in this effort. But they had to know what they wanted for their society, and more important how too achieve them in practical terms. Paper qualifications alone would not be enough. Pragmatism and practical qualifications and experience would also be needed. In this respect the Malays were still lacking. The future in his view was full of challenges and obstacles, but if they were allowed to divide the Malays, then they would fail in their quest to better themselves. For example, he said, the implementation of the NEP had brought benefits to all strata of the society. But there exists now among the Malay intellectuals themselves a division of views on the NEP. It had been alleged by some that the NEP had benefitted only a privileged few. The Prime Minister, Dr. Mahathir, expressed the hope that the Congress, comprising the elite of the Malays, in its various deliberations would be forward looking and that it would come up with pragmatic proposals on how to lead and improve the society into the 21st century. In the quest for Malay improvement he emphasised:

> We do not intend to seize the rights of others but we are entitled to our rights. .... to be economically strong, Malaysians from every level must be committed. This could only be achieved through a sense of patriotism based on love for the country, which is acceptable to all, and not on narrow nationalism based on ethnic-centricity. When we talk of entering the 21st century, we should not be discussing about Malay problems but we should discuss them in the context of a Malaysian society if national integration is to succeed.[84]

In the two day session many proposals were presented for discussion. Datuk Asri Haji Muda, the former president of PAS and Hamim (a Kelantan based party) and now of UMNO, in his lecture entitled "The Malay political scenario: Then and Now", said that Malays had no alternative but to maintain their political power to ensure their future and survival. UMNO, PAS and other Malay or Muslim based parties according to him must find common ground for them to come to terms with and cooperate for the sake of Malay unity and survival. On the same theme, the Editor of Utasan Malaysia, Chamil Wariya, in his paper "Malay leadership in Face of the Future", said that UMNO was the only viable Malay party that could ensure the political survival and future of the Malays. Dr. Abdul Malik, Professor at the University of Malaya, stressed that the process of building a true Malaysian society must take into account the history and existence of the non-Malays. The Minister himself said that the education policy of his ministry is futuristic and that students are being prepared to market their skills to meet future needs and requirements. With respect to the corporate sector, Datuk Haron Kamar Endot, President of the Bumiputra Executives and Entrepreneurs Association, in his paper prepared jointly with the late Encik Lajman Haji Sirat: "The Bumiputra Economy in the 1990s", tabled many far reaching proposals for the strengthening of Malay participation in this sector. With respect to poverty, Sharil Abdul Karim, a professor of economics, urged in his paper "Poverty in Malaysia: Between Imagination and Reality" that the programmes

---

[84] *Mingguan Malaysia*, 2 July 1989.

of the government should be divided into two categories, one for infrastructural purposes and another for direct poverty eradication. Professor Annuar Razak in his paper "Future problems of the village and some solutions" took to task several government agencies for failing to effectively implement programmes to help the poor. Datuk Mokzani, Datuk Kahalid Ibrahim of PNB and Dr. Abdul Halim of Bank Islam also raised thought provoking comments, while others only nitpicked on Bahasa Malaysia saying that it should be called Bahasa Melayu. Dr. Farid Onn and Dr. Nik Safiah Karim complained that after 32 years of independence many professionals are still unable to speak and write the language properly. It is noteworthy that no speaker seems to have raised the issue of the serious unemployment problem facing the Malays, especially Malay graduates. What policies should be adopted and implemented to create full employment for Malays and non-Malays alike seems to have escaped the attention of the participants. At the end of the session Maria Samad, a well known journalist, complained that the assembly, "was just another gathering of well intentioned people who lacked vision and direction. They were unable to steer the discussions to the level suggested by Dr. Mahathir".[85] One speaker at the Congress was quoted as having said:

> the participants at the congress reminded him of ULAMA in the early 19th century who wasted their energies debating how chickens should be slaughtered in accordance with Islam or whether Muslim women should put on a PURDAH in public. Yet here we are living in an age of science and technology. It is a question of priority, otherwise you face a crisis .... The Malays were still as unrealistic as they have always been.[86]

The resolutions adopted at the end of the Conference included the following:

> to stress the Malay self-concept upon the young generation from the standpoint of history and socio-psychology as well as instil a sense of optimism in their future;

> to use a multi-dimensional approach and not merely income level in defining rural poverty as well as using different variables to measure rural and urban poverty;

---

[85] *New Straits Times*, 8 July 1989.
[86] *Idem.*

to urge UMNO to improve its mechanisms so as to attract and assimilate
more Malay technocrats and professionals into its ranks;

to attain higher quality and infuse thinking into education and to impress
on the need to excel as part of an effort to get rid of mediocrity among
Malay students;

to uphold the status of the Malay language while stressing the importance
of learning other languages;

to set up a corporate sector committee in which Malay intellectuals in
various fields, especially from the private sector, will be pooled and their
expertise utilised as ready input for institutions of higher learning;

to maintain nationalism as the basis of Malay struggle but recognise Islam
as a dynamic complementary and catalyst factor in development, and

to coordinate the functions of the various Ministries and agencies as part
of the programme to reform the agricultural sector and avoid duplications.

## Summary

In sum, it appears from this review of positions held by the various
influential groups that the Malays are standing pretty much alone in
their defence of the NEP. Indeed the Malays are beleaguered with
nowhere to turn for help or sympathy for their cause in the face of
the onslaught sustained by the well organised and economically
advanced non-Malays and their allies. The Malays perceive that the
NEP is designed for their benefit, even though they are properly
concerned by the implementation of the policy. It is perhaps
surprising, however, that the Malays have not come out more
strongly in defence of the NEP, locally and abroad and, given that
they have been in control of the government all along, that they
have not insisted more vigorously that the NEP was implemented
more rigorously, consistent with its original objectives. In the
meantime, while much has been achieved, valuable opportunities
have been lost. Now the problems are more complex and the
solutions are therefore more painful all round; vested interests are
more entrenched and the economy more complex. The international
environment in the 1980s has also been less favourable than it was
in the 1970s.

Disunity amongst the Malays in the last decade or two goes a
long way to explain the inability of the Malays to put their act
together for the improvement of their common destiny. In the past,
when the Malays have managed to suppress what may appear to

outsiders, perhaps even to themselves, as petty intrigues, prejudices and squabbles, they have been able to focus their energies on the bigger issues and to advance their common political and economic cause. But disunity among the Malays is a historical "adat" from the time of Hang Tuah all the way. It is something in which they excel without even trying. It is born out of their instinct, perfected by the history of practice. Sometimes they recognise the folly of their petty squabbles at the expense of bigger rewards. With hindsight they realised, for example, that while they were fighting and killing each other about who should have the rights to collect the tolls on sampans plying in the tributaries of the Perak river, the colonial masters took from under their very noses the Kinta tin field, reputed to be one of the richest tin fields in the world. To-day the stakes are much higher with the economy getting richer with development and internationalisation; it is worth countless Kinta tin fields. But by the looks of it, particularly with the demise of the original UMNO, the history of squabbling amongst the Malays is repeating itself. While they are pulling the kris against each other, and each justifying his own side by appearing to be more religious than his brothers on the other side, they are denying their common destiny. It was the practice of the colonial masters to encourage such pettiness and divisions among the Malays by dividing them and by diverting their energy to other, seemingly more important but irrelevant matters. It is no accident that they encouraged increasing doses of native religion as an instrument for diverting their energy from economic pursuits and providing a philosophical basis for their acceptance of their status of poverty and inequality. Now this role has been taken over by the ulamas and mullahs of PAS/ABIM and even by some within UMNO itself. Indeed, the more gullible of the Malays have come to accept their status of poverty and inequality as divine will and destiny and to believe that it even would be against the teachings of Islam to improve one's lot, particularly if this in any way could be seen as imitating decadent and secular Western ways of life. As a result, the Malays have been weakened politically and economically. When for the first time since Hang Tuah the Malays were able to unite on a country wide basis under the banner of UMNO, led by Dato Onn, Tunku Abdul Rahman, Tun Razak and others, they achieved wonders for themselves. They managed to drive their masters out and achieved Merdeka. They were therefore placed in a position to better manage and chart their own economic destiny. Only now they would not have the convenience of the colonial bogey man to blame. Today, more than 30 years later, colonial domination can no longer be accused of being in their way, at least not directly and openly. Whether the Malays now stand or fall, it will be their own making.

## Other Voices

### The World Bank

In 1969 and 1970, when the Government was sorting out its response to the social and economic problems that had found such dramatic expression in the riots of May, 1969, Malaysia's friends abroad and in international development agencies were at best passive and mute, at worst critical and obstructionist. The elaboration of the NEP was very much a national domestic challenge to which Malaysia's political leadership rose remarkably constructively, comprehensively and consistently. Once the NEP was firmly adopted and expounded in the Second Malaysia Plan 1971 to 1975 and its Mid-Term Review, however, it was received internationally, at least by some, with understanding, if not full support and approval. As already recalled, Malaysia found, for instance, that the shift in general development philosophy of the World Bank in the early 1970s towards more attention to distributional aspects paralleled in some respects the thrust of its own NEP. The relationship between the World Bank, as leader of the international development community, and Malaysia was good and productive in respect of both the bank's lending operations and its policy analysis and advice.

The World Bank also commissioned or supported several studies of the Malaysian economy, including some that focused on the NEP and contributed to a better understanding of the statistical and factual basis for its introduction. These contributions came out about ten years after the emergence of NEP and generally confirmed, often in much detail, the policy and statistical analysis on which Malaysia had taken its decisions on NEP in 1969 and 1970.

In his study for the World Bank in 1979, Jacob Meerman recognised the reality of the political economic situation in Malaysia on the ground that:

> The pursuit of this goal (i.e. the rapid elimination in the striking disparities in wealth) was politically feasible because of the anomalous situation of Malaysia in which political power was largely disassociated from economic wealth: the political leaders of Malaysia were blessed by the coincidence that striving for social justice for Malays or Bumiputras

... also furthered the interest of their own constituency, the poor and largely rural Malay majority.[87]

In another study published by the World Bank, Kevin Young, Willem C.F. Bussink and Parvez Hassan focused specifically on the NEP.[88] Having put the policy under detailed examination, using a variety of tests, the authors concluded:

> What emerges from this analysis is that the government's strategy for development sustaining rapid industrial growth and focusing public programs on the poor — can enable Malaysia to meet the targets for reducing povery and restructuring society. Given the internal consistency of the government's plan, the question is whether the strategy can be successfully pursued. Although Malaysia has many things in its favour, the discussion suggests that meeting the targets of the New Economic Policy will require vigorous government efforts in promoting rapid industrial growth and implementing more effective programs that reduce poverty directly[89] ... To reduce the incidence of poverty from 49 per cent of households in 1970 to 17 per cent by 1990 (is an ambitious target). Given the rapid rate of population growth expected over this period — the number of households is projected to increase 3.3 per cent a year — attaining this target will be a formidable task.[90]

> The income disparity between the traditional agricultural sector and the rest of the economy in Peninsular Malaysia widened from about 1:2.5 in 1960 to more than 1:3 in 1970. ...the riots (of 1969) probably had their roots in tensions arising from the widening income disparity between the Malay and Chinese communities — the one predominantly rural, the other predominantly urban.[91]

> Under these circumstances it seems appropriate to conclude that the objective and the process of restructuring are more important than the specific numerical targets. The main goal is to foster national unity, which would be jeopardised if the enforcement of targets are to cause a slowdown in economic growth. Thus the efforts to reduce identification of race with economic function should be continued.[92]

[87] Jacob Meerman, *Public Expenditure in Malaysia — Who Benefits and Why*, a World Bank Research Publication, Oxford University Press, 1979, p. 19.
[88] Kevin Young, Willem C.F. Bussink and Parvez Hassan (eds.), *Malaysia — Growth and Equity in a Multiracial Society*. A World Bank Country Economic Report, Johns Hopkins University Press, 1980.
[89] *Op.cit.*, p. 60.
[90] *Op.cit.*, p. 61.
[91] *Op.cit.*, pp. 31-32.
[92] *Op.cit.*, p. 8.

The discussion of alternative growth strategies ... affirms the necessity for government to pursue a strategy of rapid growth if the targets of the New Economic Policy are to be attained.[93]

In sum, the New Economic Policy, with its emphasis on reducing poverty and restructuring society in the context of rapid economic growth, provides a policy framework favourable to moderating income inequalities. In fact, it can be convincingly argued that the thrust toward modernisation and the eradication of poverty, together with the insistence that no one should be left behind in development, already implies a policy to moderate income differences. It may thus be desirable to formalise this implicit policy, perhaps as a third objective of the New Economic Policy. To do so would allay any lingering fears among the poor and among middle income earners in non-Malay groups that they may not benefit, or may even lose out, under the New Economic Policy.[94]

Similarly, in another revealing study for the World Bank[95], Depak Mazumdar reports:

Chinese employees have an earnings advantage over the Malays in the urban economy of Malaysia ... There is a perceptible segregation of the two major communities into broadly defined occupational groups, but the underrepresentation of Malays in semi-skilled and skilled blue collar jobs is balanced by their over representation in the public sector in a range of white collar jobs... The discussion of the racial segregation of employees by establishments in the two sample regions suggested that the observed pattern was consistent with the predictions of the Becker hypothesis of employer discrimination.[96]

In 1983, Sudir Anand, also on behalf of the World Bank and drawing on the data from the 1970 Post-Enumeration Survey, again reconfirmed the general and statistical findings of the earlier studies, both by the World Bank itself and by others including the DNU in 1969-70.[97] He warned, however, that "90 per cent of the inequality in the country arises from disparities in income *within* each racial

[93] *Op.cit.*, p. 73. This is in line with the argument of the OPP, striving for growth with equity, but not growth first and distribute later.

[94] *Op.cit.*, p. 124.

[95] Depak Mazumdar, *The Urban Labour Market and Income Distribution — A study of Malaysia*, a World Bank Research Publication, Oxford University Press, 1981.

[96] *Op.cit.*, p. 200-201.

[97] Sudhir Anand, *Inequality and Poverty in Malaysia — Measurement and Decompositon*, a World Bank Research Publication, Oxford University Press, 1983.

group. Thus it is not very helpful to invoke the relatively large income disparity ratios *between* the races in attempting to explain individual income inequality in the country."[98]

When these findings appeared from the World Bank, they confirmed what was already well known and generally accepted in Malaysia, namely that the functioning of the economic system resulted in what amounted to structural discrimination against the Malays. Without a conscious, alternative policy, such as the restructuring efforts of the NEP to increase Malay employment in the modern sector, nobody, least of all the myriad small and medium scale Chinese companies, would employ them. In the government services it is different, of course, but here there clearly had to be a limit to the number that could be absorbed, Malay or non-Malay. And without restructuring of capital ownership and control, neither would employment restructuring at all levels of operation and in all sectors be attainable, nor would rough income equality, given that income in Malaysia derives as much or more from returns to capital, rent etc. as from employment.

## MIER (Malaysian Institute of Economic Research)

MIER was established as an independent non-profit research organisation. Although it is less than five years old, its impact is much felt in economic and business circles in Malaysia, much of this through its seminars, debates and publication of papers. The Institute has prepared what is known as MIER's Income Doubling and Distribution Plan, 1991-2000, or in short IDDP, which was presented to the public in August 1989. IDDP postulates a growth rate of almost 10 per cent per annum, so as to double per capita income by the year 2000, fully eradicate absolute poverty throughout the land, and attain approximate parity in average household incomes of Bumiputra and non-Bumiputra. Moreover, according to the MIER model, by the year 2000 there would be near full employment of the labour force (at five per cent unemployment) through growth and efficient utilisation of human resource, and better life for all through improved education and better and more general access to basic services, such as health, water and electricity.

In some respects, including its limitations, the IDDP is akin to the numerical illustration we presented in chapter 4. It is noteworthy for the light it may throw on the potential of rapid growth for structural

[98] *Op.cit.*, p. 96.

change, but it neither addresses directly policies for ethnic balance, nor is it convincing in the asserted indirect impact of growth on ethnic income distribution. Specifically, the IDDP recommends that the restructuring of ownership objective and targets of the NEP be de-emphasised in the 1990s, but fails to develop any credible substitute for these policies. It would seem, for instance, that the amendments of the National Land Code in 1987, allowing foreigners greater opportunities to purchase properties in Malaysia, utilising a large proportion of local loans for the purchase, were hardly consistent with the declared intention to effect a better distribution of assets and therefore of income.[99] Similarly, the lifting of the ICA (Investment Coordination Act) clause, so as to exempt companies with capital of less than \$ 2.5 million or employing less than 75 people from any obligation to employ Malay labour, has removed control over 75 per cent of local manufacturing establishments; taken by itself, this was hardly a change of policy conducive to accelerating the entry and progression of Bumiputra in the modern sector. It is arguable, of course, that each of these and similar departures from the thrust of the NEP strategy may be justified as temporary aberrations to overcome transient difficulties and adverse changes in external conditions; our point, however, is that any realistic strategy must face up to such issues and provide a credible alternative to the continuous and persistent pursuit of the NEP strategy for growth and ethnic equality. The MIER is currently engaged in a major effort to develop the IDDP so as to encompass alternative scenarios for growth, presumably also alternative policy packages. If so, the work of MIER can become a most needed major supplement to the planning work within Government itself.

## The Malaysian Economic Profession

A sample of the most recent views of the economic profession on the NEP could be gauged from the papers and interventions presented at the 10th Malaysian Economic Association Convention held in Kuala Lumpur on August 7, 1989. The theme of the convention was "Malaysian Economy beyond 1990: An International and Domestic Perspective". It was intended to provide an open forum for a frank exchange of ideas among the economists of the

---

[99] As Katijah Ahmad, a board member of MIER, comments: the foreigners pick up real estate at bargain basement rates given the weak ringgit.

country on key issues facing the country. In his speech launching the Convention the Prime Minister said:

> We have repeatedly mentioned the important role of political stability in promoting economic growth. The fact is that it is the NEP which has made political stability possible after the race riots of 1969. Such was the stability during the period of the NEP that actually economic growth is higher during the NEP years than before the NEP was formulated. In Malaysia it would be fatal to ignore the economic disparities between the races and consequently to do nothing to correct these imbalances. Because we are stable now it is easy to think that the stability is unrelated to the NEP. The suggestions to drop the NEP altogether is the result of this kind of shallow thinking... The expectations of the Bumiputras have not been fulfilled. They may be at fault themselves but other factors outside their control were also responsible.

Leading participants were largely the same professionals whose views have been referred to in the foregoing sections of this chapter. Basically their interventions were variations and refinements of the same themes. Dr. Lim Lin Lean, for example, asked the government to shift its focus from the restructuring objective to the poverty eradication objective, and presented a persuasive argument. Dr. Zainal Aznam of MIER pursued the poverty theme, and suggested that the economy had already entered its income equalising phase even twenty years ago at the time when the NEP was first introduced. Professor Jomo K. Sundram felt that the achievement of the poverty eradication objective had been exaggerated by the government. All agreed that the poverty thrust of the NEP should be continued in the post 1990 era, but more effectively implemented, while disagreements continued about the restructuring objective.

## The National Economic Consultative Council (NECC)

To resolve these conflicting views and claims and counter-claims in current debate, including the accusation by the MCA and others that the statistics published on the NEP have been fudged by the authorities, the government in early 1989 convened the National Economic Consultative Council (NECC), or Majlis Perundigan Ekonomi Negara (MAPEN), under the Chairmanship of Tan Sri Gazali Shafie. He is an UMNO elder statesman of vision and experience, known also for his technical competence, who had been an influential member of the cabinet under various Prime Ministers. The NECC was given the task to develop community consensus recommendations and the government assured the public that it would seriously consider incorporating the advice of the NECC in its post 1990 economic strategy. In his launching speech, while recounting some of the successes of the NEP, the Prime Minister stressed that the goal of any strategy for Malaysia had to be the attainment of a viable balance in this plural society. Nobody wants to be left behind.[100] The Committee members were selected from various walks of life and from different political parties, representing a cross section of the Malaysian society. Some have crossed the political lines back and forth and have changed sides with the changing wind, others were present as elder statesmen. Many of the diehards of the various camps were there, initially also spokesmen from the DAP; later some members left in protest, including those from DAP. The fact that so divergent groups could be brought together at all in one Council is in itself an achievement. It is to be expected that, in a typically Malaysian fashion, at the end of the day, the NECC will come up with something pragmatic and workable for the nation as a whole. If anybody has perfected the art of compromise, it is the Malaysians.

## Summary

In this chapter we have tried to outline the basic positions of the various main communities towards the NEP. In general, the non-Malays are against the NEP, the Malays for. The non-Malays are therefore agitating for its abolishment. If the NEP is to be continued, they maintain, it should be modified so as to include prominently policies to ensure non-Malay proportionate representation in institutions and economic benefits in which now the Malays are dominant, including in particular the civil service, the defence and police forces, land settlement etc. The common ground of agreement with the Malays is the poverty objective. All are agreed that this should be a central element in any future Plan after 1990. As a non-Malay initiative for an alternative post-1990 plan, the MCA has submitted its proposals to the NECC. The MIC and Aliran have done likewise. One faction of the Malay liberals, whose stance is not dissimilar to that of the non-Malay, has also made its proposals in the form of a National Growth Policy. Finally, the MIER has offered an ambitious model for the 1990s. Without exception, all these alternative plans are "Growth first and distribute later" type of strategies.

---

[100] *New Straits Times*, 20 January 1989, for full text of speech.

It appears to have become a pattern that the DAP would first lead in the assault on the NEP, followed in the later years by the MCA and the Gerakan, all in a well coordinated manner, intentionally or otherwise. The result of the sustained attacks, political as well as intellectual, has been that there have been notable retreats in recent years in several key areas, like the ICA and the Land Code.

The Malays are conscious of the need for modifications in the NEP so as to deal effectively with its acknowledged weaknesses, most conspicuously in the emergence of a group of wealthy Malays whose richness reflects their connections to the powers that are rather than their business acumen. In their drive for economic equality vis-à-vis the other communities the Malays urge that the planning in the 1990s and beyond must be growth oriented, but with primary concern for ethnic equality.

However, in 1990, the Malays do not stand together politically as they did in 1969 and 1970, when they were all united in their search for what became the NEP, and when they were able to prevail — at least for a time. To-day, UMNO leaders are in favour of the NEP, and would like to carry some of its major elements into the future. Some influential Malay "liberals" are in favour of disbanding the NEP and replacing it with a policy more firmly focussed on growth. Other Malay intellectuals are preoccupied with issues such as culture, religion and language. The PAS and ABIM group has no economic strategy to speak of, while Angkatan 46 is still too much in its infancy to be able to produce an agreed, comprehensive strategy. But the DAP, an associate partner of Angkatan 46, has had its own strategy of a "Malaysian Malaysia" in place for many years. At this point it seems that if UMNO or Angkatan 46/PAS were to confront each other in a general election, the Chinese community is in a good position to gain whatever the outcome: either MCA or DAP would form part of the government and be strongly placed to push for their not too dissimilar policies for advancing the cause of their community. It is a fail safe strategy. This could further enhance their already dominant position in the economy.

It remains to be seen what the NECC will come up with in its report for post 1990 Malaysia.

# CHAPTER 6

# THE FUTURE

## The Setting

In the 20 years since the riots of 1969 and the introduction of the New Economic Policy, there have been profound changes in the political, social and economic situation of Malaysia. Commensurate changes are to be expected in the next 20 years and policies must be prepared to meet them. This is a complex task in a country peopled with a restive and vocal population of extraordinary diversity: culturally and religiously as well as ethnically, and with an economy in rapid transformation and growth. The ethnic composition of the population itself is in course of rapid change and this is one of the factors that will have to be taken into account in looking to the future and planning for it.

What follows is based on the continued operation of a market based economy growing rapidly with its sights on the world as well as on the domestic market. It is written in the knowledge that Malaysia has to find its place within a region that itself is in considerable ferment, where the fortunes of individual states have been directly influenced by political turmoil and by general economic progress as well as by setbacks that they have experienced. The definition of national interests in these circumstances has, at times, been only tentative, yet Malaysia has followed a consistent policy of gradually intensified cooperation, rather than integration, within her ASEAN connections. These have been designed to ease members' interactions amongst themselves while largely leaving policies bearing on relations outside the region to be determined by individual members' perception of their own national interest. In the process Malaysia has been growing out of her colonial past and realising the need and opportunity for her integration into the world economy.

Development strategies and policies have to be seen in a political setting. In 1970, party political divisions were less complex than today. Changes in the social fabric and in underlying economic interests have led to a dispersal of party loyalties, particularly amongst Malays, far greater than in 1970. There are now great divergencies of view: not only between parties representing Bumiputra interests and those representing the concerns of the Chinese, but also within each of these and between them and other political organisations, as we have detailed in chapter 5.

One dimension of the growing diversity of party political allegiance, is the perceived confrontation of religious convictions and traditions with the demands of a rapidly growing and modernising economy. Religious life and expression has been an accompanying aspect of the evolution of the human race throughout the ages and with, alas, at times, devastating consequences to society from misdirected or misused religious fervour. While in Malaysia in recent years, much of the heightened intensity of religious expression may be more a reflection of events elsewhere than of conditions of spiritual life domestically, it is a potential danger to social harmony and indirectly to the development of the economy.

## Objectives

National unity, as envisaged by Rukunegara, is the basic objective and primary need for the future. This applies not only to inter-communal unity but, equally important, to resolving the various elements of dissension within ethnic groups. Adoption of policies for the avoidance of communal conflicts and for fostering a sense of common identity among and within races is a necessary condition of progress. To these ends successful economic policies are needed, as are complementary social policies for the avoidance of communal conflicts and for the furtherance of accommodation and harmony among and within ethnic communities. There is a whole range of policies and actions that can advance or block the cause of national unity, both by Government and by its citizens in going about their daily lives, and some of these may not as yet have been explored — or sufficiently explored.

In this book about the NEP we deal directly only with *economic* policies. However, it is their relationship to the basic objective of cohesion, if not unity, of Malaysian society which has governed the thrust of the NEP as a whole and the selection of its components. In fact, the NEP itself, no less today than when it was first designed, must be seen as the economic policy dimension of the drive towards a viable, stable and prosperous nation. Within the field of economic policy, it may be helpful to consider four major objectives one by one:

*First*, the economic inequalities *between* the Malays and the non-Malays, as well as those *within* the communities themselves, continue to require correction. This is necessary, not only in the interests of equity and fair dealing, but to avoid the danger of social, economic and political tension which could ultimately lead to political instability.

*Second*, the continued presence of real poverty, which in some states is wide-spread, is a feature of economic life in Malaysia, which is not acceptable to any political party or group in the country. It is recognised, however, that time and effort are needed to bring about a definitive reduction, not to say eradication, of poverty throughout the land.

*Third*, the experience of seeing large numbers of Malaysians exposed to the hardships and indignities of unemployment has brought about a general realisation that the creation of job opportunities for all, particularly for the young and for new entrants to the labour market, is an important objective.

*Fourth*, rapid growth in output, with supporting growth in exports to cement Malaysia's place in the world and provide for import requirements, is seen by most, if not all, as being needed to make everyone better-off. To some, growth is seen as an objective in itself, while others see it mainly as a means to an end. In most circumstances, differences of this nature matter little, but where and when policies for growth hinder or delay the advance towards the attainment of more fundamental goals, such as those described above, policy differences arise. Such differences are sharpened when — as is often the case — the positive and the negative impacts of growth-inducing policy measures, and of the other policy thrusts, are felt by different groups, in Malaysia sometimes by different ethnic groups.

Consistent with — and indeed as part and parcel of — the pursuit of the four main objectives listed above, Malaysia has introduced and developed a set of policies which are characteristic of the NEP. In later sections we review the relevance of some of them for the 1990s and consider the implications for policy and planning. It is in the nature of economic policies in this area that they raise controversy and debate. And so they should. Their further elaboration and implementation require political skill and cooperation, informed through analysis and debate — not political confrontation. Moreover, they will have to be closely monitored so that the public can judge for itself whether the country is achieving its goals. This may also be a means to base judgments on facts rather than on prejudices, as has so often been the case in the past.

The commentaries that follow are made in the spirit of the NEP, which has often been assailed but which has shown itself, in spite of some shortcomings, to be an effective policy for dealing with the economic problems of Malaysia. However, it has to be accepted that approximate parity will take time to accomplish and will not be attainable in only a few years. In the last 20 years some progress has been made in reducing racial disparity and the foundations are now in place for further and speedier progress, but further time is clearly needed to complete the process.

## Inequality

Inequality in terms of income as well as assets remains large in Malaysia compared to other developing countries in the region and beyond. The significance of inequality is a matter of perceptions as well as statistics. While many economic and social issues evident in Malaysia are also present in other developing countries, including very unequal distribution of income and assets, the Malaysian situation has the added dimension that there are very marked differences between ethnic groups which today, as in 1969, are matters of great concern. Even after 20 years of NEP, the average standard of living of the Chinese Malaysians, their incomes and assets and their opportunities for gainful employment are far in excess of those of their Indian compatriots, with the Bumiputra trailing behind. There has been only a modest abatement in the past 20 years in ethnic income inequalities, but there have been significant changes in their composition.

The most significant change over the 20 year period has been the reduction in the number of Malaysians who have to eke out a living below the poverty line. In a later section we stress the need to push for further advance in this respect in the coming years, noting the real difficulty of coming to grips with a remaining "hard core" poverty. Given that the misfortune to have to live in poverty, thus defined, is disproportionately a Malay problem, there is no question that progress in this area to date and in the future will also contribute to the reduction in racial inequalities, both as measured numerically and as perceived by the population.

Important as progress in the eradication of poverty in Malaysia has been and remains for the future, it is also clear that the statistics and perceptions of inequality now will be more affected by what happens to relative conditions of work and life for the much larger groups who have already rid themselves of abject poverty. Into this large group also enter the households who move up across the poverty line, and much more than proportionately this is bound to continue to be the Bumiputra. Those below the poverty line have seldom the energy for effective political organisation on their own, but, as they emerge from a life and death struggle, they will have the capacity and inclination to express themselves against inequality, unfairness and injustice which, with frustrated hopes and aspirations, may be fired into violence. Indeed, it is to the needs and potentials of this group that policies for the coming years increasingly will have to be addressed.

In the 1970s and 1980s it was largely through a shift of people from low to higher productivity occupations ("traditional" to "modern" sectors) that general economic progress and poverty reduction were achieved and racial income inequalities contained. Such shifts will continue to be important; in fact, in a growing Malaysian economy there is still a large surplus of labour — mostly Malay — in rural traditional occupations which in coming years will move into better rewarding activities in modern sectors of the economy. As this shift proceeds, however, further progress will have to come increasingly from an advance in productivity *within* sector groups. Improvement in racial economic disparities depends now more than ever on the speed and extent, relatively to other Malaysians, of upward movement of Bumiputra productivity and income within sectors. This is a dimension of planning and policy which was important in the NEP as originally conceived and as seen during implementation to date; our point is that it is now going to be even more critical to develop and put into effect special policy measures to support such career acceleration for the Malays.

In this connection it is important to realise that the experience of the 1970s and 1980s, particularly the mid-1980s, points to the difficulties of achieving and maintaining a measure of full employment, particularly for the Malays. Any growth in unemployment would tend to offset some of the gains from productivity and income advances for the employed. With higher unemployment for the Malays this would slow the move towards racial balance. Again, therefore, in addition to general measures to contain unemployment, special concern is called for to ensure that unemployment does not fall disproportionately on the Malays.

Rural Malaysia in the foreseeable future will continue to be populated more than proportionately by the Bumiputra. Rapid growth in agricultural productivity, as has been achieved in the past decades, remains an important objective also for the future, both as a force for economic growth generally and for steady improvement in the conditions of life of Malays, including their position relatively to the other main groups. However, as shown in the last decades, more and more Malays will find their livelihoods in industry, trade and other non-agricultural pursuits. As we have seen, on balance, this will be a move to higher productivity activities and thus lay the foundation for an easement of racial disparities. However, the relative share of non-labour inputs (interest, profit, management etc.) in net value added in industry is typically higher than in agriculture and other traditional activities. Therefore, with the continuing shift of Malays to the non-agricultural sector also goes a shift to livelihoods relatively less dependent only on rewards to labour through employment, and more dependent on the share in non-labour rewards from ownership, management and control. The focus on these latter dimensions in the NEP in the past thus becomes even more necessary in the future.

The relative success of the poverty eradication drive of the past is also likely in the future, more than hitherto, to place in sharper focus another dimension of inequality, that of the conspicuous and growing income and asset maldistribution *within* each ethnic group. Again, this change in the perspective is largest for the Malays, for whom the issue of large disparities in standards of living among brothers is new in this form. In recent decades, however, they have experienced how much the economic and political system, including the NEP as practised, has worked to produce, on the one hand, an extraordinarily wealthy group of rulers' families and other Malay entrepreneur insiders and, on the other, open unemployment for increasing numbers of Bumiputra, including ever larger numbers of young and educated Malays.

In the analysis that led up to the NEP, as well as in the implementation of the NEP in the 1970s and 1980s, much was made of regional differences in levels of development and poverty, as well as in racial composition, as between states. In the mid-1960s, Kelantan and Trengganu were at the bottom of the league with a per capita GDP less than one-third of what it was at that time in Selangor (including the Federal Territory). By the mid-1980s, the GDP per capita of Trengganu had moved dramatically to the top to roughly equal that of Selangor, while Kelantan stayed behind as before. Trengganu's spurt was a reflection of the discovery and development of oil off its coast, but also of the impact of this on other sectors of activity. However, the incidence of poverty in Trengganu even now is as high as in the financially and economically very much poorer state of Kelantan; about one in three households in both these states live below the poverty line as against one in twelve in Selangor. In any federal state, such extreme disparities are bound to find expression in politics and in policy, as indeed they have in Malaysia.

There are, unfortunately, narrow limits to what in practice can be achieved through central government policy to reduce, or reduce more rapidly, regional disparities. Certainly, preferential and generous allocation of funds for worthwhile development projects and programmes in the lagging states or regions will help. However, money is not at all enough, as is borne out by the fact that Trenggannu, its new found wealth notwithstanding, appears to have made no significant extra dent so far in the extent of poverty in that state. As in comparisons of development levels and growth rates between countries, so also for regional balance: it is the economic, human and institutional development potential (or changes therein) *within* the state or region which largely determines the outcome. Direct aid and support can be helpful elements, as can the general conditions of interchange and interaction with the rest of the country and farther afield, but these are rarely decisive for rapid development. Of course, the realisation that regional policies at best take a long time to show results, adds to, rather than detracts from, the importance and urgency of efforts at the Federal level to affect a change by consistently analysing regional development implications of plans and programmes and — where an option is available — to give preference to the backward region. At the same time it is for Federal and State authorities, separately and together, to seek to foster *in situ* development, particularly in the economically weaker states, through human resource development and institutional change.


# Poverty

Poverty in its worst form is gradually diminishing in Malaysia, but there is still some way to go. In the urban areas, recorded poverty is now fairly low. In some respects, this is surprising for unemployment levels are not low and many might be expected to be in economic difficulties. Presumably, the effects of unemployment are being mitigated by support from relatives or friends. Statistically, for the most part, poverty now remains as a very serious problem only in rural areas; unfortunately, it is here that, in its residual state, it is most difficult to attack. Over half a million families in rural areas, mainly Bumiputra, are still in poverty. This is considerably less than was the case in 1970, when there may have been more than 3/4 million families affected, but there are still far too many poor today. The problem is exacerbated by reason of being concentrated in particular areas and this means in practice in particular States. In considering what can be done about tackling the last vestiges of poverty, it is necessary to take a rather long look ahead, and to do this with an eye to phasing operations that will ultimately make economic conditions in rural areas more closely comparable to those in urban surroundings.

The first phase is concerned with continuing to help those in poor paying traditional types of agriculture, such as padi cultivation and rubber tapping. Both the holdings of land available for cultivation by farmers growing padi and the yields obtained are low. If adequate incomes are to be obtained, both yields and acreage need to be increased. It has proved possible to help rubber tappers by replanting with more productive species but this has been offset by the reduction in prices resulting mainly from competition from synthetics. The introduction of new methods of cultivation can contribute to raising incomes, but ultimately the attainment of satisfactory living standards will depend on increasing the areas of land available to smallholders. In fact, much new land has been brought into cultivation but it is increasingly evident that there is a limit to the extent to which the area can be speedily and economically increased even though land is available. Less new land is now being developed than previously and targets have been reduced.

Where it appears land is plentiful, in Sabah and Sarawak, the limited availability of settlers and high costs act as constraints; where, in Peninsula Malaysia, these factors might be less of a problem, scarcity of land is an obstacle. Thus, opening up land must be expected to make a diminishing contribution to the reduction of poverty in future years. This apart, some residual poverty will prove exceptionally difficult to deal with because those suffering from it will be of more advanced years, reluctant to seek their fortunes elsewhere and, perhaps, resistant to new methods of cultivation. To remove poverty at this end of the table will require other methods of relief than increasing production. The structure of agriculture is likely to change considerably and consideration needs to be given to this in relation to residual poverty.

In some respects, the improvement in living standards will change the concept of poverty. Aspirations will be enhanced, and the concept of relative poverty will replace that of absolute poverty in peoples' minds. What is this likely to entail for agriculture? It is almost certain to mean that many fewer people will expect to make their way in agricultural pursuits. In advanced economies only about 5-10 per cent of the working population may be needed in agriculture and, often, even less. If only ten per cent of the present working population of Malaysia were to be employed in agriculture, there would be scope for only about 650,000 farmers and not the nearly 2 million employed at the present time. In other words, employment would have to be cut by something like two-thirds. Even if this were done, the amount of land operated per person would average only about 20 acres, say 8 hectares. With labour intensive crops this might enable a good living to be gained, but for many forms of cultivation it is quite small. The rundown in labour may occur naturally, but it may also be necessary for some government intervention to facilitate an orderly reduction. If output could be maintained after a cut in the labour force of about two-thirds, rural incomes would come within range of those obtainable in urban occupations but, as urban incomes are almost certain to continue to increase, still further efforts would be needed to achieve and retain some semblance of parity.

Ultimately, these prognostications represent a considerable change in thinking about rural development and the transfer of labour to the modern sector of the economy that it entails. How long might it take for the modern sector of the economy to absorb the present extent of surplus labour in agriculture of the order of 1 million or more workers as indicated above? The answer to this is uncertain. The non-agricultural sector of the economy has been absorbing labour at the rate of about 200,000 persons per year in recent years, which have not been very propitious years for the transfer of labour, but it has been sufficient to absorb the natural increase in the labour force. If this absorption could be raised to 270,000 which would imply an increase in previous rates of growth from say 6 per cent per annum to about 8 per cent, which is not beyond the bounds of possibility, the transfer would take about 20 years — the time span of a Second Outline Perspective Plan 1990 to 2010.

This view of the reduction of poverty in the rural sector suggests various accompanying consequences. One of these is that the period when wages will rise with progress towards total economic modernisation can not be very far off. In the next decade at the very least, wages will begin to rise in the agricultural sector of the economy.

Various adjustments will be needed to respond to this, including continued efforts to raise productivity, not only in the agricultural sector but also in the modern sector of the economy. A realisation that population will fall in rural areas, with all that is implied for physical planning, settlement and land use, is a further consideration. In adapting to these changing circumstances Malaysia will benefit from the experience that has been gained in opening new tracts for development and by "in situ" development and from the existence of institutions concerned with these things.

As development proceeds, poverty will take on a more simplified aspect. Poverty amongst the Chinese is now very low and further progress will go some way to eliminating what remains; much the same may be the case for the Indians for whom absolute poverty is very little greater than for the Chinese. The NEP with its attack on poverty was never meant to confine attention to the poverty of the Bumiputra to the exclusion of other ethnic poor. There can be no question of excluding them in the future either and no reason for doing so. The continued efforts to eliminate poverty are to be seen as part of an integrated programme applied without discrimination.

If all goes well, this will mean that in about a decade or two at the most it will be possible for poverty to shrink to very small dimensions. If this is to happen, however, special attention will have to be given to the states of Kedah, Kelantan, Perlis, Perak and Terrangganu, where poverty is much higher than elsewhere, and, of course, to the position of Sabah and Sarawak. This leads us into a very difficult field, that of regional development. Improvement will certainly result from continued economic development along accustomed lines, but there may well be a residual element of poverty here, as in other places, that will not be readily treatable by general economic action and policies. In other places, a proportion of those remaining in agriculture in unrewarding jobs will also continue in poverty which may, by then, be remediable by some degree of temporary state subsidies. Those incapable of earning a living, wherever they may be, will have to be aided in similar fashion.

## Unemployment

Understandable concern has been expressed about the high levels of unemployment that have occurred in recent years. Both the levels of unemployment and the concern expressed need to be put into perspective. Unemployment levels of more than 8 per cent recorded during the years of recession or slow growth in the mid-1980s can not readily be compared with levels in other countries, for unemployment statistics are notoriously compiled on a multiplicity of bases. Moreover, opinions as to whether unemployment levels are high or low depend very greatly on the perception of those making the judgement and on the experience of different countries. An unemployment level of 8 per cent would not have appeared high in industrialised countries in the 1930s or even in some of such countries in the 1980s. Nevertheless, the level of unemployment in Malaysia is much more serious than such comparisons might suggest. In the first place, although the figures of employment appear to be designed to cover the whole of the labour force, there may not be very much overt unemployment in the countryside; there the problem is much more likely to be underemployment and unremunerative employment than open unemployment in its most acute form. It may be surmised, therefore, that the actual incidence of unemployment is strongly concentrated on those seeking work in the urban areas, and, if statistics of this were more readily available for inspection, the level of unemployment might appear very high. Secondly, within any environment the incidence of unemployment is much greater in relation to certain sectors of the community, particularly the young, than others. Thirdly, while in industrialised countries unemployment benefits may be quite substantial in relation to basic needs, no such provision exists in Malaysia and the unemployed are forced to seek support from friends, relatives or charity. If such support is not forthcoming there is nothing on which they can fall back.

While the level of unemployment is partly a reflection of chronic inability to provide employment for a rapidly expanding labour force, it is also affected by fluctuations in the rate of growth of output and, in consequence, the number of jobs that may be added in response. A level of unemployment of little more than 5 per cent of the labour force was recorded in the early 1980s. At that time, the GDP was increasing remarkably rapidly, at little short of 10 per cent per annum, compared with its more usual rate of expansion of about 6 per cent. When the rate of expansion of GDP fell to 3.9 per cent in 1983 and when output actually fell in 1985, unemployment rose to over 8 per cent and only recently, with a resurgence in output, has it begun to decline.

According to this analysis, the level of unemployment is largely a function of three factors: the expansion in the labour force, the increase in output generated and the accompanying movements in productivity. Of course, this is an oversimplistic view, other factors are involved and could disturb the mechanism. A mass movement out of agriculture to the towns in search of more remunerative employment could introduce another dimension in line with the pressures that development in many African countries has engendered. But this does not seem likely when it is possible to earn a reasonable level of remuneration in many agricultural operations and when those in the least remunerative of them may be approaching retirement and be reluctant to tear up their roots.

This suggests that the level of unemployment may, therefore, continue to be determined by the factors outlined above. At present the outlook for some reduction in unemployment levels appears to be reasonably favourable. It is true that the labour force will continue to increase at about 3 per cent per annum for some years and that there may be some increase in participation rates, although these are already high; but if productivity were to increase at no more than 3 per cent per annum, which is rather more than it appears to have done in the past, an increase of 7 per cent in output per annum should suffice to prevent unemployment rising and might be sufficient to permit some decline. If a greater increase in output could be achieved, unemployment might be reduced to more manageable dimensions. Nevertheless, it is not to be expected that a higher increase in output would necessarily bring about a commensurate decrease in unemployment, for the supply of labour and the transference of labour from agriculture to other sectors of the economy would undoubtedly increase in response to anything approaching labour scarcity.

Consideration also needs to be given to the level of wages paid in the modern sector of the economy as a proportion of net output. In the manufacturing sector in Malaysia it appears that the wage bill is an unusually small proportion of net value added. It seems that in many industries it may account for no more than one-third of the value added. The opportunities to expand employment depend greatly on the international competitiveness of modern industry in Malaysia. The level of wages will, therefore, govern the rate at which activity can be expanded.

If the economy grows at 7 or more per cent per annum, unemployment should be reduced. But it is not to be expected that the resulting numerical levels of unemployment will ever be extremely low. Adequate mobility of labour presupposes that there will be movement from job to job and in the course of seeking employment some unemployment is bound to be recorded. As a matter of judgement for Malaysia, unemployment of up to 5 per cent might constitute a residual level reflecting the need for mobility and the time taken to search for first time employment by those moving into the modern sector of the economy.

Irrespective of the level of unemployment, it is to be expected that the incidence of it will continue to be felt more by some groups than others. In 1985, for example, the unemployment rate was 7.6 for the Bumiputra, 7.0 for the Indian population and only 5.6 per cent for the Chinese.

If previous patterns are maintained, it will be those moving from traditional occupations that will be first affected, inevitably the Bumiputra, and the young, and in greater proportion than their representation in the population. This is a reflection, to some extent, of the need for the young and those in badly paid occupations to seek work in the modern sector of the economy. From the ethnic point of view, difficulty in overcoming racial discrimination will also be a contributing factor. For the most part, unemployment may be expected to be of limited duration for many of those looking for work, particularly when the demand for labour is expanding rapidly, but there will inevitably be individual instances when this is not the case and where special measures will be needed to facilitate mobility, such as those instituted for unemployed graduates.

In the early stages of development, educational attainments make it easier to secure employment. This is not necessarily the case as development proceeds and it no longer seems to apply in Malaysia. Of those in employment in 1987, half had education to secondary level or beyond. Therefore, educational attainment can no longer be expected to provide a satisfactory safeguard against unemployment.

In the end, the only way in which unemployment can be kept in check is by the creation of an adequate level of jobs. In the case of the Malaysian economy, demand management of a Keynesian type is unlikely to be able to make a very significant contribution to reducing unemployment; notwithstanding, it is important to maintain conditions conducive to a continued high rate of investment. Nevertheless, the provision of jobs will depend to a considerable degree on the supply side of the economy. In these circumstances, policy to alleviate unemployment is likely to have to continue to take the form of training or retraining schemes to equip those experiencing difficulty in obtaining employment with skills which are in demand. More broadly, this also has the implication that education itself has to be conducted with an eye to imparting some skills of value in earning a living.

Unemployment in Malaysia has the additional dimension that racial discrimination needs to be curbed in order to ensure that the incidence of unemployment is not borne unevenly. The proposals to monitor employment both in relation to numbers and the wage bill discussed below also have a bearing on the incidence of unemployment.

# Growth

The necessity for rapid growth in the economy in order to reduce poverty and promote greater racial equality was a cardinal principle of the NEP. In the past, as we have seen, growth was rapid and closely in line with aspirations. It made a major contribution to the economic well-being of the Bumiputra and allowed them to make some progress relative to other ethnic groups, but it did not eliminate poverty and it left considerable inequality in the distribution of income and assets. The growth camp in the political arena contends that what is needed to maintain the process towards viable national unity is a strong rate of growth, and it goes on to contend that if this were achieved, no other major policies would really be necessary. Very high rates of growth are contemplated and assumed to be possible. At times the thinking behind this approach appears to be that what other countries have done Malaysia can do and can do better. It is easy to be beguiled by the surface plausibility of such arguments. The development of the LDCs is not to be regarded as some race in which the prize goes to those who develop fastest, whether with or without the attainment of greater equality in income. A much more measured approach to the process of development is needed, fully to take into account the circumstances of different countries. In the case of Malaysia, poverty is much too evident, but it is not of the crippling intensity as that evident in other parts of Asia or Africa. Its eradication does not dictate a desperate attempt to attain some all-time high in the growth stakes: rather does it suggest a continued attempt to combine high rates of growth with well-constructed attempts further to reduce poverty by methods directed specifically to that end. To depend only on growth to reduce poverty and *a fortiori* to promote greater racial equality would be a crude policy indeed.

The concern for future growth rates raises both political and economic issues and we have benefitted from some work recently prepared by the MIER. In a paper from 1988 Datuk Dr. Salih has presented a balanced view of the form that economic policy might take, with strong emphasis on the directions and policies that would be required to improve the position of the poor and achieve national unity, to the extent that economic policies could be expected to contribute to this aim.[1] Nevertheless, the rate of growth put forward in the paper, nearly 10 per cent per annum, seems rather too

---

[1] *The New Economic Policy after 1990*, revised version of a paper presented at the MIER 1988 National Outlook Conference, Kuala Lumpur, 29-30 November 1988.

optimistic; as does the implied capital-output ratio of 3.5. The rate
of growth of the NIEs is likely to get increasingly difficult to
emulate as world competition in the industrial sphere increases, and
with so many emerging nations appearing as major industrial powers,
it will be difficult for all to keep up high rates of growth. It is also
not realistic to suppose that capital-output ratios can be kept down
by substituting cheap labour to a marked extent.

Capital-output ratios in modern industry are often very largely
dictated by technological factors and the opportunities for capital
saving are correspondingly limited.[2] It is not realistic to expect, at
present levels of development and as labour gets more expensive,
that capital-output ratios will fall. In preparing a perspective plan it
might be better to proceed on the assumption that the capital-output
ratio could be four or more and the rate of growth in output up to
eight per cent rather than ten. In some respects, this is not an
important issue. Whether Malaysian incomes double in ten years or
in thirteen[3] is not critical at this stage of her development, so long
as poverty continues to fall and ethnic inequality is reduced. It is
true, of course, that faster rather than slower growth will make this
easier to attain. Further it has to be noted that growth by itself will
not suffice to remove poverty without attendant other measures to
remove inequality. Arithmetic models of the type used in chapter 4
and by the MIER can readily be used to demonstrate how growth
can extinguish racial imbalances but this is, unfortunately, more a
reflection of the shortcomings of such models, which do not really
address the problem, and the many factors that are neglected in a
necessarily oversimplified view of how an economy works. There is
a need to extend these types of models to address these issues.

The Malaysian economy is now showing considerable resilience
and the foundations are there for further rapid growth. To a large
extent this will be determined by forces over which the government
has little close control. The economy is open to the world. The

---

[2]  An illustration from Malaysia is provided by the electrical and electronic industry
where most of the foreign equity was concentrated on the assembly of chips which
were relatively labour intensive. By the 1980s the industry was diversified into wafer
fabrication and the production of a whole range of consumer goods which were
relatively capital intensive. See *Malaysia Economic Report 1989-90*, p. 110, for
details.
[3]  The estimation of 13 years is based on a rate of growth of output of 8 per cent
per annum and a population increase of 2.6 per cent per annum as postulated in the
paper referred to. But it may be noted that the rate of increase of the work force at
the beginning of the 1990s is estimated to be about 3.1 per cent (see *Malaysia
Economic Report 1989-90*, p. 9).

benefits from oil, the proceeds of export crops, the returns from export markets are all highly dependent on world prices and world markets. The Government can certainly do something to help to provide economic conditions conducive to growth but it does not really have the capability of determining growth rates to any marked degree; very few governments do. Thus, to base an economic plan on this or that rate of growth, as it is so often tempting to do, is not so much to determine that rate of growth as to postulate it. One of the characteristics of a good economic plan is to recognise what rate of growth may be feasible and to build about that. If such estimation proves to be good or bad, changes can be made and policies changed but such adjustment processes are never costless and policies based on rates of growth outside the capacity of the economy can be very costly. If greater than expected rates of growth do prove to be possible, it will be much easier to accommodate and adjust to this than if the reverse proves to be the case. At this stage of Malaysia's development it would be sensible to plan on a rate of growth of 7 to 8 per cent and not to build hopes on some great leap forward.

It is evident that an accelerated rate of growth will require a continued high rate of investments and savings. A rate of increase in output of up to 8 per cent per annum will tax even Malaysia's capacity to save and will require gross investment rates of the order of 35 per cent or more of the GNP. This is a very high ratio and few countries can sustain investment at this level for a considerable length of time. Singapore has succeeded in forcing domestic savings to a totally exceptional and probably not sustainable level in excess of 40 per cent. Even Japan is saving only a little in excess of 30 per cent of GDP. But it may not be beyond the capacity of Malaysia to invest 35 per cent of the GDP for a time. In 1989, if estimates prove to be accurate, about 27.5 per cent of the GDP is likely to be invested and to this should be added the surplus in the balance of payments which was expected to amount to nearly 7 per cent of the GDP. Thus, in favourable circumstances an investment proportion of 35 per cent of GDP might be sustainable for a limited period. This implies, of course, that the impetus to invest is not reduced by the export of capital. The openness of the Malaysian economy extends, in practice, to capital movements as well as other transactions. It is also going to be critical that the international terms of trade do not deteriorate from their 1989 levels to a marked degree. A further factor is the maintenance of profitability which, amongst other things, depends on approaching labour scarcity and pressures for wages in the modern sector to rise.

The foreseeable rate of growth in the next decade can not be regarded as a panacea for the elimination of racial imbalances. Even very rapid growth would not achieve this, for there will be areas of activity that are left outside the scope of growth and for which special measures will be needed to reduce the incidence of poverty and racial imbalance. Without this there is a strong danger that growth will serve not to reduce inequality but to increase it, with those in the industrial sector of the economy increasing their income much more rapidly than those in the agricultural sector; and while many may move out of agriculture into industry, those remaining are very likely to continue to be impoverished without government intervention and unless agriculture can succeed in maintaining and extending the remarkable progress it has made in the past.

Without an ethnically better balanced economy the progress of growth could break down. Those that contend that the NEP is an impediment to growth seem to be in danger of deceiving themselves in relation to this. The NEP policy, as was contended in chapter 4, is not vastly different, in its modern form, from a strategy that is ostensibly growth orientated. Many of the measures associated with the NEP: elimination of poverty, better health and education etc. are all conducive to growth. So is emphasis on agricultural development and the need to redress the balance between town and countryside and between different areas and states of the country. What the opponents of the NEP seem to have particularly in mind when expressing their antagonism to it, appears to boil down to two specific measures: the regulation of industrial ownership and the system of quotas imposed for the employment of Bumiputra. Of these the regulation of industrial ownership appears to have been the most contentious.

## Malay Rights, Preferences and Discrimination

The Constitution defines a number of rights of Malays and other Bumiputra, providing preferential treatment in certain areas, including land alienation and administration, granting of licences and permits, access to educational and training facilities etc. As foreseen at the time of drawing up the Constitution and as practised over the years, these articles were intended to provide the legal base for secure and equal opportunities for Malays in the economic life of the nation — over time on an equal footing with other groups of citizens, in particular the Chinese. The NEP, as initially conceived and subsequently laid out in Plan documents, gave further content and specificity to some aspects of Malay preferences, including in particular a system of provisions for ownership and employment quotas, as well as budgetary allocations directed specially to assist the Malays in their economic pursuits. The administrative implementation of the NEP was characterised by flexibility and also by accommodation in its application to changing economic and political cirumstances, most notably seen in the retreat in the mid-1980s from the stipulations then in force for Malay equity participation in investment and even Malay participation in employment.

The explicit preferential arrangements in favour of the Malays are intended to counter what may be termed structural discrimination in economic life against them. As a matter of record, the outcome of economic forces combined clearly shows that the Bumiputra as a group are way behind the other major groups, in particular the Malaysian Chinese, in participation in the modern economy, in national growth and development, in control and ownership of capital and investments, in income and standards of living. It was the recognition of this built-in disadvantage of the Bumiputra in the economy at the time of negotiations for Merdeka in the 1950s, and in 1969/70 when the NEP was designed, that led to the introduction of explicit rights and preferences for the Bumiputra and their acceptance, more or less willingly, by all major parties. Without understanding of the existence and severity of such structural discrimination, the policies of explicit preference in favour of the Bumiputra would also not be understood and accepted. If and when structural discrimination as between ethnic groups has been largely overcome through restructuring of employment and ownership, management and control, income and asset distribution, there will be no longer any need for overt and specific preferences, at least no argument that can be based on considerations of social and ethnic balance and equity.

It is in the nature of specific rights and preferences for Malays and other Bumiputra, that where they are actually brought to bear (or even where there is fear that they will be applied), they are properly and understandably perceived as discrimination by those who do not enjoy such rights and preferences. This is true anywhere where some, but not all, of the population are legitimate and direct beneficiaries of preferences or affirmative action. The parties against whom discrimination of this nature is exercised may nevertheless lend their support to such provisions, as an agreed means to further accepted objectives, as indeed was done by all parties prior to Merdeka, when they accepted, as a central national objective, the build-up of Malay capacity to participate in the economic life of the nation at par with the Chinese and other nationals. However, those subjected to discrimination would want to be assured that the preferential provisions are not being misused in practice for purposes other than those agreed and, also, that they are designed and implemented so as to be cost effective. Given that the direct costs of the application of rights, quotas etc. are borne by those who are excluded from preferential treatment, in particular the Chinese, while the direct benefits redound to the Bumiputra, it becomes particularly important that the pursuit of the agreed national objective is and is seen to be effectively served by the system of preferences and discrimination actually imposed.

In 1969/70, there was no doubt in the minds of the framers of the NEP that a move towards national unity — and indeed to a viable society — had to include a clear, if gradual, easing of racial economic inequalities, accepting that this required management that included more explicit and intensified preferences and discrimination than in the past. At the initiation of the NEP in 1969-70, the estimate of income inequality was expressed as a ratio of average per capita income of non-Malays to Malays of 7 to 4. While subsequently this estimate was found to have been a clear understatement of the lag in income of the Malays, even the ratio of 7 to 4 (indicative of non-Malays having 75 per cent higher average standards of living than did the Malays at that time) was so large that the need for corrective action was firmly impressed on the politicians — and the NEP took shape. Today, after 20 years of NEP which have brought some easement, and with somewhat better statistics, the average income inequality between the major ethnic groups is again estimated to be at roughly the level of 7 to 4, just about the same as was assumed in 1970. As far as the awareness of racial disparities are concerned, therefore, and as these influence national unity, the basis for the judgement on the need for and importance of an NEP strategy for national unity appears very similar today compared to what it was in 1970. It remains an eminently political decision to determine how far the present situation is consistent with continued overt preferences and discrimination, intensified or eased.

Policy makers today can draw on the twenty years' experience of the NEP, including the effectiveness or otherwise of the various discriminatory provisions as formulated and implemented in the 1970s and 1980s. They can also draw on the lively, if not always focused debate about the NEP, which has been conducted in Malaysia with so much intensity and feeling. It is here not only a question of a balanced assessment of real costs and benefits, but also of perceptions as felt by individuals directly concerned, as expressed by intellectuals and other opinion makers, and as variously interpreted within the political and administrative system. What can emerge from analysis, therefore, is not at all a blueprint for the future, but only a commentary on choices to be made. To this we now turn, taking up a number of separate issues involving Malay rights and preferences, not necessarily in order of their importance and certainly not in an attempt to be all inclusive.

## Land

In the Constitution, land alienation and administration are subjects of special attention, safeguarding traditional systems of land use, including the prerogatives and responsibilities of the rulers and — by delegation — the state governments. As in most other countries, there is in Malaysia a strong attachment to the land: the cultural identity of the Bumiputra is closely linked to the land and the village. At the same time, land is the basis for much economic development, and traditional rights and practices often are challenged in the process of growth and modernisation. Non-Bumiputra Malaysians, particularly those with modest standards of living, are clearly subjected to discriminatory treatment in this field. Not only do the Bumiputra have an overwhelming head start, both as owners (or in control) of most of the land for smallholder cultivation and as workers gaining a livelihood in agriculture, but the access of non-Malays is also very limited indeed when it comes to new land for agriculture. This has been hard to accept by the excluded, most clearly in relation to willing agriculturalists in the New Villages. It would seem that the practice of Bumiputra preferences in the past in this case may have been carried too far, beyond the point where benefits no longer outweigh the costs. At least, land policy is a case which illustrates the need to analyse — economically and socially, as well as politically — the costs as well as the benefits of policies now pursued.

## Public services

As a result of history and tradition, the security forces (police and armed forces) as well as the central civil service are heavily manned and directed by Malays. This mainly reflects explicit discrimination in recruitment and promotion which is not generally or readily accepted by the non-Bumiputra. With respect to discrimination in the security forces, perhaps also in the civil service, the Malay justification sometimes appears to be essentially political: these are the instruments of ultimate control of the society. For the non-Malays this argument is definitely not permissible; this kind of discrimination calls in question their loyalty as individuals and as ethnic groups to the nation of which they are citizens.

A different and more plausible argument has been voiced, namely that this is the main field of employment in the modern sector where the Government itself does the hiring. Therefore, as long as the Malays are not in fact absorbed in the private modern sector, dominantly controlled by the non-Malays, in numbers and at levels commensurate with those of other ethnic groups, the exercise of preferential recruitment and promotion of Malays to the security forces and civil service is necessary to provide some offsetting force. Analytically this is a valid position, although it is in the nature of seeking to cancel a negative by imposing two. In any event, it illustrates that there is real scope for mutual accommodation: the Malays might accept more non-Malays in the public services as and when the non-Malays accept more effective arrangements, including quotas, for more Malays in the private sector, also at higher levels of control and income. While no abrupt change in numbers may be practicable, it would seem timely to seek gradual accommodation on this point in the interest of nation building.

## Employment

During the period of the NEP to date, the rapid growth of the modern sectors of the economy has attracted and accommodated a large influx of Bumiputra. In this important respect, a major objective of the NEP has been well served. There is, however, still some way to go to affect the full measure of employment restructuring in aggregate numbers of Malaysians of different ethnic groups in the modern sectors of the economy. Moreover, further progress may now be more difficult to achieve as such disparities in employment patterns become narrower. If, as we assume, the objective of restructuring employment patterns is maintained and is to be reflected in the management of development towards an ethnically better balanced economy, then this is hardly the time to leave aside such policy instruments as are available and have been tested in the past and have proven to bring results. Nevertheless, we read into the history of the last few years a weakening in the application of such instruments, both in the provisions of the ICA and in the administrative application of employment restructuring coersion and suasion vis-à-vis the private sector.

Employment restructuring, then, is in the first place a matter of ensuring entry of Malays into modern sector activities, so as to correspond more closely to their share of the overall labour force. Secondly, it is a matter of creating conditions and incentives that eventually will allow rough parity to be reflected at all levels of operation within the enterprises of the modern sector. In this second respect progress is dependent on investment in general and specialised education, as well as in training and experience. Progress, therefore, necessarily takes time, but can be speeded up by Government action, including also programmes in partnership with the private sector, as well as exercise of suasion on the basis of persistent monitoring of progress in individual enterprises and industry groups. As experience from the NEP period to date shows, this type of action can be an effective force for restructuring also at higher levels. However, as we look back over the period of the NEP, we find that the scope for such action has not been actively explored. Thus, for instance, while returns required from enterprises give a basis for monitoring the ethnic composition of their labour force — and for a dialogue on further improvements in that balance — the same kind of returns with appropriate breakdown do not seem to have been used — at least not as actively — to push for advancement of Malays as between levels of operation and responsibility within the enterprise.

Similarly, with a relatively small addition in the information returned from enterprises on ethnic composition of their labour force, namely information on wages, salaries and other benefits received, the authorities and the enterprises would have at their disposal a set of data that would closely link employment patterns to income disparities within enterprises and for groups and enterprises. Such data, in turn, would provide most helpful inputs into the Government's review of progress in creating an ethnically better balanced economy; it equally would provide a basis for setting time specific targets for such progress at the levels of individual enterprises and industry groups and for developing cooperative programmes of action on training and advancement of lagging ethnic groups. While politicians must accept that progress in this respect can move only as widely and speedily as is consistent with efficiency, enterprises must actively exploit and seek to create such opportunities for acceleration of Malays into higher echelons. This is an area for give and take which again illustrates the potentials of public and private sector cooperation. Laws and formal regulations will be needed, as are institutions to organise and administer the effort. Most of those needed are already on the books, but the most decisive element will be the degree of attention and priority given to the task by those politicians and administrators who will have to give specific content and bite to the provisions. In turn, this depends on political commitment and steadfastness of purpose.

## Ownership

The stipulation in the NEP of targets for 1990 of percentage shares of ownership of Malaysian capital assets, notably in equity, of 30:40:30 by Bumiputra, other Malaysians and foreign interests respectively, has been a focus of the debate on the implementation of the NEP. It is not clear from the statistical evidence exactly how far the move towards better racial balance in this respect has advanced. However, the increase in percentage ownership of share capital held by Bumiputra appears to have come to a halt in the last five years well short of the target of 30 per cent; official figures used in fact show less than 20 per cent, but this is most certainly an underestimate. Foreign interests have reduced their share to under one-quarter, i.e. also well below the target of 30 per cent. By contrast, there has been a massive increase in non-Bumiputra holdings in the 1980s to 50 per cent or more, exceeding the target by about one-quarter. Particularly troubling, of course, is the aborted progression in the Bumiputra share, which itself is not unrelated to the roll-back in the implementation of the NEP in the mid-1980s and to the efforts of Government to divest part of the assets of trust funds for the Bumiputra to private parties. While, at the time, these changes in policy may have been well advised to spur the recovery of overall private investment and to provide an environment with incentives for higher efficiency of operation, they have delayed the attainment of a better balanced distribution between Bumiputra and other Malaysians in the country's capital stock and control of the economy. Therefore, at this point of time it is necessary to raise the question of re-introducing and re-strengthening the NEP provisions and practices for a more balanced asset distribution. Again, this is very much a question for political judgement and decision, the answer to which only in part depends on the economic consequences of alternative courses of action.

For what it may be worth in the circumstances of the 1990s, the experience of the policies for improved asset distribution pursued in the years up to the mid-1980s suggests, on the one hand, that on the whole there was no significant negative impact from these policies, as practised, on overall investment and growth rates. Most criticisms of the NEP on this score are overdrawn. On the other hand, the benefits in terms of improved racial *income* distribution, while real, were probably quite modest, particularly since, to a considerable extent, this particular flow of benefits intensified and financed the shift to a more skewed and inequitable distribution within the Malay group. Moreover, the manner in which some Bumiputra equity holdings have been acquired, the emergence of a select group of individuals and even political party interests as powerful owners of much of such equity and, with some notable exceptions, the reported lack of professionalism and business acumen displayed in the direction and control of companies taken over, raise serious questions about several aspects of the NEP policy of equity restructuring, at least of the practices of its implementation and its results. Thus, there are strong and valid reasons for reconsideration of the NEP approach to asset restructuring, not so much targets set for achievement as the practices of their pursuit. Yet, without a greatly stepped-up Malay share of ownership and control of assets, there is no possibility of ever achieving for the Bumiputra a share of income and control of the economy anywhere nearly commensurate with their share in population. Even assuming that employment patterns in modern activities, also at higher levels of responsibility and income, could eventually come to be in reasonable accord with population patterns, half or more of net value added in the economy will continue to accrue predominantly to the non-Malays. Perhaps even more important than the consequences for racial income disparities will be the realisation by Malays that control of the economic destiny of Malaysia in this respect will escape them.

One-third of Bumiputra ownership of corporate capital is now held through trust funds, as distinct from equity held by individual Bumiputra. Questions have been raised about the benefit to the Bumiputra of such holdings; and since the early 1980s, the share held collectively in this way has been reduced, in part through a deliberate policy of disinvestment. While in the interest of efficiency and flexibility some disengagement of Federal and particularly State Government ownership and control of enterprises in Malaysia may be well advised in many cases, there has been some unjustified extension of this kind of argument to funds held in trust for Bumiputra ownership and control of units of production and trade within the market economy. It appears that the disinvestment of such holdings often has been difficult to carry out without contributing to the further acceleration of economic imbalance in asset and income distribution *within* the Malay group; moreover, it has proved difficult to devise and operate a procedure for transfer to Bumiputra individuals or groups, which avoids the fact and appearance of favouritism. The very purpose and intent of the equity ownership restructuring was to ensure that effective control and management of the growing economy gradually redounded more equally to the Bumiputra and to as wide a group as possible. However, individual Bumiputra, except the already rich and powerful, can hardly gain control and management of modern enterprises through acquisition of decisive share holdings. Collectively, however, through trust funds, it is possible to wield influence through significant equity stakes: in general meetings of shareholders, in representation on boards, in the determination of strategies of operation and management, in selection of chief operating officers etc. This is the way the Permodalan Nasional Berhad (PNB or in English The National Equity Corporation) operates with considerable success and that experience could be more widely applied. If — as has been suggested — PNB is now as fully committed and extended as efficiency and control permit, a set of parallel PNBs might be established, at both Federal and State levels.

In the last several years, the determination and the effort to restructure capital ownership and control so as to better reflect the composition of the population and to reach at least the target of a 30 per cent Bumiputra share appear to have run out of steam. Unless there is some renewed vigour in this area, the fears of the Bumiputra of what they see as internal colonialism replacing British domination may again surface and threaten social and economic peace. But broad national support for asset restructuring is unlikely to be forthcoming — or for that matter earned — unless the malpractices of operation of the instruments of policies for equity restructuring are recognised and effectively curbed.

## Social Policies

The debate in Malaysia on the impact of the NEP in the past and on its scope and content for the future has so far been conducted somewhat separately at two levels. First, there has been the *economic* debate centred on the consequences of NEP for overall growth and development, for levels of investments, for incentives and productivity, for distribution of income and assets. Second, the NEP has also been a central topic in the *ideological* and *political* debate, reflecting ethnic group interests, shifting party political circumstances etc. Debate at both levels is, of course, important and legitimate. However, each would gain in depth and relevance by being extended into matters of social development and social policy. Moreover, the debates at the economic and political levels would have a better chance of coming into more interaction, if they were informed by a growing body of scholarly analysis, carefully reviewed experience and critical insight about the structures and dynamics of social change.

Social science has come a long way in Malaysian universities and research institutions in the last couple of decades. Much is now known, but little has been achieved — perhaps for lack of trying — in bringing this body of knowledge to bear on the issues of ethnic economic disparities as barriers to national unity. As a result, the administrative and political leadership has not been in a position to give much feed-back to the scholars and institutions to help define issues of policy relevance for study and research. There now appears to be a situation with considerable scope and opportunity for gains to be made from intensive interaction between policy makers and the social scientists. As a beginning, perhaps, the social science research community in Malaysia might be invited to make a contribution in the form of scholarly assessments of social consequences — positive and negative — of particular policies; for example, sociological studies of experiences from the way housing projects are organised, or from ethnic discrimination in university acceptance, or even studies of reactions of Malay villagers and urban workers to the fact of conspicuous wealth being amassed by other Malays.

## Planning and Monitoring

Overall growth and structural change in the economy are traditional and well developed areas of economic policy and planning analysis in Malaysia. However, the record of planning specifically related to the ethnic dimension in the NEP is less than impressive, so is the development of published statistics with ethnic breakdown. It is unclear how much unpublished statistical material for ethnic groups in fact is available in Malaysia from censuses and surveys, but in any case it has not, it seems, been much drawn upon for NEP planning purposes. This is an area in which greater investment of resources and openness to public scrutiny and debate in coming years promises high returns in the search for effective instruments of management to gradually ease racial economic imbalances and to further national unity. Effective policy to support and strengthen the shift to an ethnically better balanced economy must build on an information and data base that is steadily being improved and extended, as well as up-dated.

Such a data base for the past would need to be used for extrapolations and projections into future years, relating the latter to those of official plans but with extension and supplementation in part informed by market studies, including assessment of export potentials, and by evidence from inter-country comparisons of the evolution of patterns of production and demand.

Three sets of data and projections are central to an NEP analysis:

- Data and projections on the overall growth of the economy — as experienced over the past and as projected for the future — detailed as fully as possible by individual industry or activity categories. (In 1969 a set of 23 sectors were used, for expository purposes grouped together in 5 sectors: Traditional Rural, Modern Rural, Traditional Urban, Modern Urban, and Government.) The main concern would be with value added by industry category and with the primary input components.

- Data on employment and wage levels and patterns by ethnic categories and by industry group for past and future years, detailed, estimated and projected in essentially the same way as for value added etc. above.

- Data on ethnic breakdowns for non-wage primary inputs (profits, interest, management etc.) by activity categories.

It would be necessary to develop these sets of statistics so as to allow them to be combined, specifically to ensure that equivalent industry groups are used for all three sets. This would allow planners to study the interrelationships that emerge over time between, on the one hand, growth rates and growth patterns and, on the other hand, employment levels and wage rates — as well as returns to capital and management — by industry and ethnic groups. The analysis would focus — *inter alia* — on inter-relationships between sectors (internally and with foreign countries) in terms of input-output and demand structures; technical and economic potentials of individual activity and product lines; interactions between economic growth, employment and labour force participation rates, overall and by ethnic group; education, training and productivity aspects of growth and development, overall and by industry sectors as well as by ethnic groups; volume and price developments of foreign trade as well as internal terms of trade, again in their relationships to changing economic growth levels and patterns.

Such an approach would help clarify the impact of individual policy action, of strategic approaches, and of choice between options for policy on the levels of income, employment etc. and on their ethnic distribution. The socio-political dimensions of this kind of planning would enter the analysis both in the choice of alternative policy strategies, which are judged to be relevant and illustrative, and in the interpretation of the results that emerge from alternative sets of policy assumptions.

Planning for a vigorous and balanced economy along the above lines would have several advantages over the more traditional planning practices of the past which have given but partial consideration to NEP objectives. It would allow a more policy oriented monitoring of change and progress, in that the major policy actions and impacts would be explicitly specified in the planning exercise. For this an appropriate planning model of the economy might be an advantage. The purpose would not be to provide forecasts of what might happen in the future, so much as to trace the consequences of various outcomes of policy actions in relation to levels of activity in the various sectors of the economy and other factors. A major aspect of this would be to show results in terms of particular targets for growth and other variables on ethnic patterns of employment and on the distribution of income and assets between ethnic groups. By aggregation at various levels, achievements in the reduction or otherwise of racial income disparities could be derived and monitored, as could ownership patterns, employment promotion of lagging ethnic groups etc. Depending on the outcome of such analyses and monitoring, adjustments in policy and policy mix could be considered on a more informed basis. Such review of NEP as has taken place in the past two decades has had at best a tenuous link to the policy actions themselves. Given the way planning has actually been undertaken, the monitoring of NEP so far has been deficient and of little help to policy makers.

## Seizing the Opportunities

The agenda for policy and action for development and restructuring in the 1990s and beyond is a heavy one. Yet, the challenge is clear, also in terms of the response that is needed. Moreover, it is well within the capacity of the political and governmental, executive and administrative systems to respond adequately.

In 1969 and 1970, the chart for the advance into the future was much less clear than it is today. At that time, new policies had to be designed without having the benefit of experience from tested approaches in Malaysia — or for that matter, without much experience from other countries similarly placed. The political leadership, in adopting the NEP, had little more to rely on than their own instincts and judgements and some imaginative but only tentative analysis from the technicians. Now that the results from two decades of implementation of the NEP are in, decisions for the coming years can be based more confidently on lessons from the past: What works — and works as intended — and what does not seem to work? What balance of components is needed to bring about improvements? What are the costs — real and perceived — of particular actions? Are self-sustaining improvements brought about or is a particular policy just a holding operation? What are the dangers of lack of consistency of approach and persistency of effort?

The NEP has stood the test of time. Yet, there is a clear need for an open and thorough review of its components, if not its thrust, in the light of the relatively rich experience now at hand, not only from Malaysia but worldwide, and the changing opportunities and constraints foreseen for the coming years. In the sections above we have made some suggestions, but what is covered there does not add up to a full programme. This can only come through debate and argument involving all major parties and interests, much as what is encompassed by the NECC. (No report from the NECC has been available at this time of writing.) It must also be based on careful analysis and data, such as can be done comprehensively and with authority by the Government's own statistics, planning and policy institutions. Malaysia is fortunate in having well qualified economists, social scientists and planners to do such work, if only they are firmly guided to address the principal issues for political deliberation and resolution.

The four major economic thrusts for Malaysian development under the NEP are central objectives for the 1990s and beyond as they have been in the past: first, the reduction of inter-ethnic inequalities and of intra-ethnic maldistribution of income and assets, second, the further reduction of poverty, third, the containment of unemployment, and fourth, the furtherance of economic growth. Their attainment will make heavy demands on the politicians. They will have to be able to present and advocate their political preferences and programmes in terms of the interests of all Malaysians, not only the narrower group interests. In so doing, they will have to put on the line short-term political gains in popularity amongst their supporters — particularly in respect of policies affecting ethnic disparities — for more basic and long-term contributions to national unity and development. Politicians and the public at large will have to accept that approximate parity between the ethnic groups will take time to accomplish and will not be attained in only a few years: the Malays will have to accept that for quite some time to come the Malaysian Chinese will be working and living at markedly higher levels of productivity and income; the non-Malays will have to accept that Malay rights have to be firmly and persistently exercised also in future years until the Bumiputra have overcome the handicaps in the modern economy under which they are now labouring.

Understandably, it is not easy for Malaysians fully to accept the constraints placed on the pursuit of individual and special group interests by the overriding needs of national cohesion and eventual ethnic equality. A necessary condition for acceptance is that the costs and benefits of actions taken or even proposed are as fully clarified and debated as possible. A better system of monitoring of actions taken and of results obtained could be of considerable help. This would require collection of more and better statistics relating to issues of national unity and ethnic imbalances, intensive professional and objective analysis and scrutiny of the data produced, as well as wide publication and open debate of the findings. In these respects — even after 20 years of NEP — Malaysia has a long way to go. As the debate is now conducted, assertion is often the substitute for carefully examined statistics, prejudice for fact.

For this kind of monitoring and debate, Malaysia does have, of course, the capability in ample measure to do the work; it also has a number of institutions that could in fact do it: the Statistics Department, the EPU and other parts of the Prime Minister's Department, for specific aspects perhaps also the Central Bank, the Ministry of Finance and even the Auditor General and others. Yet, the job is hardly done seriously, neither in sufficient detail nor with sufficient width.

One reason for this is the lack of political clearance for such work and the great reticence in sharing such information as is available with the public. It is difficult to understand and accept this attitude and it militates against constructive debate and the building of informed consensus on diagnosis and treatment. Without creating new institutions, but through political and administrative resolution, a practice might be initiated of preparing annual and ad hoc reviews of the course of implementation and results of the NEP as a whole and of its constituent parts. Such reviews are needed, not only in respect of statistics and of economic policy actions, but also of legal, administrative, budgetary aspects of the NEP. However, the professional quality of the reporting and the candour and independence of the reviews prepared would determine the degree of acceptance of the findings and ultimately their value for the evolution of policy generally and NEP specifically.

# FOUR SELECTED DOCUMENTS
# FROM 1969-70

*With minor presentational changes these documents are reproduced
in the following pages as they appeared originally*

# POLICIES FOR GROWTH WITH RACIAL BALANCE[1]

## The Background

Economic and social policies of the coming decade can play a major role in modernising Malaysia and ensuring a degree of political stability. But the events of May 13th and of the election that preceded them clearly suggest that a continuation of past policies in a "back to normalcy" spirit will not be good enough.

When independence was achieved in 1957, there was an implicit agreement between the dominant Malay and Chinese components of the Alliance Government, and the essentials of this agreement remained in force up until the 1969 election. Briefly stated, political power was to remain largely in Malay hands and this power was to be used to promote Malay economic interests so as to reduce and eventually eliminate the gap between the Malay and non-Malay economic position. Modern trade and industry, on the other hand, were to be allowed to develop with a minimum of government interference, even though it was recognised that this policy would mean that most modern businesses would remain in Chinese (or foreign) hands. Tax revenue was to be used in part to build the infrastructure for the modern sector and in part to promote Malay welfare. Public expenditures, however, were not to be allowed to expand to a point where they might jeopardise balance of payments equilibrium or internal financial stability.

The pursuit of these policies did in fact achieve a large measure

---

[1] This paper, written by J. Faaland within a few weeks of the riots of 13 May 1969, was only a personal first assessment. However, the paper was subsequently circulated widely within Government. It was instrumental in formulating issues for debate and became a reference document in subsequent elaboration of analysis.

of real success in terms of economic growth and development; moreover it gave the country twelve years of relative political stability. But, in retrospect, it is recognised that the policies were not good enough. There was some government expenditure to promote Malay income; various kinds of direct controls were applied (employment quotas, preferential licensing, etc.); and specialised institutions (FAMA, Bank Bumiputra, MARA, etc.) were established. Employment quotas did create jobs for thousands of Malays, but they did not touch the vast majority of the Malay population which was in the rural areas. The specialised institutions also provided some Malay employment, but they were operated too inefficiently to have a significant favourable impact on rural marketing, credit, and the like. The end result of these efforts was that population growth wiped out the few gains that were made and rural Malay incomes failed to rise significantly. The increasing gap between rich and poor in turn had the political effect of pushing many Malay intellectuals and politicians within  UMNO toward advocacy of increasingly radical solutions.

These political trends within the Malay community were quite apparent to the Chinese and Indian communities and were a source of increasing concern. More important, the original arrangement of the 1950s that provided a favourable climate for Chinese businessmen had little appeal to the Chinese and Indians who were labourers, teachers, and professionals. This majority, who were not businessmen, did experience rising incomes, but the number of new jobs created did not keep up with the number of new entrants into the labour force and hence unemployment rose. Rightly or wrongly, this job squeeze was blamed increasingly on the Malay income promotion policies of the government, in particular on the direct controls favouring the Malays. Furthermore, the Chinese and Indian communities were more and more able to express their dissatisfaction through the ballot box (due to the rapidly increasing proportion of citizens and registered voters).

The effect of these trends was obscured in the 1964 elections by Indonesian confrontation, but not in 1969 when a substantial majority of the Chinese and Indian communities voted against the Alliance Government. A feeling in the Malay community of having been played out by the more aggressive Chinese, of losing out, had been growing for some years. This concern that the Malay population might be relegated to a permanent status of economic, social and political inferiority seemed to many Malays to be confirmed by the outcome of the elections, particularly in Perak and Selangor. The Chinese, in their turn, were elated. Foresight, perhaps even different handling of the crisis, might have prevented the violence of May 13th, but even without the riots, the underlying political balance had been shattered.

The main challenge that faces the government today is that of constructing a new alliance of moderate elements (Malay, Chinese and Indian) within the nation. But the new alliance must be built on a rather different base from the old one. At the centre of this new arrangement must be a series of policies that will be genuinely effective in raising Malay incomes and providing for Malay entry into the modern sector on the basis of real equality. So far few such policies have arisen either from within or without the government. There is a shift in emphasis toward dealing with the unemployment problem among Malay youths, but this shift will do little for the 94% of the Malay work force that is employed.

## Constraints and Options

The remainder of this paper is devoted to a discussion of a series of policies that might be really effective in meeting at least the minimum aspirations of the Malay population. But from the outset of this discussion it should always be kept in mind that certain political and economic policies put definite limits on the kinds of policies that can be pursued.

First and foremost among the political realities is the fact that nearly half of the people of West Malaysia as a whole and nearly two out of three of those living west of the mountains and south of Kedah (but including Penang) are non-Malays - see Table A. 1. With the exception of a few wealthy businessmen and highly trained professionals, most of these people have no place else to go or at least no place to which they would go voluntarily. A policy designed to promote the emigration of Chinese and Indians, therefore, is bound to fail to change substantially the percentage distribution of the population. Such a policy would instead cause an outflow of the most skilled and enlightened, leaving behind a discontented mass of the less-educated. The predictable result would be the rise of left-wing parties that would base their programme on an appeal to communal discontent and communal solidarity against the other races. The present DAP programme, by comparison, would come to appear moderate.

If the government were to go a step further and attempt to promote emigration by severe repressive means, it would almost certainly mean civil war and possibly the effective partition of the country. It is difficult to see how either side could win such a confrontation in the sense of having firm and unchallenged rule over the whole country afterwards. The relative strengths of the two sides are too near even and not just in numbers alone. Malay control of the government and army would be offset by the superior organisational ability and guerrilla warfare capability of the Chinese. Both sides would have comparable financial resources. Either side, if it appeared to be losing, could appeal to counterbalancing outside support (Indonesia in the case of the Malays, Singapore and eventually Communist China in the case of the Chinese).

The most important economic reality that limits the options open to the government is the fact that leadership in the modern sector is almost entirely in the hands of non-Malays and is going to remain so for some time. Industrial ownership, management, and technical staffs are almost entirely Chinese except for a few Europeans and Americans. Commerce, foreign and domestic, at all levels is either in British or Chinese hands with the latter increasingly dominant. There are few or no Malay estates. Malay participation in construction is largely confined to unskilled and semi-skilled jobs. And university graduates in the sciences, medicine, and engineering are almost entirely Chinese or Indians. Only in the government are there large numbers of Malays in managerial type positions and even there the Malay roll is heavily concentrated in the area of general leadership (e.g. the MHFS) while technical jobs remain largely in the hands of the non-Malays.

The only way this situation could be changed rapidly would be if the government socialised all or most industry and commerce as was done say in Burma (where the Chinese population was quite small). The results of such a step, as in Burma, would almost certainly mean stagnation and decline in the modern sectors for many years to come. Further the Malaysian economy is far richer than that of Burma at the time of socialisation and thus the decline in the Malaysian modern sector would be more dramatic and the consequent political effects more severe. Even with socialisation the changeover to Malay control would be largely a superficial one. Technical jobs would continue to be held mainly by Chinese and Indians, not because of the exercise of any kind of monopoly power by these groups, but Malay technicians, at least in any number, simply don't exist.

These political and economic realities clearly set limits on how far a responsible government can ignore the vital interests of the non-Malay population. In the sphere of politics, stability depends heavily on the willingness of a substantial portion of the Chinese and Indians to continue to support moderate political programmes, either those of

## TABLE A.1
## DISTRIBUTION OF POPULATION IN WEST MALAYSIA
(June 1967)

| State | Malays | Chinese | Non-Malays Indians | Others |
|---|---|---|---|---|
| Kelantan | 619,857 | 37,639 | 8,074 | 11,635 |
| Terengganu | 349,836 | 22,916 | 4,711 | 1,275 |
| Kedah | 627,336 | 186,552 | 87,811 | 23,436 |
| Perlis | 90,541 | 21,160 | 2,135 | 3,770 |
| Total | 1687,570 (80.4%) | 268,267 | 102,731 (19.6%) | 40,116 |
| Pahang | 242,609 | 146,216 | 31,283 | 5,444 |
| Johor | 644,678 | 525,007 | 97,057 | 31,220 |
| Total | 887,287 (51.5%) | 671,223 | 128,340 (48.4%) | 36,64 |
| Selangor | 418,964 | 667,736 | 274,433 | 47,748 |
| Perak | 658,065 | 712,783 | 239,596 | 26,161 |
| Penang | 217,339 | 428,689 | 89,747 | 16,284 |
| Melaka | 207,053 | 162,112 | 33,212 | 7,949 |
| N.Sembilan | 216,359 | 204,119 | 76,912 | 12,639 |
| Total | 1717,780 (36.4%) | 2175,439 | 713,900 (63.6%) | 110,781 |
| Total | 4292,637 (50.3%) | 3115,009 | 944,941 (49.7%) | 187,561 |

the Alliance or of some alternative moderate grouping. This need in turn requires a mechanism for political expression and organisation through which Malays and non-Malays alike can choose their spokesmen and leaders. It probably also requires a rearrangement of the powers and responsibilities of the local, state and federal governments, so that these leaders can exercise real power in areas that directly affect their constituents (perhaps including the local police). Malay political dominance may still be maintained at the federal level and to a lesser degree also at the state level, by ensuring that election districts are so drawn that Malay areas are over-represented. It goes without saying that, in addition to or as part of these measures, the physical security of the entire population, Malay and non-Malay, must be guaranteed.

In the economic sphere there must be clear limits set on the amount of interference with the modern private sector, particularly industry, that is to be applied. Otherwise that sector will not play its vital role in the modernisation of Malaysian society, both Malay and non-Malay. Furthermore, a rapid increase in unemployment among young Chinese and Indians will be at least as politically explosive as a comparable increase in Malay unemployment. Thus not only must extreme policies be avoided such as ones that would throw presently employed Chinese and Indians out of work replacing them with Malays, but there must also be provisions for increases in Chinese and Indian employment.

Within the broad limits of these political and economic realities and given a moderate government, however, there is a wide variety of Malay development policies that can be pursued. But first the goals of these policies must be made clearer.

## Strategies and Goals

An effective Malay development policy must begin by recognising that the Malay community is not one homogeneous group, but several different groups who find themselves living in very different social and economic situations and whose needs are not identical.

A central feature of all economic policies must be the increase of rural income and employment together with and as part of an attempt to slow Malay migration to the cities. A second major feature of policy should be slowing rather than facilitating Chinese and Indian migration into areas that are now overwhelmingly Malay (principally the East Coast plus Kedah and Perlis).

It is not suggested that one should attempt to permanently segregate the races in Malaysia. Over the long run the only hope for political stability will be the existence of a high degree of integration, but integration of people whose abilities and interests are similar enough to benefit from the experience and to live in peace. Just who should be encouraged to integrate and who should not, ought to be decided on the basis of an investigation of the likely results and not by sweeping generalisations and rules. Certainly, however, the integrated group should include at a minimum all those who are highly educated as well as some substantial proportion of the urban skilled population.

One approach that has to some extent been tried in the past is to promote urbanisation through growth of the modern sector, while at the same time attempting to increase the percentage share of Malays in that sector. No consideration appears to have been given, however, to whether the resulting integration would lead to genuine racial harmony. To the degree that this policy has been carried to a point where it has encouraged urban migration it has been counterproductive. Even if the income of Malays is raised significantly by employing them in urban jobs, there is still likely to be an increase in discontent, in part because of the difficulties involved in the adjustment to an unfamiliar way of life, but even more because the wide income differential that separates the unskilled Malay from the rest of the urban population will be made glaringly apparent. In the future, therefore, any attempt to help the urban unskilled Malay population must be designed in such a way as not to encourage a new influx from the rural areas.

University graduates and other skilled urban Malay residents present a number of problems which are substantially different from those of other Malays. It is this group that now provides and will continue to provide the political and government sector economic leadership of the country. Thus it is crucial that a significant portion of this group become as highly skilled as the individuals' own intellectual resources allow.

The specific policies that can be used in pursuit of the general goals are numerous, but the most important ones are four in number. Briefly stated they include: a thorough going land reform and support to smallholder farmers; a major effort to accelerate new land development; a larger and redirected education effort; and a policy of rapid industrialisation. In addition to these four main programme areas, there would be a number of *ad hoc* measures of a shorter term nature designed to provide Malay employment, enhance Malay incomes and stem migration to the cities.

Given this variety in situations, problems and needs it is of importance — when discussing policies to improve Malay income and employment prospects and to provide for Malay participation in the modernisation process — to separate at least four Malay groups, viz:

1. Rural Malays on the East Coast and in Kedah and Perlis,
2. Rural Malays on the West Coast except Kedah and Perlis,
3. Urban semi-skilled and unskilled Malays, and,

4. Educated Malays particularly those with University-level (as well as MARA) education.

The precise nature and combination of suggested policies, the four major policies as well as *ad hoc* measures, vary considerably depending on which of the four Malay groups they are designed to affect. In the following we seek to clarify the policy requirements for these main groups.

## Rural Income and Welfare: Policies for the East Coast, Kedah and Perlis

The main economic problem in the East Coast and in Kedah and Perlis is that incomes are low and rather stagnant. Unemployment and underemployment also exist, but are of less importance.

The first major feature of a development programme for these parts of the country relates to land ownership and tenancy, incentives to improve agricultural technology, and credit and marketing facilities for the small producer. While the data are weak and information incomplete, a significant barrier to progress and improved conditions of rural life is that half the land is being farmed by tenants under very insecure conditions of tenure. Rents rise with productivity (and probably even without a rise in productivity) and tenants often remain on a given piece of land only for a few years. Under such circumstances, improvements are of interest to farmers only if their fruits are quickly realisable. Long-term investments of effort and labour benefit mainly the land owner, not so much the tenant. Even if substantial capital investments are undertaken by the government, farmers may be slow to respond if much of the extra income will end up in the hands of others. The widespread use of the T.O.L. (Temporary Occupation License) presents similar problems for farmer incentives and thus for farmer incomes as does the tenant/landowner relationship.

To the extent such a situation prevails, any really successful rural development policy for this region must begin with or at least include adjustments in the landowner/tenant relationships. If thoroughgoing land reform seems to be too drastic, there are a number of lesser steps that will at least eliminate the present system's worst features. A guarantee of security of tenure to tenant farmers and the establishment and enforcement of maximum fixed rents would both go some way toward insuring that productivity gains would not end up benefitting only the landowners. An existing law providing security of tenure and rental maximum provisions for paid farmers apparently has not been adopted and enforced.

The major barriers to land reform in any country are political. Only a major and continuing effort will do the job. Many countries have land reform legislation, but few have land reform. Effective enforcement requires continued vigilance, a large staff of inspectors, good land records, etc. but most of all it requires the determination of the political leadership to carry it out. Although the initial barriers to reform are political, the potential gains for political stability are enormous.[2]

The second major feature of an East Coast development programme would involve much more rapid land development. This is not the place to outline such a programme which apparently in any event is high on the priority list of government. Suffice it here to stress three points.

First, land development must proceed at such a pace that a high proportion of the increase in the labour force in the East Coast states can be and will be given opportunities for gainful employment in land clearance, development and settlement. For the East Coast states proper (Kelantan to Eastern Johore) this would mean well over 100,000 acres of new land development each year. Clearly, FLDA can only do a part of this, State schemes for smallholders must be encouraged, as well as public and selected private estate developments.

Secondly, land development programmes for individual farmers must give the settlers large enough holdings to provide them with attractive incomes — allowing for the probable advances in technology in the near future as well as in the general levels of income. The current allocation of acreage in FLDA schemes of only 8 acres for rubber smallholders needs to be increased by perhaps 50% (and something of the same order for oil palm holdings). Even though the targets for land development would have to be that much higher to settle a given number of families, such an upward revision of size of holdings would make economic sense in the pursuit of the basic objectives of providing the Malay population with high standards of living in rural activities and also containing the migration to the urban centres to manageable levels. Moreover, even if land development for a sufficient number of new settlers on adequately-sized holdings can only be achieved with a longer delay, it is probably better from a political point of view to make sure that

---

[2] Land reform in Japan, for example, turned a peasantry on the edge of rebellion into the core support of the Liberal-Democratic Party, the group that has not yet been effectively challenged in post-war Japan.

at least some of the population feels prosperous than to have all new settlers somewhat better off than before but still below Malay income in other occupations.

Third and perhaps most important to be stressed, East Coast land development must not only be designed for the ultimate benefit of the Malays, it must be led and, for the most part, implemented by the Malays (with, of course, limited technical support from non-Malays). Two implications follow: in the first place the States' prerogatives to control land alienation and development should be respected and strengthened; the Central Government must curb its well-intentioned but misdirected efforts and attempts to override States' hesitations to alienate land in the national interest when the benefits to the States' own authorities and citizens are unclear or indirect. The second implication is that land development programmes on the East Coast must not put considerations of low costs, etc. so far to the forefront that it becomes necessary to transfer large numbers of non-Malays to carry out the land development, housing and infrastructure components of the programmes.

The above emphasis on States' rights is not intended to suggest that the Federal Government has little or no responsibility for effective and rapid land development. The Federal Government clearly must seek ways to deal with notorious inefficiencies or other malpractices in State land policies. Also, it is the Federal authorities rather than those of the individuals States that can best assess the needs for inter-state movement of settlers. Our point is that the most effective way for the Federal Government to operate — in other than the most immediate short-term — is to work on and through the State authorities. Close contact and frequent dialogue between State authorities and Federal agricultural and planning agencies are often surprisingly effective in bringing about consensus on the nature and solution of problems.

The third major feature of an East Coast development programme should be an ambitious infrastructure construction programme. While this is not the place to list specific projects, it is obvious that the programme would include a road building effort — particularly the feeder road system — rural electrification, and the like. The main point to make here is that such a programme should be large and should be launched without delay. As for land development it is important that considerations of costs should not dominate to such an extent that infrastructure development on the East Coast would require large numbers of non-Malay workers. Also, the Federal Government should not allow major works (e.g. East-West Highway) to be delayed for months and years just to make room for the time-consuming process of obtaining foreign finance for feasibility studies; the cost in terms of delay in development is hardly commensurate with the cost in terms of financing such studies from Malaysia's own resources rather than from foreign assistance.

The fourth major feature of a development programme for rural Malays — in particular but not only those living on the East Coast states, in Kedah and Perlis — is to seek out policies assisting rural farmers to increase their productivity and income. A number of policies and programmes fall in this category, including improved extension services for better agricultural practices, multi-cropping and inter-cropping; expanded processing assistance; improved marketing facilities;[3] restraint in the cost and price inflating protection of the domestic market given to industries located in the relatively advanced West Coast states; etc.

Perhaps the most striking example of current policies which are detrimental to improvement in productivity and income in the rural areas is the discrimination now operating against rubber smallholders in rubber replanting and newplanting. Smallholders as a group themselves have to finance all the support paid out to those smallholders that replant, while estates are subsidised; moreover, a very low limit is set on the area for which smallholders can replant rubber under the support scheme. Such policies make no sense at all in terms of equity or economics, at least not within the context of an overall development strategy as advocated in these pages.[4]

The implementation and follow-up of a development programme for the East Coast, Kedah and Perlis as characterised above by its four major features raises a number of questions and problems. Here we shall deal with only four:

First, given a greatly expanded programme of land development coupled with the several measures to increase agricultural productivity advocated above, what will happen to product prices and therefore rural incomes? In particular, since most new land in fact is assumed to be used for rubber, what will happen to rubber prices? The answer, of course, is that rubber prices will be lower than

---

[3] It may be worth considering a concentration of FAMA efforts in the East Coast areas where marketing facilities are inadequate or too rudimentary to cope with an emerging and growing cash crop economy, rather than on the West Coast where marketing facilities are already highly developed and hence where FAMA intrusion at least in some measure may tend to increase marketing costs and lower rural income.

[4] At the present time when rubber prices are high, the emphasis should be on smallholder *new* planting, while the *re*planting programme should be strongly supported and encouraged when rubber prices are less attractive.

without the proposed development. In our judgement, however, the effect on the world rubber market of the expansion in output in Malaya which we are here concerned with will be very small. Moreover, the effect on the balance of payments of a small price fall will most certainly be offset by increased quantity. Further, to the extent a lower price emerges, this will tend to discourage other nations from undertaking major planting programmes since they cannot match Malaysia's low costs. Estate profits will fall and this will have some effect on private investment in other sectors, but rubber profits, more than other modern sector profits, appear to leave the country in large amounts in any case. Thus fear of declining prices should not be a barrier to pursuit of such a programme. Some new land will of course be planted in oil palm and other cash crops. How far such crops can be pushed depends on the research effort undertaken (MARDI) as well as on one's judgement of likely future price developments, the existence of processing facilities, etc. The point to make here is that, if there are definite limits on how far oil palm can be pushed from a marketing point of view, there are not likely to be any such limits on rubber for the foreseeable future.

Second, if Chinese (and Indian) workers from the West Coast are not to be used in any great number in East Coast development of land and infrastructure, it becomes all the more important to organise, train and discipline Malays for effective and large-scale participation in such work. Evidence from a number of State schemes suggests that there is no reluctance on the part of Malays to go into the jungle to clear land for their own settlement, and judicious Federal as well as State support for road and other facilities may pay off handsomely. For larger infrastructure work and clearing schemes the work might be done by newly-formed army construction battalions. Such components are a regular feature of most armies and they will not be any more superfluous to the main military task in Malaysia than in most other countries. More important, army services is extremely popular among Malay youths and hence making them a part of the regular army (they would also get some military training, have the same ranks, uniforms, etc.) might compensate for what they would consider too arduous if wages were the only reward.

It may also be desirable for these construction battalions to be given heavy equipment. Labour saving devices are not desirable in principle, but they should be used if the alternative is a markedly slower land development programme. In fact, in some cases machines used intensively on critical bottleneck jobs (e.g. land clearing, land preparation for double-cropping, etc.) will create employment opportunities by speeding the process. Further, the presence of some heavy machinery might make the work more appealing to Malay youths (they would learn how to operate such machinery, would rightly feel they were more a part of the modern sector, etc.).

Third, once the East Coast development programmes are well underway, will it be possible to provide the large number of extension workers, administrators and technicians of various types that are needed if the return on the investment is to be realised? Failure to provide adequate support staff will mean not only that the potential benefits of the new projects will be underutilised, but that even the benefits that are realised will be poorly understood and appreciated. If such proves to be the case, the inconvenience of changing one's ways may seem to the farmer to outweigh the benefits; as a result the overall social and political effect may be negative, as has apparently been the case so far in the Muda area.[5]

Fourth, a critical aspect of the programmes and policies outlined above is that, if in combination they are not carried out at a high enough rate to be really effective in raising incomes of the rural Malays in the East Coast states, Kedah and Perlis, then they are hardly worth the effort. If, however, they are to be implemented in sufficient measure to bring about a real improvement in rural life, then they are going to be very expensive. Some aspects of the financing problem are discussed in a later section.

## Rural Income and Welfare: Policies for West Coast (except Kedah and Perlis)

Many of the policies for the East Coast must also be applied on the West Coast. The discussion in this paper of a programme of development for rural Malays in the West Coast states can therefore be shorter, concentrating on the points of significant difference in emphasis and in methods of implementation.

Land tenancy may be less pronounced on the West Coast (there are, however, few good studies). But even if this proves to be so, there are still good reasons for pushing land reform in the West as well as the East. The difference between the incomes of rural Malays

---

[5] As an explanation for the drift of political sentiment in the Muda area the excessive over selling of the benefits that would eventually accrue to farmers — long before any benefits could even begin to be felt — may be more important.

and urban Chinese and Indians is far more apparent on the West Coast and the consequent desire by Malays to migrate to the cities is that much greater. Land reform could raise the incomes and reduce the migration of many who now have little reason for not giving city life a try.

Land development must have high priority also in the West Coast states. Much of this development should be designed to increase the size of existing holdings, but new holdings of substantial size can also be developed, some by degazetting forest reserve land suitable of modern agriculture. The major difference between this West Coast programme and that in the East is that the land clearance work in the West may be contracted out to the private sector. There is no significant danger of encouraging an influx of Chinese and Indians into largely Malay areas, the Chinese and Indians are already there. Further the private sector can do the job far more rapidly and efficiently, particularly given the fact that the proposed East Coast Programme will tax the government's implementation capacity to the limit. It may, however, be desirable to set Malay employment quotas for those private contractors partly to deal with West Coast Malay unemployment, but also to train a cadre for the East Coast schemes.

Again as in the East, there is no need for land development to concentrate on rubber alone. Oil palm and other crops can also be pushed. In fact it is likely that there will be a concentration of these other crops on the West Coast where marketing and processing facilities are much more highly developed and there is no reason why this concentration should be vigorously resisted. Where newer crops are involved it would be desirable to see that some of the land is allocated to Chinese who can then perform an entrepreneurial function, the benefits from which can gradually be passed on to the Malay community. Marketing of these newer crops should be left to the private sector since considerable imagination and risk-taking will be required.

Investment in infrastructure development in West Coast states need not to the same extent as for East Coast states lead rather than follow the growth of economic activity. Even so, infrastructure development in West Coast states will inevitably be high, but it is reasonable in these states to be more cost-conscious, allow some delays in order to obtain foreign finance and generally to make sure that costs are minimised. In construction as for land development, however, it would seem desirable to set Malay employment quotas for private contractors (and of course for PWD) to provide a measure of training and participation.

For the rural Malay in the West Coast states the smallholder rubber new planting and replanting programme may be the most important component of the effort to raise levels of income and improve rural life. It should also be relatively easy to implement. As described earlier, an effective smallholder new planting and replanting programme requires long overdue policy changes — including subsidies to rather than taxes on the smallholder sector. However, such changes and expenditures should give higher long run returns in terms of improved rural incomes and political stability than virtually any other form of government action.

Even if all these policies are carried out immediately and vigorously, there will still be a time lag of several years before the impact of some of them (but not all) will be felt. Hence survival during the next decade probably also means taking a number of immediate steps to employ rural youths, particularly those who have already been educated away from their rural origins but are not sufficiently trained to be teachers, extension workers, and the like either on the East or West Coast. Some of these should be recruited into the new army battalions being formed after May 13th and education requirements for the military could be designed so that recruitment came mainly form this group (officers, of course, should not be recruited from this group). Some could go into the new army construction battalions created for East Coast development.

## Urban Semi-Skilled and Unskilled Malays

The measures described above should raise the willingness of people to remain in the rural areas, but there is no reasonable prospect of their entirely choking off the flow into the cities of Malay workers who are qualified for only limited kinds of urban jobs. This flow will remain above the available number of jobs.

To the extent that anything has been done about this problem in the past, it has involved attempts to force these workers on the modern sector. Furthermore, this pressure on the modern sector has been rather unbalanced. Only relatively large-scale industrial and other business organisations, i.e. the most advanced part of the modern sector, can be systematically inspected and pressured to accept Malay workers. Pioneer industries, in particular, have had to bear the brunt of this effort.

Some such policy to promote Malay modern sector employment is of course, necessary. Partly it is because there is some prejudice against Malay workers even when they are just as good as non-Malays in a particular job. Partly it is due to the fact that many kinds of training must be done on the job and Malays should certainly be given a chance to participate in such training.

The central issue is not whether there should be quotas, but how high they should be and whether they should be looked on as a means of solving the urban unemployment problem. There are several good reasons for saying that these quotas should be kept say below 25% of the work force, and that they should not be thought of as a significant means of solving the unemployment problem. They should instead be thought of as a means of ensuring that Malays get training that will qualify them for participation in the modern sector on a basis of genuine equality. Participation on a basis of glaring inequalities in performance is not going to promote political stability among people who will have to find non-economic ways of compensating for their inner sense of technical inferiority. Nor, need it be added, will such a system promote industrial growth. If they have the effect of slowing industrial growth significantly the net result may well be no net increase in the number of Malays employed over and above what would have happened with a more moderate set of quotas.

The key point, however, is that the number of Malays who can make effective use of industrial training opportunities is significantly lower than the number of unemployed urban Malay youths. Further, if quotas are set at say 40%, the training that the best of the group will receive will be markedly inferior to what it would have been if the quotas were set at 20%. Instead of the modern industrial techniques and work habits of the non-Malays dominating the factory, it will be the rural work habits and discipline of the Malays.

The other major urban employer is the government. There is still some scope for placement in the public sector but the government cannot for long continue to play an important role here. There is a limit to the number of errand boys, drivers, secretaries, etc. that the government can use. People with real skills are another matter, but they have no trouble finding employment in any case.

There are also various service jobs available that semi-skilled and unskilled Malays can perform. One could issue more taxi licenses, but then, of course, the income of those with licenses would go down. Parking meter attendants is an even more trivial source of employment. Commercial establishments and other service organisations that operate on a shoe-string and employ, in addition to the owner, perhaps one of his sons and a second cousin can hardly be expected to take on an unskilled Malay unless they themselves see the need for him. Thus the main hope for major increases in urban employment must come from rapid growth of industry and other sectors of the modern urban economy (transport, commerce, etc.); this is discussed in a separate section below.

There remains the question of what to do with the unemployed urban Malays. One answer is to put barriers in the way of their entry into the cities. But most of the obvious methods would cause more political difficulties than does the existence of substantial unemployment. One possibility would involve city zoning regulations that abolished squatter-type dwellings (for security reasons) and allowed new buildings in general to go up only if they met certain clear standards. The standards could be set high enough so that only those with jobs or savings could meet them. For Malays with jobs this would be no hardship since Malays generally put greater effort and pride into their homes than do either Chinese or Indians at the same levels of income. Another possibility is an urban public housing programme for Malays, but one where the apartments would only be given to fully employed individuals or those connected with specific organisations (such as much present housing for government employees). This measure would be counter-productive if it had the effect of freeing other housing for recent arrivals, but not if it were combined with a tight zoning law that kept squatter housing to a minimum.

A second set of measures — even more difficult to administer properly — would be to give preference in urban jobs to long-term urban residents. To some degree government hiring of unskilled personnel for urban jobs could be skewed in favour of long-term urban residents. Perhaps the labour exchange could be encouraged to make a greater effort to find jobs for those who had been on the rolls a long time (but not according to any fixed seniority principle so there would still be plenty of uncertainty and to long time urban residents. Recruiting for the urban police force, where backgrounds are presumably carefully checked, could be done primarily from urban youths.

None of these measures of course, will solve the problem completely and they won't even seriously dent it if they are not combined with the major effort outlined above of the rural areas. Urban centres will have to continue to live with unemployment for some time to come. How well they will do depend heavily on the quality of the political leadership and of the police. To attempt to solve the urban Malay unemployment problem by accelerating the growth in Chinese and Indian unemployment among the unskilled will almost certainly make urban stability an impossibility.

## Education Policy and the Employment of Educated Malays

Education policy can play a role in meeting the needs of the rural population and of the unskilled urban Malay. Also, the educational system is the source of the Malay (and non-Malay) leadership elite. A much-strengthened education system for the Malay is perhaps the most basic means to ensure his rightful place in a modernising economy and society.

For rural Malay one important step that can be taken is to increase the number of qualified teachers in rural areas. The number of teachers in primary schools has not increased significantly during the past four years (up less than 3%) while the number of primary school students has increased by 14%. Given present educational technology in the country, this has meant an inevitable loss in quality. In addition to improving primary education, this increase would provide employment each year for a thousand or more graduates of teacher training and similar schools.

There should also be some revision in rural school curricula to make them more relevant to rural needs. The object of education, at least at the lower levels, should be to provide children with the tools that will make them better farmers. Arithmetic should be centred around problems of long-range household and farm financial planning to take just one example. The curriculum should definitely not be oriented towards sending these students on to the university, MARA or other higher level schools in urban areas. Some students will, of course, go on to such schools. At lower educational levels the needs of this latter group can be met by ensuring that the rural oriented education is of high quality. At the secondary level the best solution is to provide some residential schools on the East Coast whose quality in college preparatory education and science-oriented programmes is very carefully controlled, i.e. in no way inferior to that provided in existing West Coast facilities. For these schools and classes high quality education is absolutely crucial if they are not to become factories for the production of maladjusted youths unqualified for modern sector employment and unwilling to farm. The maintenance of such quality probably requires competitive entrance examinations and also a substantial component of Chinese teachers and students in the schools.

Highly educated and really able Malays do not present an employment problem. The government can use far more than it has at present, and undoubtedly will continue to be the major employer for this group. There is no danger that the supply will get too large in the foreseeable future. The development of the University of Malaya is crucial to the future of the country and steps must be taken to maintain its quality and to ensure that in certain faculties the best of the Malay youths benefit from it. This means setting quotas that guarantee admission to some percentage of Malays (say 20 or 30%),[6] but it also means keeping a tight lid on the number allowed into such weak fields as Malay studies. In addition it means a real effort to upgrade the faculty largely irrespective of the resulting racial mixture.

The new university in Penang is already starting operations and final decisions have been taken to set up the National University which is to commence its operations next year. Malaysia will no doubt need three (or even four) universities in the future. Over the next few years all three universities will be competing — it seems desperately — for very scarce qualified teaching and research staff as well as for students that can really benefit form University education. In this situation it is most important that expansion of facilities, staff and student body is not allowed to lead to disasterous consequences for quality. For the new National University the dangers are particularly grave; unless pressures for rapid build-up of facilities, staff and student body are contained, the National University could become not a source of strength but of badly-educated malcontents.

In the context of this paper - and assuming the pressures for an impossible rate of expansion can be controlled -it is worth urging that consideration be given to locating the National University on the East Coast. While further measures would be required to attract and develop academic staff if the institution is not to be located in Kuala Lumpur, a decision to set up the National University on the East Coast would give evidence of the government's determination to bring the Malays into full participation in the country's economic and educational growth. Moreover, if the National University is to be established in Kuala Lumpur it may become a channel for the most promising youths in the rural sector to move to the more highly developed urban areas of West Coast states, rather than an institution for training of the cadre of educated and highly skilled youths on which the East Coast states depend for the improvement of life in the Malay society.

A great number of the graduates of post-secondary schools will come from MARA, Serdang, etc. Provided that these students are well-trained in the relevant skills and are willing to go into the rural

[6] Past experience suggests this can be readily accomplished by admitting Malays whose position in a ranking of all applicants would not have secured admission for them, but who nonetheless meet all other requirements.

areas, employment should not be a major problem. Previous sections of this paper have pointed out the need for more teachers, extension workers, people to keep land reform records, and the like. There is room for thousands of new jobs in these areas each year.

The difficulty is that too many of these students prefer Kuala Lumpur or at least do not want to return to the rural areas. There is no easy solution to this problem, but locating some sixth form and post-secondary schools or perhaps branches of such schools on the East Coast or in other rural states would help. Reorienting some of the training programmes to better meet rural needs could also make a contribution.

Some graduates should also be channelled into the urban private sector (including some of MARA's graduates), but this group is not likely to be large. The ablest Malay graduates naturally find their prospects better in government services and thus seldom show much interest in working for private companies, moreover the private sector cannot be expected to become a dumping ground for the less able. The personnel requirements for the private sector in terms of quality are at least as demanding as those of the government. Further, just as with unskilled workers, it is difficult to see that political advantages are gained in the long run by placing the less able white-collar Malays up against the best that the non-Malay sector has to offer.

It is politically as well as economically shortsighted to expand the number of the post-secondary school group beyond the capacity of the system to absorb them. The political cost of telling a secondary school graduate that he can't go on because he failed the necessary entrance examinations is certainly less than telling him several years later that he will have to take a job paying no better than he would have got with only a secondary school certificate. There is certainly no reason why the government should spend money where it clearly leads to an over-supply of graduates and thus creates or aggravates a situation with increasing numbers of malcontented youths whose aspirations cannot be realised.

The group of educated Malays includes wide differentials in ability and acquired skill and education. It must be recognised that a great many of them do not and will not become in any meaningful sense members of the leadership of the country. The income and prestige of this group, however, are high, often unrealistically so, and this fact more than any other makes them highly volatile and prone to political demagoguery. The phenomenon is an important part of the political life of most developing and many developed countries. This is typically the group which provides the leadership for political disintegration, a much less demanding task than integration and growth.

## The Role of Industry

Most of the above discussion had little to say about the role of industry in the promotion of Malay income and employment. The omission was deliberate. To make industry bear the brunt of a Malay income and employment policy will be to markedly slow its development and to seriously endanger the long-term economic future of the country. There are at present few Malays capable of and willing to handle managerial and technical jobs in industry and there are certainly few if any Malay entrepreneurs who operate on any scale. Nor, as pointed out above, are investors likely to find the prospect of a 40% or more Malay work force attractive. Those with a choice will go elsewhere and many do have such a choice.

Industrial growth is also crucial over the long run if the various schemes described above are to be financed. Present sources of government revenue are heavily dependent on the modern sector and growth of the modern sector is in turn greatly influenced by the pace of industrial development.

Even a modest reduction in the rate of industrial growth will have a major impact on industrial employment over the long run particularly since reduced growth will probably effect the rate of increase in productivity less than that of employment. The present annual rate of increase in industrial employment is 4 to 5%. The long-term employment impact of changes in that rate is illustrated by the data in Table A.2. This illustration suggests that the way to increase employment over the long run is to concentrate on raising the rates of industrial growth. Even within 10 years the differences between a 3 and 6% rate of growth in employment amounts to a cumulative total of nearly 100,000 jobs. Over 20 years the difference is nearly 300,000 jobs. Even if only 20% of all new jobs go to Malays, that is still 33,000 and 93,000 new jobs respectively for the 10 and 20 years period.

It is, of course, possible that an attempt to raise Malay employment by forcing substantially increasing numbers of Malays on existing industrial establishments could lead to higher Malay employment even 10 or 20 years hence than would be the case with lower Malay quotas and faster industrial growth. But the price would be enormous. The loss in government revenues would mean a major reduction in government programmes to increase rural income and hence an almost certain net loss in overall Malay employment opportunities (in contrast to industrial Malay employment).

## TABLE A.2
### ANNUAL INDUSTRIAL EMPLOYMENT INCREASES

*Annual Industrial Employment Increase 10 years from 1968*

| If rate is: | 3.0% | 4.4% | 6.0% |
|---|---|---|---|
| Corresponding absolute number | 8,200 | 13,700 | 21,600 |

*Annual Industrial Employment Increase 20 years from 1968*

| If rate is: | 3.0% | 4.4% | 6.0% |
|---|---|---|---|
| Corresponding absolute number | 11,100 | 21,100 | 38,200 |

Further, what then could one propose to do with the 4.25 million non-Malays in West Malaysia who will presumably be entering the labour force at a rate of 80 to 100,000 new entrants each year? They are, in the main, already in urban areas and are qualified for a wide variety of industrial jobs and industrial support jobs (e.g. commerce, banking, etc.). Further, because they are mainly in urban areas, they are more apt to be unemployed than underemployed (although some will become hawkers) and urban unemployment, regardless of race, is more politically explosive than rural underemployment. Some non-Malays can be given new or improved employment opportunities as settlers within land development schemes, but most probably not in any great numbers. Moreover, employment on estates is declining. Other employment outlets therefore have to be found for the non-Malays, both for political and economic reasons. Construction and commerce are possibilities, but increasingly the new entrants will have to be absorbed by industry.

Recently the Government has announced a new policy, one central feature of which is to develop industries in rural areas and small urban centres throughout the country. Developed as well as developing countries have tried to supplement development in the main industrial growth points by policies to encourage industrial activity also in relatively laggard parts of their countries. The common experience is that this is costly and difficult and that the results are at best very slow in coming. This does not make the policy wrong or unimportant, but it is also important not to be misled in terms of the role industrial development outside the main centres can play. It is quite unrealistic to claim for this element of the new economic policy much of a contribution to the modernisation process in the rural economy or to the creation of employment opportunities for the rural population.

There are, of course, a number of opportunities for industrial development for instance in the East Coast states that should be taken: rubber and palm oil processing facilities need to be established and might well be subsidised by the Government; wood based industries from sawmilling to fiber plants could be encouraged; it may well be found necessary and worthwhile to set up publicly-owned and operated factories or for the government to enter into a partnership with private industries, etc.

It is important to note, however, that the entrepreneurs for most such industrial enterprises — and indeed for the myriad small market oriented workshops and industries that could be developed — are Chinese. More than the Malays they have the trade links and the ability to organise and to mobilise working capital; not having deep roots or even a base in rural life they also have greater incentives to go into these new activities.

The main thesis of this paper is that it is crucial to develop policies that will be genuinely effective in raising Malay incomes and providing for Malay entry into the modern sector on a basis of real equality. We also argue for the adoption of a strategy that slows Chinese (and Indian) migration into areas that are still overwhelmingly Malay. Given the racial imbalance in the impact of the new economic policies as explained above, we must conclude that a *general* policy of stimulating industrial growth outside the main centres is misdirected and dangerous. Support to selected industries which Malay entrepreneurs and workers have at least an equal real chance of controlling and operating is a different matter. These will largely be raw material based industries, such as those mentioned above.

The key point that should never be lost sight of is that rapid industrial development in Malaysia, if it is to take place, for many years to come and to a large extent, will be carried out by Malaysian and Singapore Chinese. Investment by Americans, Japanese and British will never be more than a small proportion of the $1,000 to $2,000 million in private investment that will be required annually and which will increasingly go into industry.

Some measures, to be sure, would promote both foreign and Chinese investment. A major speed up in the processing of pioneer industry applications, the continued provision of desirable industrial parks in places where industry and not some political group wants them, the construction of good transport facilities, cheap electricity, etc. are all efforts that would help. High tariffs do not seem to be important and frequently are altogether undesirable. Certainly Hong Kong and Singapore have got along very well without them. Foreign exchange restrictions would almost certainly discourage all investors, Chinese or foreign. An increase in profits taxes most probably would have an even greater negative effect unless it was matched by a similar increase in Singapore.

The central theme of our argument is that the goal of rapid industrial growth, if it is to be met at all, will have to be accomplished by means of essentially liberal policies which may not promote, but at least will not hamper the dynamism of Chinese entrepreneurs. In one respect Chinese entrepreneurs are going to be much more demanding than many foreign businessmen. Chinese who do not expect to spend the rest of their lives in Malaysia and who do not expect their sons to follow from where they leave off will not be particularly interested in acquiring large amounts of fixed assets in Malaysia and private investment will suffer as a result. And rich Chinese are not likely to consider living out their lives (and their children's lives) in Malaysia unless they find the quality of life for Chinese in Malaysia attractive. To be attractive, life will have to provide, in addition to physical comfort, a genuine sense of security. For Chinese, as for Malays, such security can only be provided through some form of participation in the political process, participation which allows the Chinese as well to have at least a veto in areas that directly impinge on their most vital interests (and ultimately this probably includes the field of public security). If the only guarantee of Chinese rights is the ultimate one of going into the jungle, wealthy Chinese will eventually opt out of Malaysia.

## Finance and Planning

A partial listing of the programmes discussed above leaves little doubt that together they will cost a great deal. A land development programme sufficient to employ a high proportion of new entrants into the East Coast labour force at higher than present average income levels will by itself be very demanding on overall investment resources and public funds. We have further advocated: land development also for the West Coast; a meaningful land reform which would need some subsidy; a subsidised and stepped up rubber replanting programme for smallholders; heavier expenditures on rural education; new branches of post-secondary schools and the location of the National University on the East Coast; a large construction programme for East Coast states as well as an infrastructure development in West Coast states to keep pace with economic growth there, etc.

This is not the place to spell out how a development budget should be composed for the next several years. It will not be enough for the planners to assess whether all our proposed programmes are in some sense desirable. Too many desirable projects are better than a large number of inherently undesirable projects, but too much of a good thing can still turn a short-term improvement into a long-run disaster.

The moral for the planners is that simply advocating more expenditures on desirable projects is not enough. The overall level of those expenditures must be related to expectations concerning the balance of payments and must include fall back positions if rubber prices should drop (as they will eventually), or if the capital outflow should prove serious, or some combination of these two developments (a prospect that is far from remote).

On the other hand, to err on the side of financial conservatism is to concede defeat without trying to rise to the challenge. A timid and cautious financial and economic approach to Malaysia's present problems is doomed to fail. As we have emphasised at various points, it is not enough that programmes and policies represent efforts in the right direction. Only if they are implemented with dispatch and in ample measure can they be successful in achieving the overall objective of creating a workable and lasting social and economic basis for development and political stability.

Government pronouncements of policy and the administration's conduct of policy preparation and implementation over the last three months suggest an even greater danger than inadequate or faulty macro planning. This danger is that the government and the administration will try to remedy the nation's political problems by singlemindedly pursuing goals such as "reduce unemployment" or "reduce Malay unemployment" and "raise the rate of growth of GNP". The current ad hocism of economic policy discussion and decision-making badly needs to be replaced by analysis and consideration of the framework and means of a policy that is relevant to the basic issues of racial balance in economic development and growth. It is relatively easy to state the need for better balance and particularly the need to ensure that the Malay community enjoys a fair share of the opportunities and fruits of development. It is easy to point to imbalances and inequities. The real challenge is to propose a set of policies — not just minor isolated measures — that gives promise of success to correct the imbalances and righten the inequities. This requires imagination and hard work. It also requires direction and organisation.

Much of the argument above has tried to make the point that relatively subtle shifts in emphasis in economic policies can have a major impact on their political effect, turning it in some cases from negative to positive. Moreover, many important political actions, without which the country will achieve neither political stability nor economic growth, do not have any direct economic content whatsoever. One should not, therefore, pretend or attempt to save the political situation with a new economic policy, however well designed. The ultimate guarantee of political stability and national unity must come out of a re-established and renewed political process.

# RACIAL DISPARITY AND ECONOMIC DEVELOPMENT[1]

"We must bring to the open all fundamental and sensitive problems of our multi-racial society."[2]

## Introduction

In spite of having taken "all possible measures to spread out the wealth and prosperity of our country so that they can be shared more equally among our people of various races", the Government's policies since Merdeka have been ineffective in dealing with the wide income and productivity disparity between the races. "We must, therefore, chart a new course for our nation. There is no doubt that we have to face challenging problems in the years ahead."

This paper seeks to highlight the fundamental nature of the problem of economic disparity and to assess the magnitude of the imbalance. We procede to a consideration of alternative strategies to deal with the disparity and then evaluate the potential for growth and structural change in the economy and in racial balances. The potential and projected developments have implications for the country's social and economic fabric, which we present in broad

---

[1] This document, written by J. Faaland, was issued by the Department of National Unity in November, 1969 and circulated throughout central Government departments. The separate statistical Appendix is not reproduced here.

[2] This quotation and those in the first paragraph are taken from a message from Tun Razak to TV Malaysia, Nov. 1969.

outline and, finally, we list the main conclusions emerging from the analysis.[3]

The statistical-factual basis for policy and planning relating to racial economic disparity in Malaysia is rather weak. More data will be available in a few weeks' time when tabulations from the 1967-68 socio-economic survey are ready. However, it will require a prolonged and determined effort of statistical data collection and analysis as well as much sociological research to provide the Government with reliable, comprehensive and detailed information on the racial components of such central matters as employment patterns by industry and by functions and positions within firms and industries, productivity differentials between workers in similar occupations, savings and entrepreneurial behaviour, etc. It serves no purpose to apologise for the weakness of the statistical basis of this first effort to analyse the disparity problem, but the urgent need for further basic statistical and sociological work in this area must be stressed.

The scarcity of data notwithstanding, it is still possible to get a rough picture of the disparity problem which is reliable enough for derivation of significant general conclusions for analysis and policy. The recognised statistical deficiency in no way justifies deferment of basic political decisions on overall strategy and guidelines for action to deal with the problem of racial economic disparity.

In this paper we deal with the disparity problem in terms of economics. In a full analysis it is, of course, important to consider also other factors which determine the individual and collective well-being of the peoples of Malaysia, such as health conditions generally (including infant mortality rates, malaria incidence, etc.) and educational opportunities (including proximity of schools at various levels, quality of teaching, etc.). Moreover, we only deal with economic conditions in West Malaysia. Also, in much of the analysis we only distinguish between Malays and non-Malays. These limitations rule out consideration of many important national and racial issues, but they allow concentration on a number of critical problems of racial disparity.

---

[3]  In a separate Appendix to this paper we present a number of detailed tables with estimates and projections.

## The Problem

A number of generalisations regarding the "wealth and prosperity" of Malaysians of different races are widely accepted, *inter alia*:

the "average" Malay has a lower standard of living than the "average" non-Malay;

Malays form a much higher proportion of population in rural areas than in towns;
Malays populate the relatively poorer States and occupations to a higher degree than do non-Malays;

Malays form a higher proportion of the work force in low-productivity traditional agriculture and a lower proportion of the work force in high-productivity modern industry and commerce;

within given industries and enterprises Malays — as compared to non-Malays — typically hold lower-echelon positions;

placed in similar physical situations the motivation, inventiveness, energy and productivity of Malays in many activities fall short of those of non-Malays;

Malays own (or have property rights over) only about one-third of land under agricultural cultivation;

Malays have a significantly lower share of ownership of industrial and commercial capital.

The limited purpose of this section is to present the results of efforts to quantify the consequence and impact of these expressions of racial disparities in terms of productivity and income levels of non-Malays as compared to Malays. For this purpose we use national accounts, population and employment data for the eleven States and for sectors of activity.

Table B.1 gives a breakdown of population by State and major race in 1965. For each State we give an estimate of GDP varying from around $400 per capita for Kelantan and Trengganu to $1500 for Selangor. About one in four of both Malays and non-Malays live in the three southern States of Pahang, Johore and Malacca, where GDP per capita averages about $750. However, nearly 40% of all Malays as against less than 10% of the non-Malays live in the four northern States where GDP per capita averages only about $450. At

TABLE B.1
GDP BY STATE AND POPULATION BY STATE AND RACE,
WEST MALAYSIA, 1965

| | Malay share of pop.(%) | GDP per cap.($) | Population by Race (in '000) | | | | |
|---|---|---|---|---|---|---|---|
| | | | Malay | Chinese | Indian | Other | Total |
| *Four Northern States* | 80 | 459 | 1688 | 269 | 103 | 40 | 2100 |
| Trengganu | 92 | 449 | 350 | 23 | 5 | 1 | 378 |
| Kelantan | 91 | 369 | 620 | 38 | 8 | 13 | 679 |
| Perlis | 76 | 536 | 91 | 21 | 2 | 4 | 118 |
| Kedah | 68 | 518 | 627 | 187 | 88 | 23 | 925 |
| *Three Southern States* | 51 | 762 | 1095 | 833 | 161 | 44 | 2133 |
| Pahang | 55 | 985 | 243 | 146 | 31 | 5 | 425 |
| Johore | 50 | 729 | 645 | 525 | 97 | 31 | 1298 |
| Malacca | 50 | 638 | 207 | 162 | 33 | 8 | 410 |
| *Four Western States* | 35 | 1085 | 1510 | 2014 | 681 | 103 | 4308 |
| Negeri Sembilan | 42 | 901 | 216 | 204 | 77 | 13 | 510 |
| Perak | 40 | 891 | 658 | 713 | 240 | 26 | 1637 |
| Selangor | 30 | 1493 | 419 | 668 | 274 | 48 | 1409 |
| Penang | 29 | 870 | 217 | 429 | 90 | 16 | 752 |
| *Total West Malaysia* | 50 | 850 | 4293 | 3116 | 945 | 187 | 8541 |

the other end of the scale about one-third of all Malays and two-thirds of all non-Malays live in the richer western states where GDP per capita averages nearly $1100. Without at this stage suggesting any causes and effect relationship, the Malays largely live in the parts of the country that are relatively untouched by economic development and modernisation, while the non-Malays largely live in the prosperous States.

In Table B.2 we examine racial productivity and income levels from another angle, namely, racial composition of the labour force in the various types of industries and activities. For each activity category we give estimates of value added, and of total employment and its racial composition. Combining these data we derive estimates of value added by industrial and racial groups.[4]

As shown at the bottom of Table B.2, value added per worker in the Malay-dominated activities (non-estate agriculture, fishing and public administration and defence) averages $1400, while in non-Malay-dominated activities (all other) the average is more than 2 1/2 times higher, viz. $3600.[5] Allowing for the fact that also some Malays (about one in four) work in the higher productivity sectors and some Chinese and Indians (also around one in four) work in the low-productivity sectors, we find that the average productivity of Malay labour is about $2000 as against about $3000 for both Chinese and Indians. In other words, non-Malays *on the average* have labour productivity and income 50% or $1000 higher than the Malays.

Large as this difference is, there are at least two important reasons why this measure of the disparity represents an underestimation of the difference between Malay and non-Malay average productivity and income.

In the first place, within a given industry or enterprise non-Malays on the average have a higher share of the higher echelon and higher income jobs than do the Malays. Thus in modern industry and commerce there are relatively more non-Malays in positions of clerical staff and foremen, the Malays — with notable exceptions — are relatively more prominent in the general labour categories.

[4] These calculations rest on the assumption — later to be modified — that labour productivity and income per worker for the several racial groups are equal within each industry category.
[5] Note that we are in this paper concerned with productivity and with income derived by Malays and non-Malays form participation in the production process. The related problem of income transfers between races is not considered at this stage.

TABLE B.2

VALUE ADDED AND EMPLOYMENT BY INDUSTRY AND RACE IN WEST MALYASIA, 1967

| | TOTAL ECONOMY | | | EMPLOYMENT OF | | | | | |
| --- | --- | --- | --- | --- | --- | --- | --- | --- | --- |
| | Value added ($mill) | Total employm. ('000) | Valued added per worker($) | Malays in '000 | in % of all employed | Chinese in '000 | in % of all employed | Indians in '000 | in % of all employed |
| *Forestry, Agriculture Fishing* | 2155 | 1426 | 1500 | 967 | 68 | 301 | 21 | 146 | 10 |
| Forestry | 117 | 37 | 3200 | 16 | 43 | 21 | 57 | - | - |
| Rubber estates | 665 | 232 | 2900 | 62 | 27 | 67 | 29 | 100 | 43 |
| Rubber smallholdings | 444 | 503 | 900 | 318 | 63 | 152 | 30 | 33 | 7 |
| Other agriculture & livestock | 771 | 592 | 1300 | 525 | 89 | 45 | 8 | 13 | 2 |
| Fishing | 188 | 62 | 3000 | 46 | 74 | 16 | 26 | - | - |
| *Mining, Manuf., & Construction* | 1762 | 353 | 4900 | 83 | 23 | 245 | 68 | 27 | 8 |
| Mining and quarrying | 562 | 69 | 8100 | 20 | 29 | 41 | 20 | 7 | 10 |
| Manufacturing | 860 | 222 | 3900 | 42 | 19 | 161 | 72 | 17 | 8 |
| Construction | 340 | 67 | 5100 | 21 | 31 | 43 | 64 | 3 | 4 |
| *Commerce* | 1249 | 388 | 3200 | 89 | 16 | 246 | 63 | 65 | 17 |
| *Public Administration & Defence* | 505 | 207 | 2400 | 158 | 76 | 21 | 10 | 26 | 13 |
| *All other activities* | 1438 | 419 | 3000 | 138 | 33 | 192 | 46 | 78 | 19 |
| Electricity & water | 160 | 23 | 7000 | 9 | 40 | 6 | 26 | 7 | 30 |
| Transport & communication | 268 | 92 | 2900 | 38 | 41 | 34 | 37 | 19 | 21 |
| Other services | 1010 | 304 | 3300 | 91 | 30 | 152 | 50 | 52 | 17 |
| *All industries* | 7109 | 2798 | 2500 | 1416 | 51 | 1005 | 36 | 342 | 12 |
| *Malay dominated Industries:* (Rubber,non-rubber agriculture, livestock & fishing; public administration & defence | 1878 | 1364 | 1400 | 1048 | 77 | 234 | 17 | 72 | 5 |
| *Non-Malay dominated industries* | 5231 | 1434 | 3600 | 367 | 26 | 771 | 54 | 270 | 19 |

In the second place, it is often argued that non-Malay workers are more productive, save and invest a larger share of their earnings when faced with objectively similar opportunities in traditional smallholder agriculture, in traditional urban activities and even in some modern sector activities.

Even abstracting from these important sources of underestimation of the disparity, the quantitative evidence presented in Table B.2 brings out very clearly the structural character of the overall productivity and income disparity, viz. that the non-Malays — both Chinese and Indians — to a far greater extent than the Malays are participating in the modern, urban and rural, higher productivity activities.

Moreover — and equally important — ownership and leadership in the modern sector are almost entirely in the hands of the non-Malays. Industrial ownership, management and technical staffs are almost entirely Chinese except for a few Europeans and Americans. Commerce, foreign and domestic, at all levels is either in British or Chinese hands with the latter increasingly dominant. There are few Malay estates. Malay participation in construction is largely confined to unskilled and semiskilled jobs, the entrepreneurs themselves are overwhelmingly Chinese. University graduates in the sciences, medicine and engineering are almost entirely Chinese or Indians. Only in government service are there large numbers of Malays in managerial type positions and even there the Malay roll is heavily concentrated in the area of general leadership (e.g. the MHFS) while technical jobs remain largely in the hands of the non-Malays.

For the purpose of further analysis we have grouped the many activities in agriculture, commerce, industry, government, etc. into five main sectors:

*The Modern Rural Sector* which comprises the estates, commercial forestry, trawling, and about half the mining operations.

*The Traditional Rural Sector* which comprises all agriculture, forestry, fishing and mining, not included in the modern rural sector. This sector also includes the mass of underemployed and fully unemployed rural workers.

*The Modern Urban Sector* which comprises modern type industry, construction, trade and commerce, etc.

*The Government Sector* which includes Federal, State and local government administration, public educational and health services, etc., as well as the police and military forces.

*The Traditional Urban Sector* which comprises the urban petty traders, stalls, small artisans, personal servants and the multitude of activities requiring little or no initial skill or training for entry. This sector also includes the unemployed urban workforce.

While the grouping on many points must be arbitrary, it is designed to give a picture of the structure of the economy as between the traditional, low-productivity, relatively stagnant and economically backward activities on the one hand, and on the other the modern, organised, relatively capital-requiring and more highly specialised and productive sectors. At the same time we are also interested in the location and orientation of the various activities as between rural and urban settings.

In 1967 the total labour force in West Malaysia of 3,000,000 was distributed as follows (in round numbers):

350,000 in the modern rural sector
1,250,000 in the traditional rural sector
550,000 in the modern urban sector
300,000 in the government sector
550,000 in the traditional urban sector

The racial composition of the labour force differs very significantly among these five major sectors. Malays now outnumber the non-Malays by a factor of nearly 3 to 1 in the traditional rural sector; in the traditional urban sector, however, the inverse ratio applies. In the modern rural and urban sectors the non-Malays outnumber the Malays by a factor of about 5 to 2, while in the government sector Malays outnumber the non-Malays by about 5 to 3. While half the non-Malay working force (750,000 out of 1,500,000) were employed in the modern sectors (including government), less than one-third of the Malays (430,000 out of 1,500,000) were in those same sectors. These and other estimates relating to the employment structure and its racial components are given in Table B.3 below.

For each individual industry (even further detailed than in Table B.2) we have estimates of value added per worker. Making a minimum adjustment for known or assumed differences in earnings and productivity as between Malays and non-Malays[6], we have derived estimates of value added by the Malay and non-Malay work force. These estimates are summarised in Table B.3 (on page 16) in the form of aggregates for the five major sectors.

---

[6] The productivity and income differentials as between Malays and non-Malays here refer to workers within the same industries, but with different productivities in same jobs and with different distribution as between jobs at various levels.

As already shown in Table B.2, some sectors of the economy yield a much higher value added and income per worker than do others. The information in Table B.3 supplements this picture. The traditional rural sector again stands out as by far the least efficient in terms of productivity of its labour — which is largely Malay: the productivity of labour in the modern urban sector — which is largely non-Malay — is four times as high. Overall there is a productivity and income differential in favour of the non-Malays which may be expressed by a ratio of nearly 7 to 4 or by the absolute difference of $1250. While recognising the weakness of the data and the implications of the method of estimation applied, in particular the fact that we have deliberately underestimated rather than overestimated the racial productivity and income disparity, the enormity of the task to create economic balance is evident.

Our findings so far are of course not new, the disparity is glaring and has been a constant underlying concern of Government ever since Merdeka. In the past, however, the basic realisation of the problem has not been expressed in explicit and pervasive policies, nor has the Government or its administration so far instituted or carried out any thorough and comprehensive analysis of the qualitative and quantitative elements of the disparity problem.[7] In this area as in other fields of social change failure to analyse and consider the nature and magnitude of the problem explicitly leads to ineffective, conflicting and superficial policy.

The events of May last have brought the basic objectives and implications of Article 153 of the Constitution to the forefront; they have also instilled a greater sense of urgency in the Government and the administration to cope with the country's economic problems. In particular, great efforts are made to speed up decision taking relating to industrial development and to locate job opportunities for those who are now unemployed. While these and other measures of immediate amelioration are both useful and urgent, they neither constitute an attack on the disparity problem, which is necessarily rational, nor promise any measure of success. Racial economic disparity is far too deeply entrenched in the structure and dynamics of the economy to be reduced (or even contained) as a by-product of policies to step up the rate of overall growth, of exercises in persuasion to have industrial activities more widely spread geographically, of short-term measures to find employment opportunities for selected groups, or even of uncoordinated efforts to

---

[7] A few attempts to analyse and quantify the disparity problem in Malaysia have, however, been made by non-government students in Malaysia.

increase the Malay component of the work force in selected industries. None of these policies are necessarily undesirable — although some may be counterproductive in terms of racial balance — but they do not by a very long shot add up to a policy to deal with the disparity problem.

## Strategy Choices

A strategy to deal with the disparity problem must be characterised by a series of policies that will be genuinely effective in providing for Malay entry into the modern sector on the basis of real equality and in raising the incomes of Malays at least in step with those of non-Malays. This sector seeks to draw the outlines of such a strategy.

### Growth vs. Distribution

In the past the strategy adopted has concentrated on growth rather than balance or distribution: if only the rate of growth of overall output and national income could be stepped up and maintained at a high level, then there would be enough resources produced to tackle also the distribution problems. While a high rate of growth is indeed important, it is now clear from the evidence of the past that it does not bring with it parity or balance between the races.

It is important to recognise that the pursuit of racial economic parity as a national objective in many ways limits the options to pursue the maximum growth objective. Policies designed to further better balance do not always mitigate against growth, but most do in some measure. This is readily seen in respect of direct discrimination in licensing and in public sector contracts or purchases, preferential or exclusive allocation of land or other rights, stipulation of racial quotas for the work force of industrial firms, etc. There is also conflict between the objectives of growth and balance in terms of use of resources: the burden of taxation to raise resources in support of the Malays can become counterproductive in terms of overall investment, growth and entrepreneurship; devoting financial and real resources to increase the productivity and economic capacity of the Malays to some extent means foregoing development in other more productive lines of activity; etc.

In the following we assume that the Government — in full awareness of the costs in terms of overall growth — wishes to pursue the objective of reducing the disparity.

## Redistribution vs. Participation

The strategy to date has been to concentrate on achieving rapid growth of overall production and aggregate income creation. This strategy need not exclude and has not excluded consideration of disadvantaged groups; in fact rapid overall growth can provide a larger and expanding overall resource base from which to support and subsidise the lower income groups: i.e. the rural population, those working in the low-productivity traditional sectors, the unemployed, the Malays.

The transfers and subsidies to the disadvantaged groups, which a strategy concentrating on rapid development make possible, are essentially of two types: first, transfers and subsidies to raise their levels of private and collective consumption above what their own production efforts permit, and second, transfers of resources so as to build the capacity of the disadvantaged groups to raise their levels of productivity, production and income in the future.

There is a complete lack of analysis and organised data which could give a firm basis for a judgement on the extent or absence of net redistribution of income and resources in favour of the disadvantaged groups. The real income of those living and working in the traditional sectors of the society, of the rural people and particularly of the Malays, has been adversely affected by a number of measures and policies adopted in accordance with the maximum growth strategy: the several production taxes on rubber smallholder are hardly commensurate with payments made to them; the health programme gives non-estate rural residents much lower protection from malaria and other health hazards than is provide to the urban populations and generally to those living in the modern sector; the rural people and generally all those that live and work outside the modern sectors of the economy pay a good part of the cost of subsidising (or protecting) industry without getting the benefits in terms of jobs and income in the modern sector; the rural people have on the whole lower quality teachers and educational facilities; etc. Even though there may be some offsetting factors, in our general judgement the balance of transfers operates against — not in favour of — the rural people and occupations and thus on balance against the Malays; there certainly is no major redistribution in favour of the Malays taking place. In fact therefore — if not in theory or in terms of stated objectives — the strategy of maximum overall growth is not supplemented by (significant) income redistribution in favour of the groups which do not themselves participate fully in this rapid growth of production and income.

It may well be possible to do better than in the past in terms of income and consumption transfers from the modern to the traditional sectors, form non-Malay to Malay groups. It would be completely unrealistic, however, to imagine other than marginal adjustments of consumption levels in favour of the disadvantaged groups being practicable by transfer mechanisms. It would be self-delusion to believe that the imbalances inherent in a maximum growth policy can be dealt with by such income redistribution.

The second type of transfers requires the mobilisation of resources produced in the modern growth sector for investment in improved production facilities and capabilities for the disadvantaged groups. This type of transfer involves giving priority in public development and operating expenditures to rural over urban areas, to Malay entrepreneurs over non-Malays, to smallholders over estates, to agricultural extension over advanced industrial training, etc. In considering this means to support the underprivileged groups two comments should be made. First, there is statistically no evidence that on balance such priority has in fact been given in Malaysia since Merdeka, although there are numerous cases of considerable efforts having been made in particular cases, e.g. the rural development policies of the early 1960s, the RIDA and MARA efforts, the scholarship system in favour of the Malays. However, the needs for public investment and operating expenditures to support and service the modern sector (for electricity and water supplies, for transport and communication, for university training of engineers, for commercial services, for public administration, etc.) have been so strong and urgent that the Government has had little left over for transfer to the rural sector. Second, the proof of the pudding is in the eating: whatever transfers have been affected, they have been totally inadequate to bring about a better production and income balance between the races.

Thus, on both counts (income or consumption redistribution and transfers in support of future development capacities for those who fall behind) the strategy of maximum growth has shown itself inconsistent with attainment of the objective of balance between races.

Rather than through transfers of resources created within a maximum growth strategy, therefore, the objective of creating economic balance between the races must be sought through more balanced participation of the races in such economic activity and growth as is consistent with the objective of reducing disparities. The strategy of balanced participation, therefore, places primary emphasis on the objective of parity, secondary emphasis on overall growth and national income. This of course is the inverse order of the maximum growth strategy. Rather than aiming for such mitigation of disparity as is consistent with maximum growth, the strategy of balanced participation aims for such growth as is consistent with reducing racial disparities.

This is not only a play on words. It is crucial for policy formation as well as for analysis to recognise that the strategy of maximum growth compromises balance between races, the strategy of balanced participation compromises growth. It may be possible to have some growth and some mitigation of disparities, but the two objectives are basically competing — at least within a policy objective period up to the end of this century. The disparity which already exists is so deep seated — see discussion above — that the economic distance between the races is bound to widen unless determined policies to give the disadvantaged groups considerably greater participation in the modern sectors are now accepted, even though many of these policies will tend to reduce the rate of overall growth and development of the national economy. As we shall see, on an optimistic assessment of the future, effective policies to contain and even lessen racial disparities may be consistent with an overall rate of growth in the economy of 6% annually, which would be rather better than in the period since Merdeka. But if the maximum growth objective was allowed to prevail at the expense of parity considerations, growth could be a good deal higher still, given the same set of optimistic assumptions about the future. The choice between growth and parity objectives is essentially political, but no one should be in doubt that in terms of economics it is a real choice.

## The Role of Government

Racial economic disparities being so pronounced as they are in terms of levels of income and participation in the modern sectors of growth, the solution can be found — if at all — only through determined and consistent efforts over a long period well into the next century.

The only way the situation might be changed rapidly, say by the end of the 1970s, would be if the Government socialised all or most industry and commerce as was done say in Burma (where the Chinese population was quite small) and effected a massive redistribution of wealth and income. The results of such a policy, as in Burma, would almost certainly mean stagnation and decline in the modern sectors for many years to come. Further the Malaysian economy is far richer than that of Burma at the time of socialisation and thus the decline in the Malaysian modern sector would be more dramatic and the consequent political effects more severe. Even with socialisation the changeover to Malay control would initially be largely a superficial one. Technical jobs would continue to be held mainly by Chinese and Indians, not because of the exercise of any kind of monopoly power by these groups, but Malay technicians, at least in any number, simply do not exist.

While Government will have to exercise its power, political and economic, to ensure the rapid emergence of racially balanced participation in modern economic life of the country, there also must be limits set on the amount of interference with the modern private sector, particularly industry, that is to be applied. Otherwise, that sector will not play its vital role in the modernisation of Malaysian society, both Malay and non-Malay. Furthermore, a rapid increase in unemployment among young Chinese and Indians will be as politically explosive as a comparable increase in Malay unemployment. Thus not only must extreme policies be avoided such as those that would throw large numbers of presently employed Chinese and Indians out of work replacing them with Malays, but there must also be provisions for increases in Chinese and Indian employment.

In other words, a balancing act must constantly be performed so as to find a course which is economically, socially and politically viable between the Scylla of economic stagnation and the Charybdis of racial disparity. It will have to be the job of the political authorities to strike the balance; it must be the job of the administration to analyse and present the constituent elements of the choice. In the past as well as today, the political choice is made without guidance and advice on its implications.

## Urban and Rural Racial Balances

The strategy developed above emphasises equity in racial distribution of development, more equal participation in the modern sector and stronger government action to steer the modernisation process. This strategy also has a geographical component.

As shown above, most Malays live in the less prosperous States, work in the less productive occupations and live in the rural areas where modernisation is laggard. It would be an inherent part of the strategy, therefore, to ensure that opportunities for growth and modernisation in the rural areas in fact are available to and are grasped by the Malays. Unless the Malays do in fact benefit from such opportunities for growth as exist or can be created in the rural areas where most of them work and live, the task of ever achieving parity will be well nigh impossible. One significant implication of this strategy therefore is to slow rather than facilitate Chinese and Indian migration into areas that are now overwhelmingly Malay (principally the northern and eastern States, but also rural areas generally).

An illustration of the importance of explicit consideration of this dimension of strategy for racial balance is provided by the announced New Economic Policy, one central feature of which is to develop industries in rural areas and small urban centres throughout the country. This is a sound objective in terms of geographical dispersion — perhaps also in the long run in terms of overall growth of industry — but it is most likely to be sharply dysfunctional in terms of racial economic balance. The entrepreneurs for most such industrial enterprises — and indeed for the myriad small market-oriented workshops and industries that could be developed — are Chinese. More than the Malays they have the trade links and the ability to organise and to mobilise working capital; not having deep roots or even a base in rural life they also have greater incentives to go into these new activities. A *general* policy of stimulating industrial growth outside the main centres is therefore mis-directed and dangerous. Support to selected industries, which Malay entrepreneurs and workers have at least an equal chance of controlling and operating is a different matter. The trouble is, there probably are very few such special industries. An industrial policy for rural (and small town) areas can however be highly favourable in terms of racial economic balance if Malay entrepreneurship and workers are given initial protection form the non-Malay competition which has hitherto smothered them.

## The Main Features of a Strategy

The central features of the strategy suggested above are therefore four:

1.  *to emphasise racial balance* over national growth.
2.  *to emphasise balanced racial participation in the existing and growing modern sector of the economy* over redistribution of resources from non-Malay to Malay groups (or for that matter from modern to traditional sectors).

3.     *to rely on government power to steer developments in favour of balanced participation* rather than on the full play of market forces.

4.     *to increase rural income, and reserve for the Malays the major share of opportunities for growth and high-productivity employment in the rural areas.*

Some of the further implications of a strategy for racial economic balance will appear in the account of potentials for change which are discussed in the following section. The specific policies that can be used in pursuit of the general goal are numerous, but the most important ones are four in number. Briefly stated they include: an intensified and comprehensive policy of support to smallholder farmers; a major effort to accelerate new land development; a larger and redirected education effort; and a policy of rapid industrialisation. In addition to these four main programme areas, there would be a number of *ad hoc* measures of a shorter term nature designed to provide Malay employment, enhance Malay incomes, stem migration to the cities and contain non-Malay migration to rural, Malay-dominated areas.

The present paper concentrates on the overall magnitude, structure and potential for change in the economic balance between races, so as to provide the Government with a clearer view of the options available to deal with the basic disparity issue. Once the Government decides on the major questions of priorities between growth and balance objectives and on strategies to be adopted, then programmes, projects and policies can be and must be worked out. Only then will policies be operational and effective. The purpose of the present paper is to allow Government to consider and decide the overall strategy of economic development in the country and to provide effective guidance for the day-to-day work on economic planning and policy.

## Potential for Change

### The Basis of Projections

Given the structural change of the racial income and productivity disparity, it can at best be reduced slowly and gradually and eliminated only in the very long run. In order to form a judgement on the intractability or otherwise of the disparity problem, we present in this section a set of projections for the medium-term future to 1985.

It must be stressed at the outset that the projections are based on what we consider rather heroic and definitely optimistic assumptions of what might be attainable, given strong political will to deal explicitly with racial imbalances, as well as adequate understanding of the issues, determined implementation of policies by the Government, and sheer luck in terms of favourable economic developments in world markets for products and capital. Moreover, we have based our projections on what we recognise as being:

a deflated estimate of the present disparity (as discussed above);
possibly an overestimate of the extent to which and the speed with which the basic production structure can be modernised over the relatively short period to 1985;
an ambitious set of targets relating to the degree of participation — induced or forced — of the Malay work force in this development; and probably an unrealistic assumption regarding the rate of overall growth in the economy which will be consistent with the assumed policies to ensure Malay participation.

More realistic assumptions and more modest targets could be worked into projections of this nature. The purpose and value of the approach here adopted is to determine an outer limit of what can possibly be achieved over a decade or two to meet the objective of racial balance.[8] Even so, the picture that emerges is far from encouraging.

Table B.3 summarises the projected employment and income developments from 1967 to 1985 by major sectors of the economy and for Malays and non-Malays separately. In the following paragraphs we present the main assumptions of the projections, particularly with regard to the changing structure of the economy and the employment pattern as between main sectors and as between Malay and non-Malay labour force.

---

[8] This statement is not strictly correct in terms of logic, since it excludes the possibility of drastic policies of socialisation as well as extreme measures of discrimination against non-Malays.

## The Labour Force

In 1985 the total labour force will be about 5 million, compared to 3 million in our base year, 1967. This increase by two-thirds represents an average annual growth rate of just under 3%. Since all those who will be in the labour force in 1985 are born before 1970, this is a relatively firm order of magnitude for the 1985 labour force. We expect that the Malay and non-Malay total labour force in 1985 will be of equal size as is the case to-day.[9]

### The Rural Economy

To assess the growth of job opportunities we start with the rural sectors and with agriculture which is by far the dominant labour user. West Malaysia has vast areas of uncultivated land. Application of this potential features prominently in the country's development plans and announced policy objectives. Today, however, not more than 75,000 acres of new land are being developed annually, while the potential is clearly much larger. For the purpose of our projections a total development of nearly a million acres over the eight-year period 1968 to 1975, and nearly 2 million acres over the decade 1976 to 1985 has been assumed.[10]

We further assume that as much as one-third of new land is developed for estate agriculture. Considerable technological improvements must be expected, particularly in the dominant rubber estate industry, reducing labour requirements per acre. The projected expansion of estate agriculture of over 40% in acreage by 1985 will therefore give employment in the estate sector as a whole to only up to 10% more workers than today. This leaves just under 2 million acres of new land for non-estate development, including FLDA, state schemes, youth schemes, etc. as well as for purely private smallholder development. Allowing an average of 10 to 12 acres per family, with an average of 1.5 workers per family, this would create 250,000 to 300,000 more jobs on non-estate new land.

[9] We also assume that the labour force emanating from the workers (and their families) now living within each major sector will grow at the same rate. This does of course not mean that they will all find work in the "sector of origin"; a main purpose of the following discussion is to make a judgment on where the job opportunities will be.

[10] This would require an immediate step-up of land development to 120,000 acres in 1971, thereafter increasing by 10,000 acres each year till it reaches 200,000 acres in 1979 and then being maintained at that level.

Land now being cultivated could yield much higher returns even with existing technology provided efforts were stepped-up to replant smallholder rubber, to extend and intensify agricultural extension service, to introduce better methods of farm management, to facilitate and stimulate selective diversification, to provide credit and trading facilities, to improve primary and secondary level rural schooling, to improve the health of the rural population by stepped-up malaria eradication, etc., to build rural roads and improve the drainage system, and so on. The question of how and how far such efforts to improve agricultural output and productivity of land can and should go requires much further study. This is not the place to detail such a programme. It clearly could be a very large programme, requiring a major input of human, physical and financial resources.

In existing non-estate agriculture there is today considerable underemployment as well as an estimated 100,000 unemployed. We assume that over the period to 1985 it will be possible through development of more intensive agriculture to activate some of the underemployment of the present labour force, to increase the average labour productivity on presently existing non-estate acreage by up to 3% per year, but only to provide for a marginal increase over the 18-year period in the number of full-time jobs on this acreage.

We also assume that there will be continued modernisation of forestry, fishing and mining activities within both the present modern and traditional sectors, but that the employment expansion estimated at about 75,000 by 1985 will be concentrated on the present modern sector, mostly in forestry and in mining.

In the rural sectors we have thus accounted for about 400,000 additional job opportunities to be created over the 18-year period to 1985 as follows (in round numbers):

25,000 in the estate sector
275,000 on new non-estate land
25,000 on presently cultivated non-estate land
75,000 in the modern sector of forestry, fishing and mining.

This represents a total increase of well over one-fourth in 18 years in number of jobs in the rural economy or an increase of 1.3% per year. At the same time, productivity per worker is projected to increase significantly (by an average of about 3.5% per year) in both the modern and traditional rural sectors, reflecting improved agricultural and labour productivity in an expanding estate agriculture and higher than average productivity on new land to be developed

TABLE B.3

LABOUR FORCE, EMPLOYMENT, VALUE ADDED AND DISPARITY
BY FIVE MAIN SECTORS 1967 AND 1985
(Estimates for 1967 and Projectors for 1985)

| | EMPLOYMENT | | | | | VALUE ADDED PER WORKER ($) | | | DISPARITY | |
|---|---|---|---|---|---|---|---|---|---|---|
| | Malays in thous. (1) | Malays in % of all workers (2) | Non-Malays in thous. (3) | Non-Malays in % of all workers (4) | All in thous. (5) | Malays (6) | Non-Malays (7) | All (8) | In terms of $ per worker (7)-(6) | In terms of disparity ratio (7):(6) |
| **Traditional rural sector** | | | | | | | | | | |
| Total labour force | | | | | | | | | | |
| 1967 | 928 | 74 | 327 | 26 | 1255 | 1135 | 1640 | 1215 | 505 | 1.44 |
| 1985 | 1150 | 74 | 400 | 26 | 1550 | 2080 | 2760 | 2250 | 680 | 1.33 |
| Employed labour force | | | | | | | | | | |
| 1967 | 886 | 77 | 269 | 23 | 1155 | 1180 | 1750 | 1370 | 570 | 1.48 |
| 1985 | 1100 | 76 | 350 | 24 | 1450 | 2175 | 3155 | 2410 | 980 | 1.45 |
| **Modern rural sector** | | | | | | | | | | |
| 1967 | 103 | 29 | 248 | 71 | 351 | 3455 | 3920 | 3785 | 465 | 1.15 |
| 1985 | 185 | 41 | 265 | 59 | 450 | 7115 | 7390 | 7280 | 275 | 1.04 |
| **Modern urban sector** | | | | | | | | | | |
| 1967 | 142 | 27 | 393 | 73 | 535 | 4125 | 5160 | 4885 | 1035 | 1.25 |
| 1985 | 380 | 35 | 720 | 65 | 1100 | 7925 | 9520 | 8970 | 1595 | 1.20 |
| **Government sector** | | | | | | | | | | |
| 1967 | 185 | 62 | 112 | 38 | 297 | 2400 | 2400 | 2400 | - | 1.00 |
| 1985 | 400 | 67 | 200 | 33 | 600 | 4085 | 4085 | 4085 | - | 1.00 |
| **Traditional urban sector** | | | | | | | | | | |
| Total labour force | | | | | | | | | | |
| 1967 | 142 | 25 | 420 | 75 | 562 | 1280 | 1805 | 1675 | 525 | 1.41 |
| 1985 | 385 | 30 | 915 | 70 | 1300 | 1955 | 2255 | 2135 | 300 | 1.15 |
| Employed labour force | | | | | | | | | | |
| 1967 | 99 | 22 | 361 | 78 | 460 | 1840 | 2100 | 2045 | 260 | 1.14 |
| 1985 | 275 | 30 | 650 | 70 | 925 | 2740 | 3175 | 3045 | 435 | 1.16 |

TABLE B.3 (continued)

*Total economy*

| | | | | | | | | | | |
|---|---|---|---|---|---|---|---|---|---|---|
| Total labour force | 1967 | 1500 | 50 | 1500 | 36 | 3000 | 1750 | 3000 | 2575 | 1250 | 1.71 |
| | 1985 | 2500 | 50 | 2500 | 33 | 5000 | 3645 | 5120 | 4380 | 1475 | 1.40 |
| Employed labour force | 1967 | 1415 | 51 | 1383 | 49 | 2798 | 1855 | 3250 | 2545 | 1395 | 1.75 |
| | 1985 | 2340 | 52 | 2185 | 48 | 4525 | 3890 | 5860 | 4840 | 1970 | 1.51 |

*Rural economy*

| | | | | | | | | | | |
|---|---|---|---|---|---|---|---|---|---|---|
| Total labour force | 1967 | 1031 | 64 | 575 | 36 | 1606 | 1370 | 2510 | 1775 | 1140 | 1.83 |
| | 1985 | 1335 | 67 | 665 | 33 | 2000 | 2780 | 4605 | 3385 | 1825 | 1.66 |
| Employed labour force | 1967 | 989 | 66 | 517 | 34 | 1506 | 1425 | 2790 | 1895 | 1365 | 1.96 |
| | 1985 | 1285 | 68 | 615 | 32 | 1900 | 2885 | 4980 | 3565 | 2095 | 1.73 |

*Urban economy (incl. government)*

| | | | | | | | | | | |
|---|---|---|---|---|---|---|---|---|---|---|
| Total labour force | 1967 | 469 | 34 | 925 | 66 | 1394 | 2585 | 3305 | 3060 | 720 | 1.28 |
| | 1985 | 1165 | 39 | 1835 | 61 | 3000 | 4635 | 5305 | 5045 | 670 | 1.14 |
| Employed labour force | 1967 | 426 | 33 | 866 | 67 | 1292 | 2845 | 3515 | 3305 | 670 | 1.24 |
| | 1985 | 1055 | 40 | 1570 | 60 | 2625 | 5120 | 6200 | 5765 | 1080 | 1.21 |

*Traditional sectors*

| | | | | | | | | | | |
|---|---|---|---|---|---|---|---|---|---|---|
| Total labour force | 1967 | 1070 | 59 | 747 | 41 | 1817 | 1155 | 1645 | 1355 | 490 | 1.42 |
| | 1985 | 1535 | 54 | 1315 | 46 | 2850 | 2050 | 2410 | 2215 | 360 | 1.18 |
| Employed Labour force | 1967 | 985 | 61 | 630 | 39 | 1615 | 1255 | 1950 | 1525 | 695 | 1.55 |
| | 1985 | 1375 | 58 | 1000 | 42 | 2375 | 2285 | 3170 | 2660 | 885 | 1.39 |

*Modern sectors (incl. government)*

| | | | | | | | | | | |
|---|---|---|---|---|---|---|---|---|---|---|
| | 1967 | 430 | 36 | 753 | 64 | 1183 | 3225 | 4340 | 3935 | 1115 | 1.35 |
| | 1985 | 965 | 45 | 1185 | 55 | 2150 | 6210 | 8125 | 7265 | 1915 | 1.31 |

for smallholdings, together with reduced underemployment as well as improved productivity in the traditional rural sector generally.

For the purposes of this exercise we have assumed that overt unemployment in the rural area will remain at its present (1967) level of about 100,000. Since the number of jobs in the rural area is expected to increase by about 400,000, the implied rural unemployment ratio is projected to decline from about 6% in 1967 to 5% in 1985. Our assumption of unchanged rural unemployment is somewhat arbitrary and may well need revision. However, this assumption reflects the expectation that rural workers, particularly the young entrants into the labour force, will tend to drift to smaller towns and larger cities if in fact they cannot for long find jobs in the rural economy. Total unemployment in the country is bound to increase substantially (see below), but we expect this increase to take the form of growing urban rather than rural unemployment.

In 1967 1.6 million workers found their livelihood in the rural economy, nearly three out of four of them in the traditional rural sector. Of these, however, an estimated 100,000 were unemployed and a good part of the rest were underemployed. The 1985 labour force emanating from the modern and traditional rural sectors will be 2,675,000 i.e. 1,075,000 more than in 1967. Even with new land being opened up as rapidly as here assumed and with considerable improvements in agriculture on existing land, less than 40% of the increase can be absorbed productively within the rural economy. It follows that there must be outward movement of labour of very large numbers from the rural areas, estimated at 675,000 workers (net) for the period to 1985. These migrants must find jobs in the traditional or modern urban sectors, or in government, or just join the ranks of the urban unemployed. The implications for other sectors of such migration out of the rural economy will be discussed later.

Next we must consider the racial composition of the labour force. In 1967 there were about 250,000 non-Malays and 100,000 Malays in the work force in the modern rural sector, about 3 in 4 working on the estates. We assume that policies are adopted which in fact will leave the number of non-Malays in the modern rural sector substantially unchanged in the future (at about 250,000 workers as in 1967), allowing most of the projected moderate net increase of 100,000 in 18 years in job opportunities in that sector to be taken up by Malays. Even so, in 1985 the non-Malays will still outnumber the Malays in the modern rural sector work force by a ratio of about 3 to 2.

It should be understood that the number of non-Malays in the modern rural sector will not stay at its present level without deliberate and discriminatory policies. If in fact land is being opened up for estate development to the extent assumed, there will be pressures from mangers both on existing and new estates to employ a larger rather than a smaller proportion of non-Malay workers who are already experienced in such work or at least by upbringing are attuned to a life on estates. Moreover, the total labour requirements of trawling, commercial forestry and modern mining are expected to increase, an increase in demand which in part will be directed towards non-Malays. To fill practically all the net increase in job opportunities in the modern rural sector with Malays, therefore, requires determined and persistent policies of Malay preference.

In the traditional rural economy we have identified a potential for 300,000 new jobs to be created by 1985, as many as 275,000 of them on new smallholder land. Most — perhaps 80% — of new land will, we assume, be allocated to Malay cultivators in line with the strategy advocated above. Similarly we assume that 60% of the net increase of 50,000 jobs in forestry will be available to Malays. Finally, we assume that roughly unchanged numbers of rural Malay and non-Malay workers will be occupied on presently cultivated smallholder land and that their productivity will grow through more widespread multi- and inter-cropping, shifts to higher value added products and generally more labour intensive uses of land.

If there were no net migration out of the rural sectors by 1985 there would be over 1.7 million Malays and over 950,000 non-Malays competing for the rural jobs assumed or projected above as being available in that year. Since we have assumed that the potentially unemployed rural labour force over and above the 100,000 rural unemployed today will move into the towns and cities, the rural job-creation projected would require nearly 400,000 Malay workers and nearly 300,000 non-Malays to move to the urban sectors (including government). The possibilities and consequences of migration on such a scale are discussed in a later section.

It is evident that in the traditional as in the modern rural sector we have assumed aggressive policies to speed the economic advance of Malays more rapidly than for non-Malays. It is also clear that these policies may well appear onerous, harsh and discriminatory by the non-Malays affected. Yet, the projected average absolute improvement in income per worker and productivity for rural non-Malay labour force is projected to be 80% greater in dollar terms than for the rural Malay labour force, see Table B.3.

## The Urban Sectors and Government

In 1967 the non-government urban sectors accounted for 1,100,000 workers; however, about 100,000 of them were unemployed. By 1985 the labour force in these sectors is here projected to more than double to 2,400,000, but as many as 375,000 of them will be without jobs. Of the total labour force (including the unemployed) in the non-government urban areas in 1985, the non-Malays will outnumber the Malays by a ratio of over 2 to 1 as against nearly 3 to 1 to-day. In terms of value added the urban economy — in spite of the high unemployment projected — will contribute 58% of aggregate (West Malaysia) gross domestic product, as against about 50% in 1967. By far the larger share of the increase in urban income will, of course, originate in the modern urban sector. Average productivity increase for the active work force in the traditional urban sector is projected at 2.25% annually as against nearly 3.5% in the modern urban sector.[11]

The total work force in *manufacturing* in 1967 was just over 200,000. About half of these workers were employed in modern type, organised industry, the rest were employed (or self-employed) in small-scale, low-productivity workshops and manufacturing of a back alley, rather haphazard and inefficient character with little or no possibility of getting out of the traditional urban sector into the modern economy.

Development of industry in years to come is projected to be very rapid, both in terms of employment and productivity. In the modern sector we project industrial employment to grow by over 5.2% per year with average productivity increasing by 5.5% giving a rate of growth of value added in modern manufacturing of over 11% annually for the 1967 to 1985 period. While the present Malay work force in modern industry is estimated at less than 20%, we have assumed that it will be possible — through suasion as well as coercion — to increase that proportion to 30% by 1985. It is well possible that the rapid growth projected may not be consistent with the projected increase in Malay participation. As discussed above (Section III) such inconsistency would have to be resolved by giving priority to Malay participation, and accepting the cost in terms of less rapid overall industrialisation.

[11] Including the unemployed the projected growth of average value added per worker in the traditional urban sector is below 1.5 %.

Manufacturing in the traditional urban sector will also expand, not so much from its inherent potential for growth in productivity and size as in response to the rapid growth of the urban sector itself with large numbers of poor urban dwellers trying to eke out a living from simple workshop and manufacturing activities. We have in fact assumed that with Malays constituting a growing proportion of urban dwellers, they will also gradually increase their participation in these low-productivity manufacturing activities.

For all manufacturing in the modern and traditional urban sectors combined our projections imply growth in employment averaging 4.6% annually, increasing the number of jobs from just over 200,000 in 1967 to 475,000 in 1985, average output per worker increasing from $4000 to $10,000 and total value added in all manufacturing growing at the average annual rate of well over 10%.

*Commercial activities* in 1967 employed nearly 400,000 workers, well over 300,000 of them in retail trade. Over the period to 1985 we project employment to increase considerably — by an average of 3.5 to 4% per year — in both modern and traditional type commerce, but for different reasons. In the modern sector the need for an efficient commercial service sector will increase with expansion of the modern economy generally. In the traditional sector the rapidly growing labour force and unemployment in the urban areas will increase considerably the number of people — Malay and non-Malay — who will try to find a living as hawkers, stall-operators, etc., rather than being totally unemployed. Commerce is typically a non-Malay employment area. However, with the increasing (though still minority) proportion of Malays in the urban work force, we project the Malay participation rate to increase from less than 20% today to 30% in 1985.

The non-government *services* sector now gives employment to over 200,000 workers, 60% whom were employed in low-productivity, easily entered occupations in the traditional urban sector. Little more than one in four persons employed in the service sector are Malays. Over the period to 1985, we expect the modern sector community, business and recreational service employment to grow rapidly by 4% per annum. For the traditional, low-productivity service sector we expect a 3.5% annual increase in employment, partly in response to the growing needs of the urban sector, but also — as for low-productivity commercial activities — as a reflection of the rapidly growing numbers of people coming to the urban sector and trying to crowd into those personal service sectors where entry conditions are lowest. Also, with the growing number of Malays in the urban population we project a marked increase in their participation ratio in this service sector.

*Other non-government urban sectors* include construction, electricity and water supplies and transport; these activities together employ some 200,000 workers today. These jobs, which are nearly all included in the modern urban sector and have high labour productivity, are mostly held by non-Malays. We project the rate of growth in output in these sectors to approximate the rate of growth of the total economy to 1985 and assume some increase in Malay participation rates.

*In total*, then, the non-government modern and traditional urban sectors are projected to provide gainful employment in 1985 to 1,100,000 and 925,000 workers respectively, i.e. about twice as many as in 1967. In addition, we project the number of unemployed in the urban economy to grow from 100,000 in 1967 to 375,000 in 1985 — all of whom are counted as belonging to the traditional urban sector. The structure of the urban economy as projected will change very considerably over the 18-year period. While in 1967 manufacturing contributed well under one quarter of total value added in non-government urban sectors, in 1985 it will contribute nearly 40%. This type of structural change within the urban sectors is projected to be more pronounced for Malays than for non-Malays, reflecting in particular the more rapid relative growth of the Malay labour force in the urban economy.

Projections for *Government sector* are made separately, but for many purposes Government employment may be considered as urban in nature and orientation. This sector comprises administration, education, health, etc., as well as the police and military forces. Together these activities give employment to 300,000 people, over 60% of whom are Malays. In this sector there will be considerable expansion in coming years to meet the heavy demand for security build-up, to reflect the expressed intentions of government to strengthen the education and health services, to meet the clear needs for rapidly expanding agricultural services, to strengthen the general administration capability, etc. We have projected a doubling by 1985 of the personnel in this sector. We have also assumed that through deliberate policy action the Malay share of total Government employment will increase moderately to a ratio of two Malays for each non-Malay.

## Implications for the Economic and Social Fabric

### Economic Growth

The combined effect of growth in the rural and urban sectors as described above would be to raise the gross national product (for West Malaysia) by an average rate of 6.4% annually for the 18-year period to 1985. There will, of course, be marked differences between sectors; we have for example, projected a rate of growth in the modern urban sector (including Government) of well over 7 1/2% as against little over 5% in the modern rural sector. Also, the implied overall growth rates for Malays is 7.2% as against 6% for non-Malays.

To achieve and sustain an overall growth rate of 6.4% in GDP is no mean task; in the 1960s the comparable rate of growth has been around 5%. Moreover, in accordance with the strategy of development here adopted, the objective of rapid overall growth is assumed to be subsidiary to that of achieving better economic balance. Thus at several points in the discussion above of prospects for the various sectors we have had to point to the difficulties of achieving the assumed increase in Malay participation without slowing the rate of growth in the sector. The approach adopted in this paper has deliberately been to take an optimistic view on the extent of conflict between these two major objectives; as a result we have no doubt overstated the overall growth prospects consistent with the basic strategy adopted. It may well be found in subsequent analysis that an overall rate of growth of 6% or more for the period to 1985 is not attainable — again given that the Government adopts the strategy here assumed.

### Employment and Unemployment

The structure of employment — as between sectors and as between races — would change radically over the years to 1985. The rural economy today accounts for more than half of the total labour force. In 1985 — and a rapid new land development programme notwithstanding — the rural sector will have only 40% of the labour force. This reduced importance of the rural sector in the labour force employment structure will apply to both Malays and non-Malays, thus while in 1967 two out of three Malays were in the rural sector, only about one in two will be so in 1985. As a result, the labour force in the urban sectors will increase by 4.3% annually as against

## DIAGRAM B.1
### MALAY AND NON-MALAY EMPLOYMENT AND UNEMPLOYMENT
### BY MAIN ECONOMIC SECTORS, 1967 AND 1985

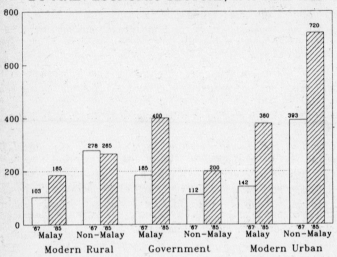

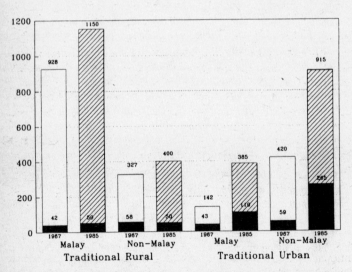

Notes: All figures in thousands. Height of columns corresponds to total labour
force in sector as indicated for Malays and non-Malays respectively. The
fully blackened area (for traditional rural and urban sectors only)
represents the unemployed labour force.

only 1.3% in the rural sectors. The changing structure of Malay and non-Malay employment by major sectors of the economy is shown pictorially in Diagram B.1.

The level of unemployment will increase very considerably over the period to 1985. While in 1957 there was a total of about 200,000 unemployed, equally distributed between the urban and rural traditional sectors, in 1985 we project unemployment to reach 475,000 in total; 100,000 in the rural areas and as many as 375,000 in the urban areas. The overall unemployment percentage (of total labour force) which was 6.7% in 1967, is projected to increase to 9.5% in 1985. In the urban sectors (including Government) one in eight (12.6%) of the labour force will be unemployed: one in ten or eleven (9.4%) of the Malays and one in seven (14.4%) of the non-Malays.

This of course is a particularly disturbing prospect, even more disturbing by the fact that it emerges from a set of optimistic projections with regard to the rate of overall growth of the economy. If, as suggested above a more realistic assessment of prospects leads to a lower estimate of GDP growth, the employment situation will of course worsen even more dramatically.

## The Move to the Cities

Successful modernisation and growth in all developing countries bring with them growth of the urban sector with problems of urban unemployment, squatters and slums. In Malaysia these problems may be somewhat mitigated — or delayed — if opportunities for rapid development of new agricultural land and for increased productivity on existing land are seized. In the present paper we have made quite optimistic assumptions in this regard. Even so, however, Malaysia will, it seems inevitably, have to live with the problems of a major drift of workers and their families from the rural to the urban economy. The drift to rural towns and to major cities is gathering momentum. Government policy may perhaps be able to contain the acceleration, but the migration is bound to be very large over the years.

In Diagram B.2 we have shown a pattern of net movement of Malay and non-Malay labour force from rural to urban and from traditional to modern activities. Net migration of this magnitude and in this pattern would be consistent with the distribution of the labour force projected above.

The rural economy cannot support the growth of its own population: we have projected a net exodus of no less than 375,000

DIAGRAM B.2
NET MIGRATION OF WORKERS BETWEEN MAIN
SECTORS 1967 TO 1985

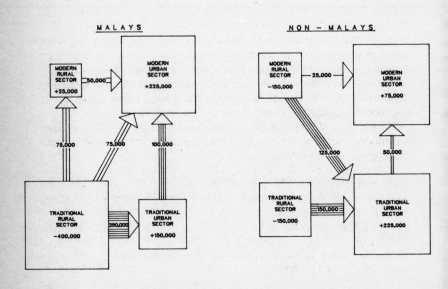

Notes: The size of blocks is proportional to labour force within the sector in
1985. Each line in an arrow represents 25000 workers. The signs —
(minus) and + (plus) refer to net out-and in-migration respectively.

Malay and 300,000 non-Malay workers and their families from the rural sectors. Even so the rural labour force (and job opportunities in rural activities) will increase by over 25% or 400,000.

Some of the excess *Malay labour force* in the traditional rural sector, perhaps as many as 75,000, will find employment on estates and in modern forestry, fishing and mining. Some rural Malay will join the security forces, move to the modern urban sector through high quality education, etc.; we have assumed that as many as 75,000 Malays will in fact so move from traditional rural sector, and another 50,000 from the modern sector of the rural economy. This means that there will be net out-migration of a quarter million Malays from the traditional rural to the traditional urban sector. Many of these will eventually be absorbed in various low-productivity traditional activities in the towns, some will swell the ranks of the unemployed and some will be able eventually to move up to modern industrial, commercial or governmental activities. We have on a net basis for the 1967-85 period assumed that as many as 100,000 Malay workers in the traditional urban sector (including some of those that come in from the rural areas) will move up to the modern industrial, commercial or Government activities.

As we have drawn the picture of developments to 1985, neither the modern rural sector of estates and modern forestry, fishing and mining nor the traditional rural economy will be able to absorb the natural increase in the *non-Malay labour force* in those sectors. We have in fact projected a net out-migration of 150,000 non-Malay workers; from each of the two major rural sectors. Some of them may be able to move directly into modern urban employment, but the majority will have to move with their families into the low-productivity, high unemployment, increasingly over-populated, traditional urban sector; a great many of them unsuccessfully seeking urban job opportunities.

## Racial Economic Disparities

We estimated above in an earlier section that in 1967 there was a productivity and income differential in favour of the non-Malays which may be expressed by a ratio of nearly 7 to 4 or by the absolute difference of $1250 per member of the labour force. Our projections show (see Table B.3 above) that with determined policies to lessen the disparity and provided the optimistic assumptions made in this paper about overall growth and Malay participation are realised in full, the imbalance as measured by the disparity ratio may be reduced from 7 to 4 in 1967 to 7 to 5 in 1985. This improvement — if it can be realised — would be a major achievement.

However, the potential reduction in the disparity ratio in part reflects the projected near trebling of non-Malay unemployed (to 315,000 in 1985) as against "only" a doubling of Malay unemployed (to 168,000). If the disparity ratio is calculated in terms of productivity of workers employed (i.e. not total labour force), then the 1985 projection gives a disparity ratio of 1.51, as against 1.40 if also the unemployed are counted in. The assumption made that the allocation of job opportunities (by market forces and government policies) is skewed in favour of Malays is therefore an integral and important precondition for the achievement of the modest improvement projected for the disparity ratio.

It is a measure of the extent of the present disparity and its basic intractability within a decade or two, however, that the improvement here optimistically projected is only in relative terms: the 1967 average disparity in favour of non-Malays in absolute dollar terms was $1250 ($3000 for non-Malay workers as against $1750 for Malays); in 1985 this absolute difference is shown to be *increased* to $1475 dollars. In absolute dollar terms, therefore, our optimistic projections show a worsening of the disparity by 225 dollars or 18% in as many years. The absolute disparity in favour of non-Malays worsens even more — by $575 or over 45% — if we consider only those who are actually employed, not the total labour force.

## Main Conclusions

The main conclusions of this analysis are discouraging, but clear. They may be summarised as follows:

a. The economic imbalance between Malays and non-Malays is already very large. Our estimate of a disparity ratio of nearly 7 to 4 or $1250 per worker today is a minimum estimate.

b. The imbalance is deeply entrenched in the structure and dynamics of the economy, indeed, it is not tractable in the perspective of a decade or two.

c. A clear change in development strategy backed by consistent, persistent and courageous implementation is required if the Government wishes to attack the disparity problem. Continuation of present policies — even their more efficient and determined implementation — will be ineffective. So will *ad hoc* and marginal adjustments in development strategy.

d. The new strategy would have to emphasise distribution and Malay participation over growth and transfers — in many cases at the cost of maximum growth.

e. The choice of strategy is a political decision, but a choice must be made. Failure to change present policies represents as much a choice as does adoption of a new strategy.

f. The new strategy assumed in this paper implies *inter alia*:
- that increased job opportunities in the modern rural sector be reserved for Malays,
- that new land be opened up at three times the present rate,
- that the settlement and economic exploitation of this land be very largely reserved for Malays,
- that industrial and commercial expansion in the rural areas and smaller towns be subjected to preferential and discriminatory, restrictive and supportive policies which will ensure that this growth will take place largely with Malay entrepreneurship, ownership and work force,
- that the Federal and State Government or their organisations act more vigorously and comprehensively to ensure Malay participation — if necessary by direct Government operations.

g. Given such a strategy and firmness, consistency and perseverance in its implementation, the achievement of parity still is at most a long-term option. Optimistic analysis shows that the disparity ratio may be reduced from 7 to 4 in 1967 to 7 to 5 in 1985. Even so the absolute income and productivity differential will increase markedly, not fall.

h. Such containment or improvement in racial balance as is projected for 1985 implies an overall growth rate of 6.4% annually, i.e. higher than in the past when the development strategy gave priority to overall growth over racial balance. This is not the only, but a major illustration of the optimism underlying the projections.

i. The employment structure will change drastically, leading to a very considerable migration from the rural to the urban sectors.

The problems of city organisation and development will be large and difficult.

j. The unemployment situation will inevitably represent a most serious economic, social and political problem.

Finally, a very first assessment (not included in this paper) shows that the prospects and problems summarised in the previous paragraph are coming upon the country very quickly. Indications are that the disparity may get worse (say by 1975) before it gets better even if the new strategy is adopted: fully, firmly and quickly. If no major shift in strategy and policy is adopted now, the disparity will of course only get worse.

# THE NEW ECONOMIC POLICY[1]

The New Economic Policy is characterised by changes in three dimensions:

(i)   reformulation of objectives and reordering of priorities;
(ii)  development and application of effective policies;
(iii) improvements in coordination and implementation of policies.

Changes relating to objectives and priorities are the most basic in the new economic policy; new instruments of policy can be forged, sharpened and developed only gradually; while implementation can be improved markedly more quickly.

This Directive presents the main elements of the New Economic Policy as now formulated. All Government Departments and Agencies are instructed to make sure that the letter and intent of this Directive are *fully* and *explicitly* reflected in all policies, programmes and projects under their responsibility. In particular, this Directive provides the basic guideline for the current work on the formulation of the Second Malaysia Plan 1971-75.

## Objectives and Targets

In the First Malaysia Plan (and reiterated in the Mid-Term Review) the Government presents a list of ten objectives. All of these remain guidelines for policy formation, but the present situation has given new urgency and priority to some of them. Today, the basic objectives of economic policy are three in number:

---

[1] This policy statement, dated 18 March 1970, was issued by the Department of National Unity as a *Directive* to all Government Departments and Agencies, providing basic guidelines for the formulation of the Second Malaysia Plan 1971-75.

(i)    the promotion of national unity and integration;
(ii)   the creation of employment opportunities;
(iii)  the promotion of overall economic growth.

It is important to recognise that these objectives are in some respects and in some circumstances competitive and conflicting, and therefore the Government will have to exercise choice and determine at what point the further pursuit of any one objective will be forgone in the interest of furthering one or the other of the remaining two main objectives.

The Government has already stated (in Development Circular No.1 of 1969) that:

> the overriding objective of the Second Malaysia Plan will be the promotion of national unity among the various races in the country and at all levels of society through far reaching development and widespread prosperity. All major plan objectives shall contribute to this end. Special emphasis will be placed on redressing imbalances in incomes and opportunities and on job creation for Malaysians in less favourable positions.

Given the overriding priority of the first objective, two major areas for analysis and decision follow. In the first place we require an explicit consideration of the implications of the national unity objective, in which a thorough analysis of targets and indicators of achievement become critical. In the second place, we need to explore — qualitatively and quantitatively — how the national unity objective relates to the employment and growth objectives; to what extent and in what circumstances will the national unity objective in fact *override* the other objectives — in other words we must analyse the nature and magnitude of conflict between objectives. Where and when the objectives are mutually reinforcing and fully supplementary no choice is required and we really only have one all-embracing objective. While this type of harmony exists widely — though not in all circumstances — as between the employment and growth objectives, each of these are often - though not all always - in conflict with the national unity objective.

While the objective of national unity as formulated above is qualitative, the employment and growth objectives lend themselves directly to quantitative measurement. In fact, employment and growth are really only derived objectives. Thus, the employment objective reflects *inter alia* the aims of providing opportunities for individual advancement and the realisation of individual potentials and abilities;

a sense of participation in the development of the community; a guarantee of a share in the fruits of development, and indeed the harnessing of human resources for growth. This latter element of the employment objective provides the link to — and the main explanation of consistency with — the economic growth objective. However, the growth objective itself reflects the basic and wider aim of providing resources for general economic well-being, for defence of the nation against internal or external aggression, for social welfare programmes, and sometimes for the greater prosperity and power of a social or economic elite. In some respects and for special groups growth may be desirable for its own sake, but its main justification is typically given in terms of the resources it provides for more basic (or higher) objectives.

In order to analyse the implications of the three major objectives on the same footing and thus provide the basis for choice between alternative strategies and for balance between the objectives, we must define at least some quantitative indicators of what kinds of changes constitute fuller achievement of national unity. The most obvious of such measures relate to racial economic balances. Are there marked differences as between racial groups in productivity, consumption, income, wealth, entrepreneurship, opportunities, etc.? If so, are these differences felt or assumed to be felt by one group or another as evidence of having lost out or of having been left out in the development process, as prejudicing the future of their group in social or political as well as in economic terms? How have these racial balances changed over time? Formulated in this way the economic objective of national unity may be expressed as *the improvement of economic balances between the races, or the reduction of racial economic disparities.*

Thus formulated, a great many important aspects of national unity are subsumed under this economic objective of racial balance: how about differences between States, between rich and poor generally, between rural and urban life, between religions, cultures, languages, etc.? Racial economic balance indicators reflect many of these elements of national unity at best imperfectly, rather like economic growth rates are only imperfect indicators of rates of improvement in general well-being. Imperfection of quantitative indicators of change in any phenomenon with a significant qualitative component is inevitable. In the case of national unity, however, changes in racial economic balances are accepted by Government as significant and central indicators of national unity. As also for the other two main objectives of employment and growth, the racial economic balance indicators of national unity need to be supplemented by analysis of changes in other social relations: in urban harmony or tension as otherwise evidenced, in racial settlement patterns for squatters and for residents in given areas, in racial elements of the retailer-customer, employer-employee, producer-trader or lender-borrower relationships, etc. All that the indicators of racial economic balance can do is to give a first quantitative approximation of the changing basis for national unity, just as overall economic growth rates are indicators of the changing basis for economic well-being or economic strength.

The three basic objectives of the New Economic Policy may now be formulated as follows:

(i)    reduction of racial economic disparities;
(ii)   creation of employment opportunities; and
(iii)  promotion of overall economic growth.

This listing also reflects the relative priorities attached to these main objectives in the New Economic Policy; racial economic balance first, employment second and growth third.

The fact that the New Economic Policy represents a fresh emphasis is clearly evidenced in the targets set for the attainment over the next few years of the three principal objectives, in particular in the change to be affected in the development of racial economic balance. Available statistical material for 1967 for West Malaysia shows that average income per capita of non-Malays exceeds that of Malays[2] by 75 per cent or even more. Moreover, since Merdeka the Malays, which constitute half the population, have received only about one-third of the increased total income that derives from growth in the economy over the whole of that decade. The New Economic Policy explicitly sets out to change this. The Government is well aware, however, that the causes of racial economic imbalance are complex and deeply rooted. Nevertheless, during the Second Malaysia Plan period to 1975 the Government is determined to force the changes necessary to effect a clear improvement in racial economic balances as against the ineffective policies to deal with this problem in the past. While, as our first analysis suggests, non-Malay average incomes exceed those of Malays by 75 per cent today, the target for the Second Malaysia Plan for reduction of this disparity must be set at 60 per cent or lower. This may appear only a modest target for improvement of racial balance; it would, however,

---

[2] The term Malay(s), wherever appearing in this paper, means Malay(s) and other Native(s).

represent a major achievement: it would not only mean that further aggravation of the racial disparity problem had been definitely stopped, it would signify that structural changes were in fact set in motion in the economy which would hold promise of eventual elimination of the racial economic imbalance which threatens to rupture the social fabric of the country.

The Government recognises that the decision to take whatever steps are necessary to achieve the target set for racial balance to some extent may compromise the achievement of maximum results in employment creation and overall economic growth. Even so, however, as a result of the development of New Economic Policy instruments and of improvements in coordination and implementation under the New Economic Policy, it is possible to set targets also for job creation and economic growth which will exceed those achieved since Merdeka. In fact, the target for job creation to the end of the Second Five-Year period in 1975 may be set as high as 3.0 per cent per annum as against less than 2.5 per cent achieved since 1957; at the same time the target for overall economic growth may be set at more than 6 per cent annually as against an average overall growth rate of about 5.5 per cent achieved since Merdeka.

The Government recognises that even if all three overall targets are achieved by 1975, major disparities between the races will still prevail (in absolute dollar terms the disparity will in fact increase), the unemployment situation will still represent a major social and economic problem, and economic growth in the non-Malay sector — while still substantial — may be somewhat slower than the resources and resourcefulness in that sector by itself would permit. We cannot in any sense fully and finally solve the basic problems of economic imbalances, unemployment and growth in the period of the Second Malaysia Plan to 1975, but the Government is determined that a solid foundation is created and a clear advance is made over the next few years to bring about a solution.

The Government considers the three main overall targets as stipulated above to be simultaneously attainable within the New Economic Policy framework. It should be clear, however, that the Government is determined that the *reduction in racial economic disparities shall be the overriding target* even if unforeseen developments occur which pose a harsher conflict than now foreseen between the three objectives.

The above targets are, of course, targets for the development of the Malaysian economy as a whole. Within the framework thus established, separate and specific targets will be set for each major sector ensuring in particular that the Malay work force is more fully and equitably involved in the growth of the economy. This will make it necessary as an integral part of the New Economic Policy to speed up the participation of Malays at all levels of modern sector activities: in manufacturing, mining, construction, wholesale and retail trade, estate development, etc. Targets and policies for each such sector must be developed over the next several months and integrated into the Second Malaysia Plan.

## Development and Application of Effective Policies

At its second meeting, the National Consultative Council expressed full agreement that a fresh approach is vital to correct the economic imbalance among the races in the country if the nation is to survive in harmony. The Council also agreed that related factors such as regional problems, nutrition, education, training and opportunities play important roles in the overall economic improvement of the poor and that these should be tackled effectively and in a systematic manner.

Perhaps the single most important characteristic of the New Economic Policy is the determination with which the Government will set up institutions, use new instruments of policy, and adopt special measures to ensure that the national objectives as discussed above are achieved. In the spirit of this fresh approach, the Government will now take a more positive and active role in the development of the country both through public sector enterprise over a wide field of activities and through the application of firm policies affecting developments in the private sector.

In exercising direction and control of both public and private sector developments, the Government will have to muster all its legal and administrative powers as well as its financial and other resources to induce, encourage and channel all efforts towards the attainment of the national objectives. The Government will use its licencing authority, budget and tax structure, financial incentives, specific regulations and other systems of incentives and controls to ensure that private sector development reflects the objectives and needs of the country.

The Government has already established a number of institutions for direct action in the economic life of the country. Institutions such as MARA, FAMA, FIDA, FLDA, MIDF, etc. will need to review their programmes and strengthen their efforts so that they make a significant contribution towards the achievement of the national objectives. New institutions such as the National Corporation and the Agricultural Development Bank must get into full operation expeditiously and effectively. Other such institutions will be set up as and when necessary.

This new emphasis on a more dynamic role for the public sector will also be reflected in the policies and activities of the various State Governments. They also must re-align their policies and programmes towards the total national effort. In this context the role of the State Economic Development Corporations needs special emphasis. They will become particularly important instruments of Government policy during the Second Malaysia Plan period in the fulfilment of the overriding objective of creating a better economic balance between races and between States.

## Policies for Agriculture, Fishing and Forestry

The agricultural sector is most important in the implementation of the New Economic Policy. Not only does this include by far the largest sector of traditional low-productivity employment, it also provides livelihood for no less than 2/3 of all Malays. In the past decade average overall growth in the agricultural sector has been about 5 per cent. While this is a creditable performance, it has not, however, contributed to the improvement of the general pattern of racial economic balance. The rapidly growing agricultural production areas have in fact been those in which non-Malays dominate, while Malays typically are engaged in the activities of low productivity gains.

During the 1960s spectacular growth rates of 20 per cent and more have been registered in the production of such commodities as palm oil and kernels, timber, poultry and eggs, pigs and pepper in all of which Malay participation is small or negligible. On the other hand, the rate of growth of padi production which is by far the most important occupation of Malay farmers, has averaged only about 2 per cent a year during the 1960s. It will therefore be a central feature of the New Economic Policy to accelerate the movement of Malay agricultural producers from uneconomic low-productivity activities into the fast growing capital-intensive and high-productivity areas of the agricultural sector. At the same time the efforts to improve productivity throughout the rural economy must be continued.

The fishing industry is expanding rapidly because of mechanisation and the application of modern techniques in trawling and other large scale enterprise. The Government will accelerate the provision of infrastructure facilities such as fishing ports, fishing training and research and step up the movement of existing Malay fishermen using outdated and inefficient fishing methods to the larger and more efficient fishing sector. A full review of Government policies relating to modern fishing will be undertaken. Consideration shall be given to the setting up of a fishing corporation to assist Malays to enter large scale, modern fishing.

In the case of timber production, in addition to the need to formulate sound overall timber and forest policies to ensure rational development, the New Economic Policy also requires that appropriate fiscal and licencing policies (for saw mills etc.) be devised to ensure balanced racial participation in this new fast-growing and rapidly expanding industry.

The Government rubber replanting grant represents a major item of public expenditure; it is also a potent stimulant of productivity improvement for the smallholders. In the past the estates more than the smallholders have been in a position to make use of this grant. As part of the New Economic Policy adjustment will be made in the operation of the cess and grant so that the smallholders are in fact enabled to speed up their replanting.

During the 1960s private sector development of the country's agricultural resources have been relatively laggard, in particular there has been little if any increase in total acreage under estate agriculture. There is now a clear responsibility on Government to ensure that estate development does in fact play an active role in the much needed acceleration of new land development. To this end the Government will continue to encourage some further private estate development. The Government will also — and on a significant scale — ensure that estates are developed under public sector auspices. The institution for implementing this policy may be the FLDA or its subsidiaries in conjunction with the State Development Corporations.

Agricultural marketing and credit present potentially powerful instruments for the implementation of the New Economic Policy. Active government involvement in the buying and selling of smallholders' agricultural products, restrictive licencing and enforcement measures can go a long way towards ensuring fair and equitable prices and returns to smallholders. The Federal Agricultural Marketing Authority should therefore be encouraged to expand its activities. Similarly Government sponsored credit institutions in particular the Agricultural Development Bank will have to be developed quickly to meet the credit needs of the small farmer and fisherman.

Agricultural credit can play a very important role in the modernisation of the whole agricultural sector, in particular the setting up of large scale and capital intensive ventures in estate agriculture, modern fishing and forestry — both at the level of primary and secondary production, processing and marketing as well as ancillary services. The Agricultural Development Bank will be the main instrument for this purpose; it will also finance such ventures on a package deal basis by developing and providing management and consultant services.

## Policies for Manufacturing, Mining and Construction

Manufacturing is a new but an important sector which will be assuming increasing prominence in the years to come. In view of the present poor participation of Malays in this sector in terms of entrepreneurship, capital and employment it is essential that more Malays should be encouraged to participate much more actively and fully in this sector. The Government must design effective policies of special incentives, support, training, etc. to make this possible.

So far Malay interests have not benefited from Government assistance to manufacturing through tax exemption under pioneer status, tariff protection etc.; as of March 1970 out of a total of over 400 companies approved for pioneer status there are less than half a dozen owned by Malay interests.

The Malay experience in trade and commerce — often a necessary prelude to active participation in manufacturing — is minimal. It is therefore necessary to institute special preferences in order to enable the Malays to compete with the non-Malays. Following are some of the measures to enable greater Malay participation in the manufacturing sector:

(a) Incentives to industry — pioneer status, investment tax credit, tariff protection, etc. — shall be made available by priority and preference to Malay interests whenever such applicants come forward, even when non-Malay applicants also declare an interest. This will mean that in some cases better proposals by non-Malay interesst will have to be rejected in order that new Malay entrepreneurs be given a chance.

(b) In order to bring forward more Malay entrepreneurs, a new policy shall be announced to the effect that more generous incentives will be offered for proposals by Malay interests in terms of tariff protection, excise, import quota regulation etc. The extent of such special Malay preferences will have to be determined so as to ensure that the development of new industries will in fact be better balanced than has been the case to date.

(c) From now on all national agencies such as CIC, FIDA and MIDF, which provide any form of assistance to manufacturing enterprises, shall deliberately practise clear preference for projects initiated by Malay interests.

(d) Consideration will be given to the announcement of specified sectors of industry in which new development will be reserved for Malay interests.

The responsibility for ensuring a racially balanced employment structure at all levels rests not only on the Government but also on the companies themselves. Manufacturing establishments are therefore required to provide training programmes for Malays for absorption into skilled employment in the firms. Such training programmes may be undertaken within individual firms or jointly by firms in a particular industry. The Government will strengthen and expand technical training institutes and will also be prepared to partially finance a workable scheme of in-service training which can be designed by the companies concerned in consultation with Government.

The Government has declared that the employment structure in factories must reflect from top to bottom the multi-racial composition of the population. It is recognised that the Ministry of Commerce and Industry has imposed the condition of proportional racial employment on firms awarded pioneer status. However, it is now necessary to initiate action to extend the condition to cover also non-pioneer firms.

The present lop-sided geographical distribution of manufacturing establishments should be corrected gradually and systematically. In this connection, Federal Government authorities shall review existing incentives for new establishments to locate in less developed areas. State Governments shall ensure that adequate supporting incentives and assistance be provided, particularly to assist development of Malay entrepreneurship and the acceleration of Malay industrial employment. It would be necessary in this connection to require certain manufacturing industries to locate themselves in less developed areas, particularly some of those industries whose sources of raw materials or markets are in such areas.

Government direct participation will take the form of equity holding, the strengthening of existing institutions and the development of new machinery for financial support and for the provision of technical assistance to Malay enterprises. The Government development budget will have to reflect these priorities.

At present there are very few Malay ventures in mining; the large scale dredging is overwhelmingly operated by European companies, while the Chinese dominate other mining methods. Nevertheless there is scope for encouragement of Malays to go into mining. Mining land in Malay Reservations represents a good base for such participation, and should therefore remain reserved. Also, off-shore areas present a new rich potential for mining, in which full participation by Malays must be ensured. State Economic Development Corporations in conjunction with the National Corporation and if necessary in joint-ventures with the private sector will have an important role to play in this development.

The construction industry offers another high-productivity field into which Malays can be encouraged to participate. It has the advantage that there are already available skilled Malay craftsmen, particularly in the East Coast, who with proper organisation and finance can provide a sound base for more active Malay participation. The Jabatan Kerja Raya will serve as a training ground for Malay skilled labour and contractors. In the initial stages especially, Malay participation in this industry will be encouraged by Government adopting a policy of giving preference to Malay firms for construction works to meet requirements of Government and Government authorities such as FLDA, Malayan Railway etc. Malay employment in this industry will also be increased through Government stipulation that contractors for Government works must employ Malays at all levels in accordance with the general guidelines.

## Policies for Trade and Commerce

This is another important sector where active Malay participation will be encouraged. This can only be achieved with assistance from the Government and cooperation from non-Malays who are already established in this sector. MARA will be strengthened or a new authority established to provide finance, technical and consultancy services to assist Malay businesses. These authorities together with State Development Corporations will construct business centres and shop houses in all towns for operation by Malay interests. This visual evidence of Malay participation in commerce will in some measure give the Malays the feeling of participation and involvement.

The Government expects full cooperation from the private sector in this endeavour by giving employment to Malays, forming joint ventures with Malays and allocating distribution agencies also to Malay interests. For this purpose the Government will consider giving appropriate incentives to encourage such cooperation.

The newly established National Corporation will have a special role to play to spearhead Malay participation in this sector. It will participate directly or in joint ventures in import, export, wholesaling and distribution business and act as a promoter of Malay business.

## Policies for Improvement of Urban and Rural Life

In recent years we have seen increasing in-migration into the urban areas and there is evidence that this flow will accelerate. Unless the urban infrastructure is capable of absorbing this ever increasing load, the urban scene will be plagued by problems of traffic congestion, inadequate housing and water supply and social problems arising out of slum and squatter habitation and the lack of employment opportunities. These will require stronger Government involvement in the development of the urban environment. New institutional arrangements will have to be made, including arrangements affecting the distribution of responsibility between local, State and Federal authorities. The Government will also have to introduce strong and comprehensive policies relating to town zoning and general city planning to cater for the different and special needs of the urban population.

More modern medical and health facilities will be provided to promote and maintain the health and welfare of people living in rural areas. To this end qualified personnel in greater numbers will be trained and posted to rural areas. Special programmes will be developed to ensure that the service of doctors and other health personnel will be available in the rural areas on a scale commensurate with what is provided in the towns. The Government will seek ways and means to educate the rural people in the needs and possibilities for improved nutrition. The malaria eradication programme for the rural areas will be speeded up. The Government will assist in the planning and establishment of social amenities, social welfare centers etc. In these and other ways the Government will give its support to the general improvement of life in these areas.

## Policies for Education

Educational development affects the nation in many vital aspects. It is a vehicle for modernisation of society and for the attainment of social goals, equal opportunity and national unity. A full statement of new policies for education will be prepared and issued separately. In this statement the educational component of the New Economic Policy will be presented.

## Formulation of Programmes by Government Agencies

These are some of the major elements of the New Economic Policy of the Government which provide guidelines to Government agencies in their further elaboration of policies and projects in their respective areas. The policies detailed above together with the statement of objectives in the first section provide the framework within which the agencies must now proceed to the preparation of their proposals for inclusion in the Second Malaysia Plan.

## Coordination and Implementation of Policies

It is extremely important to ensure that the New Economic Policy is implemented in an efficient manner in order that the objectives and targets set out are achieved in full measure and in the period planned. For this purpose the implementing machinery and procedures must be streamlined and geared for efficiency. Administrative bottlenecks and red tape must be reduced to the minimum. In this regard it is necessary, particularly for the management and operation of large projects, for Government departments and agencies to work out a system whereby their responsibilities are decentralised through delegation to subordinate, subsidiary or even operationally independent agencies.

As implementation of policies may involve participation and cooperation of various departments and agencies at both State and Federal levels, the machinery must be perfected so as to ensure close coordination amongst Government agencies. Such coordination must also be effected at the stage of policy formulation. There is today an overlap of responsibilities in this respect in several important areas such as development planning itself and training. Consideration therefore shall be given to the possibility of organisational rearrangement in which changes in the ministerial responsibilities may also be required. There must also be a machinery to secure close coordination and cooperation between the Government and the private sector. It is important that the coordination and consultation machinery provides for clear lines of responsibility so that duplication of efforts and wastage of resources is avoided.

Modern management emphasises efficiency and effectiveness for greater productivity through the application of explicit systems and procedures. These are changed and improved over time and they must continuously be adjusted to changing objectives and needs. In the implementation of the New Economic Policy, the Development Administration Unit is the main instrument for management improvement and modernisation. It is critically important, however, that all officers give of their best in dedicated, sincere, honest and loyal service.

With the new emphasis under the Government New Economic Policy, giving overriding importance to the objective of national unity, the Department of National Unity must be in a position effectively and fully to give direction to planning and policy formulation as well as to oversee that the course set is followed. For the efficient performance of this vital task the Department will be strengthened. All departments and agencies are required to extend their full cooperation and assistance to the Department in the execution of its functions.

# EMPLOYMENT, PRODUCTION AND RACIAL ECONOMIC BALANCE TARGETS FOR THE SMP[1]

## Introduction

Over the last few months the SMP Macro Group has discussed the demand components of GMP as they may evolve over the period to 1975: exports, public and private investment and consumption, as well as imports as a component of domestic demand at the levels foreseen over the SMP period. Following such a demand analysis the Macro Group has studied major components of overall financial and monetary accounts. The results of discussions so far on these issues are reported in tentative summary form in EPU: (First Draft) NDPC Paper: *The Macro Framework for the Second Malaysia Plan.*

While the macro work to date has clarified important questions of growth and finance, it does not — as far as it goes — provide much insight into the major issues of employment and racial economic balance issues. The present paper seeks to provide a framework for specific, yet comprehensive analysis of employment and balance targets and developments for the period to 1975. It does so by approaching the problems from the production side. The analysis in the present paper is in no way an alternative or substitute for the demand based analysis thus far undertaken by the Macro Group; it is a supplement to that work.

In relation to the SMP the production trends and targets have to some extent been discussed in the sectoral Inter-Agency Planning Groups, in particular for industry (but only in manufacturing) and for agriculture. This paper draws on insights gained from these discussions. It also provides a framework for focussing further work

---

[1] This paper, written by J. Faaland and dated 14 June 1970, represented an effort to ensure that the approaches and objectives of NEP were reflected in the preparation of the Second Malaysia Plan. The separate statistical paper: *Data, Assumptions, Targets and Derived Projections for the SMP* and the *Appendix table* to the original paper itself are not included in this reproduction.

on employment and racial balance targets and for consideration of impacts of specific and general policies, programmes and projects at the sectoral level.

In addition to work done by sectoral IAPGs, a direct and comprehensive analytical attack on the employment and balance issues has been made in several documents prepared in EPU and DNU, first in the paper: *Racial Disparity and Economic Development* and its *Appendix*. The present paper takes the past analysis further. In the pages that follow we give an overview on the picture that emerges from the work to date and draw some conclusions both for strategy and policy for the SMP. In the accompanying statistical paper: *Data, Assumptions, Targets and Derived Projections for the SMP* all details of data used, assumptions made and methodology adopted are given comprehensively and explicitly, so that one can readily incorporate improved data, more informed assumptions, more realistic targets as supported by decisions on specific policies to be formulated, better methodology as may emerge from discussions in coming weeks.

## Main Findings

*The New Economic Policy statement* highlights the three objectives of (i) improved racial economic balance, (ii) rapid employment creation, and (iii) overall economic growth. On the basis of provisional analysis and judgment the NEP sets minimum quantitative targets for simultaneous achievement during the SMP of:

(i)      an improvement in racial economic balance from an estimated global average of 1.75 to 1.60 or lower;

(ii)     employment creation at the average rate of 3 per cent a year or more;

(iii)    overall economic growth of 6 per cent or more.

In Table D.1 — and in more detail in the Appendix Table and in the accompanying statistical paper — we present the findings of the quantitative exercise in target setting for the SMP for production, employment and balance. As shown, the findings are fully consistent with the NEP minimum targets in all three respects. As derived from a sector by sector analysis of production, productivity, employment and Malay participation we find:

(i)      the racial economic balance indicator shows an improvement from an estimated value of 1.69 in 1970 to 1.51 in 1975;

(ii)     employment increases by an annual average of 3.0 per cent during the SMP period; and

(iii)    the average annual overall economic growth rate is found to be 7.0 per cent for the SMP in terms of volume.

*The improvement in the racial economic balance indicator* from an estimated 1.69 to 1.51 in five years is somewhat better than the NEP minimum target. Its achievement depends on three major factors:

(i)      the attainment of the projected agricultural output growth, which is considerable, and with only a marginal increase in the agricultural labour force, thus greatly increasing the average income in the rural sectors.

(ii)     the successful transfer during the SMP period of no less than 57 per cent of the "natural" increase in the labour force in rural occupations to urban activities, and

(iii)    an increase in the Malay share of the active labour force in *all* major categories of activities.[2]

*The overall employment creation* implied of 3 per cent annually falls short of the projected increase in total labour force of 3.3 per cent. As a result, unemployment is shown to increase to 292,000 in 1975 as compared with an estimated 210,000 in 1970. In percentage terms the unemployment projected represents 7.4 per cent in 1975 as compared to an estimated 6.6 per cent in 1967 and 6.3 per cent in 1970.

It is a significant implication of the targets and projections for the SMP as detailed in this study that there would be no marked difference in the changes foreseen in the overall unemployment situation as between Malays and non-Malays.

The failure to create new jobs fully in step with the growth of the labour force may require special measures. However, as here projected, the order of magnitude of the growth in the unemployment problem to 1975 should not be exaggerated. To illustrate, assume that a youth mobilisation scheme were instituted for special work programmes in which 60,000 trainees were included (both Malays

---

[2] Note that this general increase in the share of Malay participation in *all* major sectors is consistent with — even a basic condition for — the maintenance of the employment balance for the total economy at 50 per cent. The statistical explanation is, of course, that the structure of employment in shifting towards the modern urban major sectors where Malays are now numerically greatly under-represented.

TABLE D.1

SUMMARY OF PROJECTIONS AND TARGETS FOR SMP FOR EMPLOYMENT, PRODUCTIVITY AND VALUE ADDED

(Employment in thousands, labour productivity in $ of total value added per worker, aggregate value added in $ million and growth rates in average annual percentages)

| Main Sector | | Labour Force (thousands) | | | | | Labour Productivity (constant 1967 prices) | | | | Aggregate Value Added (constant 1967 prices) | | | | |
|---|---|---|---|---|---|---|---|---|---|---|---|---|---|---|---|
| | | Growth rate | T | M | NM | M share % | Growth rate | T | M | NM | NM/M % | Growth rate | T | M | NM |
| Modern rural | 1967 | | 334 | 86 | 248 | 26 | | 3269 | 3058 | 3343 | 109 | | 1092 | 263 | 829 |
| | 1970 | 2.2 | 357 | 110 | 247 | 31 | 6.7 | 3966 | 3782 | 4049 | 107 | 9.0 | 1416 | 416 | 1000 |
| | 1975 | 1.7 | 388 | 142 | 246 | 37 | 5.0 | 5052 | 4944 | 5114 | 103 | 6.7 | 1960 | 702 | 1258 |
| Traditional rural | 1967 | | 1153 | 913 | 240 | 79 | | 1235 | 1128 | 1642 | 146 | | 1424 | 1030 | 394 |
| | 1970 | 0.7 | 1179 | 931 | 248 | 79 | 6.3 | 1483 | 1349 | 1984 | 147 | 7.1 | 1748 | 1256 | 492 |
| | 1975 | 0.8 | 1219 | 965 | 254 | 79 | 4.2 | 1820 | 1673 | 2382 | 142 | 4.9 | 2219 | 1614 | 605 |
| Modern Urban | 1967 | | 592 | 153 | 439 | 26 | | 4804 | 3882 | 5125 | 132 | | 2844 | 594 | 2250 |
| | 1970 | 5.2 | 689 | 201 | 488 | 29 | 3.0 | 5247 | 4318 | 5629 | 130 | 8.3 | 3615 | 868 | 2747 |
| | 1975 | 5.2 | 888 | 304 | 584 | 34 | 3.1 | 6125 | 5227 | 6592 | 126 | 8.5 | 5439 | 1589 | 3850 |
| Traditional Urban | 1967 | | 460 | 75 | 385 | 16 | | 2246 | 2133 | 2268 | 106 | | 1033 | 160 | 873 |
| | 1970 | 4.9 | 531 | 8.9 | 422 | 17 | 1.2 | 2330 | 2213 | 2353 | 106 | 6.2 | 1237 | 197 | 1040 |
| | 1975 | 5.3 | 689 | 118 | 571 | 17 | 0.8 | 2430 | 2356 | 2445 | 104 | 6.2 | 1674 | 278 | 1396 |

TABLE D. 1 (continued)

| | Year | | | | | | | | | | | | | | |
|---|---|---|---|---|---|---|---|---|---|---|---|---|---|---|---|
| Government | 1967 | 7.7 | 297 | 185 | 112 | 62 | | 2440 | 2440 | 2440 | | | 725 | 456 | 279 |
| | 1970 | 3.9 | 371 | 238 | 133 | 64 | | 2400 | 2400 | 2400 | | 7.8 | 905 | 581 | 324 |
| | 1975 | | 449 | 296 | 153 | 66 | 2.0 | 2694 | 2694 | 2694 | | 6.0 | 1209 | 797 | 412 |
| All sectors | 1967 | 3.3 | 2836 | 1412 | 1424 | 50 | | 2522 | 1785 | 3254 | 182 | | 7153 | 2520 | 4633 |
| | 1970 | 3.0 | 3127 | 1569 | 1558 | 50 | 4.2 | 2853 | 2115 | 3596 | 170 | 7.6 | 8921 | 3318 | 5603 |
| | 1975 | | 3633 | 1825 | 1808 | 50 | 4.0 | 3441 | 2714 | 4160 | 153 | 7.0 | 12501 | 4980 | 7521 |
| Unemployment | 1967 | | 200 | 90 | 110 | 45 | | | | | | | | | |
| | 1970 | | 210 | 99 | 111 | 47 | | | | | | | | | |
| | 1975 | | 292 | 137 | 155 | 47 | | | | | | | | | |
| Total Economy | 1967 | 3.2 | 3036 | 1502 | 1534 | 50 | | 2357 | 1678 | 3020 | 180 | | 7153 | 2520 | 4633 |
| | 1970 | 3.3 | 3337 | 1668 | 1669 | 50 | | 2673 | 1989 | 3357 | 169 | 7.6 | 8921 | 3318 | 5603 |
| | 1975 | | 3925 | 1962 | 1963 | 50 | | 3185 | 2538 | 3831 | 150 | 7.0 | 12501 | 4980 | 7521 |

T = Total    M = Malay    NM = Non Malay

and non-Malays). Allowing as much as say $1000 per youth mobilised in total annual cost and even assuming that no direct economic benefits accrue, such a scheme would bring down the overall unemployment percentage below 6.0 in 1975 at the cost of $ 60 million — which is less than two-thirds of the pay increase of civil servants, etc. paid out under the "Suffian" award, etc. A scheme of this scope may possibly be worth considering — though of course with a view to achieving both training effects and some direct economic returns. It is mentioned here, however, only to illustrate the moderate and manageable increase in unemployment as here projected for the SMP.

*The overall economic growth* here projected for the SMP of 7.0 per cent in real terms would be a very considerable improvement on the performance — as well as the targets — for the First Malaysia Plan. All major sectors are projected to share in this development. Most rapid is the growth in the modern urban sector (8.5 per cent annually), but the projected growth rates for the rural sectors are also considerable (6.7 per cent and 4.9 per cent in the modern and traditional rural sectors, respectively). In fact, growth of output per worker is projected to be highest in the rural sectors (5.0 per cent and 4.2 per cent respectively), much higher than the rates projected for urban activities (3.1 per cent and 0.8 per cent for modern and traditional urban sectors respectively, and 2 per cent for Government).

The significance of this pattern of growth of output and productivity is very great, both in terms of resource allocation and resource creation in general and in its effect on the economic balance between rural and urban activities and in particular between the Malay and non-Malay labour force.

One further implication of the pattern of growth foreseen is that the economy also at the end of the SMP will be largely export-oriented. In fact the growth of output in considerable measure is in the production of export crops. Also, for manufacturing to grow as fast as is projected and consistent with racial balance objective, policies must be designed to step up production for exports considerably. (This may require re-assessment of the export forecasts for industrial products now being used.)

*The structural changes* in the economy, as implied in the projected and targeted developments during the SMP period, are very considerable. To attain and surpass the minimum macro targets set in the NEP statement constitutes a change of major importance: more rapid economic growth and employment creation than ever before and at the same time a clear cut and definitive improvement in the racial economic balance. Along with these developments will go an accelerated rate of modernisation of the economy, a very rapid migration of young people from rural to urban locations and an accelerated entry of Malay labour force into modern manufacturing, construction, commerce, etc.

(Further paragraphs on the nature and magnitude of the projected structural changes should be added, drawing on Table D.1 as well as the more detailed projections contained in the Appendix Table.)

(Also, the point should be made that the economic advance projected — while leading to an improvement in the racial economic balance indicator — still would leave the average absolute productivity and income differential between Malays and non-Malays practically unchanged. While the Malay and non-Malay total labour force are of equal size, the projected increase in total income accruing to non-Malays over the SMP period is over 15 per cent higher than for the Malay labour force.)

*The evolution of relative prices* over the SMP period is of direct relevance to the economic balance developments. The methodology adopted is based on volume changes in production and productivity. However, it is quite evident that price trends for important rural sector products are less favourable than for urban sector activities. In a supplementary set of calculations expected and assumed price changes over the SMP period have been introduced, see the paper: *Data, Assumptions, Targets and Derived Projections for the SMP*. While changes in relative prices do alter the picture presented in the present note in some respects (which may be detailed), they do not significantly affect the overall picture.

## Policy Implications

*Malay participation rates* are assumed and projected to increase in all sectors. In the modern urban sector Malay employment is projected to increase by no less than 100,000 in the course of five years (following an increase of 50,000 in the three years 1967-70). Similarly, Malay employment in Government is projected to increase by 60,000 during the SMP period. In the rural economy the Malay (as well as non-Malay) labour force is projected to increase its productivity very rapidly. Clearly, these targets can only be realised if the Malay labour force can be given training to perform these tasks, basic education and formal training as well as on-the-job training and acquisition of skills.

Moreover, not only have we assumed greater number of Malays as participants in these growing sectors, we have for most sectors assumed that Malays will move into higher productivity and income positions within industrial and commercial enterprises in such numbers that by the end of the SMP they have begun to narrow the average productivity gap between the Malay and non-Malay work force. While policies can be and must be designed and implemented to ensure that the structure of employment in industry better reflects the racial composition of the population at all levels, these policies can only be successful — not to say acceptable to their non-Malay colleagues — if the development of skills and aptitudes of Malays for effective performance as foremen, skilled operators, supervisors, clerks, technicians and management is stepped up. Thus the NEP emphasises the urgent need for training schemes to be developed in consultation and cooperation with industry. Also, special incentives — ranging from say a differential payroll tax to quota requirements at various levels of employment within enterprises — must be introduced for the improvements in Malay participation postulated to be realised.

*The position and power of the middleman* represents a problem in most developing countries. In Malaysia there are several institutions to deal with the various aspects of the middleman problem including FAMA, the Agriculture Bank, etc. The NEP emphasises the need to strengthen the existing institutions and to develop new ones in this area to give the producer a better deal and generally to make the economic system more efficient. Such institutions and policies must be rapidly and effectively developed if in fact the projected rapid improvements in production and productivity, particularly in the rural sector, are to give the rural people at large a fair share. In our projections and targets we have assumed that this will be possible and that it will be done; in fact, we have assumed that such policies will be effective to an extent where the rural producer, in particular the Malay, will derive an increased share of the total value output in the agriculture and fisheries.

*Greater participation of Malays in ownership and control* in the economy is as important in the long run for economic balance, as is an equitable share in employment opportunities. It is important first because Malay ownership and control give a better guarantee of a high degree of Malay participation in employment at all levels (see the results of the special survey of manufacturing on this point). Second, it is important because a considerable part of value added in an enterprise accrues to non-labour factors of production. For both these reasons the NEP indicates a number of measures to speed up the development of Malay entrepreneurship and to ensure growing Malay share in ownership of means of production. These measures include preferential and discriminatory arrangements in favour of Malays in the licensing of new enterprises in industry and commerce, in agriculture, forestry and fisheries, as well as the setting up of productive enterprises through public sector agencies acting as custodians of Malay interests in ownership and control in the economy. The projections and targets reported in this paper assume that policies in this area will in fact be designed in accordance with the NEP and effectively implemented. This will not be easy, it takes time for institutions and new procedures to develop and the five-year period of the SMP is not very long. Fur the future, however, it is important that the basis for expanded participation of Malay ownership and control is firmly laid in the SMP period.

Full implementation of policies to stimulate Malay entrepreneurship may require a full review of present industrial policy with a view to releasing limited administrative and organisational talents and experience to concentrate much more on the difficult tasks of nurturing Malay entrepreneurship. It is possible — indeed probable — that existing industrial policies which now engage the attention of a large number of devoted civil servants, as well as high level politicians, may have to be significantly generalised, so that applications for various supports to industry can be granted or refused more automatically.

*The implications for public finance* of the NEP and of the assumptions and targets set in this paper are very significant. In the first place the NEP, as reflected in this paper, will for reasons given above not only require a reorientation of administrative effort, but also the mobilisation and deployment of increasing amounts of financial resources through the public sector.

In the second place the growth potential which we have defined and detailed in this paper must be fully mobilised through effective demand policies. If indeed the potentials for production increase as here discussed are substantiated through further discussion, then the projections and targets for public investments and for private and perhaps also some public consumption must be stepped up considerably from the levels at which they are now being discussed. The realisation of the objectives to create employment opportunities and indeed the creation of sufficient resources for effective policies of economic balance at this level will be impossible if the full growth potential within the context of the NEP is not also realised. This is a most important point for economic policy at the moment. If indeed the Government were to err on the side of financial and monetary caution, then the basic political as well as economic potential for creating a foundation for national unity during the SMP would definitely be lost without hope.

*The balance of objectives for policy* as stated in the NEP is clearly important in itself; it also has operational significance for planning. It is clear that rapid economic growth without the minimum improvement in racial balance stipulated is unacceptable; it is equally clear that improved racial economic balance without more rapid economic growth than in the past is undesirable. The conclusion to be drawn from the analysis of economic developments over the next five years is that there is a potential for full achievement of the combination of objectives set forth in the NEP, indeed there is potential for even a somewhat better performance. It is equally clear, however, that this is a potential that will not be realised unless there is re-orientation in policy objectives and direction, as well as more activist and courageous government action in the various sectors of the economy and indeed in terms of fiscal and monetary policies.

## Future Work

At the macro level both EPU itself and the SMP Macro Group will need to get into, modify and develop the analysis on the supply side of the economy. It is suggested that the analysis reported in this paper may provide the framework for such work. In the course of such a process many modifications may have to be introduced.

While the macro work on the demand side must be continued along the lines it has been developed over the last couple of months, macro analysis from the supply side will supplement that work. It will also, as suggested above, provide a most important input into the evaluation of the overall size of the development effort that can be made and must be made during the SMP.

Along with such macro work must go sector by sector analysis of targets. This should be done in the first place with explicit reference to the impact on Malay participation in employment as well as in ownership. In the second place the analysis must lead up to a set of definite, specific and comprehensive policies and programmes through which sector targets (where necessary modified) can be realistically realised. Finally, it would be most valuable if in the discussion of developments by sectors a set of quantitative targets can be formulated for each industry or group of activities and for each agency. The double purpose of this would be first, to ensure that the targets set in the sector discussions are in fact realistic, and second, to facilitate the implementation of policies during the SMP and to measure performance against the targets set.

# SELECT BIBLIOGRAPHY

## Books & Documents

Adelman, Irma and Sherman Robinson, *Income Distribution Policy in Developing Countries — a Case Study of Korea*, Oxford: Oxford Univ. Press, 1978.

Ahluwalia, Montek S., Nicholas G. Carter and Hollis B. Chenery, *Growth and Poverty in Developing Countries*, Wash. D.C.: World Bank, 1985. (World Bank Staff Working Papers no. 309.)

Anand, Sudhir, *Inequality and Poverty in Malaysia — Measurement and Decomposition*, Oxford: Oxford Univ. Press, 1983.

Bergsman, Joe, *Growth and Equity in Semi-Industrialised Countries*, Wash. D.C.: World Bank, 1985. (World Bank Staff Working Papers no. 351.)

Chenery, Hollis et al., *Redistribution with Growth*, Oxford: Oxford Univ. Press, 1974.

Faaland, Just, *Employment, Production and Racial Economic Balance Targets for the Second Malaysia Plan*, Kuala Lumpur, 1970 (Document D).

Faaland, Just, *Policies for Growth with Racial Balance*. Kuala Lumpur, 1969 (Document A).

Faaland, Just and Jack R. Parkinson, *The Political Economy of Development*, London: Frances Pinter, 1986.

Fei, John C.H. and Gustav Ranis, *Development of the Labour Surplus Economy*, Homewood, Ill.:Irwin, 1964.

Fei, John C.H., Gustav Ranis, and Shirley W.Y.Kuo, *Growth with Equity — the Taiwan Case*, Oxford: Oxford Univ. Press, 1979.

Fields, Gary S., *Poverty, Inequality and Development*, Cambridge: Cambridge Univ. Press, 1980.

*The Future of Malaysian Chinese*, Kuala Lumpur: Malaysian Chinese Association, 1988.

Gomez, E.T., *Politics in Business, UMNO's Corporate Investments*, Kuala Lumpur: Forum, 1990.

Griffin, Keith, *Alternative Strategies for Economic Development,* London: Macmillan, 1989.

International Labour Office, *Bibliography of Published Research of the World Employment Programme*, Geneva: ILO, 1978.

Jomo, K.S., *Beyond 1990: Considerations for a New National Development Strategy*, Kuala Lumpur: Univ. of Malaysia. Institute of Advanced Studies, 1989.

Kamal Salih, *The New Economic Policy after 1990*, rev. version of a paper presented at the Malaysian Institute of Economic Research 1988 National Outlook Conference, Kuala Lumpur, 29-30 November, 1988. Kuala Lumpur: MIER, 1988.

Lewis, Arthur, *The Theory of Economic Growth*, London: Unwin Univ. Books, 1963.

Lim Kit Siang, *Crisis of Identity*, Kuala Lumpur: Democratic Action Party, 1986.

Lim Kit Siang, *Malaysia in the Dangerous 80s*, Kuala Lumpur: Democratic Action Party, 1982.

Lim Kit Siang, *Time Bombs in Malaysia,* Kuala Lumpur: Democratic Action Party, 1978. 2nd ed.

Malaysia. Department of National Unity, *The New Economic Policy*, Kuala Lumpur: the Department, 1970, (Document C).

Malaysia, Department of National Unity, *Racial Disparity and Economic Development*. Kuala Lumpur, 1969, (Document B).

Malaysia. Department of Statistics, *Yearbook of Statistics Malaysia 1988*, Kuala Lumpur: the Department, 1989.

Malaysia. Government, *First Malaysia Plan 1966-1970*, Kuala Lumpur: National Printing Department, 1965.

Malaysia. Government, *Mid-Term Review of the First Malaysia Plan 1966-1970*, Kuala Lumpur: National Printing Department, 1969.

Malaysia. Government, *Second Malaysia Plan 1971-75*, Kuala Lumpur: Government Press, 1971.

Malaysia. Government, *Mid-Term Review of the Second Malaysia Plan 1971-75*. Kuala Lumpur: Government Press, 1973.

Malaysia. Government, *Third Malaysia Plan 1976-1980*, Kuala Lumpur: Government Press, 1976.

Malaysia. Government, *Mid-Term Review of the Third Malaysia Plan 1976-1980*, Kuala Lumpur: Government Press, 1979.

Malaysia. Government, *Fourth Malaysia Plan 1981-1985*, Kuala Lumpur: National Printing Department, 1981.

Malaysia. Government, *Mid-Term Review of the Fourth Malaysia Plan 1981-1985*, Kuala Lumpur: National Printing Department, 1984.

Malaysia. Government. *Fifth Malaysia Plan 1986-1990*. Kuala Lumpur: National Printing Department, 1986.

Malaysia. Government, *Mid-Term Review of the Fifth Malaysia Plan 1986-1990*, Kuala Lumpur: National Printing Department, 1989.

Malaysia. Ministry of Finance, *Economic Report 1989/90*, Kuala Lumpur: National Printing Department, 1989.

Malaysian Industrial Development Authority, *Malaysia, Investment in the Manufacturing Sector*, Kuala Lumpur, 1989.

Marshall, Alfred, *Principles of Economics*, London: Macmillan, 1938. 8th ed.

Mauzy, Diane K., *Barisan Nasional — Coalition Government in Malaysia*, Kuala Lumpur: Maricans Academic Series, 1983.

Mazumdar, Depak, *The Urban Labour Market and Income Distribution — a Study of Malaysia.* Oxford: Oxford Univ. Press, 1981.

Meerman, Jacob, *Malaysia. Growth and Equity in a Multiracial Society*, Baltimore: The Johns Hopkins Univ. Press, 1980.

Meerman, Jacob, *Public Expenditure in Malaysia — Who Benefits and Why*, Oxford: Oxford Univ. Press, 1979.

Milne, Robert Stephen and Diane K. Mauzy, *Politics and Government in Malaysia*, Singapore: Times Books, 1980. Rev.ed.

Muzafar, Chandra, *Islamic Resurgence in Malaysia*, Kuala Lumpur, 1987.

*On the Problems of Racial Economic Imbalance and National Unity*, Report of the Economic Committee of the National Economic Council, Kuala Lumpur, 1970.

Renaud, Bertrand, *Economic Growth and Income Inequality in Korea.* Wash. D.C.: World Bank, 1976. (World Bank Staff Working Papers no. 240.)

Safie Bin Ibrahim, *The Islamic Party of Malaysia, Its Formative Stages and Ideology*, Selising, Kelantan, 1981.

*Setelah 1990: Ekonomi dan Pemebentukan Bangsa*, Kuala Lumpur: Universiti Kebangsaan, 1990.

Snodgrass, Donald R., *Inequality and Economic Development in Malaysia*, Kuala Lumpur: Oxford Univ. Press, 1980.

Turnham, D. assisted by I. Jaeger, *The Employment Problem in Less Developed Countries: A Review of Evidence*, Paris: OECD Development Centre, 1971.

*World Development Report 1989*, Oxford: Oxford Univ. Press, 1989.

Young, Kevin; Willem C.F. Bussink and Parvez Hassan, eds., *Malaysia — Growth and Equity in a Multiracial Society*, Baltimore: Johns Hopkins Univ. Press, 1980. (A World Bank Country Economic Report.)

## Articles

Abdullah Ahmad, Issues in Malaysian Politics, Speech delivered at the Institute of International Affairs, Singapore, 30 August 1986, in K.Das: *The Malay Dominance? The Abdullah Rubric*, Kuala Lumpur, 1987.

An Alternative to the NEP, *Aliran Monthly*, vol. 9 (1989) no. 5.

Aziz, U.A., Footprints in the Sands of Time: The Malay Poverty Concept over 50 years from Za'aba to Aziz and the Second Malaysia Five Year Plan, in Chee S. and S.M. Khoo, eds. *Malaysian Economic Development and Policies*, Kuala Lumpur: Malaysian Economic Association, 1975.

Bhalla, Surjit S. and Paul Glewwe, Growth and Equity in Developing Countries: A reinterpretation of the Sri Lankan Experience, in *World Bank Economic Review*, vol. 1 (September 1986) no. 1.

Chua Jui Meng, The Malaysian Chinese — the Way Ahead, in *The Future of Malaysian Chinese*, Kuala Lumpur: Malaysian Chinese Association, 1988.

David Chua, The Chinese Education and Cultural Vision, in *The Future of Malaysian Chinese*, Kuala Lumpur: Malaysian Chinese Association, 1988.

Fong Chan Onn, Economic Strategy for the Nation Towards and Beyond 1990, in *The Future of Malaysian Chinese*, Kuala Lumpur: Malaysian Chinese Association, 1988.

Gerakan Rakyat Malaysia, The National Economic Policy — 1990 and Beyond, as reviewed by Bruce Gale in *Far Eastern Economic Review*, 18 April 1985.

Kok Wee Kiat, Facing the Future, in *The Future of Malaysian Chinese*, Kuala Lumpur: Malaysian Chinese Association, 1988.

Lewis, W.A., Economic Development with Unlimited Supplies of Labour, *The Manchester School of Economic and Social Studies*, vol. 12 (1954) no. 2, pp. 139-191.

Lim Lin Lean, The Erosion of the Chinese Economic Position, in *The Future of Malaysian Chinese*, Kuala Lumpur: Malaysian Chinese Association, 1988.

Malek Merican, *Review of the NEP from the Private Sector Perspective*, paper delivered at Gemaputra Sammar Kabangsaau, Dasar Economic Baru Selapas 1990, 24-26 March 1987, Kuala Lumpur.

Maria Samad, PAS Crisis: Question of Style, Approach, in *New Straits Times*, October 3, 1988.

Papanek, Gustav, Aid, Growth and Equity in Southern Asia in J.R. Parkinson ed. *Poverty and Aid*, Oxford: Basil Blackwell, 1983.

Papanek, Gustav, Industrialization Strategies in Labour Abundant Countries, in *Asian Development Review*, vol. 3 (1985) no. 1.

Rose Ismail, Much Ado over Statistics, *New Straits Times*, August 6, 1989.

Ting Chew Peh, The Problem of National Unity, in *The Future of Malaysian Chinese*, Kuala Lumpur: Malaysian Chinese Association, 1988.

*Note that only books and other sources referred to in this book are included.*

# INDEX

## DATE DUE

The Library Store     #47-0106